THE
DIGNITY
OF LABOUR

THE
DIGNITY
OF LABOUR

IMAGE, WORK AND IDENTITY
IN THE ROMAN WORLD

IAIN FERRIS

AMBERLEY

Dedicated to a time, a place, and an event: Saturday 21 April 1979, Vinyl Junkies record shop on North Street, Darlington, buying The Human League's *The Dignity of Labour* EP.

Images in this book are by the author, with the exception of: 21, 36, 87, and 94 copyright the Trustees of the British Museum; 3, 31, 35, 42, 43, 54, 56, 63, 82, and 96 slide collection of former School of Continuing Studies, Birmingham University; 80 copyright Scala Firenze; 81 copyright Bridgeman Images; and 26 copyright Sema Basaran. I have made every effort to contact copyright holders for permissions to reproduce images here. I would be happy for any copyright holders that I may have inadvertently not credited to get in touch with me via Amberley Publishing.

First published 2020

Amberley Publishing
The Hill, Stroud
Gloucestershire, GL5 4EP

www.amberley-books.com

British Library Cataloguing in Publication Data.
A catalogue record for this book is available from the British Library.

ISBN 978 1 4456 8421 5 (hardback)
ISBN 978 1 4456 8422 2 (ebook)

1 2 3 4 5 6 7 8 9 10

Typesetting by Aura Technology and Software Services, India.
Printed in the UK.

Contents

Acknowledgements

In writing this book I have received help from a number of individuals and organisations and I would like to take the opportunity to sincerely thank them all here.

Before I started work on this book, many of the images of Roman workers discussed in this study were known to me only through photographic reproductions in academic books and printed museum catalogues and I became aware quite early in this study that simply viewing these photographic images had a curious levelling effect, interceding two-dimensional, flat images between myself and three-dimensional objects suffused with a materiality and physicality that required appreciation by the viewing of as many original artworks as I could practically contrive to see in person. Indeed, so imposing and possessing such presence were many of these funerary monuments of those who are often characterised by historians as insignificant or humble men and women, it seemed to me as if these workers had been quarried rather than born. Therefore thanks to Gianfranco Mastrangeli of the *Segreteria dei Dipartimenti e Reparti, Musei Vaticani,* who kindly arranged for me to visit the *Museo Gregoriano Profano* in summer 2014, when I viewed the reliefs from the Tomb of the Haterii, and in summer 2018 to view inscriptions in the *Galleria Lapidaria.* There I received help and guidance from Dotoressa Rosanna Barbera. For granting permission to visit the *Necropoli di Porto* at Isola Sacra, Ostia I would like to thank the *Ministero dei Beni e delle Attività Culturali e del Turismo* and the on-site custodians for their help. For answers to a number of enquiries about artworks in their care and information on viewing them I thank the staff of the *Pontificia Commissione di Archeologia Sacra* in Rome.

Acknowledgements

In addition to visiting the many museums of Rome, study visits have also been made to: Arles, Avignon, Dijon, Metz, Paris, Reims, and Sens in France; Arlon in Belgium; Igel and Trier in Germany; and to Ancona, Aquileia, Benevento, Bologna, Brescia, Capua, Este, Florence, Forlimpopoli, Mantova, Milan, Modena, Naples, Ostia, Padova, Parma, Ravenna, Reggio nell'Emilia, Rimini, Sarsina, Turin, Venice and Verona in Italy. This list of sites and museums visited is long and could have been considerably longer had I had inordinate amounts of time, resources, and money to constantly traverse Europe in search of more artworks. Sadly, I did not.

Professor Amanda Claridge and Professor Carol van Driel Murray helped with queries about particular artworks in their specialist fields. Dr Richard Hobbs of the British Museum kindly answered a query about Persian silversmiths. Dr Claire Holleran kindly provided me with a digital copy of one of her articles that I was otherwise unable to consult. Part of the discussion on the Antonine Wall legionary distance slabs in this book derives from a paper co-authored with Professor David Breeze who encouraged me to write about these artworks again.

For providing an image for reproduction in the book I would like to thank Sema Basaran. Once more, I must thank the British Museum for the creation of its wonderful web-based image research resource and for its incredibly generous facility for researchers and academics to make use of these images without charge, as I have done with a small number of images in this book. Julian Parker again gave a great deal of help in locating a number of images for the book and is thanked for his technical expertise in turning old colour slides into sharp digital images.

The staff of the Institute of Classical Studies Library, London; the British Library, London; and Swansea University library were unfailingly helpful in obtaining books and journals for my reference while researching this book. Many thanks to them all.

As always, my colleague and wife Dr Lynne Bevan read and commented on a draft of the book, much to the benefit of the finished work. At Amberley Publishing I would like to thank Shaun Barrington for commissioning this book in the first place and Richard Sutton and Cathy Stagg for their editorial work and advice in seeing the book into print.

Preface

The very existence and ubiquity of use in ancient Rome of the famous Latin acronym and slogan *SPQR*, short for *Senatus Populusque Romanus* – 'the Senate and the people of Rome' – suggests that the senatorial and plebeian classes of Rome were symbiotically and symbolically linked in the Roman imagination and in the political discourse which accompanied the Republic turning into a vast empire. But how were these links manifested in Roman culture and particularly in Roman art from the point of view of 'the people'? How were images used by some workers and professionals in the Roman world to publicly express their identities or some aspect of that identity? These are the major questions that this book sets out to address and hopefully answer.

This is the first recent book to attempt to present an extended analysis of the place, roles, and self-identities of workers, artisans, and professionals in ancient Roman society and across the Roman world in general, as reflected in contemporary images, and to interpret their positions and significance in cultural rather than purely economic terms. In order to achieve this the range of topics discussed in the book is broad by necessity, given the nature of the evidence that we possess. From the outset I need to make it clear that I will not be discussing the Roman system of slave labour, though it will be alluded to; however, in many cases cited here the individual workers discussed were actually freed slaves – freedmen and freedwomen – or the descendants of slaves. I have also taken the decision not to discuss gladiators and prostitutes (male or female) as 'workers', as in these two cases the great degree of coercive participation in both areas argues against their inclusion by reason of their working identities being thrust upon them in many cases rather than chosen, though group identity in such situations could be, and indeed appears to have been, strong in some instances. I will give brief mentions to agricultural workers in the Roman countryside, but few representations of such workers were images of real people, named people, and the images were simply illustrative or somehow metaphorical, as we shall see. Likewise, I will not be discussing images of fishermen for the same reasons.

The study encompasses consideration of both ancient contemporary written and visual sources. There is a small but interesting body of Greek and Roman writing dedicated to the discussion of the nature of work and to the philosophical exploration of work as a metaphor for broader issues and its relationship to wealth, status, and power. However, this does not necessarily mean that we understand the attitudes of all Romans to their working and professional contemporaries because some elite men of the time wrote about it. As has been the case with all of my previous books the emphasis here is on visual evidence, that is representations of workers in Roman art and particularly in the form of funerary sculptures, and as images on mosaics, wall paintings, and on a small number of decorated everyday items. I will also make constant recourse to dedicatory inscriptions which name workers and their professions, or their professional associations, and to makers' stamps that appeared on a range of items including bricks and tiles, pottery, glass, lead water pipes, metalwork, and even wooden items. Inscriptions and stamps will be treated here primarily as images, their form and purpose having been very different from the written words in an ancient book or in a papyrus record.

This book is also a story of how art depicting workers and professionals became as much a part of Roman culture as real workers played in Roman society. There can be no doubt that image and imagination together helped shape the Romans' understanding of culture and society. I believe that to a very great degree archaeological evidence and particularly visual sources both override and provide nuance to the picture provided by the Roman writers.

Remarkably, considering the significance of the subject and the relevance of economic issues today, there is no accessible general publication on workers and identity in the Roman world available in English. My guiding lights though have been the groundbreaking

1981 book *Image and Status. Roman Working Women in Ostia* by Natalie Kampen[1] and the invaluable catalogue, in German, of images of workers in Rome and Italy compiled by Gerhard Zimmer in 1982.[2] Both of these books have inspired me to consider the issue of ancient Roman workers more broadly and in a different way. There have, however, been numerous articles on various aspects of the subject published in academic journals from the 1960s up to the present day. A recent, extremely thorough book on urban craftsmen and traders in the Roman world[3] brought together numerous excellent short papers on virtually every aspect of the subject but contained little specifically on the visual evidence relating to workers' identities and what such portrayals taken together could actually have represented in cultural terms. This present book should therefore hopefully fill an evident gap in the market. It is aimed at undergraduate students studying introductory modules in Roman archaeology and history or Roman art and lay readers interested in these subjects. The book may also appeal to visitors to the museums and sites of Rome, Italy, and western Europe.

The book consists of an introduction setting out the scope and scale of the study, and detailed discussion of images of builders, bakers and food producers, and textile workers in the Roman world. Analysis of the role, status and identity of metalworkers is also presented, along with discussion of professionals such as doctors, teachers and scribes. A number of more thematic studies will also be presented, including discussion of the gendered nature of images of workers, and a final chapter setting discussion of workers and professionals in the Roman world in the broader geographical, chronological, political, religious, artistic, and cultural context of the Republic and Empire and of Late Antiquity. Comparative material relating to the portrayal of workers in other societies and in later times will also be presented and some discussion will take place on the way in which contemporary museological practices might be helping to marginalise Roman workers in museum displays today.

In the process, topics covered will include building the city, feeding the city, clothing the citizens, provisioning the city, entertaining the city, and adorning the city. In the course of this book a number of more esoteric topics will also inevitably be covered. For instance, why were the cremated remains of Eurysaces the Roman baker interred inside a funerary monument in the form of a bakery's bread-kneading bins turned on their sides? And why were there quite so many specialist job titles in Roman society, such as the *alipilus* – 'a plucker of body hair' – or the *faber ocularius* – 'a maker of eyes for statues'? The book also includes academic notes and a full bibliography to aid those who might want to pursue certain issues in more detail.

Most of the images discussed in this book were isolated works – an individual's funerary monument in a larger cemetery for instance – but even in Roman times clustering of certain types of monuments in certain specific areas of cemeteries undoubtedly occurred, as will be discussed at length in this book. If there is a methodological framework for this study it is the abandonment of the idea of a single work of art portraying a craftsman being an isolated occurrence and significant only in that respect, in favour of a series of such works having a wider significance: each one a different aspect of the same thing, rather than one final, immutable statement. It is the notion of *process*, rather than the fixed composition, that will concern us. Viewed collectively, as a group, they expressed something about ideals, illusions, desires, and imagination.

The study is I hope fully attuned to the various different ways in which cultural practices and values are experienced differently by people in different social circumstances and, of course, at different times and in different places. There is here an emphasis on the act of viewing as an embedded social and cultural practice in Roman times, as now, and the idea that art was as much a commodity as anything else sold or traded in an ancient world dominated by exchange and power. As well as attempting to parse the way certain images were viewed and experienced in the Roman world – were they formative, normal, or transformative, for instance – close reading suggests that doubt, irony, alienation, and tension were as much a product of these works as was direct meaning. Reading across the grain and against the grain then becomes almost a necessary strategy for the interpretation of such images. Producing the new need not necessarily then have involved schism, a turn towards autarkic directions, or any kind of formal withdrawal from sociality and pre-existing cultural forms: it could have been a kind of social evolution, as we shall see.

Throughout this book there is one thread to which I will repeatedly return; namely the importance and power of personal identity in underscoring Rome's response to, and evaluation of, its own character, though the narrative is not about individualism versus collectivism. The common thread helps to unite an argument that at times might have become fragmentary due to the large and diverse body of data on which this analysis is based.

Work is viewed here as a social and cultural phenomenon and to some extent a political one. However, there is no evidence to suggest that artistic expressions such as the creation of images of workers were regulated or deliberately limited in some way by the Roman authorities; rather, it would appear that freedmen and others in trades or otherwise working and singularly financially and aspirationally affluent turned to the visual in order to summon a new reality into being. Viewing practices based on connoisseurship, consumerism, erudition, nostalgia, and humour could be emulated or undermined. Traditional continuities and ruptures could somehow coexist. These were not propagandist images intended to be viewed and understood in a proscribed way. There is actually no evidence that the Roman state used culturally situated images of workers in a strategic or cynical way, as many later societies have done and continue to do. Before such images became common in Rome and elsewhere in Italy their rarity did however mark some kind of presentation of absence. Any gulf in understanding could have led to mutual incomprehension between Roman elite and plebeian viewers and audiences, each drawing altogether different conclusions while viewing the same image.

Roman art's deictic function, aside from simply being art itself, was the way in which it acted sometimes to stress the complicity between aesthetic taste and symbolic and economic power. Rome's long elite aesthetic and cultural tradition, with its complex codings of status and class, had room to encapsulate images from other classes – let us call it plebeian art or workers' art for the moment – and from other places, the latter being what we now call provincial art, all of which became coterminous. Workers' art had to be both invented and discovered; it was part of a discourse on fashion, consumption, and elite art, and finally on individual and group identities.

There were 71 Roman emperors and co-rulers between Augustus (27 BC – AD 14) and Theodosius (AD 379 – 395) and quite rightly the history and events of their various reigns and their individual biographies have dominated, and to a great extent still dominate, the study and writing of ancient history and help provide structuring principles for museum collections and displays. We understand the sequential history of the Roman world through its emperors, even though the power of the emperors was out of all proportion to their individuality and to their relatively small number in total. To put this into some kind of numerical perspective, as a comparison and contrast, from Rome alone there are 1,470 occupational inscriptions (as catalogued up to the year 1992[4]) naming ordinary, non-elite individuals and their jobs. From stamps on their wares we know the names of around 5,000 individual potters working at the samian pottery *terra sigillata* factories of Gaul. I could choose here to go on to list numbers of known named masons, carpenters, metalworkers, textile workers, doctors, clerks, and so on from more broadly around the Roman world but instead I have picked as a final example what might be thought of as somewhat of a fringe activity and minor industry in antiquity compared to these, that the names of 56 perfumers from Rome, Italy, and elsewhere in the Empire are known from inscriptions and epitaphs. It should be clear therefore that already the number of workers, artisans, and professionals from the Roman world whose names we know outnumbers and dwarfs the total number of named emperors.

This study is not in any way a history of any particular industry nor does it present an analysis of specific types of artefacts or artworks. Rather it is a study of individual workers at certain points in time and of the way that they positioned themselves within their contemporary society and forged or created identities, as far as we can gauge and understand such a set of relationships. As the numbers just presented as examples surely demonstrate, this is not some form of secret history, an unveiling of ancient workers and artisans as 'invisible' or 'secret' Romans, as some writers on ancient history have bizarrely proposed in the past. Rather they have been there in the archaeological record, hiding in plain sight for all to see, for some time. Rome was not a monument to the unimportance of its working citizens, a perpetual gesture of disrespect to people who some think lacked a sense of their own necessity. It is perhaps primarily modern museological and academic practices that have moved such people to the peripheries, as I will suggest later in the study. Again, there has often been a curious tendency in writings on the Roman economy which consider the lot of workers to either use their images purely as illustrative material or to discuss certain of these images simply as illustrations of technical processes rather than illustrations of personal and professional identities.

Again, the drawing of a taxonomy of work and workspaces in Roman urban centres has greatly exercised archaeologists and ancient historians, but often their studies have not extended to the workers themselves because of their inherently ambiguous position in Roman society. The strong interrelationship between work as an action and architecture as its support has meant that all too often the focus has been on the impact of work on the ancient city rather than the impact of workers on Roman society and culture. The physical interfaces and spatial typologies that were linked to urban development and the economy were equally relevant in terms of negotiating the development of the identity of the worker in the Roman city. I believe that work undoubtedly has important things to teach us about the categories of identity at that time.

In an academic study of any aspect of life in the past care should be taken with presenting the facts and interpreting them in their contemporary social and cultural context. Sometimes it may be tempting to view certain past actions or phenomena from a twenty-first-century perspective, although some writers overtly shun such an approach, but indeed I feel that this can often in fact prove highly illuminating. To this end, later in the book I will broaden out the field of study to encompass discussion of depictions of workers from much later times and from very different cultures and societies. The question of the nature of an ideological and politicised interpretation of such images will be addressed, as will be the issue of the limits on self-representation in the creation, consumption, and viewing of such images. In the process discussion will turn variously to Italian and French social realist art of the late nineteenth and early twentieth centuries, to the totalitarian art of Nazi Germany, Fascist Italy, and the Soviet Union, and finally to the imagistic portraits of working class people in the Roman stories and novels of the twentieth-century Italian writer Alberto Moravia. However, such parallel studies do not provide direct evidence about what may or may not have happened in the Roman era. They do though suggest possible avenues of interpretation that might equally be applied to ancient artworks and possible theoretical frameworks of interpretation that can transcend chronological contexts. A more complex but at the same time nuanced view of the Roman past in relation to class relationships in the Roman world can then hopefully emerge.

To a very great degree public discourse today is increasingly being dominated by identity politics, to the extent that it is engendering a dynamic whereby society is dividing into smaller and smaller groups and sub-groups based on given, chosen, or perceived identities. It is not simply a trait of modernity that people now might choose multiple identities, including elements such as race, gender, age, and workplace or occupational identity. Such things also occurred in the past, though whether the undertow of irony, doubt, and alienation detectable in present day identity formation can also be recognised or even existed in the past and was reflected in its use of imagery is open to question. The presentation of identity in Roman times seems to have thrived on contradiction and tension and there was a gap between ambition and achievement, image and meaning, and intention and reception. It is this conundrum, this sense of jeopardy on display which gave the form its very vitality; some were crystalline in their clarity while others basked in ambiguity, at the intersection of art and commerce. In their attempt to challenge, or at least to change opinions and perspectives, it can be seen that in presenting these scattered messages on one level everything failed while on another nothing did.

It is possible to consider this large body of evidence from both a chronological and geographical standpoint: the selection of material to discuss here is both synchronic and diachronic, corresponding to meaningful contours in the data. Of course, it took a very long time for Rome and Italy's artisanal, commercial, and manufacturing families to form themselves into a self-conscious social estate that followed the example of the elite in being able to think of themselves as people who deserved and needed to have their likenesses and lives recorded and viewed by their family and the broader community; in other words, to express a modern sensibility. In many cultures and at different times it is common to find concerns about self-identity often mixed and confused with notions of class and status. Notions about self and identity merge and mingle with the experience and enactment of social class. Erecting such monuments can never have been intended to have been a subversive or transgressive act in the Roman period. Indeed, they bridged the contemporary tension between the visual, that was art, and the material, as represented by craft.

Because the vast majority of these images of workers and professionals appeared on funerary monuments they differed from portrait statues, heads, and busts in that the framing provided by a stele, a tombstone, or the panels of the faces of a sarcophagus functioned as isolating factors on both delineation and delimitation. They displayed some measure of complicity in the cultural values that such monuments represented. Thus, although we are not generally discussing portraits as such, many of these depictions of workers and professionals which form the subject of this book did, however, share some elements with formal portraiture. The job of those portrayed was to play themselves both as individuals and as social types, a complex process of ideological negotiation. Even though the images did not seek to capture the specificity of an individual in most cases, they represented the individual by portraying a situation. Thus, they were at the same time both highly personal, particularly if the image was accompanied by an inscription of some kind, and yet strangely impersonal. They both elevated and conceptualised their subjects. However, this is not to entirely forget the hidden power of work to sometimes demean the individual worker: misery, the burden of physical exertion, exploitation, and the threat of accident or death were unfortunately ever present and very occasionally referenced in funerary inscriptions, as we shall see.

It is tempting to call the affluent freedmen class, those who could afford to commission funerary monuments for themselves or for others, a new 'middle class' in ancient Rome as some academics have done,[5] but this term is somewhat loaded and not without its attendant problems. I will therefore generally eschew its use here for those reasons.

These images are a source of insight into plebeian culture in Rome but they were not unmediated or univocal views of working life at the time of their creation and thus they do not allow us to read off social detail from them at will. The portrayed protagonists were embedded both in space and time, represented connotatively rather than denotatively and figuratively rather than functionally. When viewing them their contemporary audience is almost palpable: they could be said to have existed only as part of a response to the total resources and normative tendencies of Roman elite culture. Like all art, the images' existence relied on a cohesive, knowledgeable, and perceptive audience, their meaning lay not just in their origins but also in their destination, to paraphrase Roland Barthes. They possessed some kind of quality of directness and comprehensiveness in presenting ideas and concepts that ran both counter to and in parallel with the contemporary Roman elite discourse. While each was an isolated cultural artefact in some respects, ultimately they were embedded in a broader matrix of associations, reflecting the countless hierarchies, relationships, and associations inherent in Roman society itself. Each was an element in a continuum of social references at the time which maintained its momentum through ideology. Each contained and balanced elements of insider and outsider knowledge, often through sometimes contradictory positions. Through this, occupation and work became a cultural and social signifier, transformed not simply from an operative state into a performative one but also from a static image into a potent carrier of social and psychological meaning.

No matter how grand the funerary monument, though, social and class differentiation meant all kinds of clues were provided by the monuments as to the origins and life of the deceased, from their inscribed names, often betraying their freedmen status, and their style of dress when depicted. Demystification such as this stripped the contemporary world of overlaid elements of sentimentality and superstition, at the same time eliminating intuition and some other non-rational forms of perception, awareness, and understanding. Labouring bodies though did not belong in the clothes of the upper classes which through their design, fabric, colour and cut were meant to symbolise sedentary power. The dynamic body often was used in the artworks under discussion in this book as a way of differentiating class and indeed of celebrating class difference. As Rome acquired an empire, being Roman began to mean many more different things than it had in the early days of the Republic. Ideology, the individual, collective organisms, society, crisis in the form of constant change, and temporality all interacted together. If at one time the Roman workers' ideological consciousness might have been viewed by the city's elite as historically in conflict with their practical activities, then such a view was obviously subject to some kind of change. The transformation when it occurred provided the opportunity and context for some workers to express their individuality in public. The gap between ideological forms and economic structures was eventually bridged, and Roman ideology became a constantly coherent expression of social totality, though not of course of social equality in any way, shape, or form.

We perhaps need to consider such representations as having been part of a broader cultural sphere, and interpret them as part of the development of Roman society's complexity, as one element in the dismantling of the defensive architecture of cultural appropriation. They reflected both business and art, and themselves inhabited a space of cultural production. Images of the body in this cultural space could be seen as sources both of difference and sameness. Study of these images allows for the emergence of a fascinating parallel narrative, rather than counter-narrative, to established ways of conceptualising cultural history along event-based lines, as so often occurs in historical studies. The social production of such individuals became almost indistinguishable from their economic production.

Appreciating the decisive power of such singular works for me was some kind of call to action and a prime motive for writing this book. When the French filmmaker Agnès Varda was making her documentary film *The Gleaners and I* she saw herself in a historical continuum of work and labour that stretched from the titular gleaners, nineteenth-century female agricultural workers whose laborious and back-breaking task was to pick stones from fields before planting and glean leftovers from the field surfaces after harvest, up to the start of a new millennium. Her starting point was examination of Jean-Francois Millet's large painting *Des Glaneuses – The Gleaners –* of 1857, now in the collection of the *Musée D'Orsay* in Paris. Likewise, as I toured around the archaeological museums of northern Italy in the summer of 2018 and spring of 2019 I thought of Varda's metaphor and understood how the gleaning of evidence piece by piece in this way was a form of labour, albeit pleasurable labour, and that the dignity of labour was not altogether a redundant concept consigned to history.

Iain Ferris,
Pembrey

1

The Dignity of Labour
Presentation or Performance?

Aged sixteen and volunteering on my first excavation at the Roman site of Kelvedon in Essex, one of the first items I found while trowelling down a layer of occupation soil on the site was a piece of stamped samian pottery. Red and glossy, this pottery, also known to archaeologists as *terra sigillata*, was made in Roman Gaul in the first and second centuries AD and was exported to Roman Britain in enormous quantities. The stamp was of the potter Gippus who worked at the major samian pottery complex at Lezoux in the second century. This represented my first personal encounter with a named ancient Roman and a fascination with the idea of advertising personal identity in the past has remained with me ever since.

Engaging here with the issue of identity in the past might be thought of as perhaps being somehow arcane and esoteric, particularly at a time when identity politics is dominating public discourse and leading to an inevitable atomisation that might well result in a general cultural schism rather than the hoped-for harmony. I am largely avoiding the over-intellectualisation of the term identity in this study, or at least I hope I am, though some discussion of its use does require attention. Much of the writing on identity in the Roman world quite rightly focuses on ethnicity but discussion on that particular strand of identity is virtually absent in this book because ethnicity as a marker is not strictly relevant here nor significant among the evidence surveyed. Other typical markers of identity – gender, age, and status – will be discussed to varying degrees and all were important. The fluidity of identity in the past, as today, needed to be recognised, as did the factors which might have impacted on changing perceptions of identity and changing presentations of identity. Then, as now, people could define themselves through multiple identities depending on context and intent.

The idea of identity as being a performance, as first theorised by the Canadian sociologist Erving Goffman and subsequently elaborated on by others, is a useful tool for analysing *some* of the Roman period funerary monuments discussed in this book, and I would suggest certainly applies to the funerary stele of the Roman shoemaker Caius Iulius Helius (discussed in Chapter Three), but is highly uninformative, indeed somewhat misleading, when applied across the board to these monuments as a group. There would appear to have been a kind of desperate truth in the images and texts used by some Romans to present their working identities that makes their analysis in terms of performance glib and trite. The presentation of a working identity in the Roman world was not simply to do with status, it was an identity *in* and *of* itself: it was a cultural aspect of the Roman economy as much as of Roman society at large. A manifestation of an idea, part of the creation of a material world separate from, but part of, broader Roman society.

There must have been some very specific time, a kind of Year Zero event, when a worker or professional at Rome decided to present themselves in public through memorialisation involving a professional identity. We cannot identify this individual or ever know when this event took place. However, we can track how this event multiplied and became a bona fide cultural phenomenon in Rome and Italy and in a number of other regions of the Empire. Just as public spaces like the forum or amphitheatre became what one archaeologist has called 'entangled spaces' and others have called contested spaces where different experiences of the same spaces were had by different kinds of people, so the same thing seems to have occurred in Roman cemeteries.

In the ancient world work was something holistic, an occupation, a resource, a setting, a transformation, and sometimes also a struggle, and often all of these things simultaneously. Roman images of work usually evoked these aspects singly or in groups, depending on balance and composition, but all of these aspects were always potentially present in every such image. So many workers then lived and worked in the same premises that most distinctions between working time – economic activity – and non-working time – uneconomic activity – simply did not exist.

It is going to be apparent to the close reader of this study that craft is viewed throughout this book as a way of materialising identity, that identity and technology were enmeshed in Roman culture as well as in the Roman economy. Communities of practice came to create cultural communities.

Writing Prejudice

While present trends in the study of Roman technology are largely focused on economic and technical issues there is also a need to examine this subject from a cultural point of view, as this present study is attempting to do through an analysis of individual and group work and professional identities. What was the cultural and intellectual climate in which these workers operated? Did this change over time and with circumstances? Did abstract and abstruse philosophical intellectualisations of the value of work and the dignity or dissoluteness of the labourer have any day to day impact on real workers in real situations?[1] Were Roman Christian attitudes different to other views on this?[2] This study is all about three linked concepts – value, consent, and community – all of which were deeply contested at the time and which eventually somehow came together to define the social and cultural meaning of the economy in the Rome world.

References to workers in Roman historical and literary written sources are relatively few and tend to be incidental where they occur. When Seneca described the noise in and around the public bathhouses of Rome in the first century AD,[3] specifically castigating the sausage sellers and other street hawkers of food crying their wares, he did so with evident annoyance at these workers for disturbing the peace rather than in an attempt to describe their work. Similarly, when Artemidorus of Ephesus, writing in his curious work *Oneirocritica – The Interpretation of Dreams –* in the second century AD, wrote about tanneries and tanners[4] he did so with disgust at the handling of the corpses of dead animals and the vile odours that he claimed hung around the tanners themselves, rather than describing the hard manual labour that underpinned this economically important industry. Hundreds of thousands of anonymous slaves and labourers operated and maintained the estates and farms, tilled the fields, harvested the crops, and managed the herds and flocks in the working countryside that formed the topics of the agricultural writers Varro (in *De Re Rustica*), Columella (in *Res Rustica*), Cato (in *De Agri Cultura*) and Palladius (in *Opus Agriculturae*), for instance, but a reader might not necessarily realise this from reading these manuals.

More tellingly though, the politician and writer Cicero in his *De Officiis*[5] – *On Duties* – wrote that:

> Now in regard to trades and other means of livelihood, which ones are to be considered becoming to a gentleman, and which ones are vulgar, we have been taught in general, as follows. First, those means of livelihood are rejected as undesirable which incur people's ill-will, as those of tax-gatherers and usurers. Unbecoming to a gentleman, too, and vulgar are the means of livelihood of all hired workmen whom we pay for mere manual labour, not for artistic skill; for in their case the very wage they receive is a pledge of their slavery. Vulgar we must consider those also who buy from wholesale merchants to retail immediately; for they would get no profits without a great deal of downright lying; and verily, there is no action meaner than misrepresentation. And all mechanics are engaged in vulgar trades; for no workshop can have anything liberal about it. Least respectable of all are those trades which cater for sensual pleasures: 'Fishmongers, butchers, cooks, and poulterers, and fishermen,' as Terence says. Add to these, if you please, the perfumers, dancers, and the whole corps de ballet.
>
> But the professions in which either a higher degree of intelligence is required or from which no small benefit to society is derived – medicine and architecture, for example, and teaching – these are proper for those whose social position they become. Trade, if it is on a small scale, is to be considered vulgar; but if wholesale and on a large scale ... it is not to be greatly disparaged.

Almost inevitably, for one of the landed elite, Cicero went on to praise agriculture as something 'none more becoming to a freeman', 'none more profitable, none more delightful'. Cicero's comments, although brief, are interesting on a number of levels. Class snobbery was quite obviously the overriding sentiment on display here but he also appears to have taken any assault on his senses as a slight upon his very person, in the same way that Seneca viewed the hawkers' cries as an insult to his sense of hearing and Artemidorus probably quite rightly complained about the reek of the tanners assaulting his sense of smell.

Cicero was most certainly familiar with the scientific and philosophical writings of Aristotle from the fourth century BC; indeed, Cicero is on record as praising the style of his prose – 'a flowing river of gold'. It is curious, therefore, that the ancient philosopher's more accepting, even intrigued, stance with regard to non-elite workers in various trades and jobs did not rub off on his later Roman counterpart. It is evident from his writings about his biological studies on the northern Aegean island of Lesbos around 345–343 BC that Aristotle had consulted widely with people such as fishermen, sponge divers, beekeepers, and so on to elicit hard-won, carefully observed knowledge from them about the creatures on whom their very livings depended. Such conversations cannot have been had in an atmosphere of superiority or condescension; it is more likely that the philosopher and the workers displayed mutual respect, and that information was exchanged willingly and in a spirit of intellectual co-operation. Throughout his writings, analogies and metaphors connected with work, crafts, or tools also abound. Most famously, Aristotle had obviously paid as close attention to the quarrymen and stoneworkers of Lesbos as he had to the island's wildlife, watching intently as they measured and marked-up large rough blocks ready for the cutting of mouldings using a flexible ruler made of soft lead, much like today's rubber flex-curve. In the *Ethica Nicomachea* – the *Nicomachean Ethics*[6] – he used the example of the Lesbian rule, as this lead strip became known, as a metaphor for the importance of flexibility in rendering justice:

> For what is itself indefinite can only be measured by an indefinite standard, like the leaden rule used by Lesbian builders; just as that rule is not rigid but can be bent to the shape of the stone, so a special ordinance is made to fit the circumstances of the case.

In *De Generatione Animalium – On the Generation of Animals*[7] – he wrote: 'In animals that emit semen the nature in the male uses semen as an instrument possessing active movement, just as the tools are moved in things that come to be by craft; for the movement of the craft is somehow in these tools.'

And yet, in the ideal city state that he mapped out in one of the books of his *Politica – Politics –* there was to be no place for farmers, artisans, labourers and merchants: 'the artisan class has no share in the state, nor has any other class that is not "an artificer of virtue".'[8]

As might be expected, freedmen and the newly rich provided targets for Roman satirical writers, none more so than Juvenal and Petronius. Many readers will already be familiar with the character of Trimalchio, created by Petronius to hammer home his thoughts on the crassness of the freedmen class in Rome but we can also see a similar distaste manifested in another newly rich and ostentatious character, Juvenal's Crispinus who had once been a barber in Rome. It is also possible that these satirical sketches about rich freedmen equally reflected a more generalised anxiety about Roman elite masculinity, in which individual perceptions of male virility went hand in hand with the possession of great wealth. In other words, they say more about Juvenal and Petronius the writers or the personae of Juvenal and Petronius they created than about class and economics. In his play of *c.* 206 BC *Mercator – The Merchant –* the Roman playwright Plautus used the merchant profession of the two main male protagonists, father and son Demipho and Charinus, as a means by which to address the philosophical underpinnings of the system of slavery, though not necessarily so as to critique it. The professional language of the merchants when also applied to their love of the same woman, Pasicompsa the slave, equated her to the very commodities they traded.

If Cicero made distinctions between different types of workers and moral worth, a philosophical distinction between skill and brainpower was made by Seneca the Younger (4 BC – AD 65) in one of his *Epistulae Morales ad Lucilium – Moral Letters to Lucilius.*[9] Concerned with the part played by philosophy in 'the progress of Man', Seneca found reason in this letter to question the stance of the earlier Greek stoic philosopher Posidonius who had argued for the moral worth of skill in an artisan's work:

> ... the hammer [and] tongs ... were invented by some man whose mind was nimble and keen, but not great or exalted; and the same holds true of any other discovery which can only be made by means of a bent body and of a mind whose gaze is upon the ground.

He went on to elaborate on this theme, but his tone still seemed to suggest a latent and grudging admiration for certain kinds of innovative workers and artisans:

> We know that certain devices have come to light only within our own memory – such as the use of windows which admit the clear light through transparent tiles, and such as the vaulted baths, with pipes let into their walls for the purpose of diffusing the heat which maintains an even temperature in their lowest as well as in their highest spaces. Why need I mention the marble with which our temples and our private houses are resplendent? Or the rounded and polished masses of stone by means of which we erect colonnades and buildings roomy enough for nations? ... All this sort of thing has been devised by the lowest grade of slaves. Wisdom's seat is higher; she trains not the hands, but is mistress of our minds.

As with so many other elite Romans of his time he argued that comfort and luxury in general were venal and corrupting, something that only the very rich felt enabled to argue with a straight face. 'Follow nature, and you will need no skilled craftsmen,' he exhorted Lucilius from one of his large country estates.

The attitudes of some later Christian writers towards work and workers are also of great interest. In the writings of St Augustine, the Bishop of Hippo Regius in Roman North Africa, in modern Algeria, between AD 396 and 430, differences of viewpoint do emerge from close reading, but it is questionable as to whether this marked any kind of philosophical reorientation or profound change in broader late Roman society. Rather, it would seem that Augustine's dismissal of the idea of 'God as artisan', a creator, some kind of celestial potter moulding men from the clay of the earth as the Book of Isaiah would have it, was highly significant. Indeed, Augustine and other early Christian writers stressed the signal importance of manual labour and work in general in developing the spiritual self. It thus provided both material and spiritual sustenance for individuals, families, and Christian communities. In other words, work was a necessity that allowed the individual Christian the resources to bypass the state structures, as indeed Tertullian had earlier argued. Augustine quite tellingly pointed out that labouring hard to produce an excess of goods should in no way be seen as a sin: indeed, the profit from just such a surplus could be used charitably. Better to give charitably than to receive charity.

Saint Basil (AD 330–379), Bishop of Caesarea, Gregory of Nazianzus (AD 329–390), Archbishop of Constantinople, and Saint Ambrose (AD 340–397), Bishop of Milan, were highly influential fourth-century theologians, all of whom in their writings posited that the idea of labour itself was somehow blessed, and that because God had laboured to create the world so the earthly workers in their endeavours constantly reminded the faithful of this fact. Yet at the same time these and other contemporary Christian writers recognised that in the case of Adam's forced atonement for his sinfulness through his condemnation to onerous manual agricultural labour there was a conceptual link between work and sinfulness in certain contexts. Saint Basil argued that God gave humans the gift of craftsmanship to replace natural existing resources provided by God but which had been lost through sinning.

Finally on this topic, Augustine wrote in *De Civitate Dei* or *The City of God* that: '... some (arts) are concerned with the manufacture of a product which is the result of the labour of the artisan, like a house, a bench, a dish, or something of that kind. Others exhibit a kind of assistance to the works of God, like medicine, agriculture, and navigation...'[10] Monastic rules of the fourth and fifth centuries clearly prioritised commitment to worship over labour necessary for the functioning of the monastery, but discussion of the valuation of artisanal work in such artificial communities now takes us too far away from consideration of ideas of work in society at large at the time.

Ancient snobbery about workers and working can also be discerned from four stories linked to the Roman emperors Vespasian and Pertinax, to the Republican consul Gaius Terentius Varro, and to the fifth-century AD provincial governor Andronicus, each of which I will now consider briefly in turn. I will then consider a fifth instance concerning Vitinius at the court of Nero.

The story concerning Vespasian comes from the racy and salacious *De Vita Caesarum*, popularly known today as *The Twelve Caesars*, by the first/second-century AD writer Suetonius and therefore probably should not be taken at face value. Suetonius relates that Vespasian, emperor AD 69–79, not only had family roots away from Rome, in the Transpadana region of northern Italy, but also came from a family 'without any ancestral portraits', indeed that the emperor's paternal grandfather was a contractor providing day labourers.[11] Rather than simply being reporting of information, the lack of a family lineage, provincial roots, and family money deriving from business are presented as negative tropes by the writer.

To illustrate how engrained such prejudices were within the upper echelons of Roman society, next we can turn to the case of the emperor Pertinax who reigned for just a matter of months in AD 193 before his assassination. The historian Cassius Dio writing around the same time and a later anonymous writer in the *Scriptores Historiae Augustae* recount contemporary concerns that not only was the emperor born in northern Italy but that he was the son of a freedman father who ran a felt-making shop in the town of Alba Pompeia in Liguria where Pertinax sometimes worked as a youth. Though Vespasian and Pertinax were emperors who reigned over a hundred years apart the salacious and scurrilous gossip about their origins and links to business or trade more or less took the same form.

Gaius Terentius Varro was consul at Rome in the late third century BC, in the year 216. His modest upbringing in the city by a butcher father was grist to the mill for the Roman historians Livy and Valerius Maximus who in their writings laid into Varro for his links to this 'most sordid' trade. That he was one of the Roman commanders at the disastrous Battle of Cannae, one of the worst military defeats in Rome's history, sealed his fate in history, more so than did his modest background.

The fourth case study of elite prejudice concerns the provincial governor of Libya Superior, Andronicus of Berenice, a local man who clashed repeatedly with Synesius, Bishop of Cyrene during his gubernatorial incumbency that started in AD 411. Synesius eventually pursued his excommunication. In his letters Synesius raised the issue that not only was Andronicus serving in a province in which he was born but he was the son of a fisherman. While the Bishop claimed a clear and proud ancestry for himself, his opponent had no lineage to declare and thus somehow was not worthy of his position or respect. In a lengthy condemnatory letter the Bishop wrote that 'this fellow cannot tell the name of his own grandfather, nor even of his father, except by guess, and from a tunny fisher's perch on a crag he has come at a bound into the governor's chariot'.[12] Such petty snobbery seems totally out of place and somewhat otiose among horrific details of the governor's criminal and violent behaviour while in post.

The fifth and final story concerns an instance when provincial origins, humble artisan beginnings, and disability were merged together as weapons of character assassination in the case of Vitinius from Benevento in southern Italy who held some influence for a while at the court of Nero (reigned AD 54–68), in the process drawing the scorn of both Juvenal and particularly Tacitus: 'Vitinius was one of the most hideous monstrosities at Court ... bred in a cobbler's booth, deformed in body and scurrilous of wit...'[13]

History is surely littered with hundreds more examples of such petty snobbery, Napoleon's jibe that England was 'just a nation of shopkeepers' being among them. Rather more recently British Prime Minister Margaret Thatcher was being derided by the press as 'a grocer's daughter' but cleverly turned that insult around to suggest that this in fact had taught her frugality and 'good housekeeping'. However, it certainly had not taught her empathy or humility.

Turning now to evidence of blatant Roman class prejudice reflected in the epigraphic record, focus must first turn to an inscription from the provincial Roman town of Sarsina in northern Italy, from whose Pian di Bezzo necropolis comes an inscribed tombstone dating to the first century BC whose dedicatory inscription provides a remarkable insight into the mindset either of a somewhat bigoted elite individual, Horatius Balbus, or of the local provincial elite to which he belonged.[14] In translation, the epitaph on the tombstone in the town's *Museo Archeologico Nazionale* reads: 'Horatius Balbus ... gives burial places at his own expense, to his municipal townsmen and other residents, except for those who have hired themselves out as gladiators, have taken their own life by their own hand with a noose, or pursued a polluted craft for profit.' In many ways the issues of pollution and tainted profit very much reflect the undercurrents of class distaste in some of the written sources we have discussed above, and show that anti-worker prejudice was not simply a harmless Roman literary trope but that it was also probably part of the daily lived experience of many workers.

But such views were not necessarily universal, nor were they chronologically consistent. Indeed, also from Sarsina, though dating much later, to the second century AD, is a densely inscribed funerary altar dedicated to Cetrania Severina, a priestess of the cult of the deified Marciana (the late sister of the emperor Trajan) and wife of an *Augustalis* (a religious magistrate in the imperial cult of Augustus), that carried notice of her bequest of 6,000 *sesterces* to the three large *collegia* of the town – the *collegia dendrophorum* or timber merchants' guild, the *collegia fabrum* or builders and woodworkers' guild, and the *collegia centonariorum* or textile workers' guild.[15] This bequest recognised the significance of particular types of trade and commerce to the town and its well-being and acted as a handy juxtaposition to Balbus's surly whingeing. It is altogether possible that Cetrania Severina's stele and that of Balbus for some time stood together in the Pian di Bezzo necropolis, glaring at each other across the cemetery.

It is against this incriminatory folder of Roman pejorative writings about workers and professionals that we must evaluate the evidence left to us today, principally, though not exclusively, in the form of workers' funerary monuments. Was it really the case that the Roman elite sneered at and denigrated workers while the workers themselves often celebrated their occupations through artistic commissions? Many Roman authors wrote about art, but usually about the history of art and not about contemporary art, and therefore it is not surprising that none of them discussed this artistic phenomenon. Only in one instance can we catch a glimpse of just such an artwork under discussion and consideration, in Petronius's scabrous, fictional *Satyrica*. As the reader might have expected, the commissioner and owner of this artwork, a wall painting, is the monstrous nouveau-riche freedman Trimalchio whose overly lavish banquet forms the book's most memorable and well-known set pieces. This biographical wall painting is described by one of the guests:

There was the slave market, painted complete with placards: and Trimalchio himself, sporting long hair, was holding Mercury's staff and was entering Rome, led by Minerva. Then, how he had learned to keep accounts and had been made *dispensator*, all of this the painstaking artist had recounted along with an explanatory caption. At the place where the porch wall ended, Mercury was whisking him up by the chin to a lofty tribunal. Fortuna stood by with her horn of plenty and the three Fates, spinning their golden threads.[16]

Fighting Prejudice

In the preface to this book I noted that I had consciously decided to omit discussion of slaves from this study because of their completely anomalous position in the Roman world and the sheer complexity of the system. That the imperial slave Montanus could direct his slave Vegetus to purchase the female slave Fortunata for 600 *denarii* in London in AD 80 demonstrates how slavery replicated itself within that system on occasions.

The Roman agricultural writer Varro is reviled today for his description of slaves on a farm estate as being simply 'talking tools', there just to work and to know their place and lacking in human value. Even if household slaves were thought of and treated less contemptuously, as generally seems to have been the case, their common portrayal in Roman art, in wall paintings, on mosaics, mainly on reliefs, and their appearance as images on small items of material culture, lacks any kind of personal agency. Their identity in these instances was being chosen and presented *for* them, not *by* them. That is the distinction that means their images have a subtly different ethos and value to the workers' images that form the core of this study. Again, even though I also discuss the ancient philosophical and societal attitudes towards work and labour, apart from alluding to Varro's writings I will largely ignore the views of other Roman writers on the system of slavery and its operation in the Roman world. Quite recently, in an academic paper on images of Roman slaves on artefacts such as incense burners, lighting equipment, lamp holders, pepper shakers, and food servers, particularly for use in elite households, it was suggested that this represented the overt 'Fetishisation of human labour' at the time. I certainly cannot agree with this interpretation. Rather, I would argue that it represented the fetishisation of slave labour only.[17]

Slaves as a group were not altogether outside the contemporary money economy; many received a regular form of payment-cum-retainer from their master or mistress and some of those working in business or trade on behalf of the master/mistress, that is making them a profit, were allowed to 'earn' and retain a certain amount from these activities for themselves. The system allowed some slaves to purchase their freedom or that of others, and their allowance and earnings enabled some to do just this. Some owners so appreciated the work and character of their slaves that they legally freed them and then became their patrons. Quite commonly, some male owners freed and then married a particular female slave. Some slaves were freed as a condition in the will of their deceased master or mistress. The size and significance of this new freedmen class in Roman society grew over time, as they became a kind of de facto Roman upper working class and middle class, as did the influence of the freeborn sons of former slaves. Most freedmen and many freedwomen worked in the kinds of hands-on occupations discussed in this book, many of the highly literate ones worked in the professions, particularly the bureaucratic ones, and more still worked in routine jobs that never generated much money or satisfaction and which are not reflected in the epigraphic record that has come down to us and which is the principal source for discussions in this book.

However, many of the images that I will consider in this book are of these very freedmen and women, freed slaves in other words. We know this because the inscriptions explicitly tell us this or it can be safely deduced from the form of names of the individuals commemorated and other clues. As has been noted, these freedmen and women constituted a large and important section of Roman society, virtually an established class, and something therefore needs to be said about this class of Romans in general before specific individuals are discussed. They were certainly not some kind of invisible underclass and indeed would seem to have been both economically and culturally important in Roman society, generating wealth and acting as patrons of the arts and in building works. Power and wealth wielded influence. Of course, some individual freedmen or women might have been deluded about themselves and have had pretensions easily mocked by the Roman cultural and political elite. One has only to think of Petronius's literary creation Trimalchio mentioned above, that grotesque cultural archetype of a boorish freedman, to see how class divisions and jealousies operated openly as well as clandestinely.[18]

If elite prejudice was rife in Rome against workers, tradesmen and those who sought to make a profit away from the land, then we can see that in a number of instances rich freedmen kicked back against this snobbery, by way of the only route open to them: ostentatious display. In some ways this was an art of emancipation.

Building the City
There was no greater manifestation of being part of Rome, or of other Roman period towns and cities, than having helped build it

or renew its buildings, streets and infrastructure – and creating or presenting images of that work to others. Two particular images chronologically top and tail such a discussion, the first-century AD Tomb of the Haterii and the fifth-century or later Trier Ivory *Adventus* Relief.

Large portions of a remarkable funerary monument, the Tomb of the Haterii, that once stood on the Via Labicana in Rome, are on display today in the *Musei Vaticani*.[19] Quintus Haterius, a rich freedman of the later first century AD, would appear to have been a highly successful building contractor in the city. His family tomb carried intricate carved reliefs depicting the lying in state of his dead wife, images of numerous buildings along the Via Sacra in Rome probably traversed by his funerary procession, and of a huge building crane powered by slaves on a wheel caught in the process of constructing a tomb, along with other sculptural decoration in the form of mythological scenes, and also including statue portrait busts of Quintus Haterius and his wife. Quintus's bust, enclosed in an *aedicula*, is of a bare-chested man with a mantle draped over one shoulder. His features are rendered in the contemporary Flavian veristic style and his hair is fashionably cut and styled. A serpent lies at the foot of the bust, a symbol of death and renewal. This portrait in itself gives no clues as to the profession of the man depicted.

The vibrant and busy construction scene, often called the Tower Crane scene (Plate 1), comprises dense imagery redolent of the portrayal of a military battle on a work of Roman imperial art. Multiple viewpoints, shifting scales and perspective together evoke the constant state of transformation at the construction site. The huge Tower Crane itself is a similar device to that described by the Roman architectural writer Vitruvius, consisting of two masts connected at the top and fitted with a three-pulley block that carries a rope attached to a windlass operated by a treadmill. Five men operate the treadmill crane in this scene while four others busy themselves with the secondary system of pulleys and guy ropes that would have been used to hoist the crane. Once the crane was vertical these would have been employed to lift, position and place large stone building blocks. In experimental tests and mathematical calculations it has been estimated that such a crane could have had a maximum height of between 15 and 18 metres and that it could have been used to lift a 6.2 ton block of stone up to 13 metres into the air using at least one three-pulley block and a 1 metre diameter windlass powered by five men on the treadmill. A similar crane operated by a treadmill is depicted on a relief from Capua, which will be discussed more fully below.

Two men can be seen climbing to the top of the crane's jib in order to attach a branch to its top, in order to symbolically close off the building at its completion, what would be called a topping-off ceremony on construction sites today. Here it could have carried a further symbolic value in that the tomb on which the image appears marks the 'topping-off' of the life of its inhabitant.

Interestingly, an account of the raising in AD 357 of a huge Egyptian basalt obelisk at the Circus Maximus in Rome is given by Ammianus Marcellinus[20] who wrote that 'to tall beams which were brought and raised on end (so that you would see a very grove of derricks) were fastened long and heavy ropes in the likeness of a manifold web hiding the sky with their excessive numbers ... while many thousand men turned wheels resembling millstones', these wheels being what we would call capstans today.

The Haterii Tower Crane relief scene and the relief scene of the view of a street on the same monument, which will be returned to shortly, is not just about a family but about a family in a particular city, the metropolis of Rome, a city of light, a city of empire. Portraying the building of the city was a celebration of its streets and back alleyways, of its apartment blocks, its sumptuous houses, its temples, markets, and open spaces. When we visit Rome today it is like a city of ghosts, of people and buildings both present and absent, as was the Rome depicted on the Tomb of the Haterii.

The street scene relief from the Tomb of the Haterii is thought to be a depiction of the Via Sacra in Rome. Five buildings are portrayed, with portions of two others. But why this street and why these particular buildings? It may be that in portraying the Via Sacra the family was here commemorating the very route followed by the funerary procession. Given that we have already been presented with an unusual, intimate, and graphic portrayal of lying-in-state of a body in another relief scene it might have been expected that there could be no qualms in picturing the funeral procession down the street. Some academic commentators have argued that this was simply a portrayal of famous contemporary Flavian monuments and buildings in the city whose portrayal would allow the viewer to situate the Haterii in both time and space; a locational mnemonic device in other words. However, scholarly opinion presently favours the explanation that we are being presented here with images of actual buildings constructed by the building firm, a kind of *Res Gestae* for the Haterii family. This certainly seems to make a great deal of sense. The identification of these buildings is problematic, but the buildings portrayed are thought to be, from right to left: the Temple of Jupiter Stator in the *Forum Romanum*; the Arch of Titus (helpfully identified with an inscription that reads '*Arcus in Sacra Via Summa*'); a large arch in profile with a chariot group statue on top; the Colosseum; a partial view of a small arch or colonnade in profile, with statues of horses or a quadriga on top; and the Arch to Isis (again identified for us with an inscribed tag '*Arcus ad Isis*') that formed the ornamental entrance to the Temple of Isis and Serapis in the Campus Martius. Though at first sight the viewer might have thought that the image of the buildings portrayed here represented a continuous street scene, this was not in fact the case. Indeed, these individual structures were not a continuous or contiguous set and were in some cases many miles apart.

It has been noted that almost as much prominence is given along the street to the portrayal of statues as there is to actual buildings and structures. This need not necessarily present us with any kind of dilemma as to what this might have meant. Rather, it surely means that in public buildings in Rome the provision of statuary was part and parcel of the conception and execution of the project.

If the Haterii building firm had indeed been connected with the building of the Colosseum, one of the largest, if not the largest, building project of its time in Rome, it is no wonder they had made their fortune and were about to express their status through the commissioning of such a magnificent and expensive funerary monument that made no effort to hide their origins or professional status.

At least four centuries later than the Haterii image is the fifth-century or later Trier Ivory *Adventus* Relief (Plate 3), a complex and dense depiction of a late antique imperial ceremonial procession taking place in Constantinople where the piece was probably manufactured.[21] Since the mid-nineteenth century this small ivory panel, probably from a Byzantine reliquary, has been housed in the Cathedral Treasury in Trier, Germany. The scene relevant to discussion here might appear almost incidental to the overarching grand narrative of interlinked imperial authority and Christian piety presented as an image on the ivory, yet in many respects it is crucial. The large church building depicted here is probably the church of St Mary Chalkoprateia in Constantinople, the church in the copper market area, though not all academic commentators agree even on this.

The ivory might have been commissioned to commemorate the consecration of the church in AD 449 under Theodosius II or be a later depiction of that event perhaps. Alternatively, it might depict the arrival of the relics of St Stephen in Constantinople in AD 421. Whatever the case, outside the church an empress greets the arrival of the emperor at the head of a large procession that includes a wheeled vehicle transporting two individuals, probably bishops, together holding a large casket in which it can be assumed are contained holy relics of some kind. Behind them can be seen a bust of Christ on what is usually identified as the city's Chalke Gate. A vast crowd of spectators looks on, but on the church roofs can be seen four men putting the finishing touches to the tiling, flashing or the brickwork. For these men, the building work being undertaken is both literally and metaphorically *a sacred task*. For workers such as these men to be depicted on a luxury ivory commemorative piece and to be depicted in the presence of a Roman emperor and empress, of an image of Christ, and of holy relics, is quite extraordinary and totally unprecedented. It is perhaps making the point that though the frenzied spate of church building in both Rome and Constantinople at this time represented an imperial and elite project, it was nevertheless a project that could not be undertaken without the labour and skill of trained and experienced builders. I will return to a discussion of links between quotidian work and workers and the divine in the Roman world later in the chapter after I have presented other evidence relating to the Roman building industry.

Again, consequential images of construction workers appeared on another piece of art from Late Antiquity, the lower part of the base of the Obelisk of Theodosius set up at the Hippodrome in Constantinople, now Istanbul, in AD 390.[22] The upper parts of the base carry scenes including the emperor and his entourage in attendance at the Hippodrome. On the north-eastern face of the lower base are depicted scenes of the massive obelisk, brought from Aswan in Egypt via Alexandria where it had been in storage for over thirty years, lying full-length on the ground at the Hippodrome site. A senior official, probably Proclos as named in an inscription on the monument, directs workers to raise the great obelisk with ropes and windlasses, a task that the inscription suggests took 'thirty-two days', and on the south-western face we can see it erected in position. These images represent a remarkable and unique example of intertextuality in such a context, with the creation of the imperial obelisk monument being represented on the monument itself.

Another image of building work being undertaken, this time in the form of a fresco, can be found in the Tomb or *Hypogeum* of Trebius Justus, also known by his nickname of Asellus, near the start of the Via Latina in Rome.[23] Dating to the first decades of the fourth century AD, this tomb's decorative scheme of frescos has attracted a great deal of scholarly interest, and opinion is split between those who would interpret the overall design as a metaphorical and allusive reflection of what they interpret as the Gnostic beliefs of the family buried here and those who believe that the images can be interpreted more literally. This is not the place to repeat and weigh up the pros and cons of these academic arguments: rather, discussion will largely concentrate on those frescos which appear to suggest that Trebius Justus senior may have been the owner of a construction company and/or an architect (in the same way as the Haterii family discussed above) with his son Asellus, who died aged just twenty-one, also working in the family firm or practice.

The tomb was originally built by the parents of Trebius Justus or Asellus, that is by his father of the same name and his mother Honoratia Severina, who while they may have been Gnostics were more likely to have been Christians, as suggested by the image of the Good Shepherd in a medallion roundel on the tomb's vault. In another scene the parents of Trebius Justus present him with an embroidered cloth on which are laid out what appear to be items of jewellery or personal adornment, almost in the form of a pagan offering of *ex votos*.

The fresco panel of most interest to this study depicts the construction of a brick building, with five workmen engaged in various tasks. Scaffolding is set up around the shell of the building which is about one storey high. A man carries a large basket of bricks on his shoulder, another climbs up a ladder up against the scaffolding carrying a trug of ready-mixed mortar, two bricklayers can be seen at work with their trowels laying bricks from the scaffolding at first-floor level, one on either side of the wall, while in the right foreground a fifth man mixes mortar and shovels it into an elongated trough on a stand beside him. Of course, this scene could have been metaphorical or allusive. Indeed, visually it is highly reminiscent of the building of the Tower of Babel in so many medieval Byzantine and Venetian images.

In another fresco panel in the tomb an older man, probably Trebius Justus senior, is shown talking to another man who is identified by a painted caption as being *Magister* Generosus. The older man holds a long architect or builder's measuring rod, while Generosus holds a short rule in one hand and what might be a trowel in the other, suggesting that the two worked together regularly in professional harmony, with Generosus as a trusted site foreman, otherwise it is difficult to see why a non-family member should be picked out in this very specific way. They stand in a garden in front of a large building, possibly a building that they themselves had planned and constructed, though equally it could be their business premises or the family home.

In one scene Asellus is shown seated on a folding chair with writing tablets on his knee and a scroll in his right hand, surrounded by a large collection of writing equipment and materials set up on the ground around him. The very fact that this particular panel stresses the role of writing, literacy, and probably drawing in the professional life of Trebius Justus suggests that his profession was that of architect, the role so highly praised by Cicero. In other panels on the tomb walls Asellus is shown with farmers and agricultural produce, and an image of the transportation of building materials and agricultural produce by mules also occurs in another.

This tomb was in no way a public monument in the way that earlier funerary monuments in Rome's cemeteries strung out along the roads out from the city had been. Access would have been severely restricted, possibly only to the direct family and members of whichever religious sect they belonged to. The largely profane or neutral decorative scheme of the tomb concentrates on scenes of everyday life, or so it would appear if these scenes are taken at face value.

It is both somehow ironic and noteworthy that one of the most significant freedmen funerary monuments of early imperial

Rome – the Tomb of the Haterii – and one of the most important painted burial crypts in fourth century Rome – the *Hypogeum* of Trebius Justus – should both carry scenes of building construction. Together they testify to the ever-changing nature of the city of Rome itself and the service of its workforce over those three centuries or so.

There is no suggestion that Quintus Haterius or Trebius Justus were anything other than highly successful building contractors, though neither man identified himself with any kind of a job title in an inscription, and they would not appear to have been what the Romans would have termed an *architectus* or architect or a *mensor aedificiorum* or building surveyor, though such terms would seem to have been quite fluid in the ancient world and were not necessarily strictly comparable to our present-day ideas of what an architect is or does.

Just because Cicero praised architects, along with doctors, as learned professionals to be admired does not mean that such sentiments were universally shared at the time.[24] Just as Greek and Roman medicine is a professional field about which many contemporary books and treatises have come down to us, so we do also have a major book on architecture, *De Architectura* by Vitruvius Pollio. Leaving aside the practical aspects of this work, Vitruvius also supplies biographical information about a number of named ancient Greek architects but only about two named Roman architects, Cossutius and Mucius. It must not be forgotten that Vitruvius himself was a working architect as well as a writer, first in the army, and then designing a basilica for Fanum in the Marche region of Italy and working on some of the aqueducts of Rome under Marcus Agrippa. Many Roman architects were probably army engineers, as we would term them today. Indeed, the famed Apollodorus of Damascus was the court architect for the emperor Trajan and like so many other architects in the Roman world he honed his craft and professional skills on campaign with the Roman army before turning to grand urban design projects.

As examples, the funerary monuments of three Roman architect/builders will be discussed here, along with the anonymous depiction of a fourth architect on a North African mosaic pavement. The Hadrianic funerary stele of the building surveyor Titus Statilius Aper from Rome (Plate 2), now in the city's *Musei Capitolini*, bears a depiction of him on the front holding a scroll, perhaps of architectural drawings. Described in the inscription as a *mensor aedificiorum,* his writing equipment – inkwell and scrolls – is depicted on one of the sides of the stele and his measuring rod and scale on the other. Thus, we can see that Aper has been depicted as both a practical man and a man of learning.

Also from Rome, from the *Catacomba di Pretestato,* comes a remarkable and unusual late Roman sarcophagus in the form of a house or temple, bearing a relief of technical instruments, including a *libella* or architect's square, a ruler, compasses, a chisel and a hammer. The tiled roof of the building, its supporting columns and the partially open front door suggest allusions to both the houses of the living and those of the dead, in the same way that the Tomb of the Haterii used images of classical buildings to connect life and the afterlife, as well as professional dedication and religious observance. While this is most likely to be the resting place of an architect or builder, in the absence of a dedicatory inscription it is also equally possible that it is the sarcophagus of a non-artisanal person for whom the images of tools were highly symbolic, but symbolic only. The symbolism of craft and trade tools will be further discussed in later chapters.

Away from Rome, from Arles, and now in the *Musée Départemental Arles Antique* there, comes a second or third century AD sarcophagus dedicated to a specialist architect: 'Quintus Candidus Benignus, master builder of the Arles guild ... He had the full extent of the building art, dedication, knowledge and discretion; great technicians on any occasion declared him head of the association; nobody was more knowledgeable than that; nobody could defeat him; he knew how to construct both hydraulic devices (*organa aquarum*) and water conduits (*ducere cursum*)....' An axe and a *libella* or carpenter's square appear in relief as decoration on the sarcophagus.

On a fifth-century mosaic in the *Musée National du Bardo* in Tunis, Tunisia, can be seen an architect and his assistant. A stone column is carried on to a building site, mortar is mixed, and a stone carver works on a small column. The architect appears holding a large measuring rod in one hand while gesturing with his other hand at a now-damaged inscription, perhaps originally bearing his name, inside a wreath. Beside him sits a capital, a set square, a plumb bob and line, and a stake for setting out lines. As this pavement originally came from a Christian basilica in the region of Zaghouan it is likely that we are seeing here the building of that very structure or some allusion to work, creation, and spirituality.

Moving on from the consideration of individual major building contractors and architects in the Roman world, there are numerous other depictions of building work and building workers from Rome and elsewhere in Italy and around the Empire that will now be briefly considered. Examples of the depiction of such men as site labourers, masons, roofers and tilers, plasterers, wall painters, mosaicists, and carpenters are all known. As with all the jobs, trades, and professions discussed in this book I am not aiming to produce any kind of full catalogue of images of any particular category of worker. Rather, I am aiming to provide a sufficiently broad range of examples of each type of image to illustrate the scope and scale of the phenomenon.

It has already been mentioned above during discussion of the Tower Crane relief from the Tomb of the Haterii that there is a somewhat crude and sketchy image of another treadmill crane on a dedicatory relief from the ruins of the amphitheatre at Capua (Plate 4) which is now in the city's *Museo Campano*, the crane being operated by two men inside the wheel lifting a monolithic column shaft into place using a block and tackle, though unfeasibly the wheel and crane do not appear to be physically connected in the image. A workman kneeling on the ground in front of the wheel is shown carving a capital. The presence of a number of figures of deities, the god Jupiter and goddesses Minerva and Diana and the *Genius Theatri* (named in an inscribed caption), in attendance suggests that this was almost some kind of sacred task depicted, and indeed an inscription below this scene confirms that we are not simply viewing a mythological scene. The crude inscription reads: *Lucceius Peculiaris Redemptor Prosceni Ex Biso Fecit*, which translates as 'Lucceius Peculiaris impressario restored the proscenium after a vision'. The relief probably dates from the late third or early fourth century AD. The links displayed here between certain pagan deities and specific types of work and craft is most interesting and will be considered further below.

A first or second century AD terracotta relief found at Terracina, Lazio, and now in the *Museo Nazionale Romano* in Rome, again shows work taking place on a construction site. In the foreground two workmen are shown cutting and preparing stone blocks, one using a hammer and the other a maul. On top of a wall a man is taking hold of a stone block being winched into position using a crane. Also in that museum's collection is a second terracotta relief, from Via Cassia in Rome and probably dating slightly later, again depicting a crane in operation. Further reliefs depicting on-site lifting devices at work are reported as coming from Pratica di Mare, Rome, and Syracuse, Sicily, but the author has not seen these particular items or illustrations of them.

It is uncertain whether the Terracina, Via Cassia, Pratica di Mare and Syracuse relief panels or plaques were architectural items, relating to building dedications like the Capua relief or whether they might have been funerary items. Certainly, as we shall see later in the book, there was a tradition of displaying work-related pictorial plaques outside some of the individual tombs in the *Necropoli di Porto* cemetery, at Isola Sacra, Ostia, and such traditions may well have extended elsewhere in central Italy and beyond.

A wall painting from the *caldarium* of the bath suite at the Villa San Marco, just outside the town of Stabiae on the Bay of Naples, and now in store in the *Antiquarium Stabiano Castellammare di Stabia*, carries a depiction of a busy building site, as a large stone structure rises high above its foundations. An ox-drawn wagon, its load covered by a tarpaulin, presumably contains building materials brought to the site. A labourer hands a brick or stone to a second man atop the unfinished wall. Other men busy themselves on site lifting and carrying materials, and roughing-out and chiselling stone blocks. Others apply plaster or cut capitals. In the foreground two men operate a type of hoist known as a 'goat', lifting a large stone block up to a third man on top of the wall. Two men carry a stone block across site using wooden poles as a stretcher, two other men break stone blocks with mallets, and a fifth man in this team carries off chippings in a basket on his back. This scene probably represents the largest single number of men shown working on such a building project anywhere in the Roman world.

Dating to the first century AD the significance of this particular fresco is not immediately apparent, as it is one of a series of at least four fresco vignettes in the *caldarium*, the others being more idealised landscape scenes with structures, with the god Mercury as a recurring presiding deity. The building being constructed could be the villa bath house itself, but this cannot be proven. The scene could be purely allusive or it could be mythological, such as the depiction of the building of the walls of Troy, also incidentally involving the use of a mechanical hoist, on a wall painting from the House of Vedius Siricus at Pompeii. It has been suggested that Narcissus, a freedman of the emperor Claudius, may have owned the Villa San Marco at the time, but even if proven this would not necessarily shed light on the meaning of the building site scene.

In Rome itself it seems appropriate to briefly mention the appearance of images of the construction of fortifications, walls, and buildings on two major monuments in the city centre, on the Basilica Aemilia in the *Forum Romanum* and on Trajan's Column. A series of decorative relief friezes was probably added to the Basilica Aemilia during the restoration of 14 BC and included depictions of the building of the city walls of Lavinium, the *Rape of the Sabine Women*, the *Punishment of Tarpeia*, and various battle scenes, all images of Rome's mythical and deep past.[25] The mythic significance of Aeneas' founding of Lavinium and its building mirrored the Augustan agenda and shows the blocks of stone for Lavinium's wall being put in place by workers in the relief image, a depiction of virtually a sacred task, a ritual task. In a number of scenes on the helical frieze around Trajan's Column, dating to AD 113 and depicting elements of the emperor's Dacian Wars, can be seen soldiers of the Roman army hard at work building fortifications, digging ditches, and building defensive walls. The images of their hard work, repeated in numerous scenes on the frieze – there are nearly as many scenes of construction as there are scenes of war and destruction – are ideologically riven and represent a politically charged imperial trope in this context.[26]

While I am discussing representations of building workers,[27] it seems appropriate to briefly mention a few good examples of the occurrence of images of those kinds of support workers who would furbish and finish off the completed shells of these buildings, tradesmen such as marble cutters, mosaicists, wall plasterers and frescoists, and carpenters. I will discuss workers such as sculptors in later chapters.

In the case of marble cutters, from Ostia comes a fragment of an early fourth century AD funerary stele on which is depicted a scene in what is thought to be a marble workers' workshop where mosaic *tesserae* or pieces of marble inlay were made. The fragment is in the stores of the *Museo Ostiense*. Two men sit on low stools, both with a specialised stone hammer in their right hands, each leaning forward over an anvil-like block on which they hold a piece of stone, ready to cut them with the hammers. A basket sits at the side of one stool, to hold cut *tesserae*. In the background a workshop manager gestures to two men, ordering them to hurry off with the huge sacks of *tesserae* that they carry on their shoulders. The scene is highly specific and detailed and is unlikely to be simply allusive: presumably therefore this particular stele was commissioned for a marble workshop owner, whose name and epitaph we are sadly missing.

Of considerable interest as well is a huge late first century AD funerary stele from the necropolis of Villa San Maurizio (Plate 5), now in the *Museo Civico Reggio nell'Emilia* in northern Italy. The largest, central portion of the front of the stele is taken up with an image of a married couple, framed inside a building, in the symbolic *dextrarum iuncto* or linked-hands pose of fidelity. The inscription above identifies them as the freedwoman Pettia Ge, who paid for the memorial, and her freedman husband Caius Clodius 'Antiocho' – from Antioch and described as a *marmorarius* or marble worker. Their patron and previous master is also acknowledged, along with other freedwomen. In the register below, with a later extension of the epitaph, are depicted precise and detailed images of the five specialised tools of Clodius's trade – a stone hammer, a *libella* – a sort of A-frame level, a plumb line, a square and a stone chisel.

While we may view Roman fresco painters and mosaicists as *artists* today, in contemporary ancient Roman society such workers would have simply been viewed as skilled artisans. For this reason there is little Roman writing on these arts. While Pliny the Elder mentioned the second century BC mosaicist Sosos of Pergamon – creator of the original 'Unswept Floor' mosaic – by name in his *Naturalis Historia*, he named no Romans working in that field.

Evidence for individual mosaicists working in the Roman world is therefore rare, though through the use of stylistic and typological analysis to study mosaics archaeologists are able to posit the existence of schools of mosaicists and even suggest the location of such schools, though no workshop has ever been identified by excavation. There is a single known portrayal of mosaicists at work on a second century AD mosaic pavement from El Alia, ancient Uzalis, in Tunisia, now in the *Musée du Bardo* in Tunis. In this little intertextual vignette which forms an almost incidental scene as part of the larger depiction of life at a riverside village, a workman can be seen carrying a small basket, presumably containing stone *tesserae*, across to a second man who quite clearly is engaged in cutting the *tesserae* with a hammer and laying them onto a mortar bed.

An inscribed funerary stele dating to the first or second century AD from Perinthos in Thrace in Greece is dedicated to the mosaicist by his son Proklos. Unfortunately the father's name is not given, though it is recorded that he was eighty years old when he died. 'In many cities I have triumphed over all other mosaicists with my artistic skill, which was supported by the gifts of Pallas Athena ...' declares the Greek inscription, and Proklos the son also proudly proclaimed in the inscription that he himself possessed 'equal artistic skill' to his father, something he perhaps felt more comfortable asserting now that his father was dead.

Some mosaics carried what might have been pictorial signature traits, and quite a large number carried the artist's names as signatures, though academics do not agree how many of these might refer to the craftsmen who designed and laid the floors and how many to dedicants and patrons, but it could be that as many as seventy or eighty mosaicists' names are known.[28] The majority of examples are from pavements in Greece, Spain, Gaul, and North Africa, with only a few from Italy itself. Sometimes the formula *ex officina* – 'from the workshop of ...' – was used, sometimes something as simple as *Monnus fecit* – 'Monnus made this' – was used, as on a third-century AD mosaic from Trier in Germany. During the later, possibly fifth or sixth century, repair of a third century AD mosaic from baths at Vlisippara, near Enfida, again in Tunisia, Sabinianus Senurianus took the opportunity to advertise his repair work with two separate inscribed panels on the mosaic. On one he declared that he had designed and laid the mosaic himself, adding 'have a good bath', and on the other that the mosaic was all his own work, created without the input of a designer. A sixth century AD mosaic from Thebes in Greece is signed by both its designer Demetrios and by Epiphanes who claims to have laid the floor 'with great care'. It seems slightly unfair and gratuitous to close this discussion by suggesting that considering what a poor piece of work the repair to the Vlisippara mosaic was, with its badly rendered female bust, it is unlikely that Sabinianus was ever let loose again on his own to design a pavement.

On a third century AD mosaic at Lillebonne, France, is the signature of T. Sextius or Sennius Felix from Puteoli in Italy and mention is made of Amor, a *discipulus*, a trainee or apprentice. On a fourth century AD pavement from Carranque, near Toledo in Spain, Hirinius is named as the painter but the workshop belonged to Ma[ ]us (name uncertain). The artist signs off by declaring; 'good luck, Maternus, in the use of this room.' Another mosaic in the same building is signed as the product of the workshop of Iulius Prudens. On a third century mosaic from Chania on Crete the mosaicist identifies himself as being from Daphne (Antioch).

An undated funerary stele from Benevento in central southern Italy was set up by Carpus and dedicated to his son Hermas, a slave, who we are told fell to his death making a wall mosaic. Another wall mosaicist or *museiarius* was a freedman of the emperor Tiberius called Nicephorus who was commemorated along with his freedmen and freedwomen and their descendants on a funerary monument in Rome around the mid-first century AD. Just outside Rome, at Pantanelle on the Via Latina, is a mid-first century AD grand funerary monument to four freedmen called P. Maneilius who styled themselves as *structores paeimentari* – 'builders of pavements'.

A *marmorarius* who would seem to have cut and made what are called *opus sectile* pavements or panels is portrayed with one of his works in progress on a small marble slab of the second half of the fourth century AD, now on display in the *Museo Nazionale Romano Terme di Diocleziano* in Rome (Plate 6). It is likely that this slab derives from one of the catacombs but its exact provenance is unknown.

From Sens, in Burgundy, France, comes an extremely badly damaged funerary relief, perhaps of the second century AD, depicting a team of three plasterers and fresco painters at work, while a fourth man, probably either their direct overseer or the project architect, sits on some stairs and examines an unfurled scroll, presumably on which a plan has been drawn. The scene is set inside a high-ceilinged room. One of the labourers mixes plaster on the floor, stirring it with a long pole. Up on a trestle scaffold, the other two labourers are at work. One holds a bucket of mixed wet plaster with one hand, and applies it to the wall using a specialised plasterer's trowel called a float with the other, while the third man holds a palette in one hand, and with the other uses a paintbrush to start applying colour to the areas of dry plaster. This relief is in the town's *Musées de Sens* where it forms part of a large collection of funerary monuments bearing images of local Gallo-Roman workers and artisans, the occurrence and significance of such clusters being topics for discussion in Chapter Eight.

A small number of images of carpenters is also known: these will briefly be discussed here, though it is recognised that though many carpenters would have worked on construction projects and thus be more akin to builders, others would have specialised in the manufacture of wooden items, such as furniture.[29] Very specialised carpenters such as boatbuilders and wheelwrights will be discussed separately in Chapter Six, and the religious devotions of a guild of carpenters at Pompeii will be discussed in Chapter Eight.

In his catalogue of occupational images from Rome and Italy Gerhard Zimmer listed six examples of carpenters or woodworkers, two or three of whom were wheelwrights, and quite a number of portrayals of carpenters' tools on their own as identifying symbols. Of the other three examples one can perhaps be discounted. This late first century AD ash chest from Tivoli dedicated to C. Volcacius Artemidorus bears an image of a seated man carving, with a cow next to him and a cloaked woman looking on, with a winged figure and goat also present. This is actually a portrayal of the story of Daedalus carving a cow for Pasiphae: as Daedalus was often associated with carpenters and seen by them as a protective mythological patron it is possible that the scene here did allude to the deceased's occupation: incidentally, an image of Icarus, son of Daedalus, sat working at a carpenter's bench appears on a mid-first century AD wall painting in the House of the Vettii at Pompeii. A late first century AD grave relief from Isola Sacra, Ostia carries an image of two men operating a large saw, one man being topless, the other in a loose tunic. Whether they are carpenters sawing wood or masons sawing marble is uncertain. A mid-third century AD sarcophagus fragment in the *Musei Vaticani* in Rome carries a portrait medallion of the deceased below which is a scene of two men working at either end of a carpenter's bench, one hammering a table leg and the other using a plane. Omitted from Zimmer's catalogue is a possibly late first century AD altar relief from Rome in the *Centro Montemartini* out-station of the *Musei Capitolini*, possibly from a temple dedicated to Minerva, depicting the busy interior of a carpentry workshop, with tools hanging up on the wall. Though badly damaged, it is possible to make out at least five men at work, variously operating lathes and working timber.

A sixth figure might be the goddess herself. This could be an altar dedicated by a carpenters' guild, which would help explain the significance of the scene, or we could be seeing workers in the process of building the temple to Minerva, or it could even be a mythological scene perhaps linked to the building of the Trojan horse.

However, perhaps the best depiction of a carpenter, illustrated here, is on an uninscribed funerary stele, perhaps of the second century AD, from Reims in north-eastern France and now in the *Musée Saint-Remi* there (Plate 7). A man sits at a carpenter's workbench holding a tool, beneath the bench sits a basket for offcuts or sawdust sweepings. A set of tools sit ready in a rack on the workshop wall. It has been suggested that this is in fact an image of a shoemaker but the absence of tell-tale shoe lasts in the scene suggests otherwise.

In the *Museo Biblioteca Apostolica Vaticana* in the *Musei Vaticani* in Rome is an early fourth century AD gold on glass vessel decorated with a pictorial scene that consists of the large central figure of a man surrounded by six vignettes of carpenters at work, on a boat perhaps, sawing and planing at workbenches. As in the altar relief scene discussed above Minerva also appears on the plate which is very surprising given that this was probably an item of Christian gift-giving like other such decorated gilt glass vessels of the period. The man may well have been the owner of a carpentry business. It is difficult to understand why a craft operation should be celebrated on an item of luxury goods. However, if the figure of Vulcan could have been thought of as bridging the wide gap between the divine and the diurnal world of work, then a similar spin could have been put on the figure of Jesus as a carpenter.

In the second half of this chapter discussion began with consideration of the significance of the Roman Haterii family overtly celebrating their status achieved through the success of their building company in a funerary context. Others engaged in the building industry such as architects, mosaicists, and wall or fresco artists were then subsequently discussed. The relative worth of some of these trades and professions can perhaps be gauged by looking at the relevant entries in Diocletian's Edict on Maximum Prices of AD 301 which set out a regulatory framework for the prices of goods and services across the Roman empire in a vain effort to curb inflationary excess.[30] For instance, the Edict laid down that: a teacher of architecture should be paid no more than 100 *denarii* per boy per month (architects' work fees received no mention); a stone mason's wage was capped at 50 *denarii* a day; a worker in marble no more than 60 *denarii* a day; a wall painter should be paid no more than seventy *denarii* a day and a *pictor imaginarius* one hundred and fifty; a *musaearius* should be paid no more than sixty *denarii* a day and a *tessellarius* fifty. It has been suggested that the two different types of mosaicists listed here were differentiated because one worked on floor mosaics and the other on wall mosaics, but it is much more likely that the *musaearius* was more highly skilled than the *tessellarius*: indeed, that the role was more akin to a designer. However, both were still paid at a day rate which confirms that mosaic work was very much viewed as a craft, albeit a skilled one, rather than an art as such. A distinction between *musivarii* and *tessellarii* was also made in the AD 337 Edict of Constantine which also interestingly mentioned the need for craftsmen such as these, as well as sculptors, painters and goldsmiths, to be exempt from certain taxes in order to train their sons in their craft.

Workers and the Gods

If the Trier *Adventus* Ivory discussed above represents an extraordinary example of late Roman workers' endeavours being linked to Christian religious practice and ideology then it is worth considering here briefly some specific links between workers and a number of the pagan gods and goddesses of Rome at an earlier period. This takes two forms: an identification with 'worker deities', principally Minerva (the Roman equivalent of the Greek's Athena) and Vulcan (the equivalent of Hephaistos); and the use of moral messages conveyed through images of the gods or other mythological figures. Finally in this context I will briefly consider the figure of the Titan Prometheus and the significance of his image as a creator/maker for Roman culture.

Roman women particularly identified with the goddess Minerva, and indeed, as we shall see, in some instances this identification was actively encouraged by certain Roman male ideologies. Minerva's links to weaving not only helped to initiate girls into the Roman household but it also provided metaphors for political power, for statesmanship, and civilisation. Images of weaving were sometimes used as a political metaphor for the cohesion of Roman society under imperial rule rather than weaving simply being shown as representative of a typical, not to say archetypal, female, matronly craft pursuit. However, the goddess also came to be linked to more industrialised cloth and textile production, and to its workers, both male and female.

The owl represented the companion of Minerva and acted as a signifier of her presence. The story behind the beginning of this symbiotic association is unknown. The owl in the ancient world was considered a symbol of knowledge, of wisdom, and of learning and its ability to see in the dark also led to its acting as a darker symbol of foresight or prophecy. However, other less obvious uses were made of Minerva's symbolic owl in Roman times.

In Pompeii, as we will see in a later chapter, the processing of cloth was an important and economically highly significant local industry and the town's powerful and influential guild of fullers – the *fullones* – used the image of the owl as their symbol, thereby alluding to Minerva as the goddess of craft and weaving and as their patron. That explains, for instance, why a painted pillar from the *fullonica* of Lucius Veranius Hypsaeus displayed on each face scenes from the processing of cloth in the workshop. On one side was depicted the inspection and brushing of cloth and a man holding a cage-like structure which has been interpreted as a bleaching frame. On top of the frame sits an owl, again alluding to the fullers' guild and to Minerva.[31]

In Late Antique, fourth and fifth-century AD Roman Christian art the common image of the Virgin Mary Annunciate spinning or with a basket of wool, or both, could be thought of as being in some way part of a continuum of the Minerva/women's craft link and in its own way a moralising presentation of women's craft as a metaphor for spirituality. The writer Proclus took this analogy further in describing Mary's womb as a workshop for the making of Christ's body.[32] However, we must not ignore the evidence that objects carrying such images could have been linked to Christian women's own devotional activities and beware of always seeing them as images perhaps imposed on women as moral exemplars by men.

Depictions of the Roman fire god/smith god Vulcan, and his Greek equivalent Hephaistos, are probably the rarest in numbers of the depictions of the major deities of the Greco-Roman world for some unknown reason.[33] Vulcan was a disabled deity, with either a club foot or a mangled or damaged foot, something quite overtly shown in some Greek works, though not during Roman times. In many cultures and at many different times smiths can be seen to have had a particular and special status, often linked to magic and the supernatural, rather than simply to the worlds of work, craft, and commerce. A special legal status was often afforded these smiths, even though they otherwise had marginal and ambiguous positions within their own communities. In Roman times there is no doubt that there was an interface between craft, communication networks, and urbanisation, often manifested in images of Vulcan, or provincial smith gods, as in Gaul and Britain, for instance.

It is difficult to know how to categorise some of the depictions in Roman art of Prometheus the Titan moulding or creating men from clay, as he was attributed with doing in certain versions of his myth.[34] Images of this act of creation or manufacture are known on sarcophagi from Arles (an example now in the *Musée du Louvre* in Paris) and Pozzuoli (in the *Museo Archeologico Nazionale di Napoli*), for example, and on the decorated discs of ceramic oil lamps (for example, in the *Musei Capitolini* collections), among other media, including engraved gemstones. However, probably the best representation of this occurs on the front panel of a third century AD child's sarcophagus in the *Musei Capitolini* in Rome, from the Albani collection (Plate 8). In the centre of this busy panel, populated by numerous figures of Olympian gods and cupids, can be seen what at first sight could be a depiction of a bearded sculptor at work, holding a small clay human figure on his lap and looking to finish it off with a modelling tool. The sculptor of men here is Prometheus. A second, finished human figure stands on a plinth to one side and a third lies on the ground beyond. The goddess Minerva/Athena reaches out a hand towards the work-in-progress to oversee its provision of a soul. Interestingly, Prometheus was credited with imbuing his human creations with creative power and practical skills, and gifting them fire, perhaps making him a mythological figure that craftsmen and artisans could relate to. A variation on his sculpting or shaping humans is the relatively common image of his hammering together skeletons bone by bone like a model builder.

In ancient Athens there is sufficient evidence to suggest that Athena, as patron of women's crafts, Hephaistos, as patron of smiths in particular and artisans in general, and Prometheus, as patron of craftspeople such as potters and metalworkers and others working with fire, together as a triad sometimes received cultic attention. While this situation where 'technology therefore was given a unique degree of cultic emphasis'[35] was of a particular time and place, it is altogether possible that such a link between the Roman equivalents of these deities and craft workers was also made in later contexts in the Roman world and accounted for some otherwise equivocal depictions of one or another of these three figures. It may have been that such images, and the ideologically charged images of building on the Basilica Aemilia and Trajan's Column discussed above, helped normalise the association of images of work with Roman values and culture, and later led to the further normalisation of work images within the context of funerary commemoration.

If the figures of Vulcan, Minerva, and Prometheus can be thought of as bridging the wide gap between the divine and the diurnal world of work, then it might be that a similar spin was later put on the figure of Jesus as a carpenter. In the case of the *Musei Vaticani* gold on glass vessel decorated with pictorial scenes of carpentry discussed above it is possible that allusion was being made to Jesus' early trade. Most such items had Christian connotations and often were found accompanying burials in the city's catacombs.

Cultural Workers

But what of the other, earthly, human creators of Roman times, the subject of this book? They might not have had formal, political power but they most certainly had cultural agency to forge their own personal and occupational identities in public contexts. Indeed, the names and trades of over twelve hundred men and over two hundred women are known from inscriptions in Rome alone. The variety of occupations attested around the Roman world will strike many readers as extraordinary, with some individual funerary monuments for working people, such as the Tomb of the Haterii for a rich and successful building contractor discussed above, being remarkably grand and expensive. Less grand but equally informative are the dozens of other funerary monuments to people such as Bassilla the mime or actress from Aquileia in northern Italy, Longidienus the shipbuilder from Ravenna, again in Italy's north, and Vitalis the pork butcher from Rome, all of whose memorials will be discussed later in the study.

In the Roman world all kinds of individuals used art and images to define or maintain their identities. The most obvious group doing this was the emperor and imperial families and dynasties. The academic literature analysing the power of images from the age of Augustus, the first emperor, onwards, is enormous but will not concern us here, though it will inform many of the schemes of interpretation of some of the kinds of images with which this book is concerned. Imperial images greatly influenced the way in which Rome's elite and some provincial elites presented themselves through the commissioning of portraits and of funerary monuments. While the Roman emperor and the elite were to some extent 'doing a job', this is not the kind of job on which this study is focused. Likewise, soldiers in the army were also doing a job and their pride in that role became reflected in military funerary art too, often as a result of group cohesion and what we might call regimental identity. The study of workers and their associations or guilds – *collegia* – and the forging of individual and group occupational identities is now becoming fashionable in academic circles but most works on this subject that have appeared in print up to now perhaps surprisingly have paid little heed to the kind of visual evidence I will be using here, the primacy of these studies of Roman *collegia* being economic.

Museology has long been a field in which the display of the luxury items from the classical world has often been juxtaposed with the display of everyday items, though the craftsmanship of both types of items is generally foregrounded in descriptive interpretive panels rather than the lives of the craftsmen and women behind their creation. To paraphrase Antonio Gramsci, if those who did not produce things could not as a result produce words then perhaps the same might be applied to the production of images in the Roman world.[36] Although in a study such as this there is a danger of decontextualising individual artworks by discussing them as part of a trend, movement, or group, as I am doing with 'Roman workers' images', at all times the reader must be aware that my discourse cannot be separated from the large-scale social and ideological changes taking place in Roman society at the time. The ideological forms of Roman art rather than being dependent on strict economic determinism were equally due to the result of the relations among individuals within society, as we will see throughout this book.

In Sandra Joshel's indispensable study of the occupational inscriptions from the city of Rome – *Work, Identity, and Legal Status at Rome* – the number of inscriptions relating to the construction industry was 112, consisting of 71 carpenters and builders, 13 stoneworkers, 23 stucco workers, mosaicists, and painters, and 5 building contractors.[37] It has been this category of worker who 'built the city' that has been the main subject of my first chapter in this present study. In the next chapter attention will be turned to a much smaller, but no less important, category of workers, those who 'fed the city', that is principally bakers and butchers, thirty of whom were represented in Joshel's study, and many more of whom are represented by funerary monuments and other depictions from elsewhere in Italy and further afield in some of the Roman provinces.

2

Feeding the City
The Baker and His Wife

In the introductory chapter of this book I presented evidence for the depiction of those Romans who 'built the city', that is architects, building contractors, construction site workers, stuccoists, and mosaicists. In this chapter attention will be turned to those who it might be said 'fed the city'.

Any study of Roman workers or artisans has to include discussion of the man who today is perhaps the most famous non-elite Roman known to us, Marcus Vergilius Eurysaces, more commonly known to archaeologists and historians as Eurysaces the Baker.[1]

The tomb of Eurysaces the Baker lies just beyond the city of Rome's eastern limits, outside of, but right up against, the Porta Maggiore, and dates to around 30–20 BC, although it could possibly be slightly older (Plates 9–10). When the Tomb of Eurysaces was built the area was a Roman road junction of some complexity just beyond the city boundary, but nevertheless a cemetery ran out from here along the roads. A number of above-ground and below-ground aqueducts also converged here, some built later than the tomb but respecting it. Subsequently, having stood undisturbed for around three hundred years, Eurysaces' tomb was incorporated into the city gate forming part of the new Aurelianic city walls of AD 271–275 and the circuit's further strengthening by Honorius about 130 years later, and there it remained largely hidden until the nineteenth century when demolition works exposed it once more as a free-standing structure. However, only about three-quarters of the tomb is now still intact, and it is truncated at the east end while its roof at the west end, nearest the Porta Maggiore, is missing.

The tomb was not strictly rectangular; indeed, it would seem originally to have been a curious trapezoidal shape, presumably built this way to fit an irregularly shaped plot of land between the intersecting road system here.

The tomb originally stood over thirty feet in height, its base being partially buried today, and consists of a plain tufa base with an entrance door. The first storey above the base consists of a series of vertical tube-like cylinders, this storey being separated from the second storey by a cornice which carries inscriptions on three sides of the monument. The second storey and main body of the travertine-faced concrete tomb takes the form of a set of large circular openings, generally interpreted as images of giant cylindrical bread mixing bins set on their sides, adorned with an upper frieze relief depicting workers inside a bakery, making, baking, and stacking loaves. A low roof tops the structure. The fourth, eastern side of the tomb no longer exists. It is generally accepted that a statue of a man and woman found nearby, Eurysaces and his wife in all probability though the statue bears no inscription, probably originally formed part of the decoration on this missing face but is no longer in situ. Eurysaces was probably a highly successful freedman who made a fortune as a baker and bakery contractor for the Roman state.

Today the area around the tomb constitutes a series of busy, noisy road intersections. The setting of the tomb is now further compromised by its immediate, fenced-off surroundings being overgrown and being used temporarily by unfortunate, homeless rough sleepers. There is no signage or display board here to explain the monument to interested visitors or even to tell them whose tomb this is, though in many respects the structure's sheer size and unusual form alert viewers to its great significance. An opportunity to educate today's visitors to the tomb and casual viewers passing by is being missed here by the guardianship authorities and one wonders if the 'underselling' of this plebeian monument, in contrast to the fine display of the broadly contemporary and equally intriguing pyramid tomb of the magistrate Gaius Cestius, is part of the museological blind eye generally turned towards sites and objects linked to the Roman Empire's workers and artisans.

Returning to the unusual vertical cylinders and circular openings on the tomb's facades, at first sight it might not have been altogether apparent to a contemporary Roman viewer what these vertical and horizontal cylinders were meant to represent: they are not in any way standard Roman architectural motifs that could be seen on other buildings in the city. They evidently represented something very specific to the bakery industry and were presented to the viewer as both a kind of puzzle to be solved and as an amusing architectural pun perhaps. A number of alternative explanations for these unusual motifs have been offered by modern academics, most of whom accept that the vertical and horizontal cylinders represent the same thing seen from different perspectives. Firstly, it has been suggested that they could be portrayals of grain measures: however, this is unconvincing, as indeed they look nothing like them, to be blunt. Secondly, that the medallion-like circular cylinder motifs could represent the mouths of bread ovens. This ignores the known form of Roman bread ovens; indeed, of the form of the very bread oven depicted on the frieze on Eurysaces' tomb itself. Thirdly, and most convincingly, and now widely accepted, is the idea that the circular cylindrical motifs represent the tops of dough bins or kneading machines, seen as if turned on their sides. Close examination of the hollow horizontal and vertical cylinders on the tomb has shown that a small square hole appears in the bottom of each of them where rust stains suggest an actual fitting was once present. Dough kneading bins such as this have been found in situ in some of the bakeries of Pompeii and are notable because of the small square seating for a wooden and iron fitting that they all would have had to form the turning mechanism. It is astonishing to think that such a detail was reproduced on the Tomb of Eurysaces when the veracity of this would have been appreciated by so few people and indeed when the detailing inside the vertical cylinders would not have been visible to anyone at all.

However one identifies these elements of the tomb, as most of its contemporary Roman viewers would probably have never set foot inside a bakery such visual trickery and punning would most likely have been completely lost on them and they would have viewed these elements as purely decorative items, albeit unusual and original. Reading the inscriptions on the tomb and viewing the decorative frieze might have alerted the viewers to the possibility of the decorative cylinders as being representations of some kind of bakery machinery but beyond that incomprehension was in all probability prevalent among viewers.

The inscription, which is repeated on each of the three sides of the tomb, reads: '*Est Hoc Monimentum Marcei Vergilei Eurysacis Pistoris, Redemptoris, Apparet*', in translation 'This is the tomb of Marcus Vergilius Eurysaces, baker, contractor, public servant', though it has been suggested that the final word of the inscription – '*apparet*' – simply means 'it is obvious' rather than being a mistaken use of the word '*apparet*' instead of *apparitor* which means 'public servant'.

A separate inscribed panel found away from the tomb (Plate 11) reads: '*Fuit Atistia Uxor Mihei/ Femina Opituma Veixsit/Quoius Corporis Reliquae/ Quod Superant Sunt In/Hoc Panario*', translated as 'Atistia was my wife; a most excellent lady in life; the surviving remains of her body are in this breadbasket'.

It is most likely that Atistia was Eurysaces' wife and most academic authorities accept this premise. Again, it is generally assumed that the inscribed panel was related to a stone or ceramic cinerary urn – 'this breadbasket' – in the non-standard form of a breadbasket, which had once been placed inside the tomb. Given the punning nature of the architectural adornment of the tomb, a breadbasket cinerary urn inside seems apposite. Curiously, and surely not coincidentally, a cinerary urn 'in the form of a cylindrical basket' which may have been the very 'breadbasket' referred to in Atistia's epitaph was discovered at the site in 1838, put in store, and is now thought to be lost or at least unlocatable.

Once more academics are generally united in assuming that the statue group of a man and woman found near the tomb in 1838 and now in the *Centrale Montemartini* outpost of the *Musei Capitolini* in Rome is of Eurysaces and his wife and derives from the damaged face of the monument. The statue has an unfortunate history, the head of the female figure having been stolen, and never recovered, when on display in the Giardino Pantanella in the 1930s. Eurysaces then it would appear wished to be seen by viewers of his tomb as both a rich and successful professional man with no qualms about splashing his cash on a bizarre and ostentatious funerary memorial as well as a conservative, doting Roman husband. The question as to whether he was a free-born Roman or a freedman does not alter this duality in the presentation of his legacy and memory.

Most important here though is the nature and content of the narrow decorative frieze that probably originally ran around all four sides of the monument, but which now survives complete along the west side, virtually complete along the south side, and in a truncated form along the north side. All the scenes depict activity inside a large bakery.

On the south frieze, reading the action from right to left, are scenes of consigned grain arriving at the bakery, state officials checking grain receipts at a table, two donkey- or horse-mills in operation grinding grain, the sieving of flour, and the overseeing of the sieving and checking of the quality of flour at a table (Plate 12). On the north frieze, reading from right to left, we see a worker in the bakery using a kneading machine to prepare dough, workers preparing and forming loaves on a series of trestle tables, and finally a baker using a wooden or metal peel, as they are now called, to place loaves in a large bread oven (Plates 13–14). On the west frieze, reading from left to right, can be seen the carrying of loaves of bread in baskets to a weighing station, and the weighing of the loaves of bread overseen by toga-clad officials, an important task to be undertaken as an assurance that customers and citizens were not being cheated by the bakery company. Finally, the bread is carried off out of the premises for delivery. Academic opinion is split over the identity of some of the men in this particular scene. The figures here in togas, obviously not ordinary bakery workers dressed in this way, might represent Eurysaces and his overseers inspecting the goods before they leave the bakery premises, a form of quality control in other words. Alternatively, the togate figures are more likely to have represented state officials making an inspection as part of the operation of the state contract that the bakery had, as indicated by Eurysaces description of himself as a *redemptor* or contractor in the monument's inscription.

Worth noting is the fact that not one woman is evident among the forty-five or so bakery workers and officials or overseers depicted there. This is the largest number of workers portrayed in any single individual Roman work of art. The majority of the images that form the subject of this study are usually portrayals of individuals rather than of groups. In terms of other group images one can think of the workers portrayed on a relief of a bakery from Bologna, discussed more fully below, of the building site workers, probably slaves, operating the giant treadmill on the building relief from the Tomb of the Haterii and in other construction site scenes discussed in Chapter One, and the group of workers in the wall paintings at the fullers workshop of Verecundus of Pompeii. Some of Eurysaces' bakery workers depicted here would undoubtedly have been slaves and perhaps this knowledge would have allowed contemporary viewers of the frieze to admiringly appreciate Eurysaces' personal and professional journey or *cursus* or to fume with outrage at the public effrontery of this upstart freedman.

While I generally eschew extended discussions of artistic style and questions of aesthetic taste when writing about Roman art, in this particular instance a detour to talk about such things is justified. If we accept that the original monument did indeed carry the *Centrale Montemartini* portrait reliefs of a married couple and the Atistia inscription in the *Museo Nazionale*, then it would appear to be some kind of hybrid monument linking ideas from elite art and that strain of art that has been called 'plebeian' or freedmen art. Eurysaces has made sure that his name and occupation, the latter not just being 'baker' but also much more importantly 'contractor', appeared on both sides of the tomb, so that viewers on both sides would know who he had been. Again, the couple in the portrait relief appear in formal, probably expensive attire, yet at the same time workers in the bakery appear in their workwear or in many cases the workers are bare-chested due to the heat in and around the ovens. Eurysaces seems to be using the monument to promote a past identity, that of a working baker, and a final identity as some kind of baking magnate. There is no mention in the inscription as to whether Eurysaces was a freedman, though it is generally assumed by scholars writing today that he was. This omission must therefore have been quite deliberate and is therefore very telling indeed. The formal elite costume was perhaps here being used as some kind of distancing device, yet no matter how far away wearing this costume took Eurysaces from his more humble beginnings that distance was always going to be bridgeable in the eyes of many, if not most, of the elite Roman viewers of his tomb. As one academic commentator has written: 'Obedience, industry, and honesty all contribute to the presentation of Eurysaces, even if frugality and restraint of ambition are absent.'[2]

At one time discussion of this tomb centred on these issues of artistic style and class hierarchy and taste in ancient Rome, with the artworks of the frieze being held up as examples of what in the late 1960s was termed *arte plebea* or plebeian art.[3] Indeed, most of the other funerary monuments of workers discussed in this book would also have been categorised as such. Subsequently, the Tomb of Eurysaces became the subject of discussions centred around architectural form. This present study views the monument almost exclusively in terms of its contribution to the discussion of identity and its representation in the Roman world. Analysis of the monument's context, appearance, inscriptions, and artworks has revealed a highly complex attempt by Eurysaces to situate himself within Roman society under a number of distinct but interrelated identities.

If the cylindrical basket cinerary urn attested as being found near the Tomb of Eurysaces is not from the tomb but is part of another, separate monument to another baker then it is altogether possible that the Tomb of Eurysaces proved to be a focus for the siting of other Roman bakers' tombs and monuments. Certainly from this area comes a fragmentary decorated marble sarcophagus, now in the collection of the *Musei Vaticani* in Rome, on which is carved a scene of a horse mill for grinding flour in operation. An inscription relating to another baker called Ogulnius – *pistor* (baker) and *simi[laginarius]* (flour dealer) – has also been recovered from excavations nearby. The partial inscription also includes the word *amicus* – friend – but it would be purely speculative to suppose that he might have been a contemporary and friend of Eurysaces.

Archaeological excavation to the east of the Tomb of Eurysaces has uncovered evidence for an extensive industrial area dating between 50 BC and AD 40, comprising hall-like structures, containing at least seven animal-driven mills and ovens, suggesting to at least one authority that this could represent Eurysaces' own vast bakery complex and that he was literally buried at work.

Another successful baker in Rome whose life was commemorated by an impressive tomb of the late first century BC or early first century AD was Marcus Iunius Pudens, though his monument carried no images of his occupation and it is only from the inscription on the tomb that we know his occupation as *pistor magnarius pepsianus*, that is 'baking contractor of digestive bread', obviously a specialist baker for the kind of niche market that only a cosmopolis such as Rome could support at the time. His name indicates that he was a descendant, perhaps a few generations removed, of a freedman, and on the monument we learn that he and his wife Claudia Earine had their own freedmen in their family group or household.

The Staff of Life

Discussion of the Tomb of Eurysaces quite naturally leads on to a more general discussion of the broader context of baking and the importance of the provision of bread in the city of Rome and more widely across Italy and around the Roman empire.

At least fifteen other images connected to bakers, bakeries, or to the milling of flour for the making of bread are known from Rome and Italy[4] and can be briefly considered here. Images though very much represent the tip of the iceberg in terms of the number of actual household and commercial bakers there would have been in Rome. The fact that there was a *collegium pistorum* or association of bakers from at least the reign of Trajan underscores their number, social status, and economic importance at the time. The names of over thirty bakers and butchers in Rome are known from funerary inscriptions and dedications. At least ten of the bakers worked in their own premises, outside of domestic settings. Some of those others dubbed *pistor* or baker may have been household slaves tasked with that role. Three of the later fourth century AD Regionary Catalogues of Rome record the number of commercial bakeries in the city at the time as around two hundred and fifty.

From Bologna, and now in the *Museo Civico Archeologico di Bologna*, comes a now partial and fragmentary third century AD marble panel, presumably part of a sarcophagus, carrying a two-tier relief of activities inside a bakery, involving milling, the processing of sacks of flour, the sieving of flour, the forming of loaves, and their baking (Plate 15). At least seven men appear on this relief. Also in the same museum collection, part of the cache of funerary stele from the *Muro del Reno* from near Bologna comes a funerary stele whose decoration includes a *modius* or corn measure.

Quite recently, another funerary relief depicting baking has come to the attention of archaeologists through its open display over an oven in a present-day restaurant in Trastevere in Rome, found on the site by the father of the present proprietor some time before 1950.[5] As on the reliefs from the Tomb of Eurysaces depicted here are scenes of bread making, including two men carrying sacks of grain to a horse mill, with the horse also being depicted, grain being poured into the mill out of a sack by a third man, the kneading of dough by three men at a low table with raised sides, the forming of loaves by a further team of three men on an open-sided table, and the placing of loaves in an oven, or the removal of baked loaves, by a man with a long bread peel. A tall basket piled high with cooling loaves sits to one side of the bread oven. Altogether ten men appear on the relief and, as with the Eurysaces friezes and the Bologna relief, the exclusive portrayal of men undertaking this work might suggest a gender bias for male workers in the bakery industry for some reason. The Trastevere relief is thought to date between the mid-first century BC and the late first century AD.

The second or third century AD sarcophagus of L. Annius Octavius Valerianus from the Via Appia and now in the *Musei Vaticani* carries on its front long panel a busy set of scenes centred around the bearded figure of Valerianus himself who we must assume to be a landowner or at least an estate manager rather than a baker or baking factor like Eurysaces. Groups of men variously work in the fields in the upper register of design and in the lower they appear to be delivering grain to a bakehouse where it is processed by a screw-driven handmill and then put into an oven. The inscription on the sarcophagus is simply a jaunty farewell to Hope and Fortune rather than any kind of occupational inscription. The scenes of work here must therefore be interpreted as being purely illustrative and generalised.

Millers themselves are rarer than bakers in our database of images of workers and artisans. Depictions of horse and donkey mills, usually with the animal portrayed rather than an overseeing miller or assistant, are surprisingly common, appearing on, for instance: a now-fragmentary mid-third century AD sarcophagus from Vigna delle Tre Madonne in Rome and now in the *Musei Vaticani* (Plate 16); the first century AD urn holder of Publius Nonnius Zethus of Ostia, again in the *Musei Vaticani* collections; the mid-first century AD funerary stele of Publius Pontius Iucundus from Verona (now in the *Museo Maffeiano* there); and the third century AD funerary stele of M. Carceius Asina of Narbonne in Roman Gaul and now in the *Musée Archéologique de Narbonne*. A category of worker image which will be discussed more fully in Chapter Seven is that of cupids or *putti* undertaking human working tasks, and indeed they can be seen at a donkey mill in a wall painting from Pompeii.

On the left hand side of the cinerary urn holder of Publius Nonnius Zethus of Ostia mentioned above for the depiction of a donkey mill it carries, also appear two *modii* or corn measures, some sieves, and a measuring rod, placing it in the category of depictions of 'tools of the trade' which often act as ciphers for the depiction of a particular profession, as will be discussed in a number of places elsewhere in this book.

A baker placing a loaf in an oven appears on one end of an undated and unprovenanced sarcophagus at the Villa Medici in Rome, a horse mill appears on the other end panel, while a small image of two men loading dough into a mixer of some sort in the middle of the front panel. A miller does appear beside his mill and the horse driving it on a terracotta plaque mounted on the facade of Tomb 78 at the *Necropoli di Porto*, Isola Sacra, Ostia. A sarcophagus panel from the Mausoleum of the Scipioni, on Vigna Sassi, Porta Latina, Rome and now in the *Museo Nazionale delle Terme Diocleziano*, has images on the long front side of a man emptying grain into a *modius*, a second man levelling off a *modius* of grain, and a third man supervising a horse mill.

No funerary memorials to bakers, either with occupational inscriptions or pictorial scenes of baking, are known from outside Italy which might be significant in terms of the social status of workers in this profession away from the centre. However, it has been suggested that one of the relief scenes on the third century *Igeler Säule* or Igel Column, near Trier might depict four men working inside a bakery rather than in a domestic kitchen.

There can be no doubt that the Tomb of Eurysaces the Baker must have been a hugely expensive monument to commission and pay for, as indeed doubtless were the other bakers' and millers' funerary monuments discussed here, and that this somehow was a reflection of the singular importance of bread in the Roman diet and economy, even within Roman culture more broadly. The right to eat bread, to enjoy 'bread and circuses', was ingrained in the Roman mentality. The production of bread, its selling, and sometimes its gifting were all equally significant on different levels.

Representations of the selling of bread, though it is uncertain as to whether this is being sold from a bakery or through a third party in a shop or on a market, come from Rome (a partial relief now built into Palazzo Merolli), Ostia (in the *Museo Ostiense*), and Pompeii, in the form of a wall painting from the *Casa del Panettiere* or House of the Baker (Plate 17). Notable also at Pompeii is the *graffiti* on the precinct wall of the Temple of Apollo that reads '*Verecundus libarius hic*' and '*Pudens libarius*', that is 'Verecundus and Pudens sell their sacrificial bread here'.

At this point it is worth noting that while bakers largely produced loaves of bread for daily use they may also have been involved in the production of what we might term non-utilitarian breads, rolls, and cakes which were specifically produced for sale as religious offerings, as Verecundus and Pudens seem to have done. This additional sideline may have further increased the social cachet and status of Roman bakers, in the same way perhaps that butchers were also involved in a certain amount of non-utilitarian business in butchering the carcasses of sacrificed animals, as will be discussed further below.

While we do not have a great deal of direct environmental archaeological evidence about the use of breads and cakes in religious or ritual activities in Rome, at Pompeii a small amount of work points to interesting possibilities that could be extrapolated back to the city.[6] Analysis of excavated and sieved samples from dated archaeological deposits at a number of houses led to the identification of bread crumbs in ritual deposits at the House of the Vestals and at the House of Hercules' Wedding where a whole ring-shaped biscuit and fragments of a poppy seed cake were most tellingly also found. Similar charred crumbs and complete cakes and biscuits were found at the temple of Demeter and Persephone at Monte Papalucio, Oria in southern Italy. Whether such votive items were made at a bakery and purchased or were made at home we cannot know.

Of course, within Christianity the symbolic significance of bread became even more pronounced, with bread becoming the material manifestation of Christ's body – the host – though it is not possible to isolate any Roman images from Late Antiquity which directly illustrate this. However, other symbolism associated with bread in Christianity does exist. A painting from the *Catacombe dei SS. Marcellino e Pietro* shows Christ holding a staff of some kind, surrounded by risen loaves of bread in baking tins, probably as an illustration of the multiplication of the loaves. Over thirty-eight examples of the depiction of this event in frescos are known from the catacombs of Rome, while the breaking of the bread, the highly symbolic *fractio panis*, is depicted in the *Catacombe di Priscilla*. It is altogether possible that some of these paintings could have been commissioned as being appropriate to mark the burial place of a Roman Christian baker.

While the discursive discussion of individual bakers and of scenes of bakeries operating in Roman art here points to a social and economic importance for bakers at Rome and in the provinces, such importance also usually invited official oversight, control, and often censure, and indeed we have already seen state officials overseeing certain aspects of bakery production on the decorative frieze on the Tomb of Eurysaces the Baker in Rome. Bread, bakers, and politics could and did mix.

The community of bakers in Pompeii used a painted election slogan on a house external wall to express their support for one of their own members, Caius Iulius Polybius, who was standing for election as *aedile*, a local magistracy, and promised the town his *bonem panem*, that is quality loaves, were he to be elected. Owner of what is known to archaeologists today as the House of the Chaste Lovers in the town, Polybius seems to have conducted some of his commercial operations from this house, if the skeletal remains of a number of donkeys found here are of working animals from a donkey mill.

Beyond its taxing and the oversight of its supply the Roman imperial authorities sometimes used this control to further contribute to their individual ideological and political programmes. The best example of this relates to the alimentary food programme inaugurated by the emperor Trajan (AD 98–117), to help feed the children of Roman Italy.[7] Indeed, on the great Arch of Trajan at Benevento in southern central Italy, dating to AD 114–118, this scheme was overtly promoted and the link between bread and imperial largesse became personified in one of the relief images adorning the monument on which the emperor hands out dole to mothers, fathers, and their children, with what appear to be loaves of bread set on a tray to his side (Plate 18). The production of bread seems to have gained more attention from the imperial authorities in the early third century AD when the emperor Septimius Severus (AD 193–211) substituted bread for grain in the city of Rome's long-established free food for the poor programme, the *annona*.

The interruption of the supply of bread could and did occasionally lead to a backlash against authority. Just as in a later chapter an account will be given of a riot involving mint workers in Rome, so there is evidence from the eastern empire of two occasions when riots involving bakers took place. A remarkable inscription from Ephesus dating to some time in the second century, probably around AD 200, records part of an edict issued by the Roman proconsul of Asia Minor:

... Thus it comes about at times that the people are plunged into disorder and tumults by the meeting and insolence of the bakers in the market place, riots for which they ought already to have been arrested and put on trial. However, since it is necessary to prioritise the city's welfare far more than the punishment of these men, I have decreed in an edict that they must act reasonably. I therefore order the bakers not to hold meetings as a faction or to be leaders in recklessness, but strictly to obey the regulations made for the public welfare and to provide the city with the necessary supply of bread without fail.

A warning setting out punishment for further, future transgressions followed.

Almost two centuries later the writer Libanius (AD 314–94) recorded the details of unrest in his home city of Antioch, again in Asia Minor, in AD 387, arising due to shortages of corn and thus soaring increases in the price of bread.[8] The citizens were rightly disgruntled and provoked civil unrest, appealed to the governor who, in turn, urged the city's bakers to be 'more just' in their pricing, wanting to placate the citizens and at the same time not further antagonise the bakers. However, things subsequently got completely out of hand and the governor had no choice but to directly intervene. Mass floggings of the town's bakers took place in punishment for their intransigence in ignoring the governor's plea for price reductions and Libanius recounts that he himself stepped in to halt the floggings before they led to further, more severe rioting.

Flesh of My Flesh

While meat was not as significant a foodstuff in the Roman diet across all classes as bread, bakery goods, and grains were, nevertheless it was still an economically important product whose sale left an indelible mark on the very fabric of the city in the naming and location of the *Forum Boarium*, the cattle market, and the *Forum Suarium*, the pig market which would have been both wholesale and retail spaces.

A number of funerary memorials, though most in the form of inscriptions rather than decorated stele, to Roman butchers have been found, possibly as many as seventeen, including an unprovenanced one to the first century AD pork butcher Tiberius Julius Vitalis, for instance.[9] Now at the Villa Albani in Rome this funerary relief is highly unusual in the context of workers' and artisans' memorials in that different types of image appear on the right and left-hand sides of the relief, on the right being an image of a large face-on head and bust portrait of Vitalis, with his name inscribed on the base of the bust, while on the left of the relief we see Vitalis at work chopping up a pig's head on a raised block in his shop, with cuts of meat hanging on hooks behind him. In the portrait he is formally dressed and in the shop scene he wears loose working garments. Between the two scenes someone has later added a neat inscribed *graffito* – '*Marcio Semper Ebri*' – 'Marcus is always drunk'. It would seem to have been just as important to Vitalis or his heirs that he was portrayed with two identities, that of a respectable, fashionably dressed and coiffed man represented in the image of a portrait bust and as a working man or business owner. Here the spheres of both culture and commerce vie for our attention, as they did in a broadly similar way on the Tomb of Eurysaces the Baker.

A second interesting, uninscribed funerary relief comes from Trastevere in Rome and probably dates to the first half of the second century AD (Plate 19). It is now in the *Staatlichen Skulpturensammlung* in Dresden, Germany, and again is a relief depicting the inside of a butcher's shop. In this case we see the bearded male butcher at work chopping a joint of meat on his block with a large cleaver. A set of scales hangs from a frame, along with a second cleaver. A range of cut joints of meat and a pig's head hangs on hooks from the frame. A basket for offcuts sits on the shop floor to one side of the chopping block. On the far right hand side of the scene is a woman with an elaborately braided hairstyle sitting in a high-backed chair. She is writing on tablets resting in her lap and may therefore be identified as a bookkeeper, though some authorities have suggested that she may simply be a customer with a shopping list, which seems less likely an interpretation, or that she may have been the butcher's wife to whom the funerary monument was also dedicated.

A third relief from Rome once more carries a depiction of a shop scene [10]. This particular relief could either have been a shop sign or once more might have been derived from a funerary monument. This relief is now in the unaccessible *Museo Torlonia* collection in storage in Rome and depicts two female game butchers or poultry dealers, though the classicised and idealised appearance of the women suggests that they are in fact goddesses rather than mortal working women. The relief is divided into two zones by a pillar: on the left hand side of the relief hang six carcasses of dead birds and animals, including two suckling pigs, a hare, and two geese; on the right hand side are the two young women, one standing and pointing to an inscription on the back wall of the shop and the other seated on a low-backed chair and plucking a bird hanging from the ceiling over a small table. The inscription is a four line quotation from Virgil's *Aeneid*, whose reference to remembrance of an individual and everlasting memory suggests a funerary purpose for the relief, if indeed it is a genuine Roman piece of a Hadrianic date and not an eighteenth-century pastiche piece in the Roman style, as some authorities have suggested. Again, if genuine, the disparity between the appearance of the women and their dirty task might be explained if they were deities or mytholological figures preparing a funerary feast rather than employees in a butcher's shop.

A fourth, now-lost and unprovenanced Roman funerary memorial of uncertain date to a butcher is recorded as a drawing in the Dal Pozzo-Albani collection of drawings of classical antiquities in the British Museum, London. The image drawn here is very much in keeping with the others discussed above, though in this case the butcher is chopping a joint for a gesturing customer while a second butcher or assistant serves another customer.

Away from Rome itself, notable examples of the portrayal of individual butchers have also been found in Ostia and Bologna, for example. The Ostia example is represented by a portion of a long pictorial second century AD funerary relief set in an ansate panel depicting a butcher at work in his shop, with chopping block, scales, and hanging joints of meat, and two pigs foraging on the other side of the relief, the two scenes being separated by the letters *DM* – the common funerary formulation *Dis Manibus*. From Roman Bologna, and now in the *Museo Civico di Bologna* there, comes a large memorial funerary stele of the first half of the first century AD to Quintus Valerius Restitutus, a freedman and *sevir*, his wife, and to Lucius Metellus Niceros, at the bottom of which appears a scene in a butcher's shop, with blocks, a butcher cutting or grinding meat and hanging joints (Plate 20). It is not altogether certain though whether Restitutus was himself a butcher. A boundary stone with a bull on it may be from the same burial plot.

Butchers were also probably involved in a certain amount of non-utilitarian business, in butchering the carcasses of sacrificed animals This additional sideline may have further increased the social cachet and status of Roman butchers, in the same way perhaps that bakers were also involved in a certain amount of non-utilitarian business in baking votive bread loaves, rolls, and cakes, as has been discussed above. Perhaps the butcher Lucius Aurelius Hermia from the Viminal Hill in Rome was so successful in this respect that he felt no need to have himself depicted working in his shop or represented by the tools of his trade. His first century BC funerary relief, now in the British Museum in London, in fact consists of a lengthy explanatory epitaph accompanied by small but full-length portraits of Lucius and his wife Philematium dressed as a higher-status couple (Plate 21).

The meat from animals sacrificed in religious rites would have been cooked and eaten, sometimes in formal public feasts, so that the animals could at least be said not to have entirely died in vain. Open public banquets followed the *Saturnalia* and the *Compitalia* each year for example, while more exclusive banquets were the order of the day for the other six Roman annual festivals that included feasting. Huge quantities of cooked meat were apparently distributed at triumphal processions and sit-down meals at tables set for hundreds, indeed occasionally for thousands, were common at such events in both the Republican and imperial eras in Rome, with an estimated 200,000 people having feasted at Julius Caesar's triumphal banquets.

Usually a cut of meat from the slaughtered animal or animals would be offered to the gods by burning on an altar. The rest of the meat would be retained for subsequent events. Very often the eating of the rest of the meat from sacrificed beasts in a formal feast would be part and parcel of an event, the cementing of the social fabric following the ritual. Once clearance had been gained from the *haruspex* the animal was butchered and its meat divided up for a number of different purposes. Most commonly, the entrails were cooked, cut up, sprinkled with salt and wine as the live beast had been, and then burned on the altar as the god's rightful portion. Variations on this basic rite involved the burying of the god's portion or its casting into water. The majority of the carcass was now formally deconsecrated by a gesture from the sacrificer and could then be cut up, cooked, and eaten at a feast or even sold at the market in some cases. Every single festival in the Roman religious calendar, from the major *Saturnalia* to minor or niche events, would have involved animal sacrifice on some scale and feasting on sacrificial meat as part of the rites and butchers would need to have been present as part of the team on all such occasions.

Likewise, meat from more exotic animals slaughtered in the arena was also distributed or sold afterwards for consumption, as certain contemporary commentators revealed. Some may have been reserved for distribution to the soldiers barracked in Rome. Christians though were forbidden to eat arena meat, sullied as it was with conceptual and ideological baggage that they abhorred.

Feeding the City

Bakers and butchers as important categories of workers feeding the city of Rome and other urban communities throughout Italy and the broader empire were chosen to illustrate in this chapter how closely economics and cultural production became interwoven within Roman society after the first century BC. There were many other categories of food producers and suppliers that could also have been discussed here, along with farmers and growers, suppliers, and wholesalers. Shop workers, market stall traders, and street hawkers-those who sold food and other goods-will be discussed in a later chapter, as will be the carters, shippers, transporters, seamen, and dockers who moved foodstuffs and goods around on the roads and rivers or by sea. Sandra Joshel in her study of occupational inscriptions from the city of Rome, along with the 30 recorded bakers and butchers, lists 46 dealers in meats, fish, general produce, oil and wine.[11] Some of these dealers were quite niche in their areas of specialisation: for example, she records an *anatiarius* or dealer in ducks, an *aviarius altiliarius* or dealer in fattened birds, a *macellarius* or provisions dealer, a *mellarius* or dealer in honey, a *negotiator fabarius* or dealer in beans, a *negotiatrix frumentaria et legumenaria* or female dealer in grains and pulses, a *negotiator olearius ex Baetica* or dealer in olive oil from Baetica in Spain, a *negotiator penoris et vinorum* or general dealer in food and wine, a *negotiator vinarius* or dealer in wine, a *pomarius* or fruit seller, and a *salarius* or dealer in salted fish. All of these very specific job titles were recorded from formal inscriptions, the vast majority from funerary contexts, and it cannot be stressed enough how significant this is in terms of demonstrating the ubiquity of this remarkable phenomenon of presenting occupational identities among the freedman and plebeian classes at Rome, or at least those who could afford to commission such inscriptions.

Outside of funerary contexts those whom I have deemed to have been 'feeding the city', whether Rome itself or cities elsewhere in the empire, often left their mark or image in other ways. Indeed, in a later chapter I will discuss those traders in foodstuffs and commodities such as wine, olive oil, and *garum* or fish sauce, whose products were packaged and shipped in marked or stamped ceramic vessels known as amphorae.

The fact that many of the fish sauce amphorae carried a maker's stamp and often also what is known as *tituli picti*, that is painted commercial inscriptions relating to manufacturers or shippers of the product inside, allows a remarkably nuanced picture to be created of both manufacturing centres and trading links and of the forging of individual identities among the producers and shippers of this product, as with wine and olive oil as we will see later. The names of a number of *garum* wholesalers are known, of whom the most famous is probably Aulus Umbricius Scaurus whose fine, sprawling house in Pompeii near the Porta Marina, in which he probably lived from the early to mid-first century AD, possibly up to the eruption of AD 79, was testament to the lucrative nature of the trade. Almost a third of the *garum* amphorae, sometimes also called *urcei*, so far excavated from Pompeii were derived from his manufactory premises. Scaurus, obviously not ashamed of his occupation in the least, even commissioned an unusual black and white mosaic for the secondary atrium of his residence, depicting four *garum* amphorae, some of which bore *tituli picti* naming the product – 'the flower of *garum* made of mackerel' and 'the flower of *liquamen*' and 'the best *liquamen*' – and three of which named Scaurus, a fine piece of self promotion and intertextuality.[12] A *titulus pictus* at Pompeii also named one Aulus Umbricius Abascantus, who we can assume to have been a freedman of Scaurus, perhaps his works manager. *Tituli picti* on a number of amphorae naming Scaurus have been found in the wider Campanian region and at Herculaneum, the villas of Boscoreale and Boscotrecase and even as far afield as southern France at Fos-sur-Mer, Bouches-du Rhône. A scientific analysis of remains inside one of the amphorae from

Scaurus's house revealed that the sauce had been made from bogues, local small fish that abound in the waters around the Bay of Naples in the summer months.

As this chapter has hopefully demonstrated, certain foodstuffs and products – bread, meat, wine, olive oil, and fish sauce mainly – were of such importance and significance in the Roman world that their production and supply allowed many individuals to earn a living producing, selling, or shipping them and indeed in some cases to make a fortune from doing so. These individuals often came to identify with their occupations to such an extent that they used their occupational titles or images associated with their trade or business to present their identities in public or funerary contexts. Occupational identities could also be forged, maintained, and embellished by the setting up of occupational *collegia* or guilds, creating a sense of communal occupational identity in certain areas of the Roman economy.

Roman society placed a huge socio-cultural significance upon the production and sale of certain key foodstuffs, on 'feeding the city', allowing individuals operating in that sphere to openly create and present their occupational identities, if they wished to do so and could afford to. Likewise, those who 'clothed the city', that is textile producers and sellers, wool and cloth merchants, and leatherworkers, shoemakers, and cobblers, also had a marked social cachet that reflected their economic significance as members of an empire-wide industry. Workers in this field will be considered in the next chapter.

3

Threads
Clothing the City

Having considered those who it might be said 'built the city' and 'fed the city' in the last two chapters it is now appropriate to consider those Roman workers who 'clothed the city'. It is very unlikely that anyone would have made their own clothes in the Roman world, and therefore the textile industry as a whole can be expected to have been one of the biggest industries at this time, employing thousands of workers and allowing hundreds of entrepreneurs to profit from this lucrative trade. Such a picture is very much reflected in the archaeological evidence and in particular in the funerary monuments of many of those involved. In this chapter an examination will be made of the cultural significance and social cachet of the textile trade, concentrating on evidence relating to specific named individuals. The opportunity will also be taken to discuss not just textiles and clothing but also the leather-working industry and its associated trades, including shoe making.

Roman clothing was highly codified and reflected the social and class stratification of Roman society. The type of cloth used for a garment, its cut and style, its colour, and its accessorising were all highly significant and often deeply symbolic. Shoes, hairstyles, and adornment were of equal importance in defining individual and class status and identity. In the last decade perhaps more academic attention has been paid by researchers to the Roman textile industry and its products than to any other aspect of the Roman economy and readers will see this academic endeavour reflected in the very large number of articles and monographs on Roman textiles cited in this book's bibliography.[1]

It has already been mentioned in the introductory chapter that just as the association of smithing with the Roman god Vulcan and related deities would appear to be one of the reasons for the popularity of the portrayal of metalworking in Roman and provincial art, so the same has been suggested to have been the case with the link between the goddess Minerva and textile working, as demonstrated on the decorative frieze of the *Forum Transitorium* or Nerva's Forum in Rome.[2] The ideological programme of this frieze represented a moral message to the women of Rome not to transgress as Arachne had done against Minerva, and the images of the frieze situated moral behaviour alongside home-based textile crafts as the linked ideals of the Roman matron. Minerva also became associated with the factory production of textiles, again as has been mentioned with regard to her importance to the fullers or *fullones* of Pompeii and other Roman towns and cities.

In this chapter there will be no further discussion of home-based textile crafts but rather attention will focus on images relating to the Roman textile industry, taking in the production of raw materials such as wool and flax, the production and making of cloth, textiles, and finished garments, dyeing, and fulling and cleaning. In the second part of the chapter I will discuss images of those involved in the production of footwear. In Sandra Joshel's study of occupational inscriptions at Rome she records no fewer than fifty-five inscriptions relating to 'producers of cloth, that is spinners, weavers, wool weighers, spinning supervisors, dyers, and fullers, and an astonishing eighty-three 'makers of clothing'.[3] Of the specialised job titles she records within this group note should be taken of an *auri vestrix* or tailor of clothes in gold cloth, a *centonarius* or patchwork maker/ragman, a *mercator sagarius* and a *negotiator sagarius* or dealers in cloaks, a *negotiator lintiarius* or dealer in linens, a *negotians siricarius* or dealer in silk, a *plumarius* or embroiderer/brocader with feathers, a *sagarius* or maker of cloaks, a *sarcinatrix* or mender/seamstress, some *vestiarii* or tailors, and a *vestiarius tenuiarius* or tailor of fine clothing. If we now turn to Gerhard Zimmer's catalogue of images of Roman period workers and professionals in Rome itself and more broadly in Italy he lists no fewer than 15 examples, only 2 of which come from Rome, 3 from central Italy, 2 from Pompeii, and 8 of which come from northern Italy significantly, with 3 of those from Milan.[4] There can be seen to have been a number of different types of commemorative image when the images appeared in funerary contexts: images of textile-working tools, on their own or in work scenes; less-common literal work scenes either in workshops or in the packing and transportation of textiles and clothes; and images of textiles or clothes being quality checked, displayed to customers and clients, and on sale in a shop premises. Examples of these different types will be discussed below.

During research study trips for this book it quickly became apparent during my visits to the museums of northern Italy in particular that the region's finances in the Roman period were evidently heavily tied in to the economics of the textile industry, particularly in the first and second centuries AD, though this industry continued in importance for the region well into the fourth century. The Po Valley in the late Iron Age had become hugely significant in terms of producing wool from its numerous and vast flocks of sheep and linen from the flax grown there. This activity accelerated in the Roman period and raw materials and finished garments were produced and traded across Italy and further afield, and epigraphic evidence confirms an incredible concentration in northern Italy as a whole of cloth producers and merchants, both individually and as represented by *collegia* of wool washers, wool combers, wool carders, and textile and clothing dealers. At Roman Modena stamped loom weights, often bearing names, attest to the need of some workers in the textile industry here to openly express their occupational identity in this highly original manner.[5]

Evidence for the industry also comes from written sources such as Pliny the Elder's *Naturalis Historia* and is demonstrated by entries in Diocletian's Edict On Maximum Prices of AD 303 concerning suggested maximum wages for the various types of workers engaged in the textile industry through all its various stages of production.[6] Maximum prices of raw wool, linen, and silk are also given, along with prices of sometimes very specific regional textile items such as the *birrus Britannicus*, a kind of hooded woollen cloak obviously produced in Roman Britain and famous throughout the empire. Epigraphic evidence and funerary monuments for some of those individuals involved in the industry add a great deal of nuance to our understanding of the overall picture.

The foundations of many particular Roman images sometimes partly lay in the cultures and belief systems of other pre-Roman Italic societies. Human labour in Etruscan and other historic and prehistoric

Italian societies was often articulated and mediated through artistic expression. In the case of northern Italy one of the most unusual mediums for doing this was through the creation of rock art petroglyphs or carvings in the societies of Valcamonica in northern Italy.[7] I am not claiming at all that there are direct influences on much later Roman culture to be found here. As with my discussions in this book of modern novels and artworks depicting workers I am simply proposing that looking at these works can provide comparative ideas and suggest ways of interpreting and understanding.

In Valcamonica carvings of human figures were common at all periods from the Neolithic to the Iron Age, suggesting the cultural importance of work and craft production, and perhaps its significance on a symbolic level as well. A number of ploughing scenes in the rock art, with the ploughs being pulled by oxen, may not simply have been illustrative but could have been linked to the expression of fertility and links with the land and natural phenomena. The construction of masculinity in this society was linked to the key activities of metallurgy, warfare, and hunting, particularly in the Iron Age. Numerous rock art hunt scenes testified to both hyper-masculine display and the importance of deer in the diet and in the cosmological beliefs of the people here. Of most significance here is the fact that images of women and looms appeared commonly, showing the economic and ideological importance of textile production in this northern Italy society at this time, though the animals from whose fleeces the weavers gathered their wool were not represented.

A number of artworks carrying images of sheep in the broader context of images of textile production will be discussed in this chapter, but it is worth pausing briefly to mention here the portrayal of a sheep on its own on the mid-first century BC funerary relief of C. Cafurnius Antiochus, named in the inscription as a *lanarius* or wool worker and trader, and his wife. The relief is in the *Palazzo di Fide Propaganda* in Rome. The clasped hands of the devoted couple appear above the image of the sheep but no working tools appear. The animal here represents the occupational identity of the man. I wonder if some of the other funerary stele with images of sheep I noted during my museum study visits also might have alluded to the Roman textile industry?

But an even greater number of images of workers involved in the textile industry as broadly defined above come from the

Roman province of Gaul, and particularly *Gallia Belgica*. Indeed, it is here that we find the most significant monument in this category, the so-called *Igeler Säule* or Igel Column, a massive and impressive funerary monument still standing today in the small town of Igel near the major Roman centre of Trier in Germany[8] (Plate 22). A full-scale replica of the monument, colourfully painted as it may well have been in Roman times as revealed by the analysis of traces of paint on the original monument, stands in the central courtyard of the *Rheinisches Landesmuseum* in Trier. Commissioned by the local Secundinii family, evidently wealthy local merchants and wool factors, some of the decorated friezes on the Igel Column depict cloth manufacture and trading and thus testify to the great economic importance of sheep and wool in the Treveran region in particular and in the Roman empire more generally.

Dated earlier than, but close to, AD 250, the multi-storeyed, tiered sandstone Igel Column stands around seventy-five feet in height and is sited still in its original location on the left bank of the River Moselle. Architecturally the column consists of a stepped base on which rests a sandstone tower, comprising base, podium, vertical storey with pilaster frame, frieze, attic, pediment and pyramidal roof with figures atop. The surface area of the monument is almost entirely covered by carved decoration and relief friezes and panels.

The stepped base is covered in small motifs representing sea or river creatures and deities, perhaps alluding to the nearby Moselle, its linking with the Rhine and its access to the North Sea in the Netherlands. Three generations of the family, six or seven individuals, were clearly involved in the cloth trade according to the now-partial dedicatory inscription on the front of the south face of the monument and the main decorative panel. The monument was set up by Lucius Secundinius Aventinus and Lucius Secundinius Securus, still alive at the time of the dedication, and who presumably are the two men taking leave of a younger male relative in the main front panel relief. Heads or busts of three other, probably now-deceased family members, appear here in medallions and the scene is flanked on both sides by pilasters which are themselves decorated with erotes. The other three faces have main vertical panels that contain relief depictions of classical myths, respectively of Perseus and Andromeda, Achilles being dipped in the River Styx, and the apotheosis of Hercules, with zodiacal symbols and images of the four winds.

Below the main panels, on the socle of the tomb are images, on each face, respectively of a chest for storing cloth, a textile workshop, a textile warehouse, and the transporting of bales of cloth by wagon. The narrow frieze over the main vertical panels bears images of a family meal, workers in a kitchen preparing food, clients or customers paying money in an office, and once more a scene of the transportation of cloth bales on pack animals. On the crowning attic finished cloth is displayed (Plate 23), workers are depicted in an office, two men ride on a wagon, and finally on the fourth face Eros is depicted between two griffons.

On the four pediments that top the attic are represented the death/rape of Hylas, the death of perhaps Rhea Silvia, and busts of the sun and moon, all topped off by a figural capital with giants, a pine cone, and Jupiter as an eagle carrying off Ganymede.

The large number of purely mythological scenes on the monument, with almost half of the decorative scheme having been given over to scenes of classical mythology, related to stories involving death, love, and the afterlife. These were startlingly juxtaposed with more mundane scenes of cloth inspection, its transport by land and water, and its sale. The celebratory meal may well have represented the funerary feast partaken at the time of the dedication of the monument, a scene linking the sacred and profane aspects of the monument's imagery.

But there are some other iconographic elements of the decoration that do not easily fit this categorisation, such as the deaths of Hylas and of Rhea Silvia, but further discussion of those elements here is really beyond the scope of this present project. Suffice it to say, this monument speaks volumes about the wealth, status, and aspirations of the Secundinii family. The monument successfully marries the kind of iconography of workers, artisans, and merchants with which this book is primarily concerned, with a wide range of motifs and tropes derived from classical Roman culture and its mythology and art. It is provincial art, but at the same time in the same tradition as the much earlier Tomb of the Haterii at Rome discussed above in Chapter One.

The three vertical parts of the monument have decoration that implies that the lowest tier represents the river and seas, the largest middle tier the land that the Secundinii lived in, and the uppermost tier the heavens above. Its artistic programme, mixing the quotidian and the mythological, suggested that the family's business dealings on earth assured their immortality in the afterlife.

Other successful and wealthy textile merchants would also appear to have been commemorated in a less grandiose and ostentatious way on three funerary stele from Roman Milan and on a sarcophagus and funerary relief from Ostia. The three Milanese funerary stele, two in the collections of the city's *Museo Civico Archeologico* (Plate 24) and the third reset and built in to the later Porta Nuova (Plate 25) are mid to late first century AD in date and are all inscribed with the dedicatees' names and relationships and one carries five portrait busts of the deceased and others. However, in all three cases the most significant images for us appear towards the bottom of the stele where small vignettes comprise two figures in each case undertaking the unfolding and display of bolts of cloth. Given how often it appears in funerary imagery, there being further examples from Rome and Turin for instance, it would seem that large pieces of finished cloth, bolts of cloth, were emblematic of the textile industry and textile trading. Such bolts also appeared in shop scenes, hanging up or stacked up ready to be sold or being displayed to customers. In other scenes where one or two individuals appeared to be inspecting cloth it might be assumed that these were factory managers or owners signing off on the quality of the finished product. One such shop display scene from Vigna Strozzi in Rome and now in the *Gallerie degli Uffizi* or Uffizi Gallery in Florence involves a shop supervisor looking on while two male shop workers hold a length of cloth for display to two seated men who are attended by a male servant. This relief forms a pendant pair with another relief from the same site and in the same museum collection depicting a transactional scene in a shop or market hall specialising in textiles and cushions.

The two funerary artworks from Ostia comprise a sarcophagus panel now in the collection of the Getty Villa, Malibu in the United States, dating to the late Antonine period, AD 161–180, and a presumably more-or-less contemporary relief in the collections of the *Medelhavsmuseet* in Stockholm in Sweden (Plate 26), both commemorating the same man, Titus Aelius Evangelus.[9] On the relief panel from the front of the sarcophagus are Roman marriage imagery and scenes of daily work. The sarcophagus of Titus Aelius Evangelus, evidently a prominent local wool merchant in the town or its hinterland, and his wife Gaudenia Nicene is virtually unique in this respect. On the front panel is depicted a funerary banqueting scene with busy peripheral activity. Here we see the bearded Evangelus, reclining on a couch holding a goblet of wine with one hand and a bunch of grapes in the other which he proffers to a woman, presumably his wife. She approaches the end of the couch, holding her own wine cup in one hand and a funerary garland in the other. A small creature, variously identified by different authorities as either a dog or a goat, stands on the floor at her feet, partially obscured by her legs. Behind Gaudenia Nicene sits another bearded man engaged in some sort of textile-related craft activity, with what may be a wool winding frame in front of him and a ball of wool on a table nearby. Behind him is a tree and possibly two further animals, one reaching up into the tree to nibble at its leaves, but this area of the sarcophagus is unfortunately damaged, so identifications of the creatures are unclear. Their stances suggest that they are indeed goats. Other unusual scenes appear on groundlines both in front of the kline and behind it. In front appear representations of scales. Behind we see a cockerel, a man in a Phrygian cap leading a horse through an arched entranceway, with another cap-wearing man and a woman present. In the foreground, towards the edge of the panel, sits a young man on a chair winding wool, a wool basket visible on the floor under his chair. Images of sheep appear on the sarcophagus sides.

The scene on the front of this sarcophagus appears to represent a not altogether successful melange of a number of different types of symbolic representation: that is, standard funerary symbolism and funerary feast symbolism, biographical symbolism relating to trade or business, pastoral symbolism, and mythological symbolism of some kind. But not all is clear.

As to the funerary relief now in Stockholm the bearded Titus Aelius Evangelus, named in the dedicatory inscription along with his wife Ulpia Fortunata, his daughter Gaudenia Marcellina, and one Ulpius Telesphorus, is portrayed here alone in a workshop processing wool and making yarn. Baskets of raw material and finished material sit on the floor. A bag and a set of weighing scales hang on the wall. Obviously Evangelus married twice.

It is quite remarkable that so many of those working in the Roman textile industry chose to represent their professional identity on their funerary monuments. Even more remarkable perhaps is the fact that this was often done to represent quite specialised sectors within the overall textile manufacturing industry. The grave monuments of some of these more specialised workers will now be discussed.

The Roman textile industry would have needed to employ a huge number of specialists at different stages of production. One such specialist group of textile workers about whom we know the most is the fullers, especially the fullers of Pompeii who have received a great deal of attention from academic researchers in recent years, possibly to some extent out of actual proportion to the economic importance of the industry at the time [10]. The processing and washing of new cloth and garments using urine, chemical preparations, and water formed part of the work of a *fullo*, but much more time would have been spent on the washing and cleaning of worn clothes. Fullers were to all intents and purposes basically launderers. Much of the academic literature deals with the identification of fullers' premises and the working and layout of these establishments. Despite the particular disdain of certain Roman authors towards the fulling industry in general, at Pompeii the fullers' guild was an active and, it would seem, important presence in the social fabric of the town and was not shunned by all of its better-off citizens. Indeed, the establishment of new headquarters of the guild in the forum at Pompeii was partly subsidised by a local woman Eumachia, a member of a rich and successful local family who probably owned a tilery and pottery in the town and who married into an influential local elite clan. Eumachia's individual largesse was commemorated by the erection of a statue of her here dedicated by the *fullones*.

Equally remarkably, two of the most striking images in the overall canon of images of Roman workers relate to the depiction of cloth fullers, one from Forli in northern Italy and the other from Sens in Gaul. From Forli, and now permanently on display in pride of place in the *Museo Archeologico Civico 'Tobia Aldini'* in Forlimpopoli, is part of a small uninscribed relief of the first half of the second century A.D. on which is depicted work in a *fullonica* (Plate 27). Certainly very different in style from the Sens depiction described below, in terms of the naive and stylised depiction, nevertheless the same kind of set up is on display. A naked man can be seen standing in a large tub or vat. To one side of him stands a wooden rack or rail of some kind on which an item of cloth is hung to dry or to be brushed or felted. At the top of the relief and obviously intended to be accepted by the viewer as being inside the fullery is a beehive-shaped, probably wickerwork, frame which is a familiar piece of specialised drying equipment depicted elsewhere in fulling or textile manufacturing scenes in Roman art.

In the *Musées de Sens* in Burgundy in France is displayed an unprovenanced second century AD relief from a funerary monument depicting in its bottom register a fuller at work, standing in a large wooden tub (Plate 28), and in its upper register a man scraping cloth draped over a frame in a task called cropping the nap. The large, bulky fuller wears a short tunic beneath which one can sense a muscly torso. He grips handles at the side of the tub as he treads cloth or clothes. Cloth or a garment hangs up on a drying rail behind him. The relief is uninscribed. What is assumed to be a relief panel from the same monument carries a depiction of a man shearing sheep, so perhaps originally the monument was designed to illustrate all stages of textile production from raw wool to the finished cloth.

A late first century AD stele from Trieste and in the *Museo Civico di Storia e d'Arte* there might also be related to fulling. The stele is very classical in design and bears an inscription which shows that it was dedicated to Caius Hostilius Frugio. Underneath the inscription is a small image of a tub or basin and a wooden drying rack with cloth hung on it. The inscription does not state an occupation for the deceased. In addition to these images fullers are also represented in inscriptions, either individually or by their guilds. After consideration of the epigraphic evidence from Italy, it has been calculated that from Pompeii there are twenty-three inscriptions related to fullers, nineteen from Rome as catalogued by Sandra Joshel, two from Palestrina, and just one from Ostia.

There are also a number of fulling scenes represented on a samian vessel from Bern in Switzerland, including the now familiar workers in tubs and one scene of clothes laid out to dry. Such a vessel is likely to have been a one-off. Who could such a bowl have been made for? Its manufacture would have required the cutting of new and very individual stamps for decorating the pot and therefore the cost of commissioning such a pot would have been relatively high. There is certainly no evidence to indicate that the samian factories produced pots decorated with genre scenes involving Roman workers or of craft and industry as a matter of course.

I am not particularly interested in the absolute veracity of these various fulling scenes or of the technical specifications of the equipment portrayed. However, there can be little doubt that these scenes on funerary monuments and on the Bern pot are more-or-less technically correct in the portrayal of processes and equipment. Given the biases against fulling because of its polluting nature it is reassuring to see that such class discrimination did not altogether throttle or inhibit the professional pride of some of those working in this trade and who commissioned depictions of their work and workplaces.

It is also worth noting that each of these fulling scenes might have invoked not just a visual reaction or memory in its viewer but possibly also an olfactory one, in that for many urban dwellers the drifting smell of the stale urine from the local fullery would probably have been an unpleasant side effect of urban life, a smell perhaps brought immediately to mind by seeing these images, a very un-Proustian madeleine-moment.

At Pompeii the workshop and saleroom of a textile factor called Verecundus has been identified in Insula IX through the remarkable survival of a wall painting of felters and wool combers at work there and a painted electoral notice,[11] while nearby another painted electoral notice probably marks out a second felter's workshop. A name tag under one of the figures in the main wall painting identifies this man as Verecundus, depicted holding up a piece of unfolded cloth for display like the funerary stele images of the Milanese textile dealers discussed above. In the centre of the painting is a furnace or boiler over which four men are felting fibres. Three wool combers sit at low tables behind, hard at work: various tools of the trade sit ready on the benchtops. A second painting here is of a sales scene with a woman, presumably the wife of Verecundus, conversing with a female customer. Another painting at the property carries an image of the god Mercury inside a building on whose lower floor a large wooden textile drying rack can be seen. Not only was Verecundus producing and selling felted textiles and made-up items here but a painted sign tells us he was selling '*tunica lintea aur(ata)*', that is highly expensive linen tunics '…. with gold thread'.

Another highly interesting funerary monument to a textile specialist is the mid-first century AD funerary stele of Caius Pupius Amicus, a *purpurarius* or dyer of purple, from Parma in northern

Italy.[12] On this tall stone, split into three in antiquity and now restored in the *Museo Archeologico Nazionale di Parma* (Plate 29), appears a dedicatory inscription, a portrait bust of the deceased, and below that a number of objects relating to his occupation, including a set of weighing scales, some glass bottles and vials of different sizes presumably containing liquid dyes or *murex* extract and what would appear to be skeins of wool carded onto rings ready for dyeing.

Powdered *murex* purple extract, derived from the *murex* shell, for the dyeing of clothes was among the most precious luxury items in the Roman world. Despite the presence of the images of the bottles on the tombstone it has been argued that Amicus was not himself a dyer: rather, that he was a trader in dyes. This seems unlikely given that had that been the case he probably would have styled himself a *negotiares artis purpurariae*, as others did on tombstones elsewhere. It has been suggested that a *purpurarius* was a managerial title for someone in a business that did not necessarily just dye garments but also traded in dyed garments, the dye itself, in pigments, used to produce paint for frescos, and even in foodstuffs, that is the meat from out of the *murex* shells which itself was a valuable commodity. While it would not have been surprising for someone in business to handle a portfolio of roles and manufacture and deal in a range of products, it is likely that most ancient *purpurarii* were linked to the textile trade nevertheless.

Amicus's tombstone is the only known example on which the professional title of *purpurarius* appears along with images associated with the profession. However, funerary memorials and dedicatory inscriptions to twenty other *purpurarii* are known from Rome and from elsewhere in Italy, including Fiesole and Puteoli. None is as elaborate as Amicus's stele, though some carry portraits of couples or mixed gender family groups which suggests that women worked in this industry, something also suggested in some of the accompanying inscriptions. Some inscriptions also tell us that certain individual *purpurarii* held public offices that attested to a high social standing and aspiration, such as Cnaius Haius Doryphorus of Puteoli whose second century AD tombstone inscription described him as an *Augustalis*, and Caius Marcilius Eros who was not only named as a *purpurarius* but also as a *quinquevir* on a dedicatory stone from Truentum, Abruzzo in central Italy. Cicero's friend Caius Vestorius of Puteoli made his fortune trading in the pigment Egyptian blue and given that Puteoli was, according to Pliny, the most significant Italian source for *murex* it is likely he traded in purple as well.

At least nine *purpurarii* came from Rome and it is recorded that the empress Livia had her own personal *purpurarius* employed in the imperial household. In Rome no fewer than four of the nine epitaphs to *purpurarii* are to members of the Veturii family, suggesting not necessarily a monopoly in the purple trade for this family but certainly a pole position in the trade.

At a lower level of evidence, information about individuals involved in the shipping and trading of textiles and cloth, clothes, raw materials for manufacture, and dyes can be gleaned from the study of inscribed lead tags which turn up regularly in excavations all around the empire, especially at port and transit sites. One of the largest collections of such tags, which it is generally accepted were tied to bags, bundles, baskets, crates, or barrels of all kinds of goods, come from Sisak (Siscia) in south western Pannonia.[13] The tags are now in the *Arheološki Muzej u Zagrebu* in Zagreb. Only those tags bearing inscriptions relating to the textile trade and to specific named traders will be discussed briefly here.

Over 900 individuals are named on the Siscia lead tags, some by a single name, most by a double name and more rarely the *tria nomina* of the citizen. Female names are almost as well represented as male ones. Whether these named people were producers of goods being shipped or intended recipients of those goods on delivery we do not know. Products being shipped, as inscribed on some of the tags included *lana* (wool), *pannum* (cloth), *tunica* (tunics), *sagum* (curtains), *paenula* (coats), *palla, palliolum* and *abolla* (various kinds of mantles), and *lodix* (blankets). Colour adjectives were also widely employed, presumably to help differentiate batches from the same source. Prices on the tag could have reflected their cost of manufacture or repair, or their cost for shipping; it is uncertain which.

Something Leather

Discussion of clothing encompasses not just textiles and garments but also the leather-working industry and its associated trades, including shoe making. The significance of the leather industry, and particularly the requirement for its products in huge quantities to service the needs of the Roman army, must not be forgotten.

Just as everyone in the ancient world required cloth or textiles for making clothes, so the same applied to the provision of leather for manufacturing shoes and other types of footwear, along with leather clothing, saddles, reins and so on. While the tanning industry was economically important its operations were often viewed as polluting and taboo, and its workers as outsiders. In Rome the large tanning district of *Septimianum* extended along the right bank of the Tiber from the Aurelian Wall all the way to Porta San Spirito. Even though no individual tanners or *coriarii* left images of themselves on funerary monuments some were not averse to naming their trade or trade association in inscriptions, six being known from Rome, three from Praeneste, and one each from Capua and Puteoli. Two other examples come from outside Italy, from Oescus in Moesia and Carthage in North Africa.

Shoes were an integral part of Roman material culture, as necessary accessories certainly, but sometimes of greater significance than mere items of clothing. Their ability to be imbued with ideas relating to fashion and status means that shoes and footwear in general could sometimes convey cultural, social, economic, and even theological concepts and information through their very appearance, form, and materiality. Interesting though such topics undoubtedly are, the discussion of the many facets of shoe symbolism lies outside the scope of this present study, other than in terms of helping us perhaps to understand the sometimes significant role of the shoemaker in Roman communities, above and beyond that simply of a jobbing artisan or skilled worker.[14]

Shoes in general were made by a *sutor*. Slippers of various sorts were made by a *calceolarius* or a *diabathrarius*, sandals by a *solearius*, a *crepidarius*, or a *sandalarius*. A particular type of Gallic shoe was made by a *gallicarius*, while a *sutor veteramentarius* repaired old shoes and other footwear and was probably the lowest status worker in the shoe trade. In total at least thirty-five different specialist trade names are so far recorded for Roman period shoemakers and leatherworkers, mainly from inscriptions, with at least ten *collegia* and *corpora* representing these trades known.

References in ancient Roman written sources, in recorded Roman street names, and on leatherworkers' funerary inscriptions as a group provide some interesting topographical information about the locations of a number of workshops in Rome, as we will shortly see in the case of Caius Iulius Helius who is recorded as working at, or near, the Porta Fontanalis off the Campus Martius. The *Vicus Sandalarius* in Rome was literally the Street of the Sandal Makers and the *Vicus Loriarius* literally the Street of the Harness Makers: inscriptions concerning leatherworkers here confirm this. Juvenal mentions leather preparation or tanning 'beyond the Tiber'. Martial mentions shoemakers in the *Argiletum* and Juvenal a shoemaker from Benevento with a workshop there, the *Argiletum* being the main street between the Subura district and the *Forum Romanum*, Pliny notes that some operated near the Temple of Castor and Pollux, and Varro mentions the *Atrium Sutorium* – the Atrium of the Shoemakers – whose exact location is unknown, though it might have also been in the *Argiletum*. The *collegium fabrum soliarum baxiarum*, a shoemakers' organisation, was based in the arcades under the Theatre of Pompey. A maker of Greek sandals is attested in Subura by an inscription, a shoemaker in the *Spes Vetus* area (near where the Porta Praenestina was later built), and a *solatarius* – a maker of women's shoes-at 'the Grove of Semele' which may have been at the foot of the Aventine Hill near the Tiber.

It is not altogether surprising then that the funerary monuments of a number of Roman period shoemakers are known, including a possible female *sutrix* from Ostia, as we will see shortly. For the city of Rome itself Sandra Joshel has recorded eight occupational inscriptions relating to shoemakers, who are usually referred to as a *sutor*, but as in so many areas of Roman artisanal production many more specialised titles could be used.[15] Among Joshel's eight shoemakers are not only three *sutores* but also a *caligarius* or bootmaker, a *crepidarius* or maker of sandals, a *solatarius* or maker of women's shoes, a *faber soliarius baxiarius* or maker of woven footwear, and an *inpiliarius* or maker of felt footwear. Joshel also lists four occupational inscriptions relating to leather workers, including a *cullearius* or maker of leather bags, and a *lorarius* or harness maker. A *negotiator coriariorum* or dealer in tanned hides is also recorded in the city and a *scutarius* or shieldmaker may well have worked with leather as well.[16]

Perhaps the most interesting of these shoemakers in Rome is commemorated on the early second century AD grave stele of Caius Iulius Helius found on Via Leone in Rome and which is now in the *Centrale Montemartini* outpost of the *Musei Capitolini* in Rome (Plate 30). Its particular significance lies in the fact that the stele bears a heroicised portrait bust of Helius, a detailed and highly informative inscription, and a representation of two cobblers' lasts. The inscription reads, in translation: 'Caius Iulius Helius, shoemaker at the Porta Fontinalis, built this monument while living, for himself, Julia Flaccilla, his daughter, and Caius Iulius Onesimus, freedman, and his freed slaves and theirs.'

The portrait bust is quite remarkable in that Helius appears here in a form of almost heroic nudity, the bust being more elongated than was generally standard practice and extends portrayal of the body just down below the chest. The aged face of his portrait, almost in the old veristic style of the Republican era, seems not to belong to the buff and muscly torso below which looks like that of a much younger man. Helius declared in the inscription that he '... built this monument while living' which confirms that the style of the portrait bust must have been exactly as he wanted it to be and it was not, as so often occurred with Roman funerary monuments, the choice of others on behalf of the deceased. Helius must have given very careful consideration to how he wanted to present himself to others after his death. The verism suggests a conservative taste somehow at odds with the sheer daring of the manly, naked torso which confirms a knowledge of the penchant for emperors and others to enhance their status and declare their taste for Greek art by appearing in heroic nudity. It is also possible that the chosen style of portrait presentation stressed a kind of hyper-masculine display and attitude that was prevalent throughout Roman male society. That a shoemaker should choose such a persona to identify with is extraordinary. However, I cannot agree with the sentiment expressed by one academic who wrote of this portrait that 'the nudity ... aspires to a different ideal of a heroic, divinely inspired power – but the allusion seems gross for the commemoration of a shoemaker.'[17]

Helius also made good use of the detail in the inscription to declare and enhance his status and identity by direct reference to his freedman Onesimus and other freed slaves, some of whom would have been granted manumission at Helius's death. It is likely that Onesimus continued to work for Helius after manumission, perhaps as a highly skilled and trained worker or as a workshop supervisor and manager. But most tellingly, and unusually but not uniquely, the inscription tells us that he was a shoemaker at the Porta Fontinalis, which was in the Campus Martius, a supposedly desirable area of the city to live in. In other words, Helius is here expressing pride in both his trade and in his city but most significantly in his specific, named area of the city. It is also possible that the viewer of the monument was intended to understand from the inscription that he ran a business in a desirable area and, from his aged and experienced face, that he had had a long and successful business career.

The two wooden shoe lasts in the pediment above the portrait bust are rendered in great detail and it can clearly be seen that one of the lasts is sitting inside a sandal. Shoe lasts constituted a more-immediately understandable signifying image for the craft of shoe making than the representation of a shoemaker's tools such as awls which would be impossible for the viewer to distinguish from the same types of awls used by leather workers in general.

The very fact that Helius's funerary monument deals with a number of different layers of identity – personal, familial, and gender-related, and with issues of status, occupational success, and geographical location – makes it one of the most interesting such occupational monuments from Rome. The issue of displaying status by referencing freedmen on their funerary monuments and in accompanying inscriptions was a common trope among the artisans and entrepreneurs of Rome, and most commonly names of between one and five freedmen and freedwomen appeared, with names of men predominating, reflecting the gender bias of the time in the urban artisanal workforce. Notable exceptions to this numbers game include the funerary inscription of the cloakmaker Quintus Caecilius Spendo which named seventeen of his freedmen and one freedwoman and that of the metal-tableware manufacturer Aulus Fulvius Dorotheus whose damaged, now-incomplete inscription named at least nineteen manumitted slaves, that is thirteen freedmen and six freedwomen.

Such epitaphs help to illustrate two main points with regard to social and economic relationships in Roman society: that the freedmen class themselves had as much of a stake in the system of slavery and manumission as the upper classes of Rome and that manumission was to some extent a driver of the artisan economy in the city. While manumission might have incentivised slaves in artisan workshops there was a much more subtle advantage to be had by urban artisans in that manumission was a tool whereby they could control the size of their workforce and dictate its make-up in terms of accumulated skills. To manage such things in a febrile urban economy such as Rome's would have brought stability and helped minimise risk.

This neatly brings us to two very different funerary monuments to shoemakers from Ostia, the first of whom is Septimia Stratonice, a possible *sutrix* or female shoemaker.[18] Dying some time in the early second century AD she was commemorated on a decorated and inscribed relief dedicated to both her and to Acilius Fortunatianus, son of the dedicator (Marcus Acilius), that probably would have been attached to a large funerary monument whose location is unknown (Plate 31). The two surviving fragments of the relief were found on the Via della Fontana in Ostia and at the town's Antonine baths. The inscription is partial and has been reconstructed sufficiently to know Septimia's and Acilius's names, the fact that she was considered a very dear friend (*amica carissima*) by Marcus, and that as his benefactress she bestowed favours on him. Her occupation, if it was indeed *sutrix* or shoemaker, is not mentioned on the small portion of the dedicatory inscription which survives. A relief portrait of Septimia sitting on a stool or low seat and holding up a shoe or a last appears on one side of the stone. It has been suggested by one authority that Septimia could be holding up a votive model of a foot, what is known to archaeologists as an anatomical or medical *ex voto*, but this seems highly unlikely.

While the funerary monument of an individual in the Roman world would be set up by the deceased's family or heirs it is possible that in many instances, unless death came suddenly or unexpectedly, a design and wording could have been chosen by the deceased individual when he or she was alive. In those cases we can safely say that the choice of stressing an occupational identity either through the inscription or through an image or images on the monument, or by both, in the case of Septimia Stratonice, was made by the craftsman or craftswoman. So much of the inscription on Septimia's monument concerns how Marcus felt about her and saw her that one wonders if the choice of presenting her occupational identity on the tombstone so overtly was in fact his alone.

The second funerary item from Ostia is the front of an earlier second century AD sarcophagus now in the *Museo Nazionale Romano* in Rome (Plate 32). The central inscribed panel tells us in Greek that Lucius Atilius Artemas and Claudia Apphias provided this sarcophagus for their friend Titus Flavius Trophimas, his name suggesting that he was a foreigner working in Ostia, something confirmed by the inscription which tells us that he was from Ephesus in Asia Minor, and for themselves. On one side of the front panel can be seen a man, presumably the deceased Titus, seated on a stool and working on a shoe or sandal on his knee. A tall cabinet behind him has a number of shoes or more probably wooden shoe lasts stacked along its top shelf. A man standing on the other side of the cabinet is generally identified as a ropemaker, holding a distaff in one hand and stretching out the rope with the other. The two crafts are not incompatible taking place in the same workshop as rope-soled sandals could have been produced alongside all-leather shoes. A second scene, involving two men playing instruments, one of them dancing at the same time, is less easy to interpret or understand. A highly personalised note is added by the inscription's insistence that Titus was as a friend 'incomparable and trusted ... the straightforward one, the cultivator of every art..'. The two men working together can be assumed to be the deceased Titus and his friend Lucius Atilius Artemas, and they are probably also the dancers. The Roman art historian John Clarke has wondered whether the three friends, two men and a woman, whom the inscription tells us 'always lived together' were a sexual threesome,[19] but this is not really the place to further pursue that particular line of inquiry.

From Roman Milan come two remarkably similar images of a man working leather, one on a second century AD funerary stele from Porta Nuova and now in the *Civico Museo Archeologico* in the city and the other on one of the side panels of a large later third century AD sarcophagus from the Milanese district of Lambrate and now in the collection at *Castello Sforzesco*, the main difference being the amount of additional detail in the latter scene. The Lambrate sarcophagus leatherworker has a much more elaborate cabinet-cum-workbench on which to work and can be seen inside a well-appointed room, framed by columns and a vaulted ceiling, with a hide hanging from a stretcher on the far wall of the room (Plate 33). This seems such an intimate image, as if we the viewers are eavesdropping on him while he steadily works away, deep in concentration. It is one of a number of images on the uninscribed Lambrate sarcophagus, including that of the Good Shepherd which locates this particular burial within a Christian milieu. The deceased also appears in an architectural setting on the long front panel of the sarcophagus and in the form of a portrait bust on the lid.

However, even though not as interesting pictorially the stele of Caius Atilius Iustus from Porta Nuova is noteworthy because the inscription on it tells us that he was a *sutor caligarius*, rather than simply a *sutor*. As the *caligarius* was a very specific term for a military-issue boot it can be assumed that Iustus made a fortune from supplying the Roman army which allowed his wife Cornelia Exoratae to commission for him his fine, large but understated grave stele with its apotropaic or protective Gorgon's head towards the top, its well-cut inscription, and its image of Iustus at work. Incidentally, another memorial inscription to a *sutor caligarius* comes from the major Roman military centre of Carnuntum in what is now Austria, dedicated to Peregrinus, a Dacian by birth and now a slave of Quintus Asinus.

Also from Milan comes an otherwise unique inscription, now unfortunately lost, relating to Caius Iulius Alcimus, a '*comprator mercis sutoriae*', that is a merchant seller of shoes and presumably of related leather goods and materials. The inscription also tells us that he was a *Ravennati*, a native of Ravenna rather than of Milan where he died. This inscription, along with the Porta Nuova and Lambrate funerary monuments, might tend to suggest that alongside textile dealing Roman Milan was an important centre for leather production in northern Italy.

At least five other shoemakers' or leatherworkers' funerary memorials from various towns around Italy were recorded by Gerhard Zimmer in his 1982 catalogue of occupational images in Roman Italy.[20] While one is unprovenanced, the others came from Tortona in Piedmont, Altino in Abruzzo, Sesto Fiorentina in Tuscany, and Capua in Campania, the latter being a memorial to a *scutarius* or shieldmaker, with the image of a shield appearing in the centre of the stele. Depictions of shoes or lasts also appear on a first century AD stele from Castiglione Falleto in Piedmont, and on the second century AD cippus of Poppedia Secunda from Avezzano, Abruzzo and in the *Museo del Fucino* there. Outside of Italy there are very few images of shoemakers, the best and least equivocal examples being a shoemaker at his bench with his tools displayed on hooks behind, though very heavily worn, on a funerary stele from Bourges in central France and now in the *Musées de Sens*, and a fragmentary relief from Béziers in southern

France is presumably from a funerary monument on which a short inscription appears along with a curved tool of some sort and an image of a cobbler's last.

Images of shoemakers also appeared in other media, for instance on a wall painting from the *Casa del Cervi* or House of the Deer at Herculaneum, where the shoemakers were cupids or *putti*, while a shoe seller can be seen on a painted panel from Pompeii now in the *Museo Archeologico Nazionale* in Naples. On a small bronze ansate panel from Aquileia in northern Italy an image of a shoemaker at work at a table has been carefully etched, his occupation made clear by the boots or lasts hanging up on the workshop wall behind him.

However, one of the most intriguing, unique, and quite recent discoveries, only published in 2000, has been a painted tomb thought to be that of a successful shoemaker or seller. It has been suggested that some of the images of shoemakers depicted on funerary monuments as individuals working alone may have been nostalgic or fanciful representations of highly successful businessmen or women in the footwear industry going back to their working roots by getting their hands dirty when in fact they had ended their careers as hands-off entrepreneurs employing others to do such work in large workshops. In support of this argument it has been noted that the fine and doubtless expensive late first century AD tomb at Nocera Superiore (Nuceria), Pizzone in Campania, central Italy known as the Shoemaker's Tomb – *La Tomba del Calzolaio* – suggests the resting place of a wealthy local entrepreneur, judged against other tombs at the necropolis.[21] Inside the tomb were two original burials, with later, presumably family insertions, inscriptions suggesting that of the Masuria *gens*. Most remarkable was the painting inside depicting a shoemaker's workshop, a unique painted funerary representation of a shoemaker at work from the ancient world. Unfortunately I have not been able to view this painting, nor can an image of it be reproduced here, and in this discussion I will have to rely on the photographs published in the final report on the excavation. Due to the condition of the painting and the colours being faded and unphotogenic even this has proved difficult. However, on the left of the painting sits the figure of a shoemaker, presumably the original occupant for whom this tomb was built, with a round raised bench in front of him, with two vertical metal rods of different lengths set in its middle, presumably a specialised kind of cobbler's workbench. In the centre of the painting is a very large piece of furniture on which rest two rows of pairs of laced shoes, boots, or high sandals. This scene either represents the interior of a shoemaker's workshop or of commercial premises where shoes were displayed and sold.

In addition, it has been suggested that the name Atilius Artemas that crops up on an inscription in the Shoemaker's Tomb could be the same individual named as a dedicatee on the shoemaker and ropemaker sarcophagus from Ostia discussed above. It certainly would be a remarkable coincidence if this was the case, though the name of the wife of Artemas at Nocera is not the same name as the female companion of the Ostia Artemas. Were this somehow eventually proved to be the same man recorded in each place, it might point towards the shoemaker in the tomb being a more significant individual than a mere cobbler working alone in a home workshop, but rather the scion of a larger business with multiple workshops and outlets in different places. This is an interesting suggestion, a supposition really, but is certainly something to be borne in mind.

In this chapter discussion has focused on two of the most economically significant industries in the Roman world, the textile trade and the leather trade. Each was organised on both a local, workshop level and on a regional, provincial, and empire-wide level through the creation of networks, in terms of the provision and procurement of raw materials and the trading and distribution of finished goods. In the following chapter attention will focus on the metalworking trades of the Roman world, a set of crafts and industries less connected than the textile trade and industry and less tied into the empire-wide trading networks.

4

Metal and Transformation
Metal Postcards

If Rome needed its architects and builders to create and maintain the metropolis, if the baking of bread at Rome was part of the political settlement between the Roman state and its people as represented by the ideological significance of the *annona*, and the production of clothes and shoes was a necessity for life itself, then in economic terms it was metalworking that constituted the highest grossing industry in the Roman world as a whole and was perhaps the most admired of the crafts. Rome would have been but a provincial Italian town without the metal swords, spears, and shields of its armies. Rome's lauding of its metalworkers and its proscriptions in the form of Sumptuary Laws against decadent eating were to find a chilling resonance much later in Hermann Goering's idea that 'iron always made a nation strong, butter and lard only made the people fat.'

The transformative power of the metalworker, using heat and physical power to change ore into metal and metal into objects, imbues such workers with supernatural powers in many cultures, and in Greek and Roman societies often led to the equation of such earthly work with the labour of the god Hephaistos (to the Greeks) and Vulcan (to the Romans)[1] (Plate 34). In the provinces other smith gods such as Taranis and Sucellus were brought into the Roman pantheon. A popular image in both Greek and Roman art in various media was of Hephaistos/Vulcan and the Cyclopes (the three cyclops) forging the armour of Achilles. Perhaps references to this are intended in scenes on Roman sarcophagi involving cupids forging armour, examples of which include a striking classical bas relief, undated and unprovenanced, in the *Palazzo Conservatori* in Rome. The creation of the armour also appears as one of many scenes relating to the Trojan Wars on the so-called *Tabula Iliaca* of c. 15 BC in the *Musei Capitolini* in Rome, on the reverse of a coin of Septimius Severus (AD 193–211), on a wall painting of the mid-first century AD from the House of Vedius Siricus at Pompeii in which Thetis receives the shield of Achilles, and on another, unprovenanced Pompeian painting in the *Museo Archeologico Nazionale* in Naples with Thetis waiting at the forge of the god to receive Achilles' weapons and armour.

For this reason it is not surprising that there is a considerable number of depictions of metalworkers, principally smiths, copper workers, and cuttlers, on Roman funerary monuments and further ones on which tools of the trade appear on their own. Gerhard Zimmer catalogued twenty-nine sculptural representations of metalworkers from Rome and elsewhere in Italy, as usual in the case of representative images of Roman workers the majority of these being from funerary contexts.[2] Many of them consist of images of men striking objects with hammers, something which is not itself intrinsically interesting. It is though perhaps surprising that some of the images are representations of specialist tools or of highly technical processes which probably would have meant very little to the casual viewer. Some of these images allow us to consider issues such as technological methodology, the types of equipment in use, engineering skills and scientific knowledge, the scale of operation depicted in terms of the size of the labour force, and the relevance of the sequencing of tasks in production or manufacture. In a number of workshop scenes the hands of these artisans appear to the viewer as the protagonists as they shape, knead, model, mix, repair, and sand and polish their creations. The sounds of work seem to blend into and infuse these silent images.

Sandra Joshel in her study of occupational inscriptions from the city of Rome records twenty-six jewellers and eighty-nine metalsmiths.[3] Specialist job titles among these include *aerarius* or coppersmith, *aerarius statuarius* or maker of copper statues, *aerarius vascularius* or maker of copper vessels, *argentarius* or silversmith, *argentarius vascularius* or maker of silver vessels, *aurarius* or goldsmith, *auri acceptor* or dealer in gold, *aurifex* or goldsmith, *brattarius/brattaria* or male/female goldbeater or maker of gold leaf, *brattarius inaurator* or goldbeater/gilder, *caelator* or engraver, *candelabrarius* or maker of lampstands, *cassidarius* or helmet maker, *clostrarius* or locksmith, *corinthiarius* or worker in Corinthian bronze, *faber argentarius* or silversmith, *faber ferrarius* or ironsmith, *ferrarius/ferraria* or male/female ironsmith, *gemmarius/gemmaria* or male/female jeweller, *gladiarius* or swordmaker, *negotiator aerarius et ferrarius* or dealer in copper and iron, *negotiator/negotians ferrarius* or dealer in iron, *plumbarius* or maker of lead pipes, *sigillarius* or statuette maker, *tritor argentarius* or silver polisher, and *vascularius* or maker of metal vessels.

Exploitation and Danger

Certain issues will come and go like the tides in this study because of its main focus on visual evidence. Two such topics are the prevalence of child labour in the Roman economy, many of these children being slaves, and the danger inherent in many jobs in the Roman world. The child gold workers Pagus and Septicia Rufa will be discussed below in this respect. Few children feature in the many relief scenes of artisanal activity discussed in this book, one exception being a young boy on the bronzesmith's workshop relief from Pompeii, again discussed in detail later in this chapter. This child, along with a sleeping dog on a cushion, may have been present in this scene perhaps to humanise it or to make it less exclusively male-dominated, or even with humorous intent. However, it might have been the case that he was an apprentice or a working child slave.

Not entirely missing from the record of Roman times are images of miners at work, extracting metal ores from the ground, either through shallow, open-cast mining or deep shaft or pit mining. A few such images are known from ancient Greece. Only one is known from the Roman period, a partial relief of the first or second century AD depicting a group of miners, some carrying pickaxes over their shoulders and wearing heavy belts or harnesses with pockets or panniers to carry ore or tools, from the silver mines at Palazuelos, near Linares, Jaén, in Andalusia, Spain, and now in the *Deutsches Bergbau-Museum* in Bochum, Germany.[4] However, an extraordinary image of a possible child miner, perhaps a slave, though this is not stated in the late first century AD stele's dedicatory inscription, comes from near the mine of Poligono in Baños de la Encina, in the Sierra Morena mountains, again in Jaén province in southern Spain (Plate 35). This stele is now in the *Museo Arqueológico Nacional* in Madrid. According to the dedicatory inscription Quartulus or Quintus Artulus, the name being uncertain due to poor carving, was four years old (IIII) when he died, even though the image of the child above appears a few years older.[5] There are a number of explanations for this discrepancy, the most likely and now widely accepted being that again the carver made a mistake and that it had been intended to be nine (VIIII) inscribed here rather than four. Everything about the image suggests that the boy was a working miner, even though this is not stated in the inscription, but other interpretations can be made. He is depicted dressed in a short, loose tunic that finishes above the knees and has bare feet. He holds a pick-hammer in one hand and a small basket in the other. 'May the earth lie lightly on you', the inscription states in translation, suggesting that he may have died in a roof fall in a mine.

Alternative interpretations of the image include the possibility that he was the son of a miner, rather than a working miner himself, and that this familial identification was being stressed here, that Quartulus or Quintus was being portrayed in an adult role that he died too young to achieve, a very common trope in Roman funerary art in Italy, or that the boy was portrayed with these particular and distinct tools because they were symbolic of the mining community to which he belonged. On a personal level, I can certainly understand the ways in which a mining community uses and identifies with certain objects, signs, and symbols, having lived for a number of years in County Durham in northern England during the late 1970s and early 1980s and in the Staffordshire Coalfields town of Rugeley during the miners' strike of 1984/5.

There is though plenty of evidence to suggest that in Spain and elsewhere in the Roman empire boys from the age of eight might have worked in the mines in some capacity.[6] The age at death of twenty-two miners in Roman Spain and Portugal is known and included among the recorded dead are Tonginus and Modestianus who both died aged ten and Titus Boutius who died aged eleven. Parts of the text of the second century AD *Lex Metallis Vipascensis*, a regulatory code for procedures in mining communities, inscribed on two bronze plaques from Aljustrel in Portugal, make reference to children being one of the groups exempt from entrance payments into the public baths.

Perhaps rather more circumstantially, it has been pointed out that a number of the shafts and galleries in some archaeologically excavated Roman mines are so low and narrow that possibly only children could work in these particular areas of the mine. Again, smaller versions of full-sized mining equipment such as picks and baskets have been found, perhaps for use by children. Finally, there is a great deal of archaeological, ethnographic, and historical evidence for women and children engaged in mining activity at different times in many different societies – one has only to think of the women miners of the Shropshire Coalfield famously photographed and sexually fetishised by Charles Munby in the Victorian era.[7]

Diverging for a moment from the subject of metalworking and mining, another dangerous occupation in Roman times was stone quarrying, and while we do not have any visual evidence as emotive as Quartulus's stele associated with quarrying, there is enough evidence in the form of altars and dedications to protective gods as to suggest the desire to somehow alleviate the dangers inherent in this work. An image of the regional provincial god Saxanus, sometimes equated with Hercules as Hercules-Saxanus, who seems to have been a hammer or pick-wielding god of stonemasons and quarrymen, appears on a votive altar dedicated to the god from Šmartno na Pohorju in Slovenia and is so far unique in the Roman world. Šmartno na Pohorju was one of the two main marble quarry sites here in the Pohorje Mountains in what was southern Noricum in the Roman period, marble deposits which were heavily exploited from the first century AD onwards. On the altar's front face can be seen the figure of Saxanus wielding his huge sledgehammer against a rockface, with a row of shaped and cut stone blocks appearing in the foreground. The altar face may appear partially unfinished, with numerous striations and uneven areas, but this would have been a deliberate choice of the sculptor who wanted to almost make the god appear to be quarrying himself out of the altar face, in a similar manner perhaps to the portrayal of the sculptor Marcus Secundinius Amabilis from Bordeaux discussed above in Chapter Five. From the same quarry comes a votive inscribed altar to Jupiter and Saxanus dedicated by Aurelius Aprilis, Aurelius Ursulus, and Aurelius Angulatus, and other dedications to the god are known from a number of sites in Germany and along the Danube. The majority of such inscriptions were made by legionaries and members of the Roman fleet quarrying tufa for quernstones at Brohltal in the Eifel area near Treis-Karden in the territory of the Treveri.

Roman labour for many, particularly slaves, represented a series of epic miseries, centred around the common use of child labour, the absence of health and safety procedures, and the ever-present fear in some occupations of an early death. Eyewitness accounts of the nineteenth and twentieth century western Industrial Revolution from Alexis de Tocqueville to Friedrich Engels show that this period was the time of a massive descriptive project, including art and image, in which criminals, the insane, women, and the poor came to be systematically studied. Writers stressed both the daily grind of poverty and its associated misery, and yet conversely alluded to the dignity of labour and the indomitable spirit and resourcefulness of the working poor. Particularly in the nineteenth century the poor were often represented in images and texts in mawkish or sentimental ways, or in a traditional, hidebound manner. The grittiness and abject misery of poverty in general and the poor as individuals deserving of interest and concern, indeed of broader society's attention, came to dominate political, social, and philosophical discourse. The Roman worker was left to commemorate himself or herself when they could afford to or wished to, defining and inhabiting the space around them in their own descriptive project.

Turning now to the actual working of metals, away from the subject of their extraction, in the Roman world depictions of forges are known from both sculptures and wall paintings; images of metalworking bellows appear on sculpture; the chasing of metal vessels appears in a wall painting; images of the minting of coins appear in both sculpture and wall painting; embossing is depicted in sculpture, as is gold beating; and images of jewellery production are found in a wall painting. Some of these images will now be considered here.

In the collection of the *Palazzo dei Diamanti* in Ferrara in northern Italy a late first century AD funerary altar carries a small image of a blacksmith and an assistant beating out some iron on an anvil and a scene so similar appears on a probably contemporary funerary stele in the *Museo Archaeologico Oliveriano* in Pesaro in eastern Italy that they might well have come from the same workshop. A third scene of blacksmithing can be found on one of the side faces of the funerary altar of Lucius Cornelius Atimetus, now in the *Museo Lapidario* in the *Musei Vaticani* and dating to the second half of the first century AD.[8] (Plate 36). The inscription on the front of the altar describes Atimetus as dedicating it for himself, for his freedman Lucius Cornelius Epaphra, and for his other, unnamed, freedmen and freedwomen. On the other side face is a highly detailed and unique portrayal of a cuttler's shop or stall, with a figure to one side presumably being Atimetus engaged in displaying his finished wares to a well-dressed, presumably elite customer. The displaying of goods as consumer desirables in this manner also occurs in a number of scenes of textile sales, as has already been discussed in Chapter Three. On a low cabinet with a drawer at the top sits a wooden display case of finished cutlery items, the case having hinged side leaves which are opened out to fully display the goods for sale. We can make out on the upper set of hooks a number of curved-blade knives or *falxes*, like pruning knives, below them a row of stright-bladed utilitarian knives for household use or for craft whittling and carving, and on the bottom row of the cabinet what appear to be sets of chisels or gouges. The image juxtaposes the non-elite producer (craftsman) with the elite consumer and in its cabinet unites the countryside, as represented by the *falxes*, the *domus* or home, as represented by the utilitarian and household knives, and the workshop, as represented by the tools for sale, bringing a pleasing circularity to the visual message here.

The Altar of Atimetus is particularly interesting in that it illustrates both the act of creation of a craft item, as represented by the blacksmithing scene, and the consumption of material culture at the time as represented by the shop scene and its confident portrayal of salesman, elite customer and a bountiful choice of items. For many years the Museum of London very cleverly displayed part of its collection of bone and wooden handled knives from the Walbrook streamed in a replica fold-out shallow wooden cabinet recreated with evident reference to the Atitemus altar.

At the *Necropoli di Porto*, Isola Sacra, Ostia two ceramic plaques were placed on the front facade of Tomb 29, the Tomb of the Verii, and a third to the left of the *columbarium* entrance, all carrying images of metalworking (Plate 37a and 37b). The tomb was dedicated to Verria Zosime and Verrius Euhelpistus and dates to the late Hadrianic to early Antonine period. The first of the two plaques on the facade depicts a bearded man in a tunic, protective leather apron, and sandals holding a metal item and standing in front of what appears to be a grinder or sharpening machine of some kind. Finished tools hang on the walls of his workshop. On the second plaque from the facade two male figures appear at different scales, each engaged in some close-work task required for the finishing-off of a tool or tool blade, one at an elaborate workbench and the other sat at an anvil. The rest of the plaque surface is taken up with the depiction of a mixed array of blacksmith's tools and finished iron tools for sale. The third plaque is much simpler in design and less crowded: on it is depicted a worker probably engaged in sharpening the edge of an implement on a whetstone which he holds in his left hand and standing in front of a similar kind of grinding machine depicted on one of the facade plaques. It is possible that one of the tomb's interior black and white mosaics depicted a grinding machine similar to that depicted on two of the terracotta plaques: this would be most unusual if that were indeed the case. Given that this type of grinding machine is not familiar as a piece of standard blacksmith's equipment today this could suggest that it was a one-off piece invented by Verrius.

Fragments of a sarcophagus and its lid recovered from inside the tomb were decorated with scenes from the myth of Meleager and the hunting of the Calydonian Boar, including a scene of feasting. It has been suggested that this is a fitting subject matter for a blacksmith's burial[9] but while I am impressed by the reasoning behind this assertion I remain unconvinced. Certainly, this myth was a very popular motif in Roman funerary art in general because of its power of metaphor and analogy. In this very specific case the argument goes that the image of the stoking of a fire at a feast reflects back upon the fire of the blacksmith's forge, that the well-tempered spears and axes of the boar hunters reflected a craftsman's skill, and that the butchering of the trapped boar required good, sharp, reliable knives of the kind a skilled blacksmith would produce in quantity.

Bronze working is represented by fewer artworks than iron working but those few that we have are particularly interesting. From Pompeii, and now in the *Museo Archeologico Nazionale* in Naples, is a first century AD relief that is either a funerary memorial piece or a shop sign of some kind (Plate 38). The action depicted involves four workers, a small child, and a dog, inside a foundry-cum-workshop, undertaking at least three separate and distinct tasks. Hanging on the wall at the back of the workshop are a number of bronze buckets and vessels: nine further vessels can be seen displayed on a shelf unit. The first worker is engaged in weighing lumps or ingots of metal on a huge set of scales hanging from the workshop ceiling, while a child, presumably his son, pulls on his tunic to attract his attention. In the top centre is a furnace, beneath which can be seen a second and third man working in unison, one holding an object on an anvil while the other lifts a large hammer above his head with both hands to beat the metal. A fourth worker sits at a low workbench meticulously sanding down and finishing a vessel. The dog lies asleep on a cushion.

A first century AD votive funerary altar found at Borgo Salute, Este in northern Italy and now in the *Museo Nazionale Atestino* was dedicated by L. Minucius Optatus who we must assume to have been a coppersmith specialising in the manufacturing or finishing of copper bowls and other vessels, though his trade is not specified in the dedicatory inscription on the altar (Plate 39). However, a small pictorial vignette of Optatus in his workshop appears towards the base of the altar in which he is shown seated on a low stool in front of a workbench. He uses a pair of pincers of some kind to hold up a large metal vessel that he is working on. Two other finished vessels hang on the workshop wall.

A more specialised type of bronze and iron working is attested on the late first to early second century AD funerary monument of a locksmith from Beligna, Aquileia in north-eastern Italy and in the *Museo Archeologico Nazionale di Aquileia* (Plate 40). Unfortunately we do not know the name of the locksmith, as the upper part of the stele which would have borne his name is now missing. In the complete carved relief panel at the bottom of the monument we see a worker operating a pair of bellows on a small hut-like furnace, the worker well-protected behind a shield-like guard of some kind. In the centre of the relief a man sits on a low stool and with hammer in one hand and tongs in the other beats out some metal. On the other side are depicted three tools of the trade and a finished lock which helps provide us with the very particular speciality of this individual smith.

From Chieti, and in the *Museo Archeologico Nazionale D'Abruzzo*, is a third or fourth century AD funerary monument to a mint master who appears in the form of a head and bust set within a scallop shell at the top of the stele, with a funerary *patera* and basin on each side. This man appears to be overlooking and thus overseeing the action portrayed on the panel below. There is pictured a scene within the mint, with a *malleator* lifting a hammer to strike something on an anvil, while a second man approaches from the right. He is probably a *supposter*, holding a punch die in one hand and a pair of metal tongs in the other. Perhaps surprisingly, this is not the only image or representation that we have of work going on inside a state mint. Two very similar mint work scenes appear on a late Roman 'contorniate type' coin or medallion of c. AD 355–410 and on an imperial *tessera* or token of largesse in the Vienna coin cabinet – the *Münzkabinett* – in the *Kunsthistorisches Museum Wien*. The coin bears a head of the first century emperor Nero on its obverse, and on its reverse a scene inside a mint where six people are present, the three figures at the centre of the scene quite evidently striking coins. A terracotta plaque from a burial at Alexandria in Egypt, now in a private collection in Rome, carries images of a mint worker's tools. A number of similar tools appear on a late first century AD stele from Rome, now in the British Museum in London. Dedicated to the freedman Demetrius and his son Philonicus it carries their portrait busts as well as the die-sinkers tools Demetrius employed at the mint under his former master P. Licinius Stolo and the emblems of a *lictor*, a role presumably played by Philonicus.

An extraordinary group of Trajanic inscriptions from the excavation of part of a large building, thought to be an early imperial mint, beside the church of San Clemente on the Caelian Hill in Rome provides a wealth of information about the organisation and staffing of the mint, particularly the stratification of the workforce in the mint and the very specific job titles, designations, and responsibilities there [10]. This particular group of dedications, on the bases of statues, dates to 28 January AD 115, and is enhanced by further inscriptions from the mint site. One of the inscriptions refers to the '*familia monetalis*', literally 'the family of moneyers', not implying that the workers here were joined in some form of touchy-feely professional bonding; indeed, far from it and almost quite the opposite. The '*familia*' here implied service, servitude, and hereditary obligation: so physically taxing was some of the work in mints that criminals could be condemned to work here. The overseer of the mint is named as Publius Aelius Felix, a freedman of the emperor Trajan, who on the base of a statue dedicated to the god Apollo is described as '*optio et exactor auri argenti et aeris*', that is 'officer in charge and superintendent of gold, silver, and bronze'. Another '*optio*', without the additional, more important, '*exactor*' title, is named on an inscribed base of a statue to Fortuna Augusta as Albanus, who must therefore have been Felix's immediate deputy.

Job titles given in the various inscriptions include *officinatores*, *signatores*, *suppostores*, and *malliatores*. The *officinatores* would appear to have been third tier supervisors, under Felix and Albanus, and probably correspond to the modern job title of foreman. The *signatores* were the die cutters. The *suppostores* seem to have been responsible for putting blanks between the dies and for removing the coins once struck. The job title *malliatores* (literally 'hammerers') speaks for itself and denotes the most physically strenuous of the tasks in the mint, striking the coins, but presumably the lowest grade of worker there. Other mint job titles known from elsewhere included *argentarii*, *scalptores*, and *conductores*.

An analysis of the sixty-three names of workers in the inscriptions tells us something about the relative numbers of each kind of official or worker in the mint, and about whether each job was apparently more appropriately undertaken by a freedman or by a slave, although interestingly none of the three named roles was carried out exclusively by either freedmen or slaves. Of the seventeen *signatores*, twelve were freedmen and just five were slaves. Of the eleven *suppostores*, seven were freedmen and four were slaves. Of the thirty-two *malliatores* just eleven were freedmen and twenty-one, almost two thirds, were slaves. No job title was given for three further named workers at the mint, though we do know that two were freedmen and one a slave, giving a total of thirty-two freedmen and thirty-one slaves working there.

The importance of the mint in Rome and subsidiary mints at various other city locations around the empire cannot be over stressed. The Roman historians Eutropius, Sextus Aurelius Victor, and the anonymous authors of the *Scriptores Historiae Augustae* provide us with short accounts of a very serious series of incidents at the mint in Rome which came to be known as the *Bellum Monetarium*.[11] These sources record that in AD 271 there was a revolt of the mint workers in Rome, led by a man called Felicissimus who was a *rationalis* or senior accountant at the mint. Under the emperor Aurelian, who reigned between AD 270 and 275, reforms were made both to the coinage, in an attempt to counteract its debasement and to establish standards for silver content, and to the bureaucratic organisation of the mint itself, the initial reforms of AD 271 presumably being the trigger for the revolt, while the fuller and more root-and-branch reforms of AD 274 presumably addressing the very problems thrown up by the revolt.

Even if the revolt initially was a localised outbreak of violence at the mint on the Caelian Hill in Rome it soon spread to become a more general and much more serious event of widespread civil unrest in the city, perhaps fomented by the plotting of certain senators opposed to Aurelian's general programme of reform and his allegedly rather autocratic manner. It has even been suggested that there was unrest at the Antioch mint, in present-day Turkey, at the same time, and if so this was presumably for the same reasons. Felicissimus was killed quite early on during the revolt in Rome, presumably by Aurelian's troops, and both historian Aurelius Victor and the *SHA* authors report that seven thousand people died during the *Bellum*, though it is uncertain whether these were overall casualties or simply army fatalities. Whichever was the case, and even allowing for a certain amount of exaggeration and literary license in the primary sources, this would not appear to have been merely an industrial dispute over harsh and unfair working practices. It would appear that the revolt was triggered by Aurelian's evident attempt to get to the bottom of widespread and serious fraud at the mint in Rome, probably involving the deliberate debasement of the silver coinage by skimming silver and replacing it with lead, and the equally illegal and sharp practice of shaving or clipping coins to retain the silver-containing metal. Aurelius Victor tells us that the mint workers made war, as he put it, 'out of a fear of punishment'. It is somewhat ironic that one of the most regularly employed images on coin issues from the Rome mint around this time was that of *Aequitas* or Equity, the personification of fair trade and honest dealings holding scales, for accurate and truthful measurement, and a *cornucopia* or horn of plenty, for honestly earned bounty. Following suppression of the revolt, the mint was shut down, those workers who had not been killed as active participants in the disorder or arrested presumably now lost their jobs, with the mint eventually reopening almost three years later in AD 274.

Moving away from this discussion of mint workers, attention will now be turned on workers in precious metal, goldsmiths and silversmiths. Though without a firm provenance, a late first–early second century relief in the *Musei Vaticani*, inscribed *Aurifex Brattiar(ius)*, is thought probably to represent a memorial to a goldsmith as the inscription tells us, though equally it could have been a shop sign. More specifically the worker could have been a maker of gold foil for use in jewellery manufacture. In the accompanying image the goldsmith sits on a low seat hammering out a sheet of metal on an anvil. A pile of what might be rolled sheets of gold sit in the corner of the workshop. The usual set of scales hangs behind him. A professional *collegium inauratorum et brattiatiorum* is attested in Rome and is likely to have been influential.

Information from Justinian's Digest, a compendium of juristic writings compiled in the sixth century AD, would appear to suggest that goldsmiths in the Roman world worked almost exclusively to order, which makes perfect sense when one considers the price of gold itself. Indeed, we also learn here that more often than not the goldsmiths carried out their commissions using gold supplied by their clients.

Diocletian's Edict on Maximum Prices of AD 301[12] distinguishes between five different types of worker in gold, all paid by piecework: the *aurifex* or goldsmith; the *artifex brattias faciens* or gold leaf beater; the *auricaesor* or gold cutter; the *auriductor in lamina* or gold embosser on sheets of gold; and the *aurinectrix* or gold spinner, presumably all five specialised branches falling under the umbrella of the aforementioned *collegium inauratorum et bratttiatiorum*. Three of these job titles are also attested by inscriptions, with a twelve-year-old boy called Pagus noted as being particularly adept at making gold bracelets, a female gold leaf beater called Septicia Rufa, and a nine-year-old female gold spinner called Vincentia being among them.

From the *Catacombe dei SS. Pietro e Marcellino* on the Via Labicana in Rome comes a terracotta relief plaque, now in the *Musei Vaticani*, curiously similar to those at the *Necropoli di Porto*, Isola Sacra discussed above. Though heavily worn, the second century AD plaque appears to show activity inside a goldsmith's workshop. An overseer directs two men each sat at an anvil either beating gold or making jewellery perhaps. A large set of scales like those of the *Musei Vaticani aurifex brattiarius* described above sits on top of a storage cabinet.

In the collection at the J. Paul Getty Museum, Getty Villa, Los Angeles is a stark and simple grave stele commemorating Publius

Curtilius Agatho, the freedman of Publius and a silversmith, according to the inscription. Dating probably to the first quarter of the first century AD and probably from Rome, though the stele is unprovenanced, he is shown facing towards the viewer, portrayed from the waist upwards. He is well dressed, clean shaven, and his hair is fashionably dressed in the contemporary Augustan male style. He holds in one hand a small, presumably silver, cup which he is polishing or finishing off. This is yet another example of that small group of work images we have which are also portraits.

Those workers producing luxury items in gold and silver probably did not work in isolation. Saint Augustine in his *De Civitate Dei* or *The City of God*[13] provided a remarkable insight into the operation of small-scale specialist silversmiths when he wrote that:

> ... like workmen in the streets of silversmiths, where one vessel passes through the hands of many craftsmen before it emerges perfect, although it could have been perfected by one perfect craftsman. But many craftsmen are employed in this way only because it is thought better for each part of the art to be learned by a single workman quickly and easily, so that all are not compelled to acquire the whole art slowly and with difficulty.

Finally for representations of metalworkers from Italy, mention has already been made of the series of first century AD wall paintings from the *Casa dei Vettii* or House of the Vettii in Pompeii depicting cupids engaged in various agricultural and industrial tasks.[14] In the metalworking scene one of the cupids stands before a furnace, holding a pair of tongs and a blowpipe whose use would have been to blow on the hot charcoal fuel in the furnace for when temporarily higher temperatures would be needed for undertaking a task such as soldering. Another cupid sitting on a stool at an anvil uses a small hammer to undertake fine work; a set of scales sits on a workbench nearby, close to a small cupboard with open drawers. Various suggestions have been made by academics as to what work is being carried out at this workbench; is it a goldsmith's bench, or that of a jeweller? It is possible that it could be connected to the minting of coins, though this is unlikely as we have seen most well-attested images of work inside mints tended to be rather formalised and somewhat different.

In the Roman provinces the largest number of funerary monuments depicting metalworkers come from Roman Gaul, including Gallia Belgica, most of these being of blacksmiths, though there is uncertainty in some cases as to whether coppersmiths might be portrayed in some of these instances. At least eighteen such depictions are known, perhaps the most interesting of which is the second century AD funerary stele of Bellicus the Smith which comes from Sens in Burgundy and is now in the *Musées de Sens* there (Plate 41). A second metalworker's stele from Sens, again of a second century AD date, carries a scene of two men working at a forge. Bellicus's memorial inscription declares that he is a *bellator* or blacksmith, a finely alliterative dedication. The top of the stele is arched, framing the cloaked figure of Bellicus who stands beneath looking straight forward towards the viewer. He holds a small hammer in one hand and to his side is a small anvil. At his feet is a pet dog.

That metal workers were highly valued in Roman society and in other contemporary societies is confirmed by the attested third century AD incursions of the Sasanian king Shapur I (reigned AD 240/242–70) across the Roman borders principally to capture 'human capital' for resettlement in Sasanian territory. Apparently among those sought out and captured were skilled artisans and their families, such as Pursai, 'an excellent craftsman ... expert in weaving and embroidering gold ornaments'.[15]

Transformations

In this chapter it has been suggested that the status of metalworkers of all kinds, from blacksmiths to gold workers, was somehow enhanced by the links in the Roman imagination between the god Vulcan and metalworkers. While goldsmiths and silversmiths in particular were probably viewed as being higher-status craftsmen, nevertheless coppersmiths or bronzesmiths and workers in iron, along with the skilled mint workers that have been discussed here, were probably greatly valued in Roman society.

It certainly has to be accepted that the vast majority of images of individual Roman workers have come from funerary contexts, as have images of artisan's tools and depictions of workshop scenes and technological processes. It is therefore briefly worth considering here what we know about workers or professionals buried with their tools or other associated professional equipment or the dedication of functional or model equipment in funerary, ritual, or religious contexts. Such a discussion, despite it being about generally anonymous dedications and offerings, might throw light on the symbolic use of images of tools on funerary monuments of named craftsmen, and the way that craft transformation might have acted as a metaphor for bodily transformation from life to death.

A distinct category of votive religious offerings from the north-western provinces of the Roman empire were miniature or model items, most commonly wheels, axes, and spears, often found at sanctuaries and temple sites.[16] Each of these three main types of *ex voto* can be assumed to have been linked with a particular deity, the spear with Mars, the axe with Mars or Jupiter, and the wheel with Jupiter. Less common model or miniature *ex votos* included agricultural tools such as scythes or pruning knives, and of most interest in the context of this present study wooden, stone, and lead mallet or hammer heads. While these might have been linked to specific deities such as Vulcan and Sucellus they might also have represented offerings by craftsmen that signified the individual dedicatee by the visual manifestation of their professional identity in the form of a model craft tool. Again, from Brough-on-Humber in England comes a model anvil made of lead, though this may be a modern rather than Roman object.

A similar type of metal model – called generically and somewhat confusingly *Mithrassymbole* (even though unconnected to the Mithraic cult) by archaeologists after a German term – is found in a number of late Roman period graves in and around Cologne. These include model ladders, keys, balance beams with hanging bowls (the single most common category), comb-shaped yokes, axes, mattocks, *dolabrae*, ploughs, saws, pitchforks, spades, scythes, transport stretchers, grills, a wagon, lizards, toads, snakes, and oxen. The meaning and significance of these symbolic items is not altogether obvious. Items can occur singly or in multiples of up to thirty. All were found in female graves, with other gender-specific grave goods, sometimes inside a small wooden box. Here symbols of work were not necessarily associated with burials of workers.

In this chapter it has been argued that metalworking was probably the most financially significant craft in the Roman world, particularly the working of gold and silver and the minting of coins, and that this was reflected in the number of elaborate funerary monuments dedicated to metalworkers and known to us today. The link of the craft to the god Vulcan and other smithing deities provided further symbolic value to the portrayal of the craft in funerary contexts and perhaps in certain other religious contexts. The miniaturisation of certain types of tools to be employed as dedicatory *ex votos* at religious sites and the burial of professional equipment and craft tools with the workers who used them constitutes another ideological link between professional identity and funerary commemoration.

In the next chapter attention will be turned to the use of makers' marks on a range of items in the Roman world, principally but not exclusively pottery vessels, and it will be argued that such marks, usually in the form of makers' stamps, also constituted images of working identity.

5

Making a Mark

Word as Image

While most of the attention in this study has so far been focused on images on funerary monuments and on inscriptions which reveal something about the self identification of a number of categories of workers, artisans, and professionals in the Roman world, another category of contemporary evidence which requires examination and explanation is the maker's mark or the artist's or maker's signature. Maker's marks or stamps could appear commonly on pottery vessels and on bricks and tiles, less commonly on metalwork and glass, often on lead water pipes, and occasionally on other items such as statues, mosaics, gems, barrels, and even shoes. However, in the discussion of stamped products below I am going to limit myself to consideration of the pottery and glass industries.

Some Roman works of art even carried identifying signatures. Why were some items stamped, marked, or signed? What did the stamps, marks, or signatures mean to their makers or to their viewers? Are these marks personalised and related to the process of professional self-identification in the same way as funerary images and inscriptions could be? All of these questions will be addressed in this chapter. I am treating these marks as both visual images and as writing.

In the Roman period even something as simple as a name can potentially tell us something about the individual named. A triple name usually implied that the named individual was a Roman citizen, and a single name might have suggested that the named individual was a slave. A name stamped on a pot could identify an individual potter who made that particular vessel. It could represent the name of the pottery workshop's owner, rather than the actual potter, although in many instances, in the case of samian pottery from Gaul and the Rhineland, when this happened the letters *OF*, for *officina* or workshop, were included as part of the stamp. It could thus represent the master of a slave potter.[1]

It has been suggested that in a world where literacy was not universal and levels of literacy in Latin were not necessarily uniform across the empire the stamps on pottery were not necessarily there *to be read* but may simply have been intended *to be seen*. In other words that they were information providers but not of detailed or specific information as such.[2] Another possibility is that a maker's stamp or mark could have been made not necessarily just to identify a potter as an individual but as an individual worker in terms of monitoring and even quantifying his output. In other words, use of a stamp could have been required by the overseer of a pottery to enable the work and production of all individuals there to be controlled. Yet another possible explanation for the use of individual maker's stamps is that a specific kind of management practice might have been in operation at a particular pottery relating to the sharing of kilns by a number of potters, a situation in which the need to be able to identify the products of individual potters among each fired batch was paramount. A pottery owner and slave owner might have wanted to track the work rate of a number of his individual slaves working at the pottery and the checking of makers' stamps could have provided a useful mechanism for doing just this. A number of legal contracts preserved on Egyptian papyri concern arrangements between individual potters and the owners of pottery factories and facilities, citing the terms and conditions for the leasing out of these facilities or for the provision of raw materials, or of contract labour. In that case it would appear that the identities of individual potters through their stamps were meticulously noted in order to provide a kind of legal proof for the fulfilment of the contract.

Much pottery in the Roman world was produced to fulfil business contracts, and one thinks in particular about contracts between civilian potteries and the Roman military which are well attested in the archaeological record and which would have involved the ordering of huge quantities of pottery vessels of all kinds. Managers at the pottery would have needed to keep detailed records of the production of pots for the contract, and military quartermasters at central storage depots and at individual forts would have needed to check over goods provided from both the point of view of numbers of pots ordered and delivered and the quality of those pots. Stamping pottery would have surely been a necessity in such circumstances. However, the vast majority of pottery in the Roman period was unstamped and unmarked. The stamped or marked vessels I will discuss here are either Arretine and samian finewares, mortaria or mixing bowls, and storage amphorae.

A maker's stamp on a pot could also have been used as a mark of quality and distinction, a guarantee of sorts for the consumer. Any archaeologist who has regularly examined *terra sigillata* or samian pottery excavated from Roman sites in Britain will be all too aware that the quality of the pots varies tremendously, particularly in the case of decorated vessels. While most samian pots were produced to high standards this was evidently not always the case. The modelling of some stamps used for stamping decoration onto the pots was often very poor indeed, particularly in the case of stamps of human figures or of animals. Often potters had employed extremely worn stamps that had seen better days and should by rights have been thrown away and replaced with fresher, crisper stamps. Sometimes the pots had been misfired in some way and would be classed as factory seconds if on sale today. There is another phenomenon to consider as well, and that is the quite common use of illegible or illiterate stamps. It is difficult to explain why unreadable stamps were sometimes used on pots as this would seem to have rather defeated the object of stamping the pot in the first place. Some types of samian pots, certain forms for instance, were never stamped. The reason for this is uncertain.

An incredibly detailed picture of the workings of the Gaulish *terra sigillata* or samian industry in the first and second centuries AD has emerged from years of study, involving systematic excavation at many of the main kiln sites, the precise cataloguing of forms and fabrics of pots produced at each site, and the indexing of potters' names and the dies of their stamps. Around 5,000 individual potters' stamps are known on samian pottery. In addition, there have been recovered by excavation at some of the major samian production sites in Gaul what are known as 'firing lists', *graffiti* lists of names scratched on the underside of stamped dishes which were fired in the kilns along with the regular load: in effect, these lists probably recorded whose pots were being fired in that particular kiln at that particular time. The lists were not public documents – the pots on which they were inscribed were not for shipment and sale – but were bureaucratic or management 'documents'. At the La Graufesenque production site one such list on a vessel stamped by the potter *Castus i* carried more than thirty different names and it must be assumed that these named men were all workers in the potter's *officina* or workshop. Altogether at La Graufesenque 163 individual names appear on various firing lists, 87 of whom are unrecorded otherwise: in other words they never had their own names stamped on fired vessels and therefore must be classed as pottery workers rather than potters as such.

There is little doubt that the taste for shiny red fine ware pottery vessels represented by the success of the samian potteries of Gaul and their industrial scale of production and output partly had its origins in the social cachet of the earlier Italian Arretine pottery. The *terra sigillata* Arretine potteries of Italy, principally at Arezzo, Pozzuoli, and Pisa, provide equally interesting information about individual potters working there. However, there is still no unanimity among academic researchers as to whether the stamps on the pots from these centres represented the names of estate owners, workshop managers, or individual potters. The recording and analysis of over 33,000 stamped Arretine vessels from various production centres and found in Rome, Italy, and sites around the Roman empire has produced a complex picture of the industry, highlighting not only the work and achievements of individual potters and workshops but also the organisational aspects that led to migration of potters between different production centres, branch workshops, and industry partnerships. The very fact that shiny red Arretine *terra sigillata* vessels generally were stamped and that is how they were recognised and appreciated by their owners perhaps partly led to the later Gaulish *terra sigillata* or shiny red samian vessels largely being stamped as a matter of course.

As an example of how prevalent the stamping of pottery was in the Roman world I want to present a case study of the Roman fort site of Binchester in County Durham in northern England, a site that I was involved in excavating and publishing.[3] As we have seen so far in this book Roman Britain does not feature at all in terms of providing examples of workers' images. Indeed, only one worker's funerary image comes from the whole province and we can therefore say little about the attitude of Romano-Britons to workers or craftsmen socially situating themselves here through naming or self identification with a professional role. However, certain types of stamped pottery vessels were as common in Roman Britain as elsewhere in the Roman empire, as were stamped bricks and tiles to a lesser degree.

At Binchester, Roman *Vinovia*, a timber fort of the later first century AD was succeeded by a stone fort in the mid-second century which continued in use up to and beyond AD 410. Excavations in the 1970s and 1980s were focused on the area of the fourth-century *praetorium* or commandant's house and its associated bath suite. The two categories of stamped pottery at the site were samian pottery from factories in Gaul and mortaria or mixing bowls, most produced in Britain. A few stamped amphorae were also found. Fifty-one samian stamps, whole and partial, were represented in the excavated pottery assemblage. In the list of stamps represented at Binchester it should be noted that when more than one potter shared the same name, as indicated by the use of different die stamps, or where one potter might have used a succession of die stamps on his work, indexers have added Latin numerals after their names, i.e. Albinus iv as below.

From the kilns at Lezoux the following potters were represented at Binchester, in alphabetical order: Aestivus; Aeturnus; Albinus iv; Banoluccus; Beliniccus iii; Cracissa; Flo-Albinus; Geminus vi; Iullinus ii; Luppa ii; Maior i; Moxius v; and Scoplus. From the kilns at La Graufesenque came stamped vessels by: Calvus i (represented by two stamps); Carantus i; Carantus i and Pugnus i together; Carbo; Censor I (represented by three stamps); Crestus (represented by two stamps); Flavius Germanus; Frontinus; Iucundus iii (represented by two stamps); Modestus I (represented by two stamps); Mommo; Ortius Paullus; Patricius i; Ponteius; Secundus ii; L. Senis; Sextius-Can (probably a joint stamp of two potters); Silvinus ii; C. Silvius Patricius; Vanderio; Verecundus ii; and Vitalis ii. From the kilns at Les Martres-de-Veyre stamped vessels were present at Binchester by: Balbinus;

Latinus ii; Paterclus ii; Reginus ii; and Severus v. From the kilns at Rheinzabern stamps present in the asseblage were of the potters: Avitus viii; Verus vi; and Vitalis viii. Finally, there was one illegible samian stamp from the site.

The following additional observations can be made about a few of the potters represented by stamps on their samian vessels found at Binchester, illustrating the complexity of the samian industry. Avitus viii is known to have worked at Heiligenberg or Ittenweiler before working at Rheinzabern. Vitalis viii came to Rheinzabern from Kraherwald. Beliniccus iii worked at both Les Martres-de-Veyre and Lezoux. Paterclus ii worked at first Les Martres-de-Veyre and then at Lezoux. Severus worked at Lezoux and then Les Martres-de-Veyre.

As for the twenty-six mortaria stamps from the site, the following potters were represented: Anaus (represented by possibly as many as eight stamps) who probably worked at Corbridge, Northumberland but who probably had other workshops in the Binchester and Catterick areas; Cudrenus (represented by two stamps) who worked at Corbridge; a potter whose stamp reads QAA but whose full name is unknown; Aminus (Mimuus or Amianus, it is uncertain which), possibly from the Binchester/Catterick area; Sarrius from Cantley near Doncaster; Viator from Castleford; Quintus Iustius Cico, possibly from Lincoln; Mottius from northern France; Quintus Valerius Veranius, again from northern France; Maurius or Maurus from Mancetter-Hartshill in Warwickshire; Marinus from Brockley Hill, Middlesex; Sollus from Brockley Hill; Bruccius from Brockley Hill; Lallaius from Brockley Hill; Albanus from the Verulamium area; and someone possibly called Biria from northern England. Two other stamps were unidentifiable.

Thus sixteen names of mortarium potters appeared on stamps at Binchester and forty-three samian potters. In terms of organisation of the two industries it is well known that the movement of potters from one major samian producing centre to another took place and indeed pots produced by a number of these individuals were represented in the Binchester assemblage. As to the mortarium potters, the most interesting to me is Gaius Attius Marinus whose pots also turned up in number on another Roman site which I was involved in excavating some years later, in the Staffordshire village of Rocester. By correlating the form and fabric of his mortaria in concordance with his stamps an interesting picture has been built up of his potting career. It would appear that he started working in the major potteries in Colchester, Essex in the later first century AD, subsequently working in the Verulamium potteries at Radlett in Hertfordshire. He is next recorded working in the English midlands at the Mancetter-Hartshill potteries in Warwickshire where he seems to have been operating between AD 100 and 130. It is possible that he then either moved to Little Chester, just outside Derby, or opened another pottery there at the same time. This ably illustrates that many craftsmen in Roman times led peripatetic existences.

As for the small number of amphorae stamps recorded at Binchester only two were complete or near-complete and yielded information about the source of their product in Spain. One was from the estate of L. F(abius) C(ilo) and the other of someone with the initials PNN: the latter is closely datable to the first quarter of the third century AD through the presence of this stamp in the *Monte Testaccio* assemblage in Rome.

An Accidental Monument

In a curious way there is a major monument in Rome to some of the empire's artisans and workers, leaving aside the obvious example of the impressive Tomb of Eurysaces the Baker. By a certain sense of default it represents something similar to Britain's Tomb of the Unknown Warrior or France's Tomb of the Unknown Soldier, in that it now represents a generalised celebration of workers' anonymity, though it was never intended to be any such thing. *Monte Testaccio* then is an 'accidental monument', but in a way it is the unofficial eighth hill of Rome.[4] The name, literally meaning 'the mountain of ceramic', refers to the vast mound that lies behind the ancient city's one-time river port facilities that included the *Porticus Aemilia*. This 'hill' is around 115 feet high and covers an area of around 220,000 square feet at its base. It is not a natural feature; rather it is a huge structured rubbish dump made up of an estimated 53 million broken pottery amphorae or storage vessels for imported olive oil, vessels which could not be cleaned and reused, testifying to the massive volume of trade which in turn inevitably impacted on the very fabric of the city in this unusual way. Perhaps started as a temporary, managed rubbish dump for discarded amphorae as early as the first century BC the site continued for this use up until around the AD 260s when the port facilities moved location.

Limited excavations in a number of campaigns have demonstrated that the hill is almost exclusively made up of fragments and sherds of what are known to archaeologists today as Dressel 20 amphorae, used for the transportation and storage of olive oil. Many of the vessel handles were stamped by the potter or pottery manufactory where the vessels were made, while amphora bodies and handles in addition also commonly carried what are known as *tituli picti*, that is painted commercial inscriptions relating to their origin, producer, or contents.

Remarkably perhaps, the names of a small number of the individuals whose marks or *tituli picti* have been recorded as present in the *Monte Testaccio* dump can be related to names on dedicatory inscriptions from elsewhere. For example, Publius Olitius Apollonius, who died at Narbonne in Gaul, was described in an inscription on a statue base as a *sevir augustalis* and as a *naviculario*, that is a shipping operator or agent. Lucius Marius Phoebus was described as a *viator tribunicius* and *mercator olei hispani ex provincia Baetica*, a shipper of Spanish olive oil, who died and was buried in Rome. These concordances represent perhaps the most compelling evidence for the scope and scale of the networks of contacts, interconnectedness, and influences that underpinned the Roman economy and socially situated its workers and artisans.

It can therefore be argued perhaps that the creation of *Monte Testaccio* marked a point at which individuality crossed over with mercantile expediency and economic necessity in the Roman world view. The rise of the freedmen class, which had by now contributed so much towards the economic success of the project of empire, meant that public space in towns and cemeteries could no longer simply be the exclusive preserve of the named great men and women from the elite classes. Now named individuals from the middle and lower classes could rightly claim space there and, if they chose to do so, could celebrate and commemorate their own identities there, including their occupational and professional identities in many cases.

Makers' Images

After presenting an extended discussion of the ubiquity of stamped pottery and the large-scale prevalence of stamping or marking pots in the Roman world it will probably now come as a surprise to readers to learn that as far as I am aware there is not a single image of a named potter at work in the Roman period or a funerary inscription to a potter. Likewise, no inscriptions to potters or dedicated by potters at Rome are recorded by Sandra Joshel.[5] This seems somehow contradictory to the evident contemporary importance placed on making a mark or stamping a name that is manifested on so many hundreds of thousands of Roman pottery vessels recovered by archaeological excavation. This could be pure coincidence or it might be of significance in itself: which is uncertain. The depiction of potters working was a common image on Greek red and black figure ware pottery and it would be unsurprising if some of these images on imported wares in pre-Roman Italy had not occasioned interest. However, we do have a potter depicted on an uninscribed funerary relief, the stele of a pottery dealer or salesman, and images of potters on two wall paintings at Pompeii and on a *terra sigillata* vessel.[6] Three *graffiti* at Pompeii might also all have related to potters.

The uninscribed first to second century AD funerary relief, possibly from Rome and now in the Virginia Museum of Fine Arts in Richmond, Virginia, United States, carries a depiction of a potter sat on a low seat at a worktable. He holds a pot in one hand and in the other a brush which he is using to apply either slip or painted decoration to the vessel. Across from him sits a woman in a high-backed chair holding what appears to be a ball of raw clay in one hand and a fan in the other. It has been suggested that the woman is holding a small loaf of bread but this seems unlikely. It can probably be assumed that the relief was originally part of a funerary monument to a potter and his wife. The inscription on the third century AD stele of Vitalinus Felix, now in the *Musée Gallo-Romain de Lyon*, records that he was a veteran of the First Legion who later became a pottery dealer in Lyon in central France, as illustrated by images of a row of pots carved on the upper part of the stone.

The two wall paintings at Pompeii are found on the exterior of the south enclosure wall of the *Officina Vasaria di Nicanor* and on the exterior wall of the *Hospitium dei Pulcinella*. The first of these images, probably from around AD 50–60, consists of the figure of the god Vulcan overseeing, presumably as the god of fire and furnaces, a potter on a small stool at work forming a vessel on a low wheel with both hands. Other finished pots sit ready on the floor around the potter, as does a rod of some kind whose purpose is uncertain. Presumably the building was a potter's house or workshop-cum-shop. The second, earlier image which could date to 100–50 BC, probably also alerts us to the presence of a pottery workshop, consisting as it does of the depiction of either four different potters working away at their wheels, implying a large-scale production facility, or the same potter depicted four times. Interestingly, a young woman also appears here carrying some finished vessels.

Finally, an African red slip ware *terra sigillata* jug from El Mahrine in Tunisia, dating to the first half of the third century AD, is noteworthy because of the scene of a potter at work on it.

The three *graffiti* in Pompeii perhaps referring to potters include a *graffito* on a large jug which reads, in translation, '... the slave of P. Cornelius Corinthus made (this)' and two rather risqué *graffiti* from the *Praedia* of Iulia Felix whose reading might require a trigger warning to protect any of my more prudish readers. The first states: 'the *scutularius* [did it] with the African woman', with *scutularius* literally being a maker of serving dishes, though whether ceramic dishes or metal dishes is uncertain. The second, longer *graffito* refers to a 'clayman' which might be a job title for someone working in a pottery workshop.[7] It reads, in translation:

> Since you've held eight jobs all that's left for you now is to have sixteen. You worked as a cook, you worked as a clayman, you worked as a pickler, you worked as a baker, you were a farmer, you worked as a maker of bronze trinkets, you were a retailer, now you work as a jug man. If you perform cunnilingus you'll have done everything.

A recent survey of evidence for glass working and glass workers in the cities and towns of the Roman empire made the very important point that glass production was highly specialised, chronologically constrained, with glass blowing only being invented as a technique in the mid-first century BC, and geographically contingent.[8] Before the late Republican period the vast majority of glass vessels found in Rome and Italy were imported from the eastern Mediterranean. In other words, production centres were few despite the ubiquity of the traded finished product. In these circumstances it is then perhaps not altogether surprising that images of Roman glass workers are few and far between.

However, some glass vessels carried impressed maker's marks but nowhere near the number of pottery vessels that were stamped. Many Greek names are recorded on certain types of better-quality vessels from the eastern Mediterranean, such as, for instance, Aristeas the Cypriot, Ennion, Meges, Paulinos of Antioch, and Zosimus. The common mould-blown bottles produced in the western provinces often carried Latin or Latinised names, such as, for instance, Sentia Secunda of Aquileia and Titianus Hyacinthus.

The inscribed third century AD tombstone of the seventy-five-year-old '*opifex arti vitriae*' or 'master of the art of glass' called Julius Alexander comes from Lyon in central France and is now in the *Musée Gallo-Romain de Lyon* there. While this particular stele carries no portrait or image of Julius at work or of the tools of his trade, nevertheless it is highly informative, the unusually long and detailed inscription also telling us that he was a citizen of Carthage in North Africa. The stele marked a grave in which the body had been buried with a number of fine glass vessels and a glass hairpin, presumably all made by Julius. Other, rather briefer funerary epitaphs to glassworkers come from Cherchel in Algeria, Salona in present-day Croatia, Sparta and Athens in Greece, and Tyre in Lebanon.

The decorated discs of three ceramic lamps from sites in northern Italy (Voghenza, near Ferrara), Croatia (Asseria), and Slovenia (Školarice-Križišĉe) all carry images of glass workers in action and glass production centred around a furnace with firing and melting chambers clearly distinguishable, and glassblowing clearly rendered in one case. It has been suggested that the third or fourth century rough outline sketch of a nine-paned glass window and a tool that appears to be a saw of some kind on the marble inscribed panel in the tomb of Sabinius Santias in the *Catacombe di Domitilla* in Rome were visual links to his occupation which the inscription refers to as *artis ispeclararie*. While this might have meant that he was a maker of glass windows it is also possible that he made such windows from the easily cut and worked *lapis specularis*, a kind of secondary gypsum. A guild of *specularii* was certainly active in Rome in the third century AD, according to the evidence of an inscription, but Sandra Joshel describes the role of a *specularius* or *speculariarius* as a 'worker in mica or isinglass', or even 'a mirror maker', rather than a window glass maker.

Portraits of the Artist

Most of those we would today call the artists of the Roman world would have been considered to have been simply craftsmen in contemporary Roman society, working in stone and bronze statuary, fresco painting, mosaic work and so on. Certainly no funerary memorial to someone styling themselves as 'an artist' is known from the Roman world. While the intertwining of alienation and creativity expected in artists today was absent, nevertheless Roman artists contrived with their patrons to reveal many truths which would otherwise have gone unnoticed both to contemporary viewers and to those who came after.

Those categories of artists, craftsmen, and producers who signed, stamped, or otherwise marked their work are curiously under-represented in terms of images of their occupations, as we have seen above in the case of potters and glass workers. Such images are relatively rare compared to those of builders, bakers, butchers, textile producers, and shoemakers, as we have seen in the earlier chapters. This seems a curiously contradictory phenomenon. The few rare examples of mosaicists who signed their pavements, including the inept Sabinianus who should never have been let near a *tessera,* and the even fewer representations of mosaicists at work have already been discussed in Chapter One. Let us now consider Roman sculptors and painters, firstly in terms of their use of signatures on their works and then in terms of images of these craftsmen at work.

In total, we know the names of 548 Roman artists, though not all from signatures on examples of their work, which compares to 1,281 known Greek artists.[9] There are also known the names of 436 Greek artists working at various locations throughout the Roman world. Of the named Roman artists, 70 were sculptors and 196 were metalworkers.

While it was not standard practice for Roman sculptors to sign their works, nevertheless quite a number of such signatures are indeed known. The majority of these though are Greek names, implying that the workshop traditions of earlier Greek art contributed significantly to the development of a truly Roman art. The picture here is quite muddy. For instance, in the first century

BC the sculptor Pasiteles, though an ethnic Greek and native of Magna Graecia, obtained Roman citizenship, so should he be considered a Greek artist or a Roman artist? Pliny the Elder in his *Naturalis Historia* tells us in passing that Coponius produced fourteen statues of figures or personifications of 'nations' for the Theatre of Pompey in Rome, in this case the sculptor having a Roman name.

The name C. Vibius Ruf(us) is inscribed on the upper part of the plinth of one of the statues of caryatids in the Forum of Augustus, evidently a Roman sculptor copying a Greek original work to order. On the second-century AD *Extispicium* Relief, now in the *Musée du Louvre* in Paris is inscribed the name M. Ulpius Orestes, and it must be assumed that this is the name of the sculptor of the relief or the head or owner of the workshop where it was produced. This is the sole example of an artist's signature on a piece of monumental relief from the whole of the Roman world. The relief was found in the Forum of Trajan in Rome but it has been suggested that it was brought there from another site in Rome in the fourth century as an item of *spolia* for reuse there. There really is no evidence for this, nor for the suggestion that the inscription by Orestes is not an artist's signature but rather the name of someone arranging its delivery in the fourth century. Possible artists' signatures also appear on the so-called Esquiline Group sculpture from Aphrodisias in Asia Minor and indeed a number of signed statues are known from the city, and the signed products of fourteen individual sculptors from its sculpture workshops are known from other sites in Greece and Italy.

One of the most significant depictions of a Roman artist, as we would term him, at work is the painted image of the so-called 'Kerch easel painter' (Plate 42), forming part of the painted interior decoration of a first or second century AD limestone sarcophagus found at Panticapeion at Kerch in the eastern Crimea and now in the State Hermitage Museum in St Petersburg, Russia.[10] It is unlikely that the burial is that of the artist portrayed here but the image is important nonetheless as a unique representation of a Roman easel painter in a studio. The man, dressed in a regional variant of Romanised costume, including trousers and a heavy cloak, sits on a stool leaning over a small ceramic burner over which he is heating up what has been suggested to be an encaustic painting tool over the flames. A gridded tripartite wooden panel sits on a pedestal beside him. An easel with a blank panel resting on it stands ready. A number of completed pictures, all portraits, hang on the wall. An assistant waits in attendance in one corner of the scene. Another easel painter preparing a botanical illustration of a mandrake appears in one of the leaves of the early sixth century AD illustrated manuscript the *Vienna Dioscorides*, which I will write about more fully in Chapter Seven, this painter probably being intended to be Crateuas, the renowned herbalist and illustrator of Mithridates VI of Pontus, rather than a jobbing Late Antique painter.

At Pompeii there is a number of images in wall paintings of female painters at work on panel pictures but it is not certain whether these women were professional painters as such or whether this was a particular trope used to illustrate female elite skills and achievements in the same way that images of women or girls writing were deployed, as we will see in Chapter Nine. Certainly Pliny makes mention of a small number of named female Greek painters, all of whom were themselves daughters of male professional painters and therefore who might have been thought of as continuing a family craft heritage.[11]

It must be assumed that two second and third century AD burials from Frankfurt-Hedderheim and Xanten in Germany were of painters of some kind, though most probably wall painters, given that the grave goods included ceramic paint pots with colour pigments inside.[12]

There are only four possible decorated funerary monuments to Roman sculptors.[13] The first image appears quite obviously to be of a sculptor at work. It appears on a funerary altar, dating to the first half of the second century AD, in the *Musei Vaticani* involving a seated man and a standing women contemplating a bust on a pedestal.

The second possible sculptor's monument is an unprovenanced inscribed mid-first century funerary relief now in the Villa Albani in Rome and dedicated to Q. Lollius Alcamenes, a *decurio* and *duumvir*. Clad in a toga he sits in a chair looking at and contemplating a stone portrait bust of a young boy. He holds something in the other hand, generally identified as a tool of some sort. A woman holding a cup or small bowl attends to a tall ceramic incense burner in the centre of the room or studio. However, the figured scene in which he appears is open to a number of very different interpretations and there is no consensus among Roman archaeologists as to whether we are really seeing an image of a sculptor at work here. While he could be an artist examining one of his own finished pieces he could equally be a Roman patrician examining one of his ancestral busts – an *imago* – and thus displaying his aristocratic credentials for all to see. In both these cases it could be suggested that the sculptors are quite literally 'making ancestors'.[14]

The third image can be found on a relief panel from the front of a second century AD sarcophagus from Ephesus, now in the *İstanbul Arkeoloji Müzeleri* in Istanbul in Turkey. Here is depicted work inside a busy sculptor's workshop: a man prepares a preliminary sketch, a man works on a togate statue, a man labours at a workbench, another man chisels a marble bust, and a young male workshop assistant stands by with tools or ready to clean up after the masters. It is also worth noting here the existence of an image of activity inside a sarcophagus maker's workshop on a slab from the *Catacomba dei SS. Marco e Marcelliano* in Rome. Dedicated to Eutropos, the master is portrayed overseeing activity in his workshop: a man on a stool drills a lion's head on a strigillated sarcophagus, aided by an assistant or apprentice. Dating probably to the fourth or early fifth century AD this slab is now in the *Museo Archeologico Lapidario* in Urbino.

It is the fourth monument, a mid-second century AD inscribed funerary stele from Bordeaux in western France in the collection of the *Musée d'Aquitaine* there, that commemorates the sculptor (*scu* in the inscription) Marcus Secundinius Amabilis, that is most clear about the physicality and reality of the deceased's occupation (Plate 43). The image was also composed with humour. Dedicated by his brother Amandus the main focus of the viewer is firmly drawn to the imposing bearded figure of Marcus, wearing a hat and tunic and seated on a work stool, inside a deep niche or recess, using a mallet in one hand and a chisel in the other to carve one of the angle capitals of the niche. He is shown literally carving his own funerary stele. Many toolmarks are visible on the face of the stone and it could be that these were deliberately left as a vital trace of Marcus's existence and occupational identity. The playing with intertextuality here is both overt and complex. It can probably be safely assumed that Marcus carved the stele himself in preparation for his death, in which case we would need to consider his image here as a self-portrait.

Finally, brief mention can be made of a most curious phenomenon that has been dubbed the 'epigraphy of appropriation', whereby the retrospective signing of Greek sculptures took place in the Roman world, perhaps in an attempt to provide 'added value' to these works or for other reasons.[15] A few examples of the phenomenon will suffice to give a flavour of the practice which spanned the period from the late Hellenistic era to Late Antiquity and which was most prevalent in Rome, though attested as taking place elsewhere in Italy and more broadly around the empire, even occurring in Greece itself. All sorts of motives can be attributed to the practice, including a display of the kind of connoisseurship along the lines of that presented by Pliny the Elder in his *Naturalis Historia* and an evolution in the definition of the concept of authorship in Roman culture. In Rome in Late Antiquity many works in both bronze and marble, none of them Greek originals, came to be retrospectively signed as '*opus Praxitelis*' – '*the work of Praxiteles*', the Greek master, when quite clearly they were not. Sometimes copies of genuine signatures were added to non-original works, and sometimes epigrams were added at a later date to original works.

This phenomenon of the bogus signing of certain statues in order to give them more social cachet, more worth perhaps, and to enhance the social standing of their owners, seems vaguely absurd and rather brings to mind the Marx Brothers continuously trying to pass off a particularly poor painting as 'a genuine Tintoretto' in one of their films.

The motor behind this 'epigraphy of appropriation' seems to have been nothing more than the desire to somehow be associated with a famous artist rather than to knowingly engage in fraudulent activity of any sort. That this somehow reflected changing conventions concerning the ownership and display of signed works is obvious but what it meant in terms of contemporary ideas of authenticity and authorship in art and craft is somewhat less clear.

I have argued in this chapter that a maker's mark, stamp, or signature was as much to be *seen* as *read* in the Roman world, and that the marking of objects in this way was as much a part of the system of communicating through images as was the use of pure visual signs and symbols. The sophisticated visual culture of ancient Rome here merged with its written culture in unusual and perhaps unexpected ways, transmitting information to those who might be able to interpret and assimilate it and even intruding into the lives of those for whom such information was otiose to their requirements in terms of simply wanting to possess an item because of its functionality, appearance, aesthetic appeal, or even simply its materiality. The use of such marks, stamps, and signatures was part of the overall phenomenon of the creation of public occupational identities for many workers, artisans, and professionals at the time.

Was this different to the earlier Greek phenomenon of signing some objects and artworks, including gems, coins, pots, metalwork, buildings, sculpture, paintings, and mosaics, cutting across all genres of Greek art? Or were the Romans influenced by the Greeks with respect to this, as signing was an established Greek cultural trait? If the Greek motivation for signing works was complex, so apparently was it too for Roman makers. While the very act and process constituted 'an inscription of identity' the motives behind it probably varied tremendously. The maker could have been demonstrating pride in their work or a certification of their skill, pride in one's occupation as an individual and as part of a community of workers in the same trade, a social motive in other words. There could have been an economic dimension to stamping/marking/signing, the process being linked to advertising, branding as we might call it today, or trademarking in a way. Some items or works might have been signed/marked at the behest of the client, to provide some kind of added value: in such situations the mark/stamp/signature would be used to enhance the status of the client rather than of the maker. In cultural terms was signing, marking, or stamping an object any different from claiming authorship in the literary culture that existed at Rome? But why did many makers, sometimes highly skilled and remarkably talented ones, chose *not* to sign, mark, or stamp their work? The answer to this last question we will never know.

In this chapter discussion has centred on two main topics: the way in which makers' marks on pottery and other manufactured and traded goods can be viewed as images as much as texts, and therefore can tell us a great deal about the formation of occupational identities in the Roman world; and how the movement of such goods led to the creation of networks of associated interests in which one kind of occupational identity interacted, merged, or clashed with others in different fields of work, expertise, and experience. The latter topic will be pursued further in the next chapter, from the point of view of those workers who built ships, boats, carts, and wagons, and those who shipped and transported goods and those who sold them. These latter two groups were not people who *made* things but people who nevertheless perhaps surprisingly exhibited pride in their occupational identities in similar ways to those who did.

6

An Empire on the Move

In the earlier chapters of this book it has been argued that certain types of work and workers were liable to be more commonly commemorated than others through the use of imagery and/or job titles on funerary monuments. When we think of Roman life and its material culture we very often think of pottery and glass vessels of certain kinds as being quintessentially Roman artefacts, particularly as so many types of vessels carried potters' names in the form of stamps. Yet portrayals of glass workers and potters were relatively few as we have seen in Chapter Five. Perhaps the goddess Minerva's links with textile craft meant that textile workers or producers or those in related fields were among the most common workers portrayed, as we have seen. Similarly the god Vulcan's links with smithing might have accounted for the regular, open commemoration of metalworkers of various kinds. Mercury was a god linked with protecting travellers and of commerce and his overseeing of these aspects of Roman life provides a fitting matrix around which to organise discussion of workers in trade and commerce in this chapter. It is possible that the significance of wine as an economic staple of the Roman economy, as an important oiler of social events, including funerary feasts and graveside commemorations, led to wine producers and traders in this particular commodity being particularly regularly portrayed in funerary and other images as we will see. Even those who served wine in taverns often featured in cameo roles in such scenes.

Mare Nostrum and Other Seas

The vast expanse of the Roman empire, the maintenance of its power, and the motor of its economy relied on its transport infrastructure: its sea and shipping routes, its roads, and its riverways. I will now consider each of these in turn. It is surely of no surprise that workers engaged in what we might conveniently call the transport and transportation industry commemorated their work both in funerary contexts and sometimes in the public spaces of their home towns.

One of the best known workers' tombstones from the Roman world is the late first century B.C. to early first century A.D. stele of Longidienus the boatbuilder from Ravenna in north-eastern Italy, now in the *Museo Nazionale di Ravenna* (Plate 44). Ravenna, the Roman port of Classe, at the mouth of the mighty River Po, was a highly significant port centre in the Republican and early to mid-imperial period, both as a merchant marine trading port opening directly onto the northern Adriatic Sea and as a base for the Roman navy, a short distance away from the town, patrolling and protecting those waters.[1]

Over eight and a half feet tall, this huge stele is very much of a type well known across Roman northern Italy. In the upper register of the stele, in a niche topped by a double arch, appear the two half-length busts of a married couple, identified by the inscription beneath as Publius Longidienus, 'son of Publius, of the tribe of Camilia' and his wife Longidiena Stactinia, freedwoman of Publius.' Longidienus is clearly described as *faber navalis*, that is 'boat builder'. Wearing a toga, Longidienus is here being presented as a respectable Roman citizen, and Longidiena's *stola*, partially covering her head, suggested that she was a typical Roman matron. Underneath the main inscription is another arched niche occupied by the portrait busts of two young men, identified by the inscription beneath them as Publius Longidienus Rufio and Publius Longidienus Piladespotus, both described as freedmen of Publius. These two paid for this monument to their *patronus* the inscription goes on to tell us.

A carved relief towards the bottom of the stele depicts Longidienus himself working on a docked boat held up by a cradle frame of wooden supports. Employing what would clearly appear to be an adze, he is depicted in the process of shaping a curving plank or rib destined for the hull of the boat depicted behind him. What is called a laced tradition of boat building using timbers like this would appear to have been an Adriatic phenomenon in the Roman period, that is as opposed to the mortice and tenon jointing employed on Mediterranean sea-going craft. In order to reach the end of the timber he is standing on a stout, lockable toolbox that obviously doubled up as a stool when necessary. I find this image particularly appealing as my late father was apprenticed as a boat builder in Montrose, Scotland after leaving school and recalled using an adze similar to this in his work. Next to the image of Longidienus at work is a third inscription, as if on a small rectangular sign or plaque, which declares: 'Publius Longidienus, son of Publius, busy at his work'. On each of the narrow sides of the stele appears an image of a finished boat.

The stele of Publius Longidienus the boatbuilder of Ravenna presents us with a number of different images and texts which read and interpreted as a whole paint a complex picture of freedman identity in the late Republican to early imperial period in a provincial centre away from Rome. The portraits of Longidienus and Longidiena are very much in the style and continuum of freedmen art that was by now well established as a cultural phenomenon in Rome.

We see work being physically undertaken by Longidienus and we see the tools of his trade in the clear and accurate portrayal of the woodworking adze and the very strong toolbox-cum-step. We see a boat in the process of being built and we see images of two completed seaworthy vessels. Unusually, we see the short third inscription suggesting that being shown busy at work is a commendable thing.

The Roman art historian John Clarke has described the stele of Longidienus as representing in its time 'an affront to elite taste', a monument that to an elite viewer might have been considered 'a pastiche'.[2] I wonder though if that would in fact have been the case, given that freedmen funerary monuments bearing family or group portraits by this time would have been relatively common in the cemeteries of Rome and of the larger provincial towns of Roman Italy. In Rome individuals like Eurysaces the Baker had already found a way of presenting the dual identity of a respectable citizen and yet one involved in commerce and production to viewers of his tomb. Longidienus was not a shipping magnate though, nor does his stele either through its inscriptions or the images employed here attempt to present him as such.

The term *faber navalis* used to describe Longidienus was the most common name for a ship or boat builder as represented on funerary or dedicatory inscriptions in the Roman world. The name *architectus navalis* also appeared, but less commonly. The first or second century A.D. stele of Publius Cattius Salvius from Aquileia, again in north-eastern Italy and once more opening on to the Adriatic, not only refers to him as a *faber navalis* or ship builder but we are also presented with an image below the inscription of a simple, crescentic, double-ended boat with a quarter rudder. However, we have no portrait of him or image of him working, as on the Ravenna stele of Longidienus. Also from Aquileia, and along with the Salvius stele in the collection of the *Museo Archeologico Nazionale di Aquileia*, is the first century A.D. stele of a helmsman or boatman who is portrayed in portrait form holding a very small, probably symbolic, tiller connected to a quarter rudder. Below his bust is the image of a two-armed anchor with a fixed stock. It is possible that this particular man could have been a ship owner. The Longidienus stele and the two discussed here from Aquileia demonstrate how significant the Adriatic was as a trade route for the Roman world. At Ostia, the river port of Rome, P. Celerius Amandus died at the age of eighteen. On his perhaps second century A.D. funerary stele can be seen various tools which suggest that he might have been or aspired to be a *faber* or *architectus navalis*: compasses, a ruler, an adze and a quarter rudder.

Gerhard Zimmer in his catalogue of images of Roman workers from Italy listed a number of other examples of memorials to individuals he considered were linked to shipbuilding,[3] including: a small image of a mastless ship and some shipbuilding tools appearing as incidental images on the stele of L. Laronius Rufus from Castelvecchio di Compito whose magistracy title, a *sella curulis* or official chair and *fasces*, or symbols of authority, otherwise dominate the memorial; a now-lost fragmentary stele from Rovigo with a small image of a boat on it; two stele each with an image of a ship-building tool on them from Ravenna; and a funerary memorial to a military *faber navalis*.

Those who owned ships or captained them are also well represented in terms of numbers of funerary monuments, and examples of various kinds catalogued by Gerhard Zimmer are known from ports and trading towns including Aquileia, Ravenna, Ostia, Pompeii, Salerno, and Terracina. The Ostia images will be discussed in Chapter Eight in a broader discussion of decorated plaques at the *Necropoli di Porto* cemetery. A second century BC stele dedicated at a sanctuary to the Dioscuri of uncertain provenance and now in the *Museo Lapidario Maffeiano* in Verona in northern Italy, thanks the gods for overseeing the safe passage of the dedicatee Argenidas, son of Aristogenidas, in other words saving him from the dangers of shipwreck. Dressed in the traditional Greek manner he is depicted standing beside a generic Greco-Roman sea-going vessel with a concave stern, pointed prow, and a high sternpost. In the same collection, from Rineia in the Cyclades, is the second to first century BC stele to Archagathos, son of Diodorus, who died in a shipwreck.

Much further afield, a mariner is celebrated on the funerary stele of Theokritos probably from Tomis on the Black Sea coast and now in the *Muzeul National de Istorie a Romaniei* in Bucharest. Dating to the first half of the second century AD the stele carries a small full length image of Theokritos, described in the inscription as a *naukleros*, a ship's captain or a ship owner or a transporter of goods, formally dressed in a local Greek-style toga called a himation, with one arm in an armsling position, again a Greek trope, standing under an arch. In his free hand he holds a scroll. Beneath is the dedicatory inscription and beneath that is an image of a ship. The inscription reads, in translation from the local Greek: '*Roupheina daughter of Jason set up this stele for Theokritos son of Theokrotos, her son, a shipmaster, also called Basileus. He lived 22 years, 9 months. Farewell.*' The vessel portrayed is a sea-going ship, rather than a boat for river passage, a double-masted craft with two steering oars apparent. The masts have been dismantled, that is unstepped in technical terms. As one authority has noted, 'the image of the ship affirms his profession as *naukleros*, but it also suggests a symbolic meaning in the finality and stillness of the unstepped mast.'[4]

A small black and white mosaic inside Tomb 43 at the *Necropoli di Porto*, Isola Sacra, Ostia depicts two ships approaching a harbour with a pharos or lighthouse, accompanied by an inscription in Greek which reads in translation 'here ends my toils'. The ships here could relate to the occupation of the deceased, particularly as other tombs connected to maritime industry are recorded here as we shall see, but equally they could simply have been intended to have been emblematic of a journey (life) ending at home (Portus/ Ostia) and bringing closure (death). A relief of a well-crewed ship at sail on one face of the first century AD Monument of C. Munatius Faustus at Pompeii may again be metaphorical in intent rather than literal, as there is no evidence that either Faustus or his wife Naevoleia who dedicated the monument to him made their fortune in the shipping business.

A number of Roman relief and mosaic depictions of vibrant port and dock scenes are known, including at least two that are generally accepted as depicting Portus, the seaport of Rome itself. The first and most busy of these scenes appears on an early third-century AD relief in the collection of the former *Museo Torlonia* in Rome, and indeed is now most commonly known as the Torlonia Relief. Here we see the harbour packed with ships and small boats. The port's famous pharos or lighthouse appears at the back of the scene. Ships are unloaded in the safety of the harbour, one employing a winch mounted on its deck, while dockers carry sacks of goods down gangplanks, and a port official sits at a desk on the quayside making a record of goods unloaded and presumably of taxes due for collection. All of this activity is overseen by the giant figure of Neptune. The decoration on the front relief panel of a sarcophagus from Tomb 90 at the *Necropoli di Porto*, Isola Sacra, Ostia moves from sea to land or land to sea, depending on the choice of the viewer.[5] At sea, on the left hand side of the panel, can be seen a harbour, a crewed ship, a man ferrying off-loaded goods ashore in a rowing boat, and the port's famous lighthouse again, while on the right hand side we find ourselves inside a harbourside tavern or eating house. The scene inside the tavern will be more fully discussed and described later in the chapter.

Images of ships occur on mosaics and in wall paintings quite commonly, usually in generic scenes, but the occasional example can be cited of a particular commercial operation going on in the scene depicted. Images of dockers unloading ships and boats appear on numerous artworks, and one such partial relief from Ostia, dating to the second half of the third century AD and now in the *Museo Nazionale Romano* in Rome is illustrated here, depicting a bearded man carrying a barrel off a docked ship (Plate 45). While this is likely to be a funerary relief it probably was illustrative of the business of a ship owner and merchant rather than a lowly dockworker. Semi-naked dockers offloading goods from a ship appear on a third century AD mosaic from Sousse in Tunisia and now in the *Musée National du Bardo* in Tunis. On the quayside two well-dressed officials check and weigh goods using a huge wooden balance supported on tripod legs. Sometimes though the cargo could be more exotic and perhaps unpredictable. On the Great Hunt Mosaic from Piazza Armerina in Sicily the cargo being loaded is live exotic animals, and is a manifestation of an extraordinary empire-wide trade in wild and exotic animals for exhibition and the animal games in the arena. The dockers here would have been specialised animal handlers, probably members of the numerous hunting sodalities who earned good money tracking, capturing, and transporting such animals. I have discussed the commodification of exotic megafauna and their trade in the Roman world in great detail in my previous book '*Cave Canem. Animals and Roman Society*' and will simply direct the reader there to learn about those Roman workers employed in that particularly niche but highly lucrative enterprise and to further discussion in Chapter Eight below.

All Roads

Following that brief survey of images of named Roman boatbuilders and shipping owners, attention will now be turned briefly to the roads, with a consideration of the depiction of a wheelwright or cart builder, of firms of carters, and of horse traders whose 'product' was so essential to the workings of the Roman economy and the shipping of goods by road and the transport of people doing business or in administrative roles that required them to traverse the *cursus publicus* or state travel infrastructure of the empire.[6]

From Fossano, Cuneo, in Piedmont, and now in the *Museo di Antichità* in Turin, is the stele of the *faber* – wheelwright or cart builder – the freedman Quintus Minicius, dedicated to him by the *marmorarius* or marble worker Publius Minicius, a relative presumably and one who interestingly wished to have his own professional identity made apparent here.[7] (Plate 46.) The inscription quite significantly informs the viewer that Quintus had worked his way up from humble origins – *ab asse quaesitum*. Dating to the end of the first century AD this stele once more in size and shape conforms to a widespread northern Italian type of the time. While towards the top are classical-style dolphins and a standard depiction of a man and woman at a funerary banquet, towards the bottom of the stele appears a very small image of a man, presumably intended to be Quintus, holding a spoked wheel. Interestingly, this was one of the works of Roman art representing an ancient artisan taken to

Rome to be exhibited at the fascist *Mostra Augustea* of 1937–38. The significance of this exhibition in museological terms will be discussed further below in Chapter Nine.

Two further funerary monuments to wheelwrights or cart makers are known, one from Aquileia, again in northern Italy, and the other from Priolo in Sicily. The Aquileia funerary relief, in the *Museo Nazionale di Aquileia* there, carries a depiction of an eight-spoked wheel, a measuring staff and compasses. The Priolo funerary altar, now in the *Museo Archeologico Regionale Paolo Orsi* in Syracuse is dedicated by Eutyches and on it appears a poorly executed depiction of a man manoeuvring a huge wheel with ten spokes while a second tiny figure stands watching. Some tools, a double-headed axe and a plane, appear below, while on one side of the altar are depicted a bow, a drill, compasses, and a measuring staff or ruler.

The Baths of the *Cisarii* or coachmen at Ostia represents one of the few examples in this study of a building not only constructed by the munificence of a professional organisation but also one where that organisation took the opportunity in the Hadrianic period to decorate the building with images of its working members, in this case with a black and white mosaic of their member drivers, their coaches, and the mules that pulled them (Plate 47). This guild of drivers provided a shuttle service of sorts between their home town of Ostia to Rome and vice versa and would appear to have been proud of their profession and hugely successful. Such guilds of coachmen are known from other parts of the empire. For instance, around AD 160 coachman Gaius Julius Crescens of Thessaloniki in northern Greece had a grave stele dedicated to him by his mourning colleagues, including Artemon the yoke maker who was head of the guild. An image of Gaius driving his rig appears on the stele above the dedicatory inscription. The monument is now in the Archaeological Museum in Thessaloniki.

Given the importance of road transport both for the professionals and for independent travellers the breeding, training, and trading of horses would have been a major industry, leaving aside the breeding of horses for chariot racing and horse racing. Scenes of road haulage involving large wagons and carts are known from quite a number of places throughout the empire, particularly the north-western provinces, as on the Igel Column (Plate 48). Examples from Gaul include funerary reliefs, presumably of road haulage company owners, in the collections of the *Musée Archéologique* in Langres, *Musées de la Cour d'Or* in Metz, and the *Musée Archéologique de Dijon*. Also in the museum at Dijon is the first century AD stele of a horse breeder and trader, depicted overseeing a sale (Plate 49). Germanus the mule driver is commemorated in an inscription of the first half of the first century AD now in the *Musei Capitolini Galleria Lapidaria*.

River Routes

Scenes of the loading of boats for the river transportation of goods are as common almost as scenes of the unloading of sea cargoes, as discussed above. They include the loading of the boat the *Isis Geminiana*, pictured in a unique wall painting panel from Ostia dating to the first half of the third century AD and deriving from *columbarium* 31 in the town's Via Laurentina necropolis. Now in the *Sala Nozze Aldobrandini* in the *Biblioteca Apostolica* in the *Musei Vaticani* in Rome the picture includes a number of painted captions to aid the viewer's understanding of the scene. The boat's name appears on the right, telling us that it was named after someone called either Geminus or Geminius. The man holding the tiller is captioned as Farnaces Magister, presumably the captain, and the man supervising the emptying of what appears to be a sack of grain into a large *modius* or measure on the deck is captioned as Abascantus. A state official looks on to confirm honesty in the measuring. Another man sits ready with a sack of grain to be measured and two further dockers carry sacks of grain over their shoulders as they progress up the boat's gangplank. An image of Mercury, as god of commerce and travel, originally formed part of the composition of the picture which has subsequently been cut down in size. It can probably be assumed that the painting was prepared for the burial place of Abascantus and that he was a ship or boat owner, a merchant in other words.

A much less hectic scene of the transportation of goods by river occurs on the painted decoration on the *lararium* at the *Casa del Larario Sarno* or House of the Sarno Lararium in Insula I in Pompeii. Pack mules carry panniers of goods down to, or away from, the riverside. There a man in a long-fringed garment supervises four workmen who are variously engaged in carrying baskets of goods and then weighing them and their contents on an enormous set of scales. A boat waits nearby on the river, already loaded with cargo, possibly waiting to be unloaded. Presumably the owner of this property was involved in river commerce of some sort on the Sarno river, possibly involving the transport of foodstuffs.

A scene of barge haulage on a river appears on a fragment of a second to third century AD funerary relief from Cabrières-d'Aigues, now in the *Musée Lapidaire* of the *Musée Calvet* in Avignon, in Provence in southern France[8] (Plate 50). This is one of two surviving reliefs from what must have been a large and impressive tomb: unfortunately the tomb itself has not been located and we are without an inscription from the site to identify the deceased which might help explain this unusual choice of relief scenes to adorn the monument. The haulage scene consists of a small, mastless boat crewed by a single bearded man who sits at the stern holding a long pole or oar. On board can be seen two large casks or barrels, presumably containing wine. Towards the prow is a large upright timber around which are tied three stout ropes. The ropes are taut and stretched out, being held by two men who are on the riverbank or tow path and who are pulling the boat along. The end of the third rope would have extended beyond the broken edge of the relief and presumably would have been held by a third haulier, now absent. As if to further stress the nature of the valuable cargo a number of wine amphorae and large bottles in wickerwork casings stand on what seem to be shelves above the haulage scene and presumably represent the decanting of the wine from barrels into smaller, more manageable vessels and its eventual safe storage in a warehouse. The other scene is less well preserved and has suffered some surface damage. Nevertheless, on it can be seen a man walking along, carrying a small sack over his shoulder and holding a lead in his other hand attached to a horse or donkey (Plate 51). The beast has a very thick rope attached to its collar and it is possible that it too is hauling a small boat or barge along a stretch of river, though it could also be hauling a wagon loaded with barrels or amphorae of wine. A small fragment of relief carrying an image of two wine amphorae may be part of this same panel or be part of a third relief panel from the tomb. That would certainly make sense given the nature of the other relief scene from the tomb. The Cabrières-d'Aigues tomb must have been the final resting place of someone involved in the important wine industry in the region in some capacity, perhaps the owner of vineyards and a winery or, perhaps more likely, the owner of a river and road haulage business.

Similar scenes of river haulage of wine barrels, involving almost identical types of boats operating presumably on the nearby River Moselle, can be seen on the *Igeler Säule* or Igel Column, at Igel near Trier in Germany, as discussed at length in Chapter Two.[9] The fragment of a funerary relief, often called the Colonzelle relief, built in to the chapel of Saint-Pierre-aux-Liens at Margerie, Colonzelle, Drome in south-eastern France and broadly contemporary with the Cabrières-d'Aigues tomb reliefs also carries a depiction of wine barrels and a haulage rope.[10] But most impressive of all is probably a now-freestanding, large sculpted model of a river-going boat or barge from Neumagen and now in the *Rheinische Landesmuseum* in Trier in Germany (Plate 52). This probably once stood as one of a pair of such boats on top of a large tomb dedicated to a wine shipper or merchant whose trade centred on the River Moselle. Dated to around AD 220 the boat, with its serried ranks of oars and animal head prow and stern is modelled packed to capacity with both wine barrels and an eight-man crew, and represents one of the most idiosyncratic non-elite funerary monuments of the Roman world, alongside the Tomb of Eurysaces the Baker in Rome perhaps.

From Arles, near to Avignon on the River Rhone, and in the *Musée Départmental Arles Antiques* there, is part of a third century tomb relief from the *Nécropole de la Pointe* depicting two workers tying up a large bale of goods for shipping with stout rope and doubtless labelling it with the kind of inscribed lead identity tags discussed in Chapter Three, presumably preparing the bundle for shipping down the river by boat or barge (Plate 53). Also from the town is a small terracotta showing a similar scene of preparing cargo, suggesting that the town was a well-known centre for such trading. The preparation of very similar shipping bales also appears on a second or third century relief from Augsburg in the Cathedral collection there on which four men tie up the enormous bundle while a supervisory clerk stands by to record the details of the load on a tablet he carries (Plate 54). The weighing of commercial bundles of goods can be seen on two funerary reliefs of the second half of the first century AD in the *Museo Campano* in Capua, southern-central Italy (Plate 55). Two small cream-coloured terracotta figures in the form of dockers carrying sacks come from Ostia, suggesting, along with the Arles figurine, that such genre figures might have been relatively popular in busy port towns like these. The final delivery of sacks of goods can be seen on a relief fragment from a mid-third century AD sarcophagus from Rome, but now in the Royal Ontario Museum, Toronto, depicting a porter delivering goods to a shop or warehouse (Plate 56).

In the case of both Avignon and Arles, these towns are both sited on the lower reaches of the River Rhone and it is likely that they were transit ports for goods from the Mediterranean that needed shipping inland and up river into central and northern Gaul and even into Germany by this route. Indeed at Arles, the centrepiece of the great Gallo-Roman museum there is a massive, around one hundred feet long, but narrow, wooden Roman barge dating from AD 50–60. Excavated and lifted from the Rhone as recently as 2004 this boat, known as Arles Rhone 3, had its final cargo still onboard, around 33 tons of building stone from a quarry at an outcrop about 10 miles away from the town.

Looking at merchants as a class of individuals much interesting information emerges about their lives, as reflected in the funerary monuments they themselves commissioned or which were commissioned by their family or heirs.[11] For instance, Tiberius Mainonius Victor, a meat merchant, and his wife Iulia Marina made provision during their lifetime for a stele for themselves and their daughter Surilla in second–third century AD Cologne. Marcus Murranius Verus from Trier who died in Lyon was a trader in wine and possibly also pottery vessels – his stele has a row of wine jugs in relief above the epitaph. Indeed, a study focused on the merchants of Roman Lyon has revealed interesting information about this one particular community of merchants. A merchant from Syria ended up living in Gaul on the Saône, dealing in goods from Lyon and Aquitania. He was not alone in this respect, as has been demonstrated by a study of the *peregrini* or outsiders who died in Lyon between the first and third centuries AD whose funerary inscriptions indicated that they were not native to the city. At least nine *negotiares* or merchants were from elsewhere: Gaius Apronius Raptor, Marcus Murranius Verus, and Marcus Sennius Metilus, all from Trier in Germany, Ioulianos Euteknios and Iulius Verecundus from Laodikeia in Phrygia, Victorius Regulus from Nemetes, again in Germany (a dealer in purple), Marcus Attonius Restitutus from Triboci in Alsace, Poppillius from Sequani in Gaul, and Valerius Sattiolus from Lingones in Gaul. Two *sagarii* from elsewhere – Gaius Latinius Reginus from Remi and Litiavus Necochoris from

Carnutes – may also have been cloak merchants rather than just simply cloak makers.

Sandra Joshel has recorded 108 dealers or merchants of different commodities represented in the occupational inscriptions from the city of Rome itself: forty-six dealers in food or wine; no fewer than thirty-five dealers in unguents and perfumes; seven dealers in leather, cloth, and clothing; seven dealers in books and paper; four dealers in metals and marble; a single dealer in slaves; and eight dealers whose specialist product was unspecified in the inscriptions.[12] These figures appear remarkably low compared to the information about merchants and traders we can glean from a modestly sized Roman town such as Lyon, just discussed, and it perhaps suggests that many of the wholesale traders, rather than just retail traders, were based in the ports and towns on the transport nodes. Certainly the presence of many merchants' offices at the *Piazzale delle Corporazioni* or Forum of the Corporations in central Ostia suggests that this might well have been the case. It has even been suggested that many of Rome's most successful merchants may well have been above identifying themselves by occupational titles and instead aspired to honorific public titles if they could be had.

Wine

Attention will now be turned to some of those who traded wine and those who were, if you like, the end users of one of the main products shipped along the seaways, roads, and rivers of the Roman empire in huge container amphorae, barrels, and casks, that is the innkeepers or tavern owners who bought and served wine in commercial premises.

While scenes of grape harvesting were very common in Roman art, many of these were simply symbolic or metaphorical. A relief scene of the operation of a wine press by two men on a funerary stele from Aquileia, now in the *Museo Archeologico Nazionale* there and dating to the first half of the third century AD (Plate 57) is so specific in the depiction of this machine that it is most likely from the funerary monument of a wine producer. The evidence for wine merchants is considerable. One of the most interesting funerary monuments on display in the *Museo delle Marche* in Ancona in north-eastern Italy is an uninscribed third century AD sarcophagus whose front panel bears three scenes set inside a classical building with vaulted roof, the supporting columns acting as frames to separate the three sets of images (Plate 58). The central image shows two men standing either side of a stacked pair of large wooden casks or barrels, presumably containing wine. One of the men is holding what might be a spigot for breeching the cask in one hand and with the other holds out a tasting bowl to his companion. The second man holds out one of his hands to receive the bowl and in the other holds a flagon or jug. They are obviously caught here in the process of tasting the vintage. A small amphora and what might be a basket sit on the cellar floor to one side. In each of the flanking arches stands an appropriate guiding deity: on the one side Bacchus, god of viticulture, with a panther and on the other Mercury, god of commerce and travel.

Again, in the same museum is a huge, more equivocal mid-first century AD stele from Castelleone di Suasa dedicated to Sextus Titius Primus and his family (Plate 59) topped by a standard northern Italian set of portraits of Primus flanked by a woman on either side, one of the women holding a small child. Underneath this is the formal inscription which informs us that Primus was a *seviri*, that is a *sevir augustalis*, an important but honorary role in the imperial cult. Such an honour was a form of formal recognition of Primus's standing in the local community and one which would have further increased his status and which probably also enhanced business opportunities for him. Just to further stress the honour, on either side of the dedicatory inscription stands a *lictor* or attendant holding a bundle of *fasces*. A number of explanations have been offered for the additional presence of two large amphorae on this stele and it seems most convincing in the context of the town and the region that they must have alluded to the wine trade again and to the way in which Primus made his fortune. It has also been suggested that the amphorae might have been intended to allude to the wine drunk at the celebration of Primus's appointment as *seviri*.

Hints that Q. Veiquasius Optatus of Alba in Piedmont was another successful wine producer or shipper come from the numerous images of figures carrying huge amphorae on their shoulders and a cart carrying a huge barrel which adorn his second- or third-century AD stele in the *Museo di Antichità* in Turin. It has though been suggested that Optatus held some some of religious title, as reflected in the words *sacrorum cultor* in the dedicatory inscription, and that the amphorae and barrel could have contained mineral water from a sacred spring. A Christian wine merchant may have been represented by the elaborately decorated carved relief panel (Plate 60 and Plate 85 for detail) from the second half of the third century AD depicting a busy scene inside a wine cellar or warehouse from the *Cimitero dell'Ex Vigna Chiaraviglio*, and now in the *Museo di Catacombe di Domitilla*, Rome.

Lower down the economic and social chain we have a number of representations of wine being served in inns from Rome, Ostia and the *Necropoli di Porto* [at least three examples – (Plate 61)], Saint Maximin and Til-Châtel (Plate 62) in France, Augsburg in Germany (Plate 63), and Mérida in central Spain, amongst others. These can more or less be taken at face value, as inn signs or as images for the funerary monuments of bar owners. Women appeared serving in two of these, the examples from Ostia and Mérida, and perhaps it can be assumed that the focus was on the women in these scenes because they were bar owners themselves.

At the *Necropoli di Porto*, Isola Sacra, bar scenes appeared on a number of terracotta plaques mounted outside tombs but of most interest is the later third century AD sarcophagus recovered from Tomb 90. For whom the sarcophagus was made remains unknown.[13] The image of the waitress or barkeeper serving a drink appeared on the front panel of this sarcophagus. To some extent this indoor scene was subsidiary to the main image on the sarcophagus panel which involved the depiction of a ship and rowing boat coming into a harbour, presumably at the local port itself, with a landmark pharos or lighthouse guiding their way. Moving to the right across the panel the decoration segues into the scene inside the tavern, again presumably at the port. Behind the tavern counter, decorated with a dolphin carving, can be seen a well-stocked bar of jars, jugs, and wine amphorae. A woman walks across the tavern to a table where two men are seated. She is carrying a glass or beaker of beer or wine and proffers it to one of the men who holds out his hand ready to take it. The second man has already been served his drink and is in the process of downing it. A small dog reaches up towards the table, flexing his front paws ready to scratch the woodwork.

While the scenes depicted here can be taken at face value as representing contemporary genre scenes quite specific to the geographical location, at the same time they include motifs and symbols quite commonly linked to funerary contexts. These include journeys across water, travelling or voyaging in general, dolphins, dogs, and funerary drinking scenes. It is as if a very local set of themes has been applied to a more universal concept. That wine would be served at funerary banquets, would often be poured as a libation onto a grave, sometimes through an amphora neck marking the place of burial, or would be used in formal and informal Roman religious rites makes images of wine growing, harvesting, shipping, or drinking sometimes curiously ambivalent.

Another category of worker is that of the shop owner and assistant, the market trader, and the street hawker, in other words workers in the retail of goods.[14] A number of people working in shops or showrooms selling textiles have already been discussed in Chapter Three while sellers of bread and other foodstuffs were mentioned in Chapter Two. I will discuss female shop or market workers in Chapter Eight. As for the retail workers and street hawkers we do not have any funerary monuments on which people named such work as their profession: indeed, it should be remembered that while we have discussed a large number of funerary memorials of workers in often surprisingly niche trades, nevertheless such trades needed to be somehow profitable for money to be set aside for burial and commemoration, possibly through a funerary club, or a *collegia* needed to pay to honour one of its members at death.

The most significant market depiction we have is of the Forum at Pompeii, as depicted in a painted frieze in the atrium of the *Praedia* of Iulia Felix there (Plate 64). Male and female traders with trestle tables and baskets selling shoes, clothes, textiles, metal vessels, bread, vegetables, fruit and hot food attract a large crowd of customers and onlookers. Why such a scene showing the economic politics of public space should have been commissioned for a private house is uncertain.

Numerous scenes of retail trading are known from Rome, Italy, and both Gaul and Germany, and many are discussed in other chapters of this book. I have chosen to illustrate two further funerary reliefs here, both from Trier and now in the *Rheinische Landesmuseum* there. Both date to the second–third centuries AD and confirm the importance of commerce to the communities in the region of the Treveri (Plates 65–66).

If we have no expensive funerary memorials to street hawkers, at least we have a number of genre representations of such sellers in action and they were occasionally referred to in contemporary written sources, usually pejoratively, and while these gave them no agency it does at least provide some evidence of recognition of their existence and role. If some of the works of art discussed in this book possibly stimulated other senses in their viewers besides the obvious optical one then in the case of the statuettes of Roman street hawkers we can at least imagine their cries and shouted exhortations to purchase their goods. Many of these hawkers would have been selling fruit or pre-cooked food.

Stored in a wooden chest in the House of P. Cornelius Tages, also known as the House of the Ephebus, in Pompeii were found four bronze statuettes of street hawkers or *placentarii* – 'bun sellers', though it is also possible that these were in fact representations of attendant household slaves, another popular subject in genre art. Now in the *Museo Archeologico Nazionale* in Naples, none of these images is in the least bit flattering, rather they are grotesque, and some degree of caricature and disdain must perhaps be read into their interpretation. These naked figures, modelled with exaggeratedly large phalluses, hold up silver trays on which the house owner probably served small delicacies for his guests at banquets. These could have been items of functional art reflecting contemporary Roman attitudes to slavery, like the lamp-bearer figure from the same house, a type found quite widely in Italy.[15]

In this chapter it has been demonstrated how the opportunity also arose for those involved not in the making and production of objects and goods but in their transportation to commemorate their professions and we have seen evidence for those involved in different aspects of road, river, and sea transportation and indeed in the building of boats and of carts, and the selling of horses. The wholesale trading of wine, one of the prime Roman commodities, has also been considered, along with the selling of wine in taverns and the retail trade more generally. The complex web of economic, social, and religious links between wine and ideas circling around life and death, and ecstatic celebration and funerary commemoration means that some images of wine production and consumption cannot necessarily be taken at face value.

In the following chapter a more thematic discussion will be presented, examining the way in which other types of images of Roman workers could sometimes be used in an allusive, illusory, or metaphorical way to convey certain messages and meanings above and beyond the literal aspects of the depictions.

7

Illusion and Metaphor

The majority of the numerous images of striving and energetic Roman workers discussed in the previous six chapters possess a vigorous energy and sense of time, place, and context that seems in many ways almost hyper-real in its intensity. However, in this chapter attention will first be turned to an analysis of certain other Roman artworks where depictions of work were metaphorical or sometimes somehow illusory. They were in many respects both out of context and out of time. The illusory art of the entertainer will then be discussed, in cognisance of the idea of identity simply being a kind of personal performance. In the second half of the chapter I will consider a number of instances of how the Roman army used images and inscriptions to conflate the idea of waging war with work, and vice versa, and how the bureaucratic recording by the army of details of physical labour undertaken by some of its soldiers helped mentally map and conceptualise the northern British frontier.

Metaphor in Action
The power of work as metaphor need not necessarily possess the umbral dread of the Nazi's slogan *Arbeit macht frei* – 'Work sets you free' – which adorned the gates of the death camp at Auschwitz-Birkenau. In Roman art there were some instances in which an image of work or of the carrying out of some professional task, duty, or role was employed to act as a metaphor for another particular act or situation. This often involved the replacement of the worker in these images by another figure, often cupids or *putti*,

147

sometimes children. The reasoning and motives behind this may have been different in each instance, but since many of these images appeared in funerary contexts some element of the juxtaposition of the present with the past or the present with the future would always seem to have been apparent.

A great deal of academic research has been undertaken on the iconography employed in the art used to decorate Roman children's sarcophagi.[1] Certain motifs and tropes occurred again and again, and there would appear to have been a fairly high degree of standardisation in both design and execution of the work, in order to provide the limited number of intended viewers of these sarcophagi a particular and managed experience in terms of recognising signs and symbols and using that recognition to express and externalise their grief. Here I will concentrate very specifically on the instances in which work metaphors were employed.

One of the most common decorative themes on Roman children's sarcophagi was the depiction of a child's life cycle in terms of a biographical narrative, with scenes of the first bath, a lesson, sometimes a chariot ride, and the departure for the afterlife portrayed, while other scenes involving the eating of a funerary meal and a gathering or *conclamatio* at the child's deathbed occurred occasionally. It is the depiction of scenes of learning that is of most relevance here, as it will be argued that these suggested early preparation for the world of professional work to come or even the placing of the figure of a child in an adult professional context that they never achieved but which their parents might have expected or desired, or just imagined. The image of the reading, presumed to be representative of part of both a grounding in literature and in rhetoric, normally took place before a male adult, either the child's father or his teacher, and it must be noted here that it is always a boy that was shown reading and never a girl, as girls would not have been allowed to enter into any form of professional role involving rhetorical submission or public speaking. On the late second century AD sarcophagus relief panel originally from Tivoli but now in the collections at the *Villa Doria Pamphili* in Rome the reading was also witnessed by Thalia, one of the three Graces, the god Mercury, and the Muse Melpomene. The theme was also pursued by the common use of the image of a scroll or a *scrinium*, and a case or chest for the storage of books and papers, again denoting education and literacy. While all the 'lesson' images involved boys, in the case of the use of the images of the scroll and *scrinium* it is worth noting that on later sarcophagi girls appeared equipped with these as well, and this might have reflected a Christian cultural attitude to female learning that differed from elite attitudes in the early Roman imperial period.

Such child to adult narratives, with their linear trajectory and sequential presentation of scenes, tended to have been favoured in the earlier imperial period, with the emphasis on later sarcophagi often changing to a more atemporal presentation of images where certain events were privileged and presented as being emblematic of larger and more complex themes.

What we are in fact seeing in these instances is no less than the activities and social values of the external adult world imposed on the world of children, as a result of the children being cut off from fulfilling their lives and adopting adult roles when reaching maturity and entering the professional worlds of letters, the law, or other roles where reading, declamation, and rhetoric were to be employed and highly valued. As has been noted, the parents of one such child might themselves have belonged to or wished to belong to the professional class and, as such, it would have been the parental interests and desires reflected in these scenes. The scenes would then have been both a record of parental status and an image of the future projected by the parents on to the child. Had the family not been of the correct status, and with the requisite wealth to accompany that status, the cost of the child's education could not have been met and the child would probably have moved into manual work of some kind.

The scenes of learning thus helped to reinforce the traditional Roman cultural values of the elite class and of aspiring freedmen. This can be no better illustrated than by the dedicatory inscription on the funerary altar in the tomb of the young boy Quintus Sulpicius Maximus, who died at the age of eleven years, five months, and twelve days in AD 94 we are told. His tomb was situated on the *Via Salaria* in Rome: the altar is now in the city's *Musei Capitolini*.[2] His skills in poetry composition and recitation, representing his tragically lost promise, were cited here at the behest of his mourning parents Quintus Sulpicius Eugramus and Licinia Januaria. His entry in a competition with fifty-one other poets earned him admiration and he 'came off with distinction'. Some of his poetry is reproduced below a niche at the front of the altar. A statue of the boy holding out a furled scroll appears in the niche.

Putti or cupids commonly appeared on Roman children's sarcophagi, most popularly in the third century AD. Hundreds, if not indeed thousands, of examples are known: Dionysiac *putti*, *putti* with garlands, *putti* playing out mythological scenes, *putti* driving chariots, *putti* in athletic contests, *putti* hunting, *putti* as gladiators, *putti* playing games, *putti* at cockfights, marine *putti*, *putti* undertaking agricultural work, and *putti* with arms and armour. Curiously, there are no examples on which they mimic or imitate a professional person such as an orator or teacher. The question must be asked, even if it cannot necessarily be satisfactorily answered, as to whether the scenes inhabited by *putti* were meant in some way to be humorous or semi-humorous or if the *putti* were themselves distancing devices, present to represent absent, that is dead, children? Were the *putti* there as reassuring, non-threatening imagistic figures that might have been thought to be bringing comfort to the departed child in its journey to another world? There is something faintly ridiculous about images of *putti* fighting as gladiators or hunting, hyper-masculine activities both, or working at a hot, dirty forge to manufacture weapons and armour. *Putti* were also very often genderless in these images, their presence in certain social situations blurring real gender roles and perhaps also at the same time subverting them, ironically so in a society so riven by formalised gender rules, behaviour, and social conventions.

A relatively common image on children's sarcophagi manufactured in Rome itself was of *putti* or cupids involved in the bearing of arms and in the manufacture and provision of arms and armour (Plate 67), though this subject was not limited to children's sarcophagi and appeared on some adult ones. This need not necessarily occasion surprise, for in a city such as Rome the presence of thousands of military officers and military veterans would have meant that such images might have had a similar future-nostalgic effect as that of boys training in reading, recitation, and rhetoric for future careers in the literate professions that they would never have. It is likely that we are seeing presented here an allusion to the war god Mars whose other roles included protection of agricultural activity, and he also had a more universalising role as father of Rome, linked to his siring of Romulus and Remus with Rhea Silvia, this paternal aspect perhaps being quite significant in the context of the commemoration of a child's death and of his or her burial.

Images of *putti* involved in the manufacture and provision of arms and armour on sarcophagi are of particular interest in the context of this book. Five children's sarcophagi bearing such images are known, and three adult ones. These busy manufacturing scenes recall the dense activity of figures in the bakery on the frieze on the Tomb of Eurysaces the Baker or the so-called Tower Crane building site scene on the Tomb of the Haterii. *Putti* working at a forge and the depiction of the fashioning of shields, spears, helmets, or a cuirass might also have been playing out the story of the creation of Achilles' armour that an educated Roman child might have been expected to have been familiar with.

It is interesting to momentarily reflect upon the contrast between the two very different sets of realities represented by the working *putti* sarcophagi being discussed here and the funerary stele of the boy miner Quartalus from Spain whose early death was discussed in Chapter Four above. Both represent different realities for children of parents from the different social strata of Roman society, and yet each attests to parental love and loss expressed through commemorative art as a distinctly Roman and Romanised phenomenon.

Putti also quite regularly appeared on sarcophagi, both of adults and children, undertaking agricultural tasks, particularly tending vines, picking grapes, often using ladders or climbing the vines, and treading grapes in vats for wine making. In these instances we can consider such images to have been linked to Bacchus/ Dionysus, although other links to concepts of rural harmony, bucolic happiness, and joy in the afterlife are often obvious or apparent. As has been noted elsewhere in this book, the connection between the quotidian drinking of wine and its key role in Roman religious and funerary rites and celebrations is complex, and was even more so in Christian contexts.

One particularly noteworthy use of *putti* and viticulture imagery occurs in the Mausoleum of Constantina (Santa Constanza) on the Via Nomentana in Rome, the burial place of the daughter of the emperor Constantine, where both the decoration of her huge porphyry sarcophagus and the magnificent mosaics decorating the vaults and ceiling of the mausoleum itself utilise such decoration profusely.[3] Constantina's mausoleum and circus-basilica originally contained her massive sarcophagus which has today been replaced by a facsimile, the original now being part of the collections of the *Musei Vaticani* in Rome. The mausoleum was probably built around AD 351 or 352.

The sarcophagus of Constantina, while still obviously an exclusive imperial artefact by nature of both its size and of the porphyry from which it was made, could not be more different from the martial decoration of the sarcophagus of the empress Helena in terms of its decoration which consists of detailed and complex scenes of *putti* harvesting grapes and garlands, again as on Helena's sarcophagus lid. On the two long sides the winged *putti*, enclosed in circular fields formed by acanthus scrolls, gather grapes and place them in overflowing baskets. Above the scrolls are further vegetal tendrils and doves, and below another cupid with grapes walks in a landscape inhabited by peacocks and rams. This abundant world of plenty almost seems to hark back to the idealised landscapes on the Augustan *Ara Pacis* monument. On the short sides the *putti* are depicted standing in a trough treading the grapes, the vinous juice flowing copiously into barrels or vessels beneath the press. Scrolls, tendrils, and clusters of grapes frame the central main motif. On the lid are found garlands suspended from two male and two female heads or masks. The decoration on all four sides of the sarcophagus and on its lid can be seen to some extent to mirror the themes of some of the stunning ceiling mosaics inside the mausoleum, with the emphasis being on the natural world and its taming by agriculture as a metaphor for its control by Roman imperial authority. Of course, such lush imagery could also have had and would have had Christian connotations, though there is no overt Christian symbolism on the sarcophagus.

Putti or cupids were also used as stand-ins for human workers in images on a number of domestic wall paintings in Pompeii, of which the most significant were created for the *Casa dei Vettii* or House of the Vettii.[4] A series of wall paintings in the form of a frieze in the *oecus* or banqueting room of the house presents a remarkable set of vignettes involving perfume manufacture, garland making, fulling and textile production, gold-smithing or coin production, and the production of wine, all conducted by *putti* rather than human labour. Whether these were all commercial activities which the freedmen Vettii brothers were personally involved in is uncertain and seems unlikely, given the diverse nature of these very different businesses. However, they do represent one of the few examples of the deployment of images of work and manufacture, albeit involving *putti* rather than real people, in a private house rather than in a workshop, outside a shop or other commercial premises, or in a funerary context. It is possible that this part of the house was used for receiving and entertaining clients and customers, and it is therefore quite conceivable that the wall paintings were designed to advertise the brothers' various businesses. However, other interpretations of these images will also be highlighted during the discussion of their content. It is worth noting first though that the frieze was a subsidiary element of the room's decorative scheme and not its intended focus; the subject of the main theme is unknown however, due to damage.

Putti or cupids involved in the production of wine is an extremely common trope in Roman art, particularly on sarcophagi as we have seen above, and such a scene appears on the north wall of the room, with what appears to be the retailing and tasting of wine in a shop stocked with amphorae taking place on the west wall, though the fresco is damaged here. Also on the north wall are *putti* bakers preparing bread for a feast to Vesta.

The *putti* involved in the fulling of wool and textile production appear on the east wall, variously treading cloth in a vat, treating or cleaning cloth or clothes, and brushing the nap of cloth hung over a rack. The finished or cleaned items are then inspected and checked, a female *psyche* appearing here in the guise of a cloth checker.

The metalworking scene, again on the east wall, has been suggested by some academic authorities to be a scene of gold-smithing or jewellery making and by others as a scene depicting the minting of coins. I am more convinced by the former identification and will therefore follow it here. The number of workers and their team make-up does not seem to match those few scenes of verified coining that were discussed above in Chapter Four. The scene of gold-smithing includes two *putti* working at a furnace, on whose firebox sits a statue head of the god Vulcan, patron of metalworkers. One *putto* opens the furnace door while the other holds an item inside the furnace with a pair of tongs while using a reed pipe to blow on the hot fuel and facilitate a surge and increase in the temperature. Another *putto* sits on a stool, hunched over a workbench or anvil on which he uses a small hammer to beat some metal item. A cabinet on which sit sets of scales and weights is in the middle of the workshop. Another *putto* weighs an item on a hand-held balance for the benefit of a seated *psyche* whose style of dress marks her out as the workshop owner or manager. To one side a pair of *putti* work together, one using tongs to hold an item down on an anvil while the other beats it with a large, long-handled hammer.

In the scene on the east wall gathered flowers arrive on the back of a goat and a team of *putti* and *psychai* make them into garlands which are then hung up on display racks for sale. Next is depicted the production of perfume: two teams each of two *putti* stand on either side of a wedge press hammering it. Other figures stir liquid in basins and containers. A *putto* sits at a table on which rests a papyrus scroll and a balance for weighing out quantities of ingredients. Behind him an open cabinet full of bottles and flasks can be seen. To one side a winged female figure or *psyche* appears to be sniffing something on the back of her raised hand, confirming that we are indeed seeing a scene in a perfume manufactory rather than of other things.

Non-occupational scenes are also present, with a *putti* chariot racing scene on the east wall and on the south wall *putti* playing, throwing toy darts. A Bacchic procession is also depicted.

It has been suggested that these wall paintings tell us as much about Roman elite perceptions of 'technical culture' as they do about work and workers as such. That is a very interesting perspective and an attractive one. It seems curious to criticise these paintings for their failure to correctly reproduce technical details of processes, equipment, and tools. The idea that the client 'was either uninterested in them or understood them only superficially' seems absurd.[5] Technology is, of course, material by its very nature but it is not separate from culturally and historically specific contexts, from dynamic social interactions, or from the making of meaning.

I wonder if the portrayal of so many very different activities was intended to somehow represent a virtual tour of various commercial locations throughout the town, a kind of pictorial map which might have made sense to visitors familiar with Pompeii's commercial landscape and layout. It could have represented the economy of Pompeii, the economic strength of its diversity. Viewers were possibly never intended to read the decorative scheme as a whole or 'read' it in a set order as we have done here. Perhaps they were meant to simply take in images of work and labour from all viewpoints in the room and again admire the toil on show here.

While many of the scenes such as the making of wine, buying of wine, and hanging of garlands could suggest allusions to the banqueting function of the room it is impossible to fit interpretation of the textile making and metal-working images into this interpretive schema. Given that the use of *putti* as images on children's sarcophagi was a well-established but not exclusive strategy of funerary commemoration of those who died too young I wonder if the images around the walls of the banqueting room in the House of the Vettii could not themselves have served a similar purpose for a mourning family, transferring their grief to images in a domestic setting? Certainly, the composition of the painted scenes involving the *putti* appears such that one can visualise them as more solid images carved in relief on stone. The figures of larger, differently dressed female winged figures or *psychai* who appear in the frescos and to whom attention is deliberately drawn by nature of their more unusual size and appearance could, as on some sarcophagi, have represented children or youths who never attained maturity but who were shown here living life beyond the time of their death in the form of images. Finally, it might be that some of these scenes were intended to stimulate or appeal to the senses of the diners, or to distill the sight, sounds, and smells of daily life in Pompeii: wine and bread to represent taste, perfume production to represent smell, the clanging of metalworking representing hearing, and chariot racing appealing to vision.

Apparently, similar scenes of commercial workshop activity centred on perfume production appeared in wall paintings in the *Casa dei Calpurnii* or House of the Calpurnii, also in Pompeii, but sadly these are no longer extant. Some such scenes also occur in paintings in houses in Herculaneum. An unprovenanced fragment of painted wall plaster reportedly from Pompeii and in the Fitzwilliam Museum in Cambridge once more shows two *putti* operating a press to process flowers for perfume. From the *macellum* or market building in Insula VII at Pompeii comes a wall painting of *putti* and *psychai* resting at a donkey mill during a festival, two donkeys having been unharnessed from the mill structure itself, in the background of the scene. The *putti* lounge around and fuss the animals.

Somewhat later, images of working *putti* appeared on one of the manuscript pages of the illustrated book known to scholars either as the *Vienna Dioscorides* or the *Juliana Anicia Codex*, a book created in Constantinople in c. AD 515 and now in the *Österreichische Nationalbibliotek* in Vienna, Austria.[6] Despite being an edition of Dioscorides' book *De Materia Medica*, with additions by other authors, this volume constitutes an item with imperial links. The introductory page bears a portrait picture of Anicia Juliana (born AD 462, died AD 527/528), daughter of the short-lived western emperor Olybrius and the powerful Galla Placidia, daughter of Valentinian. She appears enthroned, flanked by a number of personifications such as Magnanimity and Prudence, there to honour her munificence in funding church building. A *putto* hands her a book, presumably the very book in which the illustration appears. The central image is enclosed by a rope forming an eight-pointed star within a circle. The spaces between the strands of rope contain eight sets of images of *putti* engaged in building work, acting as masons, carpenters, and painters.

The links between imperial largesse and religious, in this case Christian, piety, church building, and the labour of construction workers was explicitly made on the fifth century Trier Ivory *Adventus* Relief discussed in Chapter One, though in that particular image the workers were not *putti* but real flesh and blood workers. We can perhaps see similar influences or at least an echo of them in the eighth century AD Early Islamic painted panels of construction workers on the east aisle vaulted ceiling of the great hall at the desert castle of Qusayr 'Amra in Jordan. These thirty-two panels carry depictions of stone masons, builders, blacksmiths, carpenters, and masons, the men who created the complex itself. Power, piety, money, and labour were represented here in harmony.

Shadowplayers

One group of workers which has not been considered so far in this study is that loose assembly of actors, mimes, and musicians who provided entertainment at various formal and informal events in Rome and Italy, and sometimes further afield in the empire. As was mentioned in the preface to this book I decided not to include discussion of gladiators here as their occupation was seldom a chosen one. Charioteers, boxers, athletes, and other sportsmen will also receive little coverage here, though some achieved an almost unbelievable level of acclaim during their careers and some of the most famous and renowned of them left behind expensive and elaborate tombs which reflected their social standing generated through their talent and achievements. Generic portrayals of actors and mimes were extremely common in Roman art, in both the major arts of sculpture, mosaic, and wall painting and in the minor, applied arts, and theatrical masks were equally common shorthand images for the theatrical profession and the art of theatre in general. Discussion here though will centre on specific named individual actors, mimes, and musicians in an attempt to uncover broader issues about the profession and the social standing of such professionals. It might be thought that in a profession where role-playing, disguise, and subterfuge through mask-work were de rigueur we might uncover some instances of unreliable authors of their own true identities.

Musicians in the Roman world were not necessarily always involved in profane events, and indeed would have regularly appeared in ensembles playing different combinations of instruments at sacrifices and other religious events. A small mid-second century AD funerary altar from the Via Appia in Rome and now in the *Gallerie degli Uffizi* or Uffizi Gallery in Florence is dedicated to the dwarf flute player Myropnous, and his image proudly appears on its front (Plate 68). Bearded and wearing a long, heavy tunic he holds an instrument in each hand. The accompanying dedicatory inscription in Greek calls him 'the dwarf flute player'. This is the first example of a differently abled individual to be discussed in this book and it is therefore apposite to consider the broader implications and significance of this portrait and dedication. In his groundbreaking book of 1995 *The Eye of the Beholder. Deformity and Disability in the Graeco-Roman World* Robert Garland did not discuss the altar of Myropnous but noted that dwarves would offer appear in an ancient Roman equivalent of a pantomime and terracotta genre figures of pantomime characters were popular, many of them made in Egypt.[7] However, sometimes it is difficult to distinguish these from more troubling genre depictions of grotesques and the deformed whose origins lay in the veracity and sometimes cruelty of Hellenistic art.

Quite a number of funerary monuments of mimes or actors are known,[8] giving us details of name, civic origins, and professional status, but sometimes much more detail is provided by often lengthy inscriptions such as the third century AD stele of Eucharistos of Patara, now in the *Antalya Muzesi*, Turkey, which also bears his portrait, or the fifth century AD funerary inscription from Rome, without accompanying image, of the mimic Vitalis on which he notes 'I was most famous all over the world, and it was the source of my luxury home, it was the source of my wealth ... on seeing me raging madness ceased to exist, when I approached even the sharpest pain turned to laughter ... whenever a lady saw herself imitated in my gestures she both blushed and arranged her looks' and so on. Modesty would not appear to have been one of Vitalis' gifts.

But most interesting of all to me is the stele of the mime Bassilla (Plate 69), a woman whose image illustrates how sometimes unusual occupations and lifestyles, unrestricted by general social conventions and mores, could be chosen by some women in the Roman world.[9] This stele comes from the amphitheatre at Aquileia, in north-eastern Italy and is in the *Museo Archeologico Nazionale di Aquileia*, Bassilla's remarkable story being laid bare both by her smiling image at the top of the stone and by the lengthy accompanying Greek inscription. The tombstone dates from the third century AD and is dedicated by Herakleides, a fellow 'good speaker and character mime', to his great friend the actress, dancer, and mime Bassilla. The inscription lauds her for her 'resounding fame on the stage' gained 'among many peoples and many cities' and suggests that she was in fact 'the tenth Muse', 'thus not dead'. Though now a corpse 'she has won life as her fair reward' and a resting place 'in a place sacred to the Muses'. The already touching greetings in her epitaph are further added to at the very end of the inscription: 'Your fellow performers say to you "Take heart Bassilla, nobody is immortal".'

Work and War

Of all the professional organisations in the Roman world it is probably the Roman army that has left more inscriptions, epigraphic dedications, and commemorative artworks to us than any other single body. Decorated military tombstones can provide a huge amount of information from the point of view of what kinds of personal or professional identities could be represented within the constraints of membership of a strictly defined organisational framework. Veterans' funerary stele and inscriptions likewise provide large quantities of personal, biographic detail. However, just as I am declining to discuss gladiators and prostitutes in this book, so too am I declining to allow the role of soldier to be classed here as simply a job of work in the manner of a mason or a carpenter, for instance. The Roman army included many soldiers who were in fact specialist workers, craftsmen, and artisans, or who were trained to take up these roles, as documents like the famous Vindolanda tablets show, but first and foremost each of these men was a soldier before anything else. However, I do intend to discuss military building inscriptions, in terms of how certain unique building slabs from the Antonine Wall frontier in Scotland attested to an engagement with the concept of the army's work and labour as being potentially as significant as its fighting role at this time, and in which imperial ideology and the commemoration and celebration of physical labour undertaken merged. The complex conceptual intertextuality of these inscriptions is of huge significance.[10]

The Roman state in a few instances used images and inscriptions to conflate the idea of the Roman army waging war with physical labour and work, and vice versa, as on the helical frieze around Trajan's Column in Rome (Plate 70), and the bureaucratic recording by the army of details of physical labour undertaken by some of its soldiers helped mentally map and conceptualise the northern British frontier on the Antonine Wall in Scotland.

The Antonine Wall and the remarkable series of twenty legionary distance slabs from the frontier will here be considered in terms of the significance of the unusual, perhaps unique, overemphasis on military endeavour and achievement recorded on the slabs, in tandem with an obsession with notions about work and identity reflected in some of the inscriptions on the slabs. The significance of the texts of the inscriptions on the distance slabs referring to work and labour, to physical things achieved, suggests that the idea of work as an ideological concept was presented here along with the repetitious formula on the slabs as part of a strategy for conceptualising hostile space, demonstrating control of the frontier line, and understanding conquered territory.

It was standard practice for the Roman army to commemorate its building work at forts with simple inscriptions on building stones, centurial stones, or dedication slabs. However, the three legions involved in the construction of the Antonine Wall frontier works, the Second, Sixth, and Twentieth legions, for some reason were given leave to commemorate their building work on the frontier in a much more elaborate way, with a serial programme of inscribed stones known to archaeologists today as legionary distance slabs. Twenty commemorative legionary distance slabs, mostly complete but a few fragmentary, have been recovered from the frontier so far to date. It is estimated that there were likely to have been sixty slabs in total, making a unique concerted artistic expression of Roman conquest and military might. The construction of no other Roman frontier elsewhere in the empire is known to have been commemorated in this way.

The distance slabs are of a number of types: they are either plain with an inscription, sparsely decorated and inscribed, moderately highly decorated and inscribed, or highly decorated and inscribed, but each bears the same, almost identical and somewhat formulaic inscription, introduced by the names of the emperor 'Caesar Titus Aelius Hadrianus Antoninus Augustus Pius' and the title *patri patriae* – 'Father of the Country', a formula followed on most of the slabs. The legion's name then follows with a record of their building work. The recorded lengths of built wall/frontier works vary. Again and again we see reference to *per pedum ... fecit* or *fecit ... per pedum*, that is 'completed ... over a distance of ... feet' (on ten slabs) or the distance is given in *passuum* or 'paces' (on seven slabs). The Twentieth Legion slab from Eastermains carries measurements in both *passuum* and *pedum*. Another exception in phrasing can be found on the Braidfield Farm Sixth Legion slab and the Old Kilpatrick Sixth Legion slab which introduce the otherwise unique formula *opus valli pedum*, that is it was specifically 'the rampart-work' measurement being presented here. Legionary symbols appear as decoration on many of the slabs and seven of the slabs bear narrative scenes of different sorts.

Distance slabs set up by the Second Legion which include precise details of lengths of wall built, ditches dug and so on come from Bridgeness, the largest and most elaborately decorated of all the legionary distance slabs, recording the legion having built '4,652 paces' of the Antonine Wall, from Carleith , recording a distance of '3,271 feet', Summerston, recording 'a distance of 3,666 ½ paces', Cawder , recording 'a distance of 3,666 ½ paces', and Duntocher '4,140 feet'.

Of those set up by the Sixth Legion a slab from Old Kilpatrick records '4,141 feet', another from Castlehill records 'a distance of 3,666 ½ paces', as does a slab from East Millichen, a slab from Braidfield 'a distance of 3,240 feet', and the inscription on a

Above left: 1. The Tower Crane relief from the Tomb of the Haterii, Rome. Late first century AD. *Musei Vaticani*, Rome. (Photo: Author)

Above right: 2. Funerary altar of T. Statilius Aper, building surveyor. Rome. Hadrianic. *Musei Capitolini*, Rome. (Photo: Author)

3. The Trier *Adventus* Ivory, with incidental scene of building work. Made in Constantinople. Fifth century AD or later. Cathedral Treasury, Trier. (Photo: Slide Collection of Former School of Continuing Studies, Birmingham University)

Above left: 4. Dedicatory relief from the amphitheatre at Capua, with treadmill crane. Late third or early fourth century AD. *Museo Campano*, Capua. (Photo: Author)

Above right: 5. Funerary monument dedicated by Pettia Ge to her husband Caius Clodius from Villa San Maurizio necropolis, with depictions of a marble-worker's tools. Late first century AD. *Museo Civico Reggio nell'Emilia*, Reggio. (Photo: Author)

6. Funerary plaque depicting a *marmorarius* creating an *opus sectile* mosaic panel. Probably from a catacomb. Second half of the fourth century AD. *Museo Nazionale Romano Terme di Diocleziano*, Rome. (Photo: Author)

Above left: 7. Funerary relief depicting a carpenter sitting at a specialised work bench. Reims. Possibly second century AD. *Musée Saint-Rémi*, Reims. (Photo: Author)

Above right: 8. Child's sarcophagus with scene of Prometheus making men. Albani collection, Rome. Third century AD. *Musei Capitolini*, Rome. (Photo: Author)

9. Tomb of Eurysaces the Baker, Rome. General view. 30–20 BC. (Photo: Author)

10. Tomb of Eurysaces the Baker, Rome. General view. 30–20 BC. (Photo: Author)

11. Inscription dedicated to Atistia, probably the wife of Eurysaces the Baker. *Museo Nazionale Romano Terme di Diocleziano*, Rome. 30–20 BC. (Photo: Author)

12. Tomb of Eurysaces the Baker, Rome. South frieze: arrival, checking, and processing of grain. 30–20 BC. (Photo: Author)

13. Tomb of Eurysaces the Baker, Rome. North frieze: Preparation of dough, kneading of loaves, and baking. 30–20 BC. (Photo: Author)

14. Tomb of
Eurysaces the
Baker, Rome. North
frieze: Close-up
of baker at bread
oven. 30–20 BC.
(Photo: Author)

15. Relief panel
from a sarcophagus
depicting work
inside a bakery.
Bologna. Third
century AD. *Museo
Civico Archeologico*,
Bologna.
(Photo: Author)

16. Fragment of
a sarcophagus,
probably of a
miller or baker,
carrying a depiction
of a donkey-mill.
Rome. Mid-third
century AD. *Musei
Vaticani*, Rome.
(Photo: Author)

Above left: 17. Wall painting depicting the sale of bread. *Casa del Panettiere*, Pompeii. *Museo Archeologico Nazionale*, Naples. First century AD. (Photo: Author)

Above right: 18. Relief panel depicting Trajan distributing bread as part of the *annona* scheme. The Arch of Trajan, Benevento. *c.* AD 114. (Photo: Author)

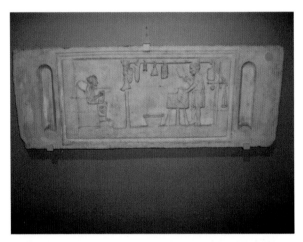

19. Funerary relief to a Roman butcher, from Trastevere, Rome. First half of the second century AD. Cast in the Ashmolean Museum, Oxford- original in the *Staatlichen Skulpturensammlung*, Dresden. (Photo: Author)

20. Detail of a funerary stele, showing an image of a butcher at work. Bologna. First century AD. *Museo Civico Archeologico*, Bologna. (Photo: Author)

21. Funerary relief of Lucius Aurelius Hermia, butcher of the Viminal Hill, Rome, and his wife Philematium. Via Nomentana, Rome. First century BC. British Museum, London. (Photo: Copyright Trustees of the British Museum)

22. The *Igeler Säule* or Igel Column. *c.* AD 250. (Photo: Author)

23. Detail of cloth trading scene on the *Igeler Säule* or Igel Column. *c.* AD 250. (Photo: Author)

Above left: 24. Funerary stele of a textile dealer. Mid to late first century AD. *Museo Civico Archeologico*, Milan. (Photo: Author)

Above right: 25. Funerary stele of the textile dealer Caius Vettius. Built into the *Porta Nuova*, Milan. Mid to late first century AD. (Photo: Author)

26. Funerary relief of the wool merchant Titus Aelius Evangelus. AD 161–180. *Medelhavsmuseet*, Stockholm. (Photo: Copyright Sema Basaran)

Above left: 27. Funerary relief with fulling scene. First half of the second century AD. *Museo Archeologico Civico 'Tobia Aldini'*, Forlimpopoli. (Photo: Author)

Above right: 28. Funerary stele with fulling scene. Second century AD. *Musées de Sens*. (Photo: Author)

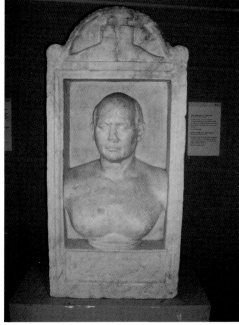

Above left: 29. Funerary stele of the *purpurarius* Caius Pupius Amicus. Mid-first century AD. *Museo Archeologico Nazionale di Parma*, Parma. (Photo: Author)

Above right: 30. Funerary stele of the shoemaker Caius Iulius Helius. Rome. Early second century AD. *Centrale Montemartini, Musei Capitolini*, Rome. (Photo: Author)

Above left: 31. Funerary relief of possible female shoemaker Septimia Stratonice. Ostia. Early second century AD. *Museo Ostiense*, Ostia. (Photo: Slide Collection of Former School of Continuing Studies, Birmingham University)

Above right: 32. Front panel of the sarcophagus of Titus Flavius Trophimas, shoemaker. A scene of ropemaking also appears here. Rome. Earlier second century AD. *Museo Nazionale Romano*, Rome. (Photo: Author)

33. Side panel of the Lambrate Sarcophagus, with relief scene of leatherworking. Lambrate, Milan. Later third century AD. *Castello Sforzesco*, Milan. (Photo: Author)

34. Vulcan on a side panel of a child's sarcophagus with scene of Prometheus making men on the front. Albani collection, Rome. Third century AD. *Musei Capitolini*, Rome. (Photo: Author)

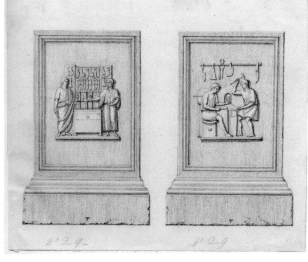

Above left: 35. Funerary stele of the child miner Quartulus or Quintus Artulus. Late first century AD. *Museo Arqueológico Nacional*, Madrid. (Photo: Slide Collection of Former School of Continuing Studies, Birmingham University)

Above right: 36. Funerary altar of metalworker and cutler Lucius Cornelius Atimetus. Rome. Second half of the first century AD. Original in the *Museo Lapidario*, *Musei Vaticani*, Rome. Drawings of side faces of the altar by Vincenzo Dolcibene (1746-1820) in the British Museum, London. (Photo: Copyright Trustees of the British Museum)

37. Terracotta funerary plaque with image of metalworking on the Tomb of the Verii, Tomb 29, *Necropoli di Porto*, Isola Sacra, Ostia. Late Hadrianic to early Antonine. (Photo: Author)

38. Funerary relief or shop sign depicting activity in a bronzesmith's workshop. Pompeii. First century AD. *Museo Archeologico Nazionale*, Naples. (Photo: Author)

39. Funerary altar dedicated by coppersmith L. Minucius Optatus, with scene of work on copper bowl. Este. First century AD. *Museo Nazionale Atestino*, Este. (Photo: Author)

Above left: (And cover image) 40. Funerary monument of a locksmith, with scene of activity inside a workshop. Aquileia. Late first to early second century AD. *Museo Archeologico Nazionale di Aquileia*, Aquileia. (Photo: Author)

Above right: 41. Funerary stele of Bellicus the Smith. Sens. Second century AD. *Musées de Sens.* (Photo: Author)

42. The Kerch Easel Painter, an image painted on the inside of a sarcophagus. Kerch. First or second century AD. State Hermitage Museum, St Petersburg. (Photo: Slide Collection of Former School of Continuing Studies, Birmingham University)

Above left: 43. Funerary stele to Marcus Secundinius Amabilis, sculptor. Bordeaux. Mid-second century AD. *Musée d'Aquitaine*, Bordeaux. (Photo: Slide Collection of Former School of Continuing Studies, Birmingham University)

Above right: 44. Funerary stele of the boat-builder Publius Longidienus. Ravenna. Late first century BC to early first century AD. *Museo Nazionale di Ravenna*, Ravenna. (Photo: Author)

45. Funerary relief depicting a docker unloading goods. Ostia. Second half of the third century AD. *Museo Nazionale Romano*, Rome. (Photo: Author)

Above left: 46. Funerary stele of the wheelwright Quintus Minicius. Fossano. End of the first century AD. *Museo di Antichità*, Turin. (Photo: Author)

Above right: 47. Black and white mosaic in the Baths of the *Cisarii* or coachmen, Ostia. Hadrianic. (Photo: Author)

48. Detail of a wagon transporting goods on the *Igeler Säule* or Igel Column. *c.* AD 250. (Photo: Author)

49. Funerary stele of a horse trader. Dijon. First century AD. *Musée Archéologique de Dijon*, Dijon. (Photo: Author)

50. Funerary relief depicting barge haulage. Cabrières-d'Aigues. Second to third century AD. *Musée Lapidaire, Musée Calvet,* Avignon. See also Plate 51 for another relief from the same monument. (Photo: Author)

51. Funerary relief depicting a bargee. Cabrières-d'Aigues. Second to third century AD. *Musée Lapidaire, Musée Calvet,* Avignon. See also Plate 50 for another relief from the same monument. (Photo: Author)

52. Funerary sculpture in the form of a wine-transporting boat from a tomb at Neumagen. *c.* AD 220. *Rheinische Landesmuseum,* Trier. (Photo: Author)

53. Funerary relief depicting two workers packing shipping bales. *Nécropole de la Pointe*, Arles. Third century AD. *Musée Départmental Arles Antiques*, Arles. (Photo: Author)

Right: 55. Funerary relief depicting the weighing and assessing of goods. Capua. Second half of the first century AD. *Museo Campano*, Capua. (Photo: Author)

Below: 54. Funerary relief depicting workers packing shipping bales. Augsburg. Second or third century AD. Augsburg Cathedral. (Photo: Slide Collection of Former School of Continuing Studies, Birmingham University)

Above left: 56. Sarcophagus relief fragment depicting a porter delivering goods to a shop or warehouse. Rome. Mid-third century AD. Royal Ontario Museum, Toronto. (Photo: Slide Collection of Former School of Continuing Studies, Birmingham University)

Above right: 57. Funerary stele fragment with depiction of the operation of a large wine press. Aquileia. First half of the third century AD. *Museo Archeologico Nazionale di Aquileia*, Aquileia. (Photo: Author)

58. Sarcophagus bearing scenes of wine tasting and selling. Ancona. Third century AD. *Museo delle Marche*, Ancona. (Photo: Author)

Right: 59. Funerary stele dedicated to Sextus Titius Primus and his family, carrying depictions of wine amphorae. Castellone di Suasa. Mid-first century AD. *Museo delle Marche*, Ancona. (Photo: Author)

Below: 60. Funerary relief with scene inside a wine cellar or wine warehouse. *Cimitero dell'Ex Vigna Chiaraviglio*, Rome. Second half of third century AD. *Museo di Catacombe di Domitilla*, Rome. See Plate 85 for close-up detail. (Photo: Author)

61. Funerary relief depicting a scene inside a bar. Til-Châtel. Second or third century AD. *Musée Archéologique de Dijon*, Dijon. (Photo: Author)

62. Terracotta funerary plaque with images of bar-keeping. Tomb 30. *Necropoli di Porto*, Isola Sacra, Ostia. Late Hadrianic to early Antonine. (Photo: Author).

63. Relief scene on funerary monument of Pompeianius Silvinus, with tavern scene. Augsburg. AD 170–230. *Römische Museen*, Augsburg. (Photo: Slide Collection of Former School of Continuing Studies, Birmingham University)

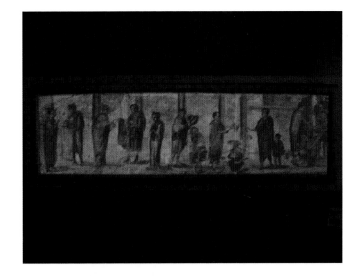

64. Wall painting depicting the buying and selling in the Forum. *Praedia* of Iulia Felix, Pompeii. First century AD. *Museo Archeologico Nazionale*, Naples. (Photo: Author)

65. Funerary relief depicting the sale of goods at a market. Trier. Third century AD *Rheinische Landesmuseum*, Trier. (Photo: Author)

66. Funerary relief depicting the sale of goods at a table. Trier. Third century AD *Rheinische Landesmuseum*, Trier. (Photo: Author)

67. Child's sarcophagus decorated with scenes of *putti* manufacturing arms and armour. Rome. *c.* AD 160. *Museo Nazionale Romano Terme di Diocleziano*, Rome. (Photo: Author)

68. Funerary stele of the dwarf flute-player Myropnous. Rome. Mid-second century AD. *Gallerie degli Uffizi* (Uffizi Gallery), Florence. (Photo: Author)

69. Funerary stele of the female mime Bassilla. Aquileia. Third century AD. *Museo Archeologico Nazionale di Aquileia*, Aquileia. (Photo: Author)

70. Scenes of Roman soldiers engaged in building work. Frieze on Trajan's Column, Rome. AD 107–113. (Photo: Author)

71. Terracotta funerary plaque with image of a miller at work at a horse mill on the Tomb of Tiberius Claudius Eutychus, Tomb 78, *Necropoli di Porto*, Isola Sacra, Ostia. Late Hadrianic to early Antonine. (Photo: Author)

72. Terracotta funerary plaque with image of a grain transport ship on the Tomb of Tiberius Claudius Eutychus, Tomb 78, *Necropoli di Porto*, Isola Sacra, Ostia. Late Hadrianic to early Antonine. (Photo: Author)

73. Terracotta funerary plaques with images of a midwife, Scribonia Attice, and the other to a doctor-surgeon, M. Ulpius Amerimnus, Tomb 100, *Necropoli di Porto*. Isola Sacra, Ostia. Late Hadrianic to early Antonine. (Photo: Author)

74. Black and white mosaic in the *Aula dei Mensores* or Hall of the Grain Measurers, Ostia. Third century AD. (Photo: Author)

Above: 75. Funerary stele with image of the sale of jewellery. Metz. Second or third century AD. *Musée de la Cour d'Or*, Metz. (Photo: Author)

Right: 76. Funerary stele with an image of the preparation of medicines perhaps or of wine, and another of carpentry. Metz. Second or third century AD. *Musée de la Cour d'Or*, Metz. (Photo: Author)

Above left: 77. Funerary relief depicting a scene of textile selling (above) and accountancy (below). Arlon. Mid-third century AD. *Musée Archéologiques Luxembourgeois*, Arlon. (Photo: Author)

Above right: 78. The *Igeler Säule* or Igel Column. *c*. AD 250. (Photo: Author)

Below: 79. Detail of a scene of workers in a kitchen on the *Igeler Säule* or Igel Column. *c*. AD 250. (Photo: Author)

Above: 80. Funerary relief or shop sign depicting a female poultry seller and grocer. Late second century AD. Ostia. *Museo Ostiense*, Ostia. (Photo: Copyright Scala Firenze)

Right: 81. Funerary relief or shop sign of a vegetable-seller. Ostia. Late second century AD. *Museo Ostiense*, Ostia. (Photo: Copyright Bridgeman Images)

Above left: 82. Funerary relief dedicated to Sentia Amaransis, a female bar owner. Mérida. First century AD. *Museo Nacional de Arte Romano*, Mérida. (Photo: Slide Collection of Former School of Continuing Studies, Birmingham University)

Above right: 83. Funerary stele of a *medica* or female doctor. Metz. Second or third century AD. *Musée de la Cour d'Or*, Metz. (Photo: Author)

84. Funerary relief of a scene in a shop where metal vessels are on sale. *Catacomba dei SS. Marco e Marcelliano*, Rome. Third or fourth century AD. *Museo di Catacombe di Domitilla*. (Photo: Author)

Above left: 85. Close-up of part of a funerary relief with a scene inside a wine cellar or wine warehouse. *Cimitero dell'Ex Vigna Chiaraviglio*, Rome. Second half of third century AD. *Museo di Catacombe di Domitilla*, Rome. See Plate 60 for view of full relief. (Photo: Author)

Above right: 86. Funerary plaque to a Christian drover or horse groom, Constantius, pictured with the horses Barbarus and Germanus. *Catacombe di Domitilla*, Rome. Fourth century AD. *Museo di Catacombe di Domitilla*. (Photo: Author)

Above: 87. Relief of the Ampudii, with images of *modii* or corn measures. Rome. First century BC. British Museum, London. (Photo: Copyright Trustees of the British Museum)

Right: 88. Sarcophagus side panel with image of the lawyer, Valerius Petronianus, at work. Milan. Early fourth century AD. Museo Civico Archeologico, Milan. (Photo: Author)

Above left: 89. Funerary altar known as The Altar of the Scribes. Rome. AD 25–50. *Museo Nazionale Romano*, Rome. (Photo: Author)

Above right: 90. Funerary relief depicting a schoolmaster. Arlon. *c*. AD 40–50. *Musée Archéologiques Luxembourgeois*, Arlon. (Photo: Author)

91. Funerary stele relief depicting a schoolmaster and pupils. Trier. Third century AD. *Rheinische Landesmuseum*, Trier. (Photo: Author)

92. Funerary stele depicting scene of accountancy, banking, or tax collection. Arlon. Mid-third century AD. *Musée Archéologiques Luxembourgeois*, Arlon. (Photo: Author)

93. Funerary stele relief depicting a scene of business dealings. Trier. Third century AD. *Rheinische Landesmuseum*, Trier. (Photo: Author)

94. Funerary stele of the Greek doctor Jason. Athens. Second century AD. British Museum, London. (Photo: Copyright Trustees of the British Museum)

95. Sarcophagus of Sosia Iuliana. Image on side panel of an occulist at work or of cultic preparations. Ravenna. Second century AD. *Museo Nazionale di Ravenna*, Ravenna. (Photo: Author)

96. The *Meditrina* funerary stele, with scene of the preparation of medicines or other products. Grand, Vosges. Second century AD. *Musée Départmental d'Art Ancien et Contemporain*, Épinal. (Photo: Slide Collection of Former School of Continuing Studies, Birmingham University)

97. Terracotta funerary plaque for Verrius Euhelpistus, depicted with an unusual metalworker's machine. Tomb 29, *Necropoli di Porto*, Isola Sacra, Ostia. Late Hadrianic to early Antonine. (Photo: Author)

Above left: 98. Funerary stele with a number of agricultural scenes, including the use of a sophisticated reaping machine or *vallus*, shown here as a detail. Late first to early second century AD. Cast in the *Musée Archéologiques Luxembourgeois*, Arlon-original in the *Musée Gaumais*, Virton. (Photo: Author)

Above right: 99. The large funerary altar of L. Alfius Statius, with depictions of an architect's or master-builder's equipment and tools. Aquileia. Early first century AD. *Museo Archeologico Nazionale di Aquileia*, Aquileia. (Photo: Author) slab from Eastermains refers to '...thousand feet', with the actual number of thousand feet not having been carved on the stone.

Of the slabs set up by the Twentieth Legion two distance slabs from Old Kilpatrick each record the building of '4,411 feet', a third from Eastermains records the soldiers building '3,000 paces (and) 3,304 feet', a slab from Castlehill makes reference to 'over a distance of 3,000 feet', as do two separate slabs from Hutcheson Hill, while an unprovenanced slab records that a detachment built frontier works 'over a distance of 3,000 paces'. Another unprovenanced Twentieth Legion slab bears an inscription mentioning 'feet' but without the precise number of feet having been inserted in the blank space on the stone.

The kind of competition between the legions referenced in the slab inscriptions was probably a reflection of pride in one's own individual unit and not necessarily pride above and beyond being part of a larger organisation, the Roman army.

Thus sixteen of the twenty legionary distance slabs known record precise building lengths, two are curiously incomplete, without the distances inscribed in the blank spaces on the stones, a nineteenth slab, from Arniebog is fragmentary and bears images but does not include the section which would have carried a panel bearing the inscription, and the twentieth, now-lost, slab was too worn for any inscription to be read at the time of its discovery and examination.

That the idea of work as an ideological concept with value was presented here for viewers is without doubt. Equally certain is the way that the repetitious formula for recording lengths of wall built on the slabs was also part of a strategy for conceptualising the frontier and coming to terms with understanding the newly conquered territory. Of the sixteen slabs recording lengths of building work the overall inscription has pre-eminence on eleven of them, while on the other five it might be thought that the presence of accompanying complex images in tandem with the inscriptions on the slabs might have had the effect of relegating the importance of the formulaic inscription or even negating it. Far from it, it would appear.

Though the slabs undoubtedly formed a series they were not stylistically consistent. Each slab was very much site-specific, pairs marking each built stretch of wall referred to in the inscription or thereabouts. They marked points in a tamed landscape, the art and inscriptions together providing a way for the Romans and others to conceptualise the frontier as a whole entity and not as a collection of discrete places in a broad untamed landscape.

There would also seem to have been some element of geographical and spatial conceptualisation involved in the design of two of the three so-called enamelled copper alloy souvenir 'pans' or small bowls linked to Hadrian's Wall. These vessels, the Rudge Cup, the Amiens Patera, and the Ilam Pan are all considered by archaeologists either to have been 'the first souvenirs' of the frontier taken home by soldiers stationed there or by civilian visitors to the wall, or to have been religious or votive items.[11] All of these 'pans' bear names of forts along the western part of Hadrian's Wall from Bowness on Solway to Great Chesters, their incision or scratching on the Ilam Pan being secondary to the vessel's manufacture: it must therefore be seen as a personalised item. Noteworthy though is an additional inscribed reference to *VALI AELI* – *vallum aelium* or Hadrian's Wall – and to *DRACONIS*, presumably Draco, its commissioner and owner. However, on both the Rudge Cup and the Amiens Patera the letters forming the names of the forts are raised and therefore had been cast as an integral part of the vessel. On the Amiens Patera six forts on Hadrian's Wall are named in red enamel (Bowness-on-Solway, Burgh-by-Sands, Stanwix, Castlesteads, Birdoswald, and Great Chesters), each name on a simple diagrammatic representation of the fort as a square of coloured enamelling. Most interestingly the frontier is represented below by a red crenellated line for the wall itself and for distance towers. A similar crenellated line can be seen on the Rudge Cup where five forts are named, the same as on the Amiens Patera, with the omission of Great Chesters.

Thus the two cups used a small number of inscribed place names to prompt the viewer to link up these site-specific individual fort names and the schematic depiction of forts and the crenellated wall and thus conceptualise the whole frontier and its material enormity from otherwise fragmentary information. Whether or not this was the case, each of the 'pans' undoubtedly represented a map to be held in the hand and viewed for whatever purpose.

These examples of precise quantification of distance on the Antonine Wall slabs and sequential naming of places on the enamelled cups would appear to have been deliberate and significant in both cases. Being able to measure distance, to quantify the distance between one point and another, one place from another, particularly in a wild frontier zone, was crucial for the Roman army. The deployment of military surveyors using the *groma* reflected the need to record precisely in order to facilitate the creation of the frontier and an infrastructure to support it.[12] Once the nature of space and distance could be measured it could then be understood and conquered. Here we see the merging of ideas about landscape, understanding, time, movement, and distance, a commemoration of specific historical interactions with landscape. The Roman legionary soldiers who conquered the territory that was to become the line of the Antonine frontier understood the natural characteristics of the land by moving across it, engaged in fighting there or in reconnaissance missions, surveying the line of the frontier and setting it out, and in building the frontier works. The local natural materials, soil, turf, timber, and stone were utilised to build the wall, ramparts and forts: the very materiality of the frontier reflected its setting and its imposition on and disruption of natural space and traditional routes. The need to then fully and meticulously document and commemorate the creation of the frontier through a serial programme of sculptural and epigraphic works in the form of the legionary distance slabs was an unprecedented and unusual decision. The elegance and effectiveness of this strategy is clear; it was a tussle between the urge to reveal and the instinct to suppress. So deep was the shading of motive and consequence that it brought a sense of resolution, a feeling of closure.

While Roman military building record stones are quite common in Roman Britain and throughout the empire, nothing strictly comparable to the Antonine Wall distance slabs is known. Most standard building records comprise an otherwise undecorated stone bearing a central inscription stating that such and such a legion or such and such a cohort or auxiliary unit built this. The need to provide any kind of precise quantification of just what was built is absent. The Antonine distance slabs record physical exertion on a precise scale whose end result was reflected in the completion of the frontier works.

In a Roman military context we can only find a parallel to the lauding of Roman military building work, and then only in images rather than text, on the decorated helical frieze depicting the Dacian Wars of AD 101–02 and 105–06 around Trajan's Column in Rome, built to honour the emperor after his death and to house his ashes. The number of scenes in which Trajan's troops chop down trees for building timber, build bridges, dig defensive ditches, cut turf and throw up ramparts, and build camps and fortifications is marked. Such scenes have been considered to act in contrast to those scenes involving light skirmishes with the enemy, full-pitched battles, and extended sieges of Dacian fortifications. In other words the juxtaposition of scenes of *construction* with those of *destruction* is a fully formed part of the narrative political and ideological programme of the monument,[13] just as it is argued that the precision quantification of military building works acts in a similar role on the Antonine Wall series of legionary distance slabs.

As we have seen throughout this book, in a world in which much of the hard labour was expected to be undertaken either by slaves or by animals it is difficult to get to grips with Roman views on the meaning of the concept of work, of work as a manifestation of an idea. A number of rather dismissive comments by Cicero in his *De Officiis* – '*On Duties*' – has already been quoted to suggest that certainly among the elite in late Republican Rome there was a strict hierarchical view of the degrees of honour, of moral worth, among the professions and workers more generally. It is hardly surprising that Cicero viewed elite landowners and gentlemen farmers as being at the centre of moral superiority while perhaps rather idiosyncratically he placed perfumers and dancers at the margins. Others railed against the taint of profit in trade and commerce in the same way that nineteenth-century aristocrats looked down on those without inherited money.

A textual source which through repetition stresses the moral value of building things is the emperor Augustus's *Res Gestae*. The *Res Gestae* probably owed its form to the tradition of funeral *elogia*, in the form of orations and later more permanent memorial inscriptions detailing the dead man's virtues and achievements. If at times routine and monotonous in its listing of detail the *Res Gestae* text surely reflected the spoken origins of the form and the hypnotic power of repetition. The three principal sections listing the buildings Augustus either built, completed after having been started by others, or restored demonstrate the Roman drive towards commemoration in posterity through architectural benefaction.

Ghosts in the Present

This present study of images of Roman artisans, workers, and other professionals centres on issues of identity and self representation, on pride in professional status as manifested in the creation and deployment of images of work and inscriptions naming jobs and professions. As we have seen, despite some elite snobbery of the kind referred to above, Roman freedmen and women were able to celebrate their lives and work mainly, though not exclusively, through the medium of funerary commemoration, on stele and funerary altars in particular. This was a phenomenon in particular in Rome but also markedly so in the Roman towns of northern Italy and in Gaul and Germany. Shop signs depicting the product being sold or its production must have been common and at Pompeii we can see that these included signs in the form of paintings on the outside of the shop or workshop premises.

But outside of freedmen funerary contexts images referencing work, labour, and physical endeavour were relatively rare. Certainly in imperial art one can only suggest the decorative frieze on the entablature of the *Forum Transitorium* or Forum of Nerva in Rome, bearing scenes of women engaged in cloth production. Rather than being somehow straightforward in appearance or intent this depiction of the story of Arachne and Minerva was specifically didactic, sending a clear message to any women of Rome who might view the frieze that transgression whether against the gods or mortal authority would most likely bring down some terrible punishment on the offender. In other words this was a moral message linked to the imagery of work.

The concept of 'hauntology', as put forward by the French literary theorist Jacques Derrida in his 1993 book *Spectres of Marx* and further developed by the social theorist Mark Fisher may have some relevance here.[14] Obviously a portmanteau word, a funny play on words with regard to the idea of 'ontology' and 'haunting', hauntology is a term for describing temporal disjunction and harnessing nostalgia for a lost future. In the context of the Antonine Wall legionary distance slabs, in a way we have nothing but traces, as the full set of slabs is absent, but the patterns that emerge from following those traces suggest that the imperial programme that underwrote the text and images on the integrated series of distance slabs was primarily concerned with lauding the achievements of the emperor as commander in chief of the army but that it had also chosen to valorise and heroise the legions and legionary soldiers themselves for the sake of ideological positions. Therefore the spirits of those soldiers were called forth in inscriptions, giving form to their future absence, the *elogia*-style repetition also suggesting the linking of those present (the viewers) to those from the past (absent and perhaps long dead).

The afterlife of the slabs, once the expansionist project represented by the Antonine frontier came apart, somehow accentuates and then distorts any reading of their meaning. In this afterlife they seem to deal with issues of family (the army), fracture, memory, and grief, and a curious strangeness infuses the seemingly real, normal, and banal message that they were originally intended to convey.

That sixteen out of the twenty known legionary distance slabs from the Antonine Wall should have carried quantified details of the building work carried out by the legionary work parties of the different units stationed there initially might not appear particularly worthy of note. However, as has been suggested above, the depiction of work in the Roman world and allusion to it in inscriptions should be considered as a social and cultural phenomenon and such a sustained programme of the precise recording of physical work undertaken to build the frontier works both situates the stones precisely in their contemporary present yet at the same time instantly places them in past time. This temporal disjunction, this playing with time, image, symbol, and text, makes the distance slabs perhaps the most enigmatic and interesting artworks from any of the frontier zones of the Roman empire. The notion of work as a political and ideological concept was starkly presented here in the form of a deliberately repetitious formula on the slabs for recording built lengths of wall as part of the imperial strategy for demonstrating absolute control of the frontier through an understanding of the psychogeography of the conquered territory.

The Tomb of Eurysaces the Baker in Rome, a key monument and signifier in this study, was built around 30–20 BC, stood clear and unobstructed until around AD 271–75 when it became incorporated within the circuit of the new Aurelianic city walls, though whether it became completely subsumed within the later build at this time and thus was now completely hidden from view is uncertain. However, certainly this was to become the case, perhaps during Honorius's further strengthening of the city's defences and the Tomb remained hidden and unknown until its startling rediscovery and re-exposure to view in 1838. At the time of its rediscovery, after being hidden from view for around fourteen hundred years, but still largely intact, it must have seemed like some curious messenger from earlier times: it was very much *of* its time and yet completely *out of time* in that there was nothing even vaguely like this incredibly original structure in the whole of Roman art and architecture as it was known and understood up to the nineteenth century. A number of authorities writing in the later twentieth century commented on the curious resemblance of the Tomb of Eurysaces to elements of the style of Italian Fascist architecture of the 1930s and 1940s and in so doing almost made it seem as if it had been a harbinger of things to come, as well as a relic of things that had been, a very good case of hauntological confusion and predication.

In this chapter discussion has ranged across a number of topics linked by the public presentation of images of work or labour, or epigraphic references to this, as a positive facet of Roman life. We have seen the way in which an education as a prelude and necessity for a professional life could be presented in a positive light in a child's funerary context, as an affirmation of Roman cultural values, and how metaphor and illusion could be employed in the creation of occupational images of all kinds. The concept of the performance of identity has been alluded to, and the linking of military identity and references to hard physical labour non-metaphorically has also been highlighted.

In the next chapter I will consider the existence of communities of workers, across specific trades and in specific geographical locations and temporal periods, where personal professional identities could be maintained and strengthened, of workers' formal and informal work organisations such as *collegia* or guilds, and of what can best be called chains of workers linked by certain types of economic interactions, often at great distances. The issues of analysing occupational groups and their identities by gender or religion will also be debated.

8

A Community of Workers

Strength in Numbers

In this chapter attention will be turned to the idea of communities of workers, formations whose very existence might have helped to create or bolster individual occupational identities in the Roman period. These communities of workers were formed within specific trades, or in specific geographical locations, and at different times. Included here will be discussion of formal and informal work organisations such as *collegia* or guilds, and of what I will call chains of workers linked by business or other economic interactions, sometimes at vast distances. Other types of workers' communities will also be discussed, including those where occupational groups and their identities can be defined by gender or even by religion, in the case of Christianity in particular.

It is greatly to the advantage of this study that the results of a detailed analysis by Sandra Joshel of a large body of 1,470 occupational inscriptions from first and second century AD Rome are available for consultation.[1] As has been made clear throughout this book the media of funerary monument epitaphs and votive dedicatory inscriptions provided workers at Rome with a means to establish or assert their individual and collective identities in a well-established tradition. This dataset includes details of people working in 259 different professions, but to think that such occupational specialisation was reflected in atomisation among the occupations would be mistaken, as in fact it led to association and bonding.

It is not as if different occupations did not interact either. When Mithrodates commissioned and had set up a commemorative stone for the young woman Psamate, 'slave of Furia' who 'lived eighteen years', he had the stonemason record there that the deceased had been a hairdresser-an *ornatrix*-and that Mithrodates himself was a baker – a *pistor* – working for the master Thorius Flaccus. Thus, from a seemingly blunt eleven-word inscription we can glean a huge amount of information about individual relationships, about a friendship or even romance, status, work, identity, and the Roman class system. Here the community of workers was a forced creation, a community of slaves brought together in an elite household, and yet Mithrodates still strove to present their individual identities through both their names and their occupational titles.

In Chapter One I discussed the geographical distribution of stele and other funeral monuments carrying images of workers and professionals and that there was a number of centres away from Rome itself where multiple representations have been recorded. In Italy such clusters occur at Ostia, Milan, Aquileia, and Bologna. In Gaul and Germany they occur at Dijon, Sens, Arlon, Metz, Trier, Autun, Bordeaux, Narbonne, Bourges, Epinal, and Augsburg. Although the general distribution and the existence of distinct concentrations such as these is in many ways simply a reflection of chance discoveries and the focusing of archaeological investigations in some cases, nevertheless it is worth considering the material from each of these places as a group and I will discuss the make-up of some of these groups in detail below.[2]

In a way such distributions of images of Roman workers are social maps. The social logic of space was as significant in the ancient as in the modern world and there was some kind of cultural syntax of space. The life and labour of the people in Rome and other cities and towns around the empire was reflected in spatial complexity both in the city's streets and neighbourhoods and in its cemeteries and burial grounds, and social cartography such as this can be viewed today through a prism of an area's physical, economic, and cultural contexts. In death, as in life, workers and professionals balanced multiple identities through producing or being associated with simple but powerful images. In iterative practices that formed a kind of mnemonic aesthetic these artworks reached out to the broader public. These though were static images, and site specific too. While we can discuss their origins and evolution we cannot talk about them in terms of circulation, as we might with reproductions of artworks. Theoretical work on the Roman town as the site of death and cross-class exchange enriches our understanding of the ancient urban communities. All images, by virtue indeed of being images, are to some extent fictions, but these grave monuments of workers were novel in that they succeeded in placing the thing itself before its viewers. They did not invoke social exclusion: rather they distilled a life of labour, of physical and/or mental exertion, of creativity, perhaps of struggle, certainly of satisfaction, contentment, and pride into a readable sign.[3]

There are certain questions that can be asked of the occupational data as a whole, though answers to these questions need not necessarily emerge from what has to be recognised as an incomplete and flawed dataset. Without a full dataset we cannot talk about the specific mechanisms and processes which allowed for the formation of networks whose members through collective action generated a distinctive culture with its own manifestations of display and commemoration. Which was the first funerary monument to a worker or professional? No definitive answer can be given in this case. Where was the first such monument set up? The answer to this question must inevitably be the city of Rome. There were certainly what might be called 'family resemblances' between many, if not most, of the workers' or professionals' funerary monuments discussed in this book. Each monument had something in common with certain of the others, but without any one stylistic or aesthetic convention being both widely shared or sufficiently exclusive to serve a demarcating function. What similarities there were had the status of conventions rather than coincidental and contingent similarities. In terms of similar monuments or types of monuments occurring in cemeteries in the same town we could suggest the ready availability of a particular type of product from a mason's yard or workshop, similar works by the same stonemason, or even the lack of imagination on the part of the commissioners of the group of monuments. Interactions need not always have been cooperative and we must consider the idea of competition and imitation, and the desire for self-distinguishment. Thus this analysis cannot ignore issues such as resources, norms, conventions, and power even inside these formal and informal groups, in the same way that we cannot ignore them when thinking about the relationships of the occupational groups to broader Roman society.

The anthropologist and sociologist Émile Durkheim proposed a theory of 'collective effervescence', whereby group action, solidarity, or agency constituted a collective creativity greater than the sum of the individuals within the group. He reasoned that this collective effervescence could bring about transformation and change, alter patterns of interaction among individuals in a group or loose coalition, and ultimately lead to the breaking of old conventions, the creation of new ways of doing things or of thinking about doing things, and even generate new ideas, values and, ultimately, new identities for the group or within the group. Outside constraints could become viewed as obsolete or temporarily suspended as a group mentality was created and took shape: old conventions could be altered or combined, transforming them to give birth to new cultural forms. He also noted that collective effervescence could also function to bolster existing beliefs, practices, and groups. Creation and stabilisation were not necessarily opposed outcomes, as that which gave life to a group or collective and its shared beliefs was also sometimes the very thing that was necessary to revivify and perpetuate them. The protagonists in this study could have been brought together in informal or formal networks, the establishment of both types of group presenting the opportunity for the exchange of ideas and a stimulus for the rationalisation of individual and group ideas focused not necessarily on status but on identification with jobs and work. Informal groups could come about through similar mechanisms.

New cultural experiments generated by situations like cultural effervescence might not necessarily last or even be of anything other than minor significance. In the case of the trend towards non-elite Romans commemorating themselves or others through the stressing of a working or professional identity this was a trend that had both traction and longevity, and which became a certifiable cultural phenomenon. Perhaps the geographical clusters of occupational images mentioned above illustrate the existence and workings of this phenomenon or of other cultural stimuli working in tandem or independently. The study requires a detailed and very concrete focus on the networks of interactivity that we have suggested existed, networks which were inevitably localised in time and space but which here are viewed as having been part of a temporal and spatially embedded network of practices. The continual and regular interaction of members of a network group such as those under discussion here would have generated all kinds of what are known as 'internal goods', both ideas and objects, and it is in the latter category of internal goods that we can locate the workers' and professionals' grave monuments.

Logic dictates that not every group or network would have thrived or grown; some might have withered and died, others petered out through lack of attending or participating members, a dip in enthusiasm, or a paucity of good or viable ideas. For collective action to generate internal goods within a network some form of critical mass would have been needed to trigger that action, and such critical mass initially would therefore be most likely to have come from a large urban population in the city of Rome, a population in which motivation and resourcing would be guaranteed. But all of these concepts – collective effervescence, internal goods, and critical mass – would have required human agency to have come into being.

Readers may well have realised by now that certain places have kept cropping up throughout this book again and again, but because of the structuring of the book broadly by types of occupation rather than by place the geographic specificity may not have been altogether clear or its relevance have been immediately understood. The opportunity will therefore be taken now to discuss the significance of the multiple appearances of occupational images at certain sites, for obvious reasons omitting Rome itself as one of these centres of clustering and Pompeii, to avoid undue repetition as most of the relevant images from here have been discussed throughout the book.

From Ostia/Portus there is the largest number of portrayals of workers and their occupations from anywhere in the Roman world, bar the city of Rome itself and possibly also Pompeii. The question arises here, as with the other groups of multiple images discussed below, about the contemporaneity or otherwise of these particular funerary images. At the *Necropoli di Porto*, Isola Sacra, Ostia,[4] a number of tombs had ceramic or carved stone plaques depicting occupational scenes on them mounted on their outside, while inside a number of the tombs contained sarcophagi carrying occupational images (Plates 71–73). A number of tombs even had what may have been occupational mosaics. Occupations portrayed on plaques and sarcophagi included a midwife, a doctor, a blacksmith, a miller, a wine merchant or bar owner, and a shipper or merchant.

The occupational material from here was as follows. Tomb 29 had three plaques associated with it and an occupational black and white mosaic, two depicting a metalworker undertaking various tasks, the other depicting a metalworker's workshop or commercial retail premises, with his finished products hanging up on the walls, the mosaic depicting the same kind of unusual workbench seen on two of the plaques, the tomb being dedicated by Verria Zosime to her husband Verrius Euhelpistus; Tomb 30 had three external terracotta plaques, two depicting scenes in a wine shop or in a wine warehouse, the deceased being named on both plaques as Lucifer Aquatari, and a third associated plaque of a water carrier; Tomb 43 had an interior black and white mosaic depicting ships, perhaps the deceased's occupation or perhaps metaphorically suggesting the life course reaching death; outside Tomb 78 were mounted two terracotta plaques and a marble inscription, the plaques depicting a man operating a horse mill and a large boat rowed by three oarsmen under the instruction of a cox at the tiller, presumably being the tomb of a miller or baker or of a shipper of grain and flour, named Tiberius Claudius Eutychus who was buried there with his wife Claudia Memnonidi according to the inscription; Tomb 86 had an interior black and white mosaic of two people in a boat; Tomb 90 contained a sarcophagus whose front panel had a scene of a harbour and workers, and drinkers in a quayside tavern; and finally, Tomb 100 had two plaques outside, one depicting a midwife delivering a baby, the other depicting a doctor or surgeon and his surgical instruments. All of these occupational artworks were on tombs within a relatively small area of the overall cemetery, as anyone who has visited the site will appreciate.

Two further terracotta plaques were recovered from the cemetery: an inscription to Calpurnia Ptolemais and Lucius Calpurnius Ianuarius was on a tomb with two terracotta plaques depicting uncrewed masted ships. An image on part of a plaque of the lower halves of two walking male figures from Tomb H has been identified as being of two porters, though the former occupation of the tomb occupant cannot be gauged from this partial image on its own.

From the necropolis of Via Ostiense at Ostia comes the so-called Nurse's Sarcophagus discussed further below. In addition, though found in two pieces, at two different locations inside the town, the funerary relief of Septimis Stratonice, probably a *sutrix* or shoemaker, must have either been removed from the Via Ostiense necropolis and reused or the stone was never put in place on a grave and was subsequently broken up for reuse.

Of course, in the town itself images of workers and professionals, sometimes subsumed in the identity of a commercial corporation or organisation, appeared on many black and white mosaics. The mosaics in the Baths of the *Cisarii* or coachmen have already been described above in Chapter Six. On the floor of the *Aula dei Mensores* or Hall of the Grain Measurers was a large third-century AD black and white mosaic showing three *mensores* overseeing the measuring of grain in a huge *modius* or corn measure, as a young boy signals to two porters to bring in the sacks of grain they are carrying (Plate 74). The subject was altogether appropriate for this busy trading hall. The many illustrative black and white mosaics that decorated the *Piazzale delle Corporazioni*, a business forum around which were ranged the offices of as many as forty to sixty trading and shipping companies based in the town and dealing with various goods, included at least four bearing images of sea-going merchant ships, one including a depiction of a dock worker transferring a wine amphora that he carries on his shoulder from a sea-going vessel to a river-going boat or vice versa.[5] Again, a scene of an official loading grain appears here, as do images of African elephants, another type of cargo brought into the port from overseas to satisfy the Roman public's appetite for animal shows. The trading of exotic megafauna such as this was a lucrative business, as will be discussed further below. Epigraphic evidence tells us that among the many *corpora* or corporations and *collegia* or guilds trading from here were ones with links to Narbonne in Gaul, Terracina in Italy, and to a number of towns in Libya, Tunisia, Algeria, and Egypt in North Africa. One company, managed by Clodius Primigenius and Claudius Crescente, specialised in *stuppatores restiones*, that is flax sail and rope trading. But was the *Piazzale delle Corporazioni* in any way a public space or was it a restricted area where the images spoke *of* and *to* only the select group who worked and traded here?

Still in the town of Ostia itself, a terracotta plaque of a crewed ship with sail up remains in situ today on Building III 14, 4, known as the *Casa di Annio*, home of Annius Felix, beneath an inscription which reads *Omnia Felicia Anni*, the Annii family being well known around the Mediterranean littoral and as far afield as the Indian Ocean as traders in luxury goods. A second, very worn, plaque on the building appears to show in the background a man sitting at a desk with a large ceramic vessel or basket on the floor in the foreground.

A number of stone reliefs from the town itself variously portray: a scene of the sale of produce and poultry from Via della Foce, perhaps a shop sign; a scene of the sale of bread from a trestle table; part of a funerary relief with images of two sows to one side and a butcher chopping up meat in his shop on the other; a scene of someone selling bread or buying bread in a bakery; a scene of two men in what might be a marble cutter's workshop; an inscribed stone to Publius Celerius Amandus with images of boat-making tools under the inscription; the upper part of a relief with a winged figure on it, above being a scene of work, with men carrying off sacks; a stone with tools on it; and part of a relief of a man carrying a basket over his back. All of these were catalogued by Gerhard Zimmer in the 1980s.

There is no doubt that Ostia/Portus for many decades represented virtually a commercial suburb of Rome and it therefore should come as no surprise that such a large number of occupational images comes from the town and its cemeteries. Unfortunately while visitors to the *Necropoli di Porto* site can view many of the original tomb plaques and in some cases casts of them in situ, most of the other items bearing Roman occupational images from the town itself are in the museum stores there and not on permanent display in the museum itself.

Away from Rome and Ostia the largest clusters of workers' images come from Aquileia, Milan, and Bologna. From Aquiliea in north-eastern Italy, once a great port outlet to the Adriatic Sea, come ten funerary monuments now in the *Museo Archeologico Nazionale* there with representations of a butcher, a potter or pottery dealer, a locksmith and another metalworker, a stone mason, a wheelwright, a boat builder, and a shipping merchant. From Milan come eight examples, including material in the *Museo Civico Archeologico* and *Castello Sforzesco*, and one further item built into the *Porta Nuova* during its restoration. These include grave stele of a butcher, three stele bearing images of textile trading, a stele of a leatherworker, and an image on the side of a sarcophagus of a leather worker in a workshop. From Bologna come at least four examples, derived from one of the *necropoli* of Roman Bologna, but being part of a larger collection known to Italian archaeologists as the *Muro del Reno* group (literally 'the wall of the (River) Reno'), discovered almost serendipitously built into a later Roman flood defence. Represented here are a butcher, a baker, a grain factor, and a builder.

Significant groupings of occupational images also occur in France, Belgium, and Germany. From Dijon come memorials to a butcher, a wine merchant, at least one bar owner, two horse traders, and two carriers or carters. From Sens in northern France come grave memorial reliefs including: a worker treading cloth in a fulling mill to wash or felt it, wall plasterers or painters, a clerk or record keeper, perhaps in a textile workshop, holding a stylus and writing tablets, a metalworker, an individual examining metal items in a workshop or shop, a mason, a cobbler, and at least one wine merchant. From Arles and Avignon, closely sited and both on the Rhône, come four relevant pieces, from Arles consisting of a relief of two men tying up a huge bundle of goods for shipping, as at Augsburg, a small ceramic model of a similar scene, and part of a funerary monument carrying a depiction of tools, while from near Avignon comes the famous funerary relief scenes of men hauling a river barge and of the storage of shipped wine amphorae in a shipper's warehouse. From Épinal come three funerary reliefs depicting what is possibly the preparation of medicinal products, including the famous *Meditrina* relief discussed in Chapter Nine. From Metz, among a number of relevant images on funerary monuments (Plates 75–76), there is a stele of a female doctor, again discussed more fully later in the book. Other centres in France with smaller clusters of occupational images include Bordeaux, Reims, Bourges, and Narbonne.

From Arlon in Belgium come funerary monuments (Plate 77) with images of brewing, fulling, cloth trading, vegetable selling, three scenes of accounting, and images of those involved in transportation.

In Germany, in the territory of the Treveri at Igel stands the Secundinii family funerary monument known today as the

Igeler Säule or Igel Column which was discussed in detail in Chapter Three and which is decorated with many scenes relating to textile production, transportation, selling, and accounting (Plates 78–79). From Trier itself come funerary monuments again bearing images of accounting and of the transportation of goods.

Roman burial grounds lay along the roads outside the towns and cities and were organised into plots which were set out sometimes along several lines running parallel to the road. The plots were marked by stone boundary markers, fences, or hedges. Each plot was owned by an individual, a family, or a group of individuals who shared the same profession, sometimes these plots being owned by occupational *collegia*. Plots were not all necessarily the same size. As might be expected the size of each plot reflected the wealth, status, and aspirations of its owner or owners. Burials within plots could be simply marked by wooden markers, amphora necks, or memorial stones or be commemorated by stele or tombstones or funerary altars or by monumental structures incorporating statuary. From the late Republic onwards there was a trend towards the building of imposing and thus highly visible funerary monuments among the elite and the most successful of the freedmen class, both in Rome and more broadly in Roman Italy.

Another type of Roman burial that has not been explicitly considered in the book so far is that of the *columbarium* tomb, a type of collective underground tomb with stacked niches for burial that was particularly a phenomenon of Augustan Rome,[6] though such tombs are also known at Ostia and Puteoli. The design of such tombs meant that artworks were seldom commissioned for placement here but the very collective nature of these burial places makes discussion of them here very relevant. Due to space, burial spots were usually identified by a funerary inscription which was usually 'cursory and formulaic', but which often included a professional title or affiliation, demonstrating just how important occupation was as a marker of Roman identity even at this relatively early period. A recent study of *columbarium* tombs has suggested that collective burial fostered group cohesion in certain sections of Roman society at the time, the group taking primacy over the individual to some extent. Almost exactly 500 *columbarium* epitaphs name the deceased's profession, less important percentage wise in the overall assemblage of epitaphs from Roman *columbaria* than legal status and familial and social relationships but more important than age at death. This seems to me a surprising statistic as a quantified marker of the construction of social identity at this time. Four times more men named their profession than women, and four times more slaves did so than freedmen. These figures probably indicate that occupational identity was particularly important for the self-perception of both men and slaves.

Where occupational groupings can be discerned in *columbarium* tombs they seem to be linked to either the burial of a shared household group or a group brought together through their association in a *collegium*. However, only six of the known tombs had any significant clusters of numbers of workers. As an example of a household group we can cite the case of Musicus, an imperial steward, buried in the Vigna Codini *Columbarium* 3 with sixteen of his under-slaves, including three secretaries, two financial officers, a household quartermaster, a cashier, two bedchamber servants, two attendants, a dresser, two cooks, a doctor, and a woman without professional title. It would appear that the Vigna Codini *Columbarium* 2 was owned by the *collegium symphoniacorum*, an association of musicians.

In many respects, the clustering of artisans or of particular trades in specific neighbourhoods in Roman towns was mirrored by the clustering of the same kinds of people at death in Roman cemeteries and burial grounds and at an earlier period in *columbaria*, as we have just seen. Just as some elite persons might never have set foot in the working parts of town, so they might have expected that such social segregation would continue after their death. While Horatius Balbus of Sarsina in northern Italy wanted to be seen to be generous and magnanimous in donating some of his owned grave plots to fellow citizens, his prescriptive list of those who need not apply showed that keeping up appearances would still have been important to him even as worms ate his flesh.

The Tomb of Eurysaces the Baker and the Tomb of the Haterii, both in Rome, and the Igel Column for the Secundinii family in Gallia Belgica mark extremes where wealth trumped status, and elite monuments were erected by non-elite individuals and their families. Many of the stele of Roman workers and professionals discussed in this book were relatively small and modest: however, some, particularly from the Roman towns of northern Italy, were very large indeed. For example: the stele of Longidienus the boatbuilder from Ravenna is 2.66m high; that of the *purpurarius* or dyer Caius Pupius from Parma is 2.28m high; and that of the wheelwright or cart builder Quintus Minicius from Turin is 1.58m high. These stele, and others like them in northern Italy, were made to be seen.

There is an astonishing degree of connectivity at play here: within certain towns; between certain towns; spatially in other ways, along certain road, river, and sea routes; on a regional level; and on a specialised level in terms of the defining of certain aspects of Roman material culture. This study has not just been about discussing individual workers or professionals but has also been concerned with the networks, both formal and informal, which sometimes connected them. The knowledge that we have of these networks is of course constrained by the location and rate of archaeological discoveries, but nevertheless sketchy block models of some of these networks can be drawn and they can be located in the social spaces of Roman society, and their formations can be tracked chronologically. There is not perhaps quite enough data to talk about components and seek evidence of cohesion or to talk of mechanisms and ties generated, but the information is all there in the growing body of Roman funerary monuments of workers, artisans, and professionals.

We cannot know how viewers of the grave monuments of workers and professionals reacted to the monuments and their clear messages about individual identity and broader identifications, with an informal or formal group. Viewers could have understood this, been baffled, or viewed the monument with complete indifference. An elite viewer might have displayed condescension, or an image could have stirred class hatred. The shared meanings generated across time by the creation of networks would have encompassed symbols, images, objects, and practices. Those outside the network might have felt somehow excluded, even if only initially, being unfamiliar with the sedimented layers of meaning which had accumulated over time. They might have felt estranged and quite unsure of how to react. Such funerary monuments might have appeared to an outsider strange, deviant, or exotic, much like the range of prescribed professions on the monument of Horatius Balbus.

Professionals like merchants, shippers, and traders often had access to new types of goods and became familiar with craft practices like painting *tituli picti* on amphorae or stamping samian vessels with potters' stamps. An interdisciplinary approach to the analysis of historic consumption, interpreting patterns discerned by the study of basic historical data in the form of probate inventories – taken at the time of death and recording the household and/or trade goods of the deceased – has been taken by Lorna Weatherill in her groundbreaking study *Consumer Behaviour and Material Culture in Britain 1660–1760* and this study can almost certainly provide a model for undertaking similar work on the material culture of the Roman world.[7]

While the value of any model lies in the quantity and quality of the available data against which it can be tested, a general reticence among Roman archaeologists up to now to undertake theoretical studies of this kind seems untenable given the undoubted value of the database from the empire. However, for the Roman world we cannot to any great extent match the kind of data provided by Weatherill's inventories, with their room by room lists of items and possessions providing a snapshot of a particular house's contents at a very precise date, at the time of their owner's death.

Weatherill's study principally involved the examination of the acquisition and take-up of new goods in Britain over a crucial one hundred years period when an early modern consumer society can be said to have emerged. This she achieved by the identification of key goods which had to be consistently listed in the inventories, and which had to be representative of other types of goods or of domestic behaviour. The goods selected for such further full analysis included basic furniture and utensils (tables, pewter, and cooking pots) to newly available goods like china. The presence of some items, like knives and forks or utensils for hot drinks, suggested gradual changes in eating and drinking habits. The ownership of books and clocks indicated cultural interests and contacts with the wider world.

Her analysis of her data allowed her to discuss a number of broader issues, both hierarchical and social ones, such as the roles of status, occupation, and wealth in the processes of consumption, as well as geographical ones such as the significance of place of residence, forms of regional variation, and the contrast between town and country. These discussions allowed for some analysis and perspective of changes over time, leading to an appreciation of the processes behind the spread of new goods throughout British society at that time. The potential worth of a model based on Weatherill's work transposed back to the Roman world is considerable. Though quite obviously objects listed in inventories and objects recovered by archaeological excavation have very different values – one is notional, a solid object represented only by lines of writing, the other quite solid and real – the broad framework of interpretation can still be applied.

Weatherill surprisingly found that consumption hierarchies and social hierarchies did not completely correspond, as might have been expected, with traders and merchants being higher in the consumption hierarchy, that is tending to be the earliest possessors of new types of goods, than the gentry and others of a higher social status, indicating that the often-quoted theory of social emulation and display as a dynamic force behind the acquisition and ownership of certain types of new goods was perhaps too simplistic.

In terms of the present study it would appear that a new freedman and freedwoman business class did emerge in Rome in the later Republic and did take the opportunity both to acquire new goods and to acquire cultural territory that had formerly been the exclusive preserve of the Roman elite, including certain types of funerary commemoration. Elite burial commemoration usually involved the provision of contextual information about the deceased, involving names, titles, familial associations, other relationships, and often offices held and honorary titles. The need to evoke context on freedmen memorials led to different strategies of contextualisation being employed, among which was the use of occupational titles and sometimes collegial affiliations. This seems a natural progression and one that presumably met little serious opposition. Weatherill's model of new goods and new ideas spreading through the contact networks of merchants and traders is an appealing way to explain how a Roman and Italian phenomenon of visualising occupational identity became a similar but different phenomenon in Roman Gaul and Germany in particular.

In Chapter Three it was noted that there is a certain amount of written evidence, including evidence from inscriptions, to allow tentative discussion of the topographical location of the leather working and shoemaking trades in Rome. That we can start to talk about the zoning of certain trades and industries in individual towns is a good starting point for being able to understand the social and cultural geography of these centres, and not just their physical make-up of streets, public buildings, houses, and infrastructure. A recent study of urban craft zoning in the Roman world[8] concluded that the apparent clustering of properties with similar craft or industrial structures and equipment could be attested archaeologically at three very different Roman towns far apart across the empire, at Pompeii in Italy, at Silchester in Britain, and at Timgad in North Africa.

However, when it comes to textual and other evidence for clustering such as inscriptions, then almost inevitably the best evidence is from Rome, including the kind of toponymical evidence such as that equating the name *Vicus Sandaliarius* with shoemaking and the *Vicus Lorarius* with harness making, again as already discussed in an earlier chapter. However, while original street and neighbourhood names can become fixed in time in any town or city at any period, as so often happens the character of a neighbourhood and its economic raison d'etre can change over time, sometimes slowly and almost imperceptibly, sometimes rapidly. Indeed, both Aulus Gellius and Galen described the *Vicus Sandaliarius* as lined with booksellers in the second century AD, yet the name had not changed: the sandal and shoemakers themselves had apparently simply moved on by then. Similarly, the *Vicus Tuscus* was written about as being a centre of shops of various kinds, including fine clothes sellers and booksellers, but which later was renamed the *Vicus Thurarius*, presumably because of a growing specialisation there in the making and selling of incense. Other attested '*vicus*' names in Rome suggesting clusters of craftsmen or traders whose profession was mirrored in the place name of their neighbourhood include the *vicus cornicularius* (horn workers), the *vicus materiarius* (carpenters and woodworkers), the *vicus iugarius* (yoke makers), the *vicus mundiciei* (makers and sellers of toilet articles and luxuries), the *vicus unguentarius* (perfumers), the *vicus argentarius* (silversmiths or bankers), and the *vicus vitrarius* (glass makers and sellers). It was not all yoke makers in the *Vicus Iugarius,* as a *purpurarius* (dealer in purple stuffs) is also recorded as trading there.

Toponyms such as these were not always attached to specialist streets, possibly because of the cultural or emotional value of a particular pre-existing name, as was probably the case with the *Via Sacra* which is reported by ancient sources as being a centre of jewellery making and selling. Gaius Ateilius Euhodus, a *margaritarius* or pearl merchant was based there, along with at least seven other pearl sellers, as was the goldsmith Marcus Caedicius Eros, Sellia Epyre sold gold decorated garments there, and the *gemmarius* or gem seller Lucius Albius Thaemella was based there. Indeed, five other gem merchants from there were buried together, their commemorative inscription confirming their link with the area. Abudia Megiste, described as a *negotiatrix* in corn and vegetables in her commemorative funerary inscription is recorded as trading *ab scala mediana*, that is 'at the middle stairs'. In *Velabrum*, below the Palatine Hill, Publius Sergius Demetrius and Gaius Clodius Euphemus had a wine business. *Ab luco lubitina* was Aulus Calvius, a cloth merchant. Wool merchant Gaius Vergilius Gentius was nearby.

Another formula for indicating artisanal or trading clusters in Rome was the use in written sources and in inscriptions of the words *in* and *inter*, here respectively meaning in and among: thus someone described as *in figlinis* or *inter figulos* would have been working in a pottery or among potters, and such formulae are known applied to bronzesmiths, scythe makers, carpenters, and basketmakers for instance.

Various other types of purpose-built commercial and mercantile structures and centres in Rome such as fora and markets (*macella*), warehouses (*horrea*), atriums, basilicas and porticoes often carried specialised names, indicating trading clusters, if not necessarily also manufacturing ones. As was mentioned earlier, Saint Augustine in his *De Civitate Dei* referred to '... the streets of silversmiths' as a broad generalisation, implying that such specialist streets could be found in many of the towns across the Roman empire. In the *horrea Agrippiana* or warehouse of Agrippa there would appear to have been a cluster of cloth merchants or textile dealers. Aurelia Nais, a freedwoman, was a fishmonger or *piscatrix* at the Galba warehouse, the *horreis Galbae,* where Gaius Tullius Crescens the marble merchant and Aulus Cornelius Priscus the cloakseller were also based.

The text of the lengthy Edict of the Prefect Tarracius Bassus of c. AD 375–76, part of the inscribed version of which is in the *Musei Capitolini* in Rome, provides a long list of names and locations in the city of shopkeepers – the *tabernarii* – and artisans 'who took for themselves (contrary to Roman customs and neglecting the edicts of prefects in the city) public money, seats at the games to which they were not entitled, and the bread of the people.' Obviously patience was running very thin at this time.

Together, this and other epigraphic evidence from Rome constitutes a considerable body of data about the economic geography of the city and its trades and workers. Roman urban life seems to have been very much shaped by the topography of work and business. Given that so many districts, streets, and buildings in Rome were named in this way and thus in the minds of all citizens connected to artisanal activity it is difficult to identify with the academic concept that such people were somehow 'invisible Romans'.⁹ But did these clusters come about through some sort of economic serendipity or was there some kind of centralised control, either by light touch or by prescription and official censure? Of course, in the case of a polluting trade such as tanning rules and regulations would appear to have been in place in Rome to restrict this industry to certain locations, though the resources and infrastructure required by the tanning industry would already have made its location perhaps as dependent on physical factors as on health and safety issues. For many craft and artisanal operations there would have been no split in terms of requiring separate sites for workshop and/or shop and residential accommodation: one property would be all that was necessary for the one man or woman or family-run operations. Therefore it would seem that to some extent the elite of the towns could dictate the locations and functions of shops or workshops, both by the use of direct legislation or in their role as property owners and landlords, and they could do this equally in terms of encouraging certain trades to locate in certain properties or areas and in discouraging other trades from doing so, thus displacing them.

There is a general lack of evidence for artisanal clustering away from Rome, perhaps not altogether surprisingly, though it has been suggested that this can at least be proven to have occurred at towns elsewhere in Italy, in Greece, Asia Minor, Judaea, and in Egypt, evidence from the latter in the form of papyrus records proving the most compelling. On the border of one of the late fifth to early sixth century AD Yakto *Megapsychia* mosaics in the *Hataj Arkeoloji Muzesi* in Antakya, Turkey is depicted a vibrant urban street scene, of a commercial district alive with taverns and the cries of fishmongers, butchers, and bakers. A similar vibrant scene, this time of quayside trading involving the sale of mussels and seafood and of wine from amphorae stored upright in sand, appears on the third century AD Oceanus Mosaic from a villa at Bad Kreuznach near Mainz in Germany and now on display in the *Römerhalle* there.

Occupational Associations

The emphasis in this book very much has been on the individual and on his or her identity as articulated through the presentation of the work or professional role of that person. While local circumstances might have created the situations where the first non-elite people were able to publicly express their identity in this way through the commissioning of particular new types of funerary monuments, as time progressed it was more likely that the impetus came from the individual's membership of a *collegium*, a professional college or guild, of some kind. Because of the importance of such organisations it will be appropriate to now examine their origins and influence, particularly in the light of much recent scholarship which has placed the *collegia* at the very heart of the Roman economic system.[10]

A *collegium* was a formal organisation, of three or more members, with legal status and could take the form of a professional guild, a religious organisation, a social club, or even simply be what are termed burial clubs, organisations whose sole purpose was to facilitate the saving of money by its members to pay for burial and/or a funerary monument, the club, after an individual member's death, taking on an organisational responsibility for carrying out the deceased's plans. Such organisations began in the Republican period and continued in importance thereafter. Some of the bigger and more significant *collegia* often committed themselves to carrying out what might best be termed public services in return for immunities from taxes and for other specific privileges.

The *collegium pistorum* or college of bakers in Rome had considerable economic, social, and political importance in the city and evolved from a purely professional association into a semi-official body which oversaw and regulated the bread supply in the city. So significant was this role that a member of the *collegium* was assigned a seat in the Senate. Other *collegia* given rights and privileges above and beyond those of most such organisations included the *corpus piscatorum et urinatorum totius alu(ei)Tiber (is)*, that is the *collegia* of Tiber river fishermen and divers whose existence is attested by no fewer than four dedicatory inscriptions from Rome.

At Rome other formally constituted professional colleges included: the *collegium saliarium* or shoemakers; the *collegium vasculariorum* or metal-vessel-makers; the *collegium vinariorum* or wine merchants; the *collegium castrensialorium* or victualers; the *collegium centonariorum* or textile and rag dealers; the *collegium farnariorum* or mowers; and the *collegium communionis minirum* or actors. At Ostia an inscription refers to Marcus Licinius Privatus, the *magister* or head of the *collegium fabrum tignuariorum* or college of carpenters, though later he would appear to have been treasurer of the bakers' guild there, demonstrating that multiple affiliations were possible across *collegia*. Remarkably a dedicatory inscription to the *collegium fabrorum* has also been found in Chichester, in southern England. Dedicated to Neptune and Minerva at their temple in the town the dedicatee was Tiberius Claudius Cogidubnus, along with the guild.

Collegia or individual members of a *collegium* could and did sponsor public building works and religious rites. In the late third century AD the emperor Aurelian placed legal prohibitive curbs on the activities of *collegia* by making membership of what had been previously voluntary associations life-long and certain public duties compulsory.

Of course, an organisation like a *collegium* could also serve to exclude certain people and to hamper their business or affect their livelihood. Certain *collegia* found themselves subject to official scrutiny, to official approval, or to official disapproval. The privileges of the *collegium fabrorum*, that is of master builders, were at one time curbed under Antoninus Pius, presumably after labour unrest. Yet by the early third century AD an inscription tells us that they were actively involved in *gratis* public building work at the Baths of Caracalla in Rome.

Callistratus, writing in the early third century AD, referred to certain *collegia* which were 'instituted to provide services required for public needs'.[11] There was no more pressing public need than the smooth running of the *annona* or food distribution charity created under the Republic and resurrected with varying degrees of enthusiasm and for various motives by many of the subsequent emperors. If the account in the *Scriptores Historiae Augustae* can be believed the emperor Severus Alexander (AD 222–35) can be credited with the establishment of quite strict official oversight of many of the Roman corporations such as wine merchants, greengrocers, cobblers, and even lupin sellers.[12]

Finally, it should be noted here that through their work in *collegia* many local freedmen businessmen found the opportunity to bolster their personal professional identities further, and further still if they used *collegium* administrative responsibilites and position as a springboard to religious magistracy in the form of being appointed to the post of *Sacerdotes Augustales*. The *Augustales* was an order of priesthood established by Tiberius to manage the imperial cult, often very significant on a local level in the provinces, away from Rome.[13] A number of the freedmen 'workers' discussed in this book proudly proclaimed their holding of this largely honorary title in their funerary epitaphs and indeed it was also suggested above that attainment of this particular religious magistracy might have been seen by some richer freedmen as a more significant identifier of their personal identity than was their profession. There is no doubt that *collegia* were significant social groupings which 'institutionalized social mobility. They allowed successful businessmen to transform economic capital into social and symbolic capital – influence, honour and prestige'.[14]

Enchainment

Because of the nature of certain aspects of the Roman economy, where ideological and cultural considerations outweighed issues like cost, efficiency, and effort, and because of the geographic extent of the empire and the diversity of its raw materials, the inter-relationships of workers in some fields were far more complex than that of clusters, networks, and associations; indeed, in some instances we might better describe these inter-relationships as a kind of enchainment. While it is easy to understand the consideration of gold and silver by the Romans as luxury materials, and thus valuable ones, it is impossible to consider, for instance, porphyry stone, *murex* shells, and exotic wild animals as anything other than culturally defined luxury items, without an obvious financial value other than in that contemporary society. Yet the discovery, exploitation, trade, and use of these latter three commodities created extraordinary linking chains across the Roman world, as significant as any economic clusters and networks we have discussed so far. People in these chains never would have met but they were linked nevertheless and would have achieved linked identities in the process. Using these three luxury commodities I would now like to briefly explore how each enchainment allowed for, or mitigated against, the expression of a specific work identity in each category and context, bearing in mind that the nature of the evidence does not allow all those discussed as being in a chain or linked together to have been necessarily contemporary. The chains are simply illustrative in nature.

Porphyry stone, the true 'Imperial Purple' stone,[15] comes from six quarries at a single location in the eastern desert of Egypt at a site that came to be known to the Romans as *Mons Porphyrites*, the road leading westwards from the quarries to Quena, Roman *Maximianopolis*, on the Nile, being known as the *Via Porphyrites*. Though other types of porphyry stone had been mined nearby by the Ptolemys the motherlode of true imperial porphyry was not found and exploited until AD 18 it would seem, when a Roman military surveyor called Caius Cominius Leugas is recorded as having discovered it. We are told as such by a remarkable dedicatory inscription left by Leugas to commemorate his founding of a temple there to Pan/Min (the Egyptian equivalent) and Serapis. This is the only record we have from the Roman world of a geological surveyor whose skills and knowledge were vital to Rome in scoping out the natural resources of newly conquered territories to maximise revenue for Rome. It is not one of our workers' images as such but rather an image in Egyptian style of the ithyphallic god Pan/Min, distinguishable by his plumed crown and flail, standing next to an eighteen-line inscription in Greek telling us that: 'Caius Cominius Leugas discovered the quarries of porphyry stone and the knekites and black porphyry and ... found also many-coloured stones and dedicated a sanctuary to Pan and Serapis, very great gods, for the well-being of his children.' The last three lines very precisely place the date as 23 July AD 18 in our calendar.

Because the quarrying here was an imperial monopoly that continued until the mid-fourth century AD the context and opportunity for the celebration of self identity through art and epigraphy must have been constricted, if not actually restricted. We certainly know that many of the hundreds of workers here living in the associated settlements would have been slave labourers and condemned criminals, including many Christians and Jews, as described by Aelius Aristides writing about the Egyptian quarries in the second century AD. But evidence also points towards many free, wage labourers being employed here, the whole operation probably being under military supervision. For instance, in the mid-third century AD an inscription was made in the Lycabettos quarry by Pancratius, a *centurio frumentarius*, a military officer, and a list of sentry duties was found inscribed on a potsherd here. Hundreds of these inscribed potsherds, known to archaeologists as *ostraca* (singular:*ostracon*), have been recovered from the quarry settlements, only a few of which reference individuals, though one *ostracon* carries a list of occupations represented at the site, including '... bellowsmen, storekeepers, hammerers, bakers, firewood collectors, carpenters, and a herald', and a single fourth century AD gravestone from the cemetery of the Lycabettos settlement was dedicated to a Christian, 'John from the hamlet of Nilos of the Hermopolite'.[16]

The enchained process in this particular case involved the discovery of the stone source, the quarrying of the stone itself, its shipping within Egypt, its shipping overseas to Italy, its transportation within Italy, its working, and its employment on imperial projects or in imperial contexts such as the use of porphyry for imperial sarcophagi. Different kinds of workers from many localities and towns would have been involved in the process.

The dye produced from the processing of *murex* shells – sea snail shells – of certain sorts became the 'purple' or purple dye that in its best form of Tyrian Purple became known as 'imperial purple'.[17] In this case the chain therefore stretched from the shores of the eastern Mediterranean and especially sites in Syria along the Levantine coastline to towns in Roman Italy such as Rome and Parma, as we have seen, and to the Roman imperial court. In Chapter Three I discussed the epigraphic evidence for traders in purple and for specialist dyers in this material and would refer the reader back to the appropriate section there to perhaps reconsider the evidence for such people operating in Italy as being evidence for the end part of another system of enchainment linking workers in one part of the empire with those in another.

Of the three systems of enchainment that I have chosen as examples to discuss here the commodification and trade in exotic wild animals – sometimes called charismatic megafauna – provides the most evidence for the linking of workers across two continents.[18]

As the Romans considered these living creatures as economic, cultural, and social commodities and political and ideological capital, so I will consider them as such here also. I have discussed the Roman trade in wild animals in some detail in one of my previous books – *Cave Canem: Animals and Roman Society* – but will briefly consider here some of the same information from a different perspective, looking at the workers involved in the trade rather than the animals and their terrible fate.

The most exotic wild beasts required for the Roman arenas came from North Africa and it is here that we find evidence for the existence of numerous hunting sodalities, as they have become called, who forged their own distinct identities, often in opposition to their rivals rather than simply in terms of self identity. The attested sodalities include the *Leontii*, the *Pentasii*, the *Tauriscii*, the *Sinematti*, the *Perexii*, the *Tharaxii*, the *Ederii*, and the *Decasii*. However, the most famous of these, represented by inscriptions on both stone and on a number of mosaic pavements were undoubtedly the *Telegenii*. Their name appears most famously inscribed on the so-called Magerius Mosaic from a large residential house at Smirat, Tunisia and now in the *Musée Archéologique de Sousse*. The main image on the mosaic is of an arena *venatio* or animal combat, a bloody combat between four leopards and four fighters with spears. All four fighters are individually named by captions, as are the four leopards. Two deities or actors dressed as deities oversee the contest, as does Magerius himself who is again identified by a caption. A herald with a tray of money to pay the combatants and the animal providers makes an announcement to the crowd lauding Magerius for providing this lavish entertainment spectacle and the *Telegenii* for realising his wishes in this way. At the end of this extraordinary speech the herald declares: 'This is what it means to be rich! That's what it is to be powerful! Yes, that's really it! It's getting dark now, may the *Telegenii* be sent back from your *munus* with their bags full of money!'

The heads of five hunting sodalities appear pictured drinking sociably together on a third century AD mosaic from a building near the amphitheatre at El Djem, again in Tunisia, this mosaic now being on display in the *Musée National du Bardo* in Tunis. While not named by inscriptions in this instance, each leader is nevertheless identified by the sodality's sign or symbol, the *Telegenii* representative being identifiable by the staff with a crescent moon. 'We three are getting along fine' the *Telegenii* leader declares.

The trade in exotic animals for the arena continued in a lesser form up to almost the mid-fifth century AD, when in AD 439 the Vandals seized the Roman's North African provinces and subsequently held power there for almost one hundred years. It has been suggested that the Telegenii had such an established and sophisticated trading and shipping network to support their hunting activity that they also subsequently and perhaps inevitably became involved in the shipping of other goods and lucrative commodities such as olive oil, though the direct evidence for this is rather slight. The name *Telegenii* is recorded in formal inscriptions, on mosaics, and even in the form of stamped mottos on pottery vessels, not only at Smirat but also at Sousse, Timgad, El Djem, Carthage, and across the Sahel.

While the North African hunting sodalities discussed above provided animals and fighters for the arenas of their native North Africa they also, of course, supplied animals to be shipped to Italy and elsewhere in the empire. Extraordinary scenes of the hunting, capture, shipping, loading and unloading of exotic animals are depicted on a number of mosaics from the Roman palatial villa at Villa del Casale, Piazza Armerina in Sicily. On the so-called Great Hunt mosaic there we can see captured animals being carried away in cages loaded onto the back of carts. It is generally accepted that the owner of the villa was somehow involved in this trade or its administration and oversight, as would have been thousands of hunters, shippers, animal keepers and so on. Specialised shippers of these North African wild animals were also based in the *Piazzale delle Corporazioni* in Ostia, as has been previously mentioned, where a mosaic pavement depicting an elephant pictorially portrays their trade to the public. Again, as an additional example, a third century AD inscription from Noricum in Austria tells us that the prominent local family the Albii were involved in the animal trade.

Even other people not directly involved could be inadvertently drawn into such chains. Pliny the Elder tells us that the famous first century BC sculptor Pasiteles while sketching caged wild beasts in transit on the Tiber dockside was mauled and almost killed by an escaped leopard.

Large *vivaria* or animal holding enclosures and pens are attested as having been present in Rome, near the Porta Praenestina for example. Inscriptions from the city refer to roles here for an *adiutor ad feras* (wild beast keeper) and a *praepositus herbariarum* (herbivore keeper), the latter role played at one time by Aurelius Sabinus. Some distance outside Rome, at Laurentum, there would appear to have been extensive holding and breeding facilities for animals intended for the arena. Inscriptions make mention of specialised animal keepers here such as a *procurator Laurento ad elephantos* (elephant keeper), a role at one time played by Tiberius Claudius Spec(u)lator, and a *praepositus camellorum* (camel keeper), a title once held by Titus Flavius Stephanus. These might have been official establishments, or they might have been private commercial concerns. In some instances, wild and exotic animals may have been bred or brought to maturity in captivity in or near Rome for the arena.

The two final links in this third chain of professional connections involved the men who fought and killed such beasts in the arena and those who butchered their carcasses for meat and other by-products, the latter group having been discussed in Chapter Two.

Working Women

There is an extraordinary group of images of Roman working women, most famously from the Roman port at Ostia, which formed the subject of a ground-breaking and thought-provoking feminist art historical study by Natalie Kampen in the early 1980s which inspired subsequent numerous academic articles on the role of the working woman in the Roman world.[19] To the Ostia examples can be added other significant such representations from the city of Rome itself, from Pompeii, and from some of the provinces, most notably Gaul and Germany, but even from Roman Spain. However, it must be stressed here that even when added together the number of images of working women from the Roman world is minute compared to the number of images of working men. Throughout this book there has been some discussion of the gendered nature of some work in the Roman world and of jobs done by working women, and it would seem appropriate here to talk about these images as a distinct group, albeit one created by academic inquiry. Discussion of these images should be contextualised against the fact that fewer women than men bore occupational titles in the overall body of occupational inscriptions from Rome and these included fewer types of occupation. Of the thirty-five occupations recorded for women most were in services or in textile-related jobs: many of the women named were slaves or freedwomen.

At Ostia Natalie Kampen identified six examples of the representation of working women, according to her definition, all dating to the second and third centuries AD.The creation of these images placed the representation of these women in the public domain, even though some of the funerary items on which some of the images appeared might be more technically thought of as private art. These Ostia representations consisted of nurses or child carers; a midwife; a waitress or barkeeper; a poultry seller; a vegetable seller; and a possible cobbler or shoemaker. I have discussed the female barkeeper above in Chapter Six and the possible female shoemaker in Chapter Three, so I will only describe the other four images here. It has been noted throughout this book that many representations of working men have been found at Ostia too and, indeed, most of these apparently date to roughly the same period, when the port was both prosperous and expanding. Its teeming workforce evidently shared to some extent in this prosperity and in celebrating the status that their jobs gave them within the overall enterprise.

The nurses or child carers appeared as part of the decoration on a now-damaged biographical sarcophagus from Via Ostiense, known as the *Curriculum Vitae* sarcophagus, now in the *Museo Ostiense* collection. The image, to the right of the central scene on the sarcophagus front, is today only partial but it can clearly be seen that three women are engaged here in caring for a number of infant children. One woman holds what appears to be a swaddled baby and looks on while the other two bathe a second child. A large bowl of water sits on the floor, and one woman is caught in the act of lifting a baby out of the bath and into the soft embrace of a towel being held ready by her companion who will now dry the child. This scene needs to be considered in the context of the overall decorative programme of the sarcophagus, as far as it can be surmised, comprising the care of an infant, the teaching of the child, and then the parents either attending the coming of age oration of their child or mourning the deceased youth. Biographical scenes such as these on sarcophagi, including the nursing of children, are so well recorded as to suggest that they were standard tropes rather than specific manifestations of any kind of reality. These images of nurses and carers represented the cadre of such working women and not specific women as such. Although the person of the midwife was largely incidental on such sarcophagi her presence was nevertheless a key component of the decorative programme's encrypted narrative.

The midwife appeared on one of two pendant terracotta reliefs set into the facade of Tomb 100, the tomb of Scribonia Attice, at the *Necropoli di Porto* at Isola Sacra, the cemetery or necropolis area just outside of Ostia, though probably serving Portus. The birthing scene is simply composed and uncluttered with detail but is nonetheless powerful. A naked woman with enlarged belly sits in a chair, supported from behind by another woman. A third female, the midwife, sits on a low stool in front of the mother in labour and reaches up between the open legs of the expectant mother as if caught at the moment of delivering the baby. On the pendant plaque a doctor treats the leg of a patient. It can be assumed from the decoration on the tomb and the dedicatory inscription – stating that it was built by Scribonia Attice for herself, her husband M. Ulpius Amerimnus, her mother Scribonia Callityche, Diocles and her freedmen and their descendants (with the exception of Panaratus and Prosdocia) – that the couple were respectively a midwife and doctor-surgeon. It is interesting that their professional identities were not brought to the viewer's attention in the inscription but rather through the more active representation of their roles via the terracotta images.

The image of the female poultry seller appears on what is known as the Via della Foce relief (Plate 80), a vibrant and busy scene of shop or market trading found at the entrance to a building on that street in the ancient port town. It was possibly a shop sign of some kind and is now in the *Museo Ostiense*. A woman and a man stand behind a stall or counter, with the woman in the foreground and the man partially hidden behind her, thus emphasising the relative importance of the two traders. To one side of the counter is a rack or gibbet on which are hung some chickens or other poultry birds. In front of the woman are two large shallow baskets containing either bread or fruit and vegetables, or indeed both. A tall cylindrical wicker container with clearly delineated air holes cut through it would appear to contain live snails, as shown by the fact that the artist has depicted one snail making its escape from the basket, though this rather large snail may simply be a rebus or ideogram. At the far end of the stall sit two monkeys.

Trade at the stall or shop seems very brisk, with one male customer being caught in the act of being served by the female vendor who holds a piece of fruit in her hand while two other men stand to one side of him, deep in animated conversation, one of these men holding a chicken in one hand that he has already purchased. Finally, in the bottom left of the panel can be seen the heads and telltale raised ears of two live hares or rabbits poking their heads out through the bars of a wooden crate in which they are housed ready for sale.

The relief depicting the vegetable seller, known today as the Episcopo Relief (Plate 81), is sadly without specific provenance, though it can probably be assumed to have come from a funerary monument of some kind, and is again in the *Museo Ostiense*. The depicted scene is less busy than the scene of poultry selling. Nonetheless it has a vibrancy that would have appealed greatly to the Roman viewer. There is only one figure on the relief, the vegetable seller herself, depicted in the very centre of the scene, face-on to the viewer, as if the viewer were indeed a customer at the stall. She stands with her left hand resting on the stall in a proprietary manner and her right hand held up in a gesture as if speaking directly to the viewer. Vegetables are laid out on a trestle table, with a basket beneath it. More produce is stacked on shelves or racks behind, both to the left and right. Some authorities have suggested that the vegetable seller has been misidentified as a woman and is in fact a man.

Although there are only six known working women relief images from Ostia Natalie Kampen was able to divide these images up into two specific categories, with additional reference to the data also provided by the representations of working men from the same town. She identified these two groups as being 'literal scenes' and 'subordinate scenes'. Literal scenes were just that: scenes in which workers were portrayed doing a specific job in a correct and natural context. In such scenes there was usually a plethora of incidental detail and acute observation. As Kampen observed, 'these localize each image enough to make it recognizable to the indigenous population'. The workers indeed would have been able to see themselves in these images and to see their town and their workplaces. However, they were presented as real but not as specific individuals in portrait form in any sense. It may have been though that the viewer, whether the subject herself or not, identified with the role portrayed much more than they would have done with a portrait of an individual. As for the so-called subordinate scenes, they stressed 'something other than work, although [they] may represent work' Kampen believed. In other words they were more complex and sometimes almost metaphorical in intent and reading.

Other notable images of Roman working women from sites other than Ostia include a first century AD funerary relief from Mérida in western Spain, now in the *Museo Nacional de Arte Romano* there, dedicated to Sentia Amaranis by her husband (Plate 82). Described in the inscription on her stele as the dearest wife, she is depicted standing by a huge wine barrel set down lengthways on trestle supports. She holds a jug in one hand, under the barrel tap, and with the other opens the tap to let wine pour out into it. Of the few Roman images of those running or owning bars or taverns this is the only one to have a name inscribed on it.

Also of great interest is an image of a female doctor on a funerary stele from Metz in north-eastern France, now in the *Musée de la Cour D'Or* there (Plate 83). On the stele the woman is portrayed dressed in a heavy cloak and holding a box presumably containing medical equipment, and she is clearly and unequivocally named as a *medica*. Unfortunately the rest of the inscription is damaged and we do not know her name.

If we are to assume that the working women portrayed in most of the works discussed above had some hand in their commissioning and in final approval of their depiction, it does not necessarily follow that every viewer would have taken away from their viewing experience the intended message of the work. A particular, identified strain of erotic voyeurism, a genuine fetishism known as mysophilia, may have been implicit in some male viewings of images of working women, in the past as in today. We only have to look at the extraordinary life of the Victorian barrister and poet Arthur Munby who pursued a lifelong interest in observing, photographing, and befriending working women in hard, physical jobs, a pursuit which was both overt, and therefore deemed to be harmless by his contemporaries, and covert in that few were aware at the time of the obsessive nature and personal sexual connotations of his mysophiliac hobby.[20] Indeed, Munby's hard-working maid, Hannah Cullwick, was in actual fact later revealed to have been his wife, though they lived to all intents and purposes the life of master and servant, in a grotesque form of public and private role playing. To return to the Roman images of working women, while this might appear to be an argument for a particularly curious instance of the male gaze being turned upon a specialised genre of imagery it is one that has not been considered previously in studies such as Natalie Kampen's and I think might be borne in mind when discussing these images today.

As demonstrated by the *Necropoli di Porto* tomb to midwife Scribonia Attice and doctor-surgeon M. Ulpius Amerimnus sometimes professional couples advertised their joint social relationship identity as well as their individual identity and occupational identity. Other examples of this are known, including: Gaius Cassius Sopater, a *linarius* or linen trader and Cassia Domestica, his wife and a *linaria*, in the same occupation, from Milan; from Turin *claviarius* or nailer P. Aebutius was commemorated alongside *clavaria* Cornelia Venusta; and in Rome Cratinus, a *lanipendus* or wool weigher, was commemorated along with Musa, a *quasillaria* or spinner.[21]

If most of the women discussed above chose to identify with their own individual occupational identity through the commissioning of images, there were many more who chose to publicly communicate their business ventures through inscriptions or through the stamping or marking of products. Almost one third of the 149 known Roman brick stamps are of women brickyard owners, including female members of the imperial court at different times, and women's names appear on stamped lead water pipes. A small number of female merchants and ship owners are known from inscriptions.[22]

Professions and Prayers

The vast majority of Roman workers' images discussed in this book have been on funerary monuments of one kind or another, thus linking the idea of the display of professional identity with the religious and social commemoration of the individual. Again, mention has already been made of the link between certain crafts and trades and specific protective gods or goddesses. Sometimes these links between work and religion were even more explicit, as I shall now explore.

This conceptual link between the profane and the sacred was made particularly well in the images employed in a number of probably first century AD wall paintings on the facade of a carpenters' shop and home (Shop VI,7, 8–11) in Pompeii. On the door jambs and nearby were painted images of protective deities including Mercury, Fortuna, and Minerva and on the facade a curious processional scene was painted[23] in which four men are portrayed carrying a large bier on top of which is an open-sided, tent-like structure containing a statue of Minerva and inside which Pygmy carpenters carry out various workshop tasks; one planes a board while two other Pygmies saw a large timber. Less easy to interpret is the presence at one end of the tent of a man, possibly Daedalus, the carpenter deity, standing over a dead body, possibly that of his nephew Perdix.

In other words we are seeing here the enactment of a religious procession to honour both the protective goddess and the craftsmen and craft that she protected. This all seems a highly improbable set up, almost a vision, until one appreciates that the working Pygmy figures inside the tent were in all likelihood actually lightweight painted wooden figures, prepared especially for the procession as images of saints might be today. Obviously this is not a veristic work scene; however, it is still highly significant in terms of its composition and context. The creation of images of Pygmy carpenters may very well have been a similar displacement strategy to the creation of *putti* workers on wall paintings elsewhere in the town and more widely in Roman sarcophagus art. They were both fiction and reality together. Pygmies appeared on numerous wall paintings in Pompeian houses and their appearance here – as painted images of carved wooden objects – should simply be seen perhaps as part of a local cultural practice of referencing Romano-Egyptian decorative fashions. The procession depicted presumably either had taken place already, and this was the depiction of one specific historical event, or such processions were annual affairs, in which case the image would have represented this religious event in a more generalised way. In either case the recording of the event and its depiction was very much within the context of Roman historical narratives more usually employed in imperial art. That the carpenter based in this house chose to display this painting publicly represented the boldest possible statement about his professional identity, his association with other carpenters, perhaps in a guild in the town, and his religious piety.

One particular issue which has been alluded to in passing in a number of places in this book has been whether there were any distinctly Christian images of workers in the Roman period, or if there was any Christianising of images in Late Antiquity, in other words a chronological pattern that can be identified.[24]

At the end of the second century AD the Christian writer Tertullian, from Carthage in North Africa, in his book *De Idololatria* – 'On Idolatry' – set down a series of prescriptions for Christians in certain occupations or lines of work. Those in the building, decorating, and engraving trade were informed that there was enough general building work for them to do without having to resort to making, decorating, or depicting idols, presumably statues of pagan deities. Businessmen were to avoid avarice, no one should set up to train gladiators, and no one should trade in meat from pagan sacrifices. Joining the imperial bureaucracy and, by extension, the army should not be entertained as an idea by a good Christian. In Chapter One I also highlighted the interest shown in the ideological and philosophical aspects of work in the writings of both St Augustine and St Basil, and it is interesting to reflect upon how ideas in theological texts might have been reflected in actual Christian religious practice, particularly the use of imagery, principally, though not exclusively, in the form of frescos and sarcophagus decoration, as a marker of both professional identity and Christian identity. Images of workers as incidental figures to broader events and subservient to more significant protagonists in a small number of Christian works of art have already been discussed above in the case of the Trier *Adventus* Ivory and the *Vienna Dioscorides* illustrated manuscript.

Among the wall paintings in the various Christian catacombs in Rome can be found a small number of images that might have been associated with specific individual workers or professionals, including a doctor or anatomist, an olive oil merchant, a baker or grain merchant, coopers or barrel makers, a carter or carrier, and a vegetable seller. It must be stressed though that these are just a handful of what might best be called 'earthly images' out of hundreds more usually concerned with biblical stories and symbolism. This suggests that occupational identity was not necessarily the most important identity for a Christian to stress in transit to the next life, though it must be noted that not all burials in the catacombs were necessarily of Christians, though the vast majority were. As Christianity aligned itself with learning and literacy there are also numerous images of reading and of teachers and pupils to be found here, and indeed such imagery was also particularly common on carved Christian sarcophagi. Images of reading will be considered as a separate category below in Chapter Nine.

In the *Nuova Catacomba* of Via Latina is the famous fourth century AD painting known today as 'the anatomy lesson', a didactic demonstration being given by an elderly bearded man holding a long wooden pointer and surrounded by attentive pupils using an opened cadaver as a teaching aid, which may mark the burial place of a doctor or surgeon, though more allusive interpretations of the scene can be offered.

In the *Catacomba di Ponziano* a fifth century AD painting carries a depiction of a naked mariner at the oars of a boat or ship transporting amphorae of either olive oil or wine. Presumably this man was a boat owner or a shipper of produce. In the *Catacombe di Domitilla* is the fourth century AD Crypt of the Bakers whose decoration includes a painting of a baker with a bushel full of grain behind him, the landing of sacks of grain, perhaps at the quays on the Tiber, and their unloading onto handbarrows. On the back of the crypt is a portrayal of the multiplication of the loaves and fishes, all of this suggesting that buried here were members of a bakers' guild or of a guild of grain merchants. Obviously a number of Christians worked in this field, as demonstrated by the at one time nearby painted image of a barley dealer at work in a mill which is no longer in situ in the catacomb.

Just inside the entrance to the *Catacombe di Priscilla* can be found what is known to archaeologists today as the Crypt of the Coopers, a fourth century AD burial place perhaps for a *collegium* of barrelmakers or wine merchants, if this can be assumed from a wall painting here that shows two groups each of four men carrying a large barrel using poles on their shoulders, with two other huge barrels depicted on the ground to one side. A probably fourth century AD portrayal of a man on a bullock cart transporting a barrel comes from the *Catacomba Maggiore* and could have been associated with a working carrier or again with a wine merchant. It is uncertain whether the ancillary fourth century burials in the so-called *Arcosolium* of the Vintners in the complex known as the *Hypogeum* of Vibia represent pagan or Christian *collegium* burials, or indeed both. The painted decoration of the vintners' tomb includes images of a man with wineskins, of stacked wine barrels, and of a sea-going cargo ship.

Moving lower down the social scale, in the *Catacombe di S. Callisto* is a fourth century picture of a woman selling vegetables from a stall. A painting of a *fossor* or gravedigger holding a long-handled pick-like implement with a curved blade can be seen at work in a catacomb by the light of a hanging bronze lantern in the *Catacombe dei SS. Marcellino e Pietro* and another *fossor* appears in a painting with his pick at rest over his shoulder, again in the *Catacombe di S. Callisto*.

A number of stone reliefs depicting tools or occupational scenes have also been recovered by excavation in the catacombs. These include: a relief from the *Catacombe di Domitilla* and now in the *Musei Vaticani* in Rome depicting a worker operating bellows at a forge and a smith hammering metal on an anvil; a small later second or third century AD relief depicting a surgeon's toolkit with huge forceps from the *Catacomba di Pretestato;* a fourth century relief panel depicting Eutropos, a maker of sarcophagi in his workshop from the *Catacomba dei SS. Marco e Marcelliano;* and a fourth century relief bearing a scene inside a shop selling metal vessels of different kinds from the same catacomb (Plate 84). A fourth century slab carrying a depiction of a *marmorius* who would seem to have made *opus sectile* pavements is now in the *Museo Nazionale Romano Terme di Diocleziano* in Rome, though it probably derives from one of the catacombs but its exact provenance is unknown. Christian funerary plaques to other workers and professionals included dedications to a number of wine merchants (Plates 60 and 85) and Constantinus the drover or carrier (Plate 86).

In the preface to this book I noted that there has often been a tendency among writers on the Roman economy to use images of workers purely as illustrative material or to sometimes discuss the more detailed of these images simply as illustrations of ancient technical processes rather than representations of personal and professional identity. For instance, the only contemporary decorated funerary monument that we have of a sarcophagus maker was quite recently illustrated and discussed in a publication simply in terms of the use of a drill by the workers depicted. Interesting and informative though that discussion undoubtedly was, it somehow seemed to be missing the point. This inscribed and decorated marble relief of the fourth century AD, now in the *Museo Lapidario, Palazzo Ducale* in Urbino, is an important

Christian artwork in its own right. Pictured standing to one side is the sarcophagus maker himself, bearded, wearing a short tunic and holding what appears to be a beaker in one hand; his other hand is raised up. Under the inscription are two workshop scenes. In the first two masons are seen working on what appears to be a popular contemporary strigillated sarcophagus. The two men are using a bow drill, a chisel rotated by a strap, to cut the marble. In order to do this one is seated on a set of portable wooden steps while the second man manipulates the bow strap. Various other tools, including a large masonry hammer, sit on the floor ready for use. Across the other side of the workshop stands a completed figured sarcophagus whose front comprises a decorated central panel bearing an inscription perhaps and a portrait head, flanked on either side by a panel containing a dolphin, still a popular funerary motif following its adoption as a symbol by Rome's Christian community.

The intertextuality here is quite fascinating, particularly the care taken to represent the form and decoration of both sarcophagi, each a very specific type. Labour, craft skill, tradition, innovation, belief, and identity all meet and merge here, and yet standing aside from his earthly role and daily labours we are presented with an image of the real man.

Presumably from a catacomb, and now in the *Museo Pio Cristiano* in the *Musei Vaticani*, is a marble plaque from the first half of the fourth century with a drawing of a large barrel on it, a Chi Rho Christian symbol and the name Seberus carved on poorly. One supposes this is yet another memorial to a Christian wine shipper or seller. From similar name or occupational plaques from the catacombs we know of a barley seller 'from the Via Nova', a locksmith, a linen weaver or *lintearius*, a cloakroom attendant from the Baths of Caracalla, and from an inscription in the *Catacombe di San Callisto* of Dionyius, a doctor and presbyter.

Of particular interest here is the much later emergence of the idea of the 'Christ of the Trades', that is as a representation and symbol of the dignity of labour and the rewards of good craftsmanship. Although this came to be manifested in an imagery employing common pictorial tropes in the middle ages, its genesis might have been much earlier. Images of Christ displaying his wounds while surrounded by the tools of various trades, in lieu of the symbols of the Passion, were common and came to be known as the *Arma Christi*: a variation included images of the body of Christ being pierced by everyday tools and instruments.

John Everett Millais' painting of 1849–50 *Christ in the House of His Parents* (also known as *The Carpenter's Shop*), now in Tate Britain, caused a storm of outrage when first displayed at the Royal Academy. Its portrayal of Christ the child displaying a wound from a nail to his mother, foreshadowing his stigmata from the cross, while around them other figures including Joseph and John the Baptist look on with concern and come to his aid takes place in a spartan workshop whose perceived disorder and dirtiness most provoked the anger of the critics and public. The floor covered in plane shavings and wood offcuts, a door supported on a trestle workhorse, tools hanging up on the wall, again all provoked negative comment, despite the picture being within the symbolic tradition of the medieval *Arma Christi* pictures. No such animosity regarding occupational images appears in the early Roman Christian tradition as far as can be gauged.

In conclusion, it has been demonstrated in this chapter that though this book is mainly about individual workers, artisans, and professionals and their identities there was a considerable overlap between individual and group identity in many cases at this time.

It has also been argued that the demonstrable clusterings of artisans working in the same trades that can be proven to have existed in some of Rome's neighbourhoods probably occurred in most towns in the Roman world. In many ways, as in life as in death, there would appear to have been foci in Roman columbaria, cemeteries, and catacombs where the burial plots of the artisanal classes clustered. The creation of both informal and formal networks of individuals working in the same field inevitably led to the strengthening of professional identities and a broadening out of the world view of the network's members. Formal *collegia* and other work and professional bodies helped strengthen and maintain both individual and group occupational identities.

This dynamic view of the role and status of technology in the Roman world foregrounds social activity and social as well as professional networks. What was occurring here in the case of those who made things, was that they were using technology to modify natural resources and materials in order to turn them into cultural products. To turn them from being *of* nature into *of* society. As can be seen with regard to Roman technology it was very much material and it existed within very specific and very well defined cultural and historical contexts defined by highly dynamic and meaningful social interactions which were often reflected in Roman art and culture more broadly and indeed needed to be reflected that way to make them somehow valid. Craft and technology provided vehicles for materialising identity for both the individual and the group.

In the next and final chapter discussion will examine the ways in which workers' images, both real and allusive or metaphorical, have been employed in other cultures, in other contexts at other times, in the hope that such such examples might help to shed light on the Roman phenomenon on which this book is focused. Consideration will also be given to other ways in which images of workers can be culturally situated, sometimes in a strategic and cynical way.

9

Roman Tales

A Cacophony of Voices

Over the course of this study I hope it has been shown how
some Roman freedmen and freedwomen of the late Republic
began to assert the open demonstration of their working or
professional identities through artwork associated with funerary
commemoration and in a few other types of context. As this
class became more influential, the free association of workers
and artisans, and their organisation into specialised *collegia*
or what we might call guilds, strengthened their position
within Roman urban society and made the celebration of their
pride in their work more overt and more widespread both at
Rome and elsewhere in Roman Italy, then beyond. Shop signs,
dedicatory inscriptions associated with non-funerary monuments
and buildings, and the stamping of products emanating from
potteries, brick and tile works, glassworks and so on, related to
this growing phenomenon. Clear chronological and geographic
trends can be discerned in terms of how provincial workers,
artisans, and professionals presented their images of identity in
public. The vast majority of images discussed in this book come
from Rome and Italy, Gaul, and Germany. A mere handful of
outliers in Britain, Spain, the Balkans, Greece, Asia Minor and
the eastern empire, and North Africa appears as isolated dots on
the distribution map.

In looking back at workers' images in art of the Roman period
we must also hold back from over-interpreting the significance of
portrayals of agricultural workers, in wall paintings, on mosaics,
and in sculptural reliefs. These images were not documentary
reports on agricultural practices of their time: rather, they were

more often than not symbolic and illustrative of the passing of the seasons and of corporeal time in general, an altogether different phenomenon linked to elite land ownership and bucolic metaphor. Images of workers toiling on estates in the countryside could simply also have been intended to reflect the wealth and status of the estate owner and have been a manifestation of the Roman concept that land ownership equalled power and control. Much later, in the medieval period and the Renaissance, similar currents of blending metaphor, elite cultural power and munificence, and religious piety would be reflected in the creation of many works of art praising agricultural toil, such as *The Cycle of the Months* by Benedetto Antelami (c. AD 1150–c. 1230) which consists of twelve reliefs carved for the Baptistery of Parma Cathedral, northern Italy.

The types of evidence drawn upon have included inscriptions, decorated tombs, decorated funerary stele and reliefs, decorated funerary altars, inscribed funerary plaques and grave markers, wall paintings, mosaics, decorated glassware, stamped pottery, tiles, bricks, lead pipes, textile shipping tags, and some small items of genre art, though examples of the latter are perhaps surprisingly few. The number of items that included actual portraits of an individual named worker or professional are few but otherwise highly significant. The evidence from mosaics is itself unusual and includes images of a wild animal shipper with a palatial villa in Sicily and merchant associations at Ostia. Cases of intertextuality are rare but again significant. For example, the only glass vessel we have that includes decorative scenes of artisanal activity carries scenes of carpentry rather than glassmaking, as we might have expected.

There are other aspects of the material that stand out, including an inherent but explainable gender bias, the rare use of portraits of the deceased, the occasional but still rare depiction of quite technical or specialised processes, and the depiction of specialised tools. The idea of the artefact as a symbol in and of itself was widespread in the Roman world, and one only has to think of the paraphernalia of animal sacrifice – the *cantharus*, *patera*, and axe that so often stood as images symbolic of individual piety, to understand and contextualise the significance of depictions of tools on funerary monuments. Images of sacrificial paraphernalia and craftsmen's tools could both be simultaneously symbolic and literal in funerary contexts. The very materiality of tools reflected the materiality of contemporary technology. Yet in most cases substance took precedence over symbolism.

The reader will hopefully now appreciate that the sheer range of jobs and occupations commemorated in Roman times was almost bewildering in its variety. As noted in the preface many specialist job titles in Roman society, such as the *alipilus* – 'a plucker of body hair', were proudly held. Indeed, one such *alipilus* at the baths in Rome M. Octavius Primigenius dedicated a free-standing tomb to himself, his wife, and his freedmen.

Discussion has also included the use of artists' signatures on art works, which has provided some interesting insights into the situation in ancient Rome and around its empire in comparison with earlier Greek material. The cultural, temporal, and geographical specificity of some of the Roman examples alerts us to the need to perhaps shed the modern connection between the signature and the idea of authentication, a connotation that seems to confuse matters to some extent when applied to some of the Roman material. Again, we have seen that less ambiguity seemed to apply to the stamping or marking of pottery, bricks and tiles, glass, lead pipes and so on, but we still need to ask why some individuals or workshops signed or name-stamped their work and particularly why others did not.

A detailed analysis of the published corpus of funerary inscriptions from the city of Rome has led to the suggestion that out of thousands of recorded epitaphs from the early empire the overwhelming majority of these inscriptions were set up by or dedicated to freedmen and freedwomen. These were not all social climbers of some kind but people who at first might have emulated elite ideology and behaviour, on a lower budget of course, and who later came to see such behaviour as culturally specific and appropriate to their own class and circumstances. Acquiring the epigraphic habit like this went hand in hand with the trend among workers and artisans to self-identify with their profession, again mainly on funerary monuments using text, in terms of citing a job title, or image, of work scenes or craft tools, or of both together.

The presentation of occupational images and identities clearly marked a point at which individuality crossed over with Roman mercantile expediency and economic necessity in the contemporary world view. Public space in towns and cemeteries could no longer simply be the exclusive preserve of the named great man and woman from the elite classes, and named individuals from the middle and lower classes of freedmen and freedwomen now claimed space there and celebrated and commemorated their identities, including their occupational and professional identities in many cases.

These portrayals of workers and their occupations were sometimes bold, sometimes almost anecdotal, so in viewing them there is less the feeling of years accrued than of selves or identities tried out. Maybe to some extent they had the power to transfigure contemporary life, with all its quotidian mess and demands, its conflicts, its ambivalences, its disappointments, and its unfinished business, into an alternative reality, seamless and permanent as the cold hard stone on which they were carved. When something could be anything it risked being nothing, and also risked tipping the phenomenon from evident complexity to cluttered emptiness. You have the inescapable impression that these images are now channelling our present, their future, telling us about a threshold moment when a whole world became obsolete and the contours of a new world began to show themselves.

These powerful artworks now tend to circulate among academics through iconographic photographs which distil an experience or a range of simultaneous experiences into singular images. These performances of identity then endure through, and as, documentation, when in fact these identities were conceived and framed as art.

The phenomenon of occupational images represented a mode of communication between individuals and the Roman elite and administration, and had the ability to link the inner world of subjective experience to the practice of making art and to the idea of art as an open-ended encounter. Just as the statues of elite Romans and emperors in an urban context became part of the geography of the city so did the images of workers become simply illustrations in a sea of such social geographic information. They were not attempts to scramble the order imposed by official and mainstream discourse, rather their purpose was first and foremost social and economic. They created portholes between the actual dynamic urban environment in which they sat and the hermetic construction of art. It was not their intended purpose to undermine old hierarchical notions of developed subject matter in Roman art, even if they ultimately did just that, nor did the commissioners of such works set out to beat new creative pathways and make fresh conceptual connections by spontaneous or intuitive methods rather than by schooled or preset ones, although we might suspect that this was an underlying motive in some cases. The temptation to view such images as documentation or reportage, as an inventorising project, must though be avoided.

The suggestion that Roman occupational images may have derived from earlier Greek models of representation from as far back as the second century BC implies a degree of cultural access that might not have existed at this level of society. However, many of those creating or commissioning occupational images were themselves of Greek heritage and the idea cannot therefore be dismissed entirely. However, certain Greek cultural traditions in this field, such as the common production of craft-referential pottery vessels, were not taken up or followed in Roman times.

Citing an occupational title on a funerary monument or depicting scenes of work or professional tools there shifted attention away from the standard elite concerns and tropes centred on birth, lineage, and family honour to ideas of productive value, skill, and often of contemporary familial relationships. Creating this strong identity for workers did not lead to the building of events in terms of forming a historical narrative, but rather it created places where people could meet each other, even if only in death, and in some ways leave enriched, being somehow free of pre-determined obsessions. To expand the field of desire like this was a principal freedom, a concept of vitality, extracting possible nourishment from the past but with the responsibility of the present. Unlike much elite art which connected to many people but had conversations with too few, this new non-elite occupational art might have had a smaller but more responsive audience.

There must also have been an 'insider' and 'outsider' perspective in viewing these artworks, particularly those where a person's trade or occupation was simply referenced by the depiction of tools or equipment, some of it sometimes quite specialised. Taken together these artworks do not produce a picture of a unified plebeian class. They did not seek to assert shared concerns across a whole stratum of society but rather within a sub-group of workers of that class. A hierarchical structure within the working plebeian class was topped by merchants and contractors. Working artisans, some freedmen or freedwomen and some not, occupied the middle ground, and slaves and apprentices propped up the structure.

But it cannot be too highly stressed, or stressed too often, that nobody had to seek permission to produce and display occupational images. No one set out or attempted to stop it. It just happened. Whatever authorised versions of the past existed were centred on outmoded notions of community. Social realism and the mission to expose and combat social ills went out of the way to blur the line between politics and parody and pastiche, between purity and danger, the mainstream and the margins, and to flatten out the world. This distinctive new discourse was both corrosive and infectious, a secular hymn to the glory of physical endeavour involving mutation, hybridity, and uncertainty in a model that prioritised collaboration and interdiscipliniarity. This pluralist position granted a kind of equivalence in which art of many sorts was made to seem more or less equal, or at its basest equally (un)important, with no one strain of art more privileged above the other.

The poison inherent in some ideas of culture, the feeling of being somehow disengaged in a world of small and individual neuroses where power and its paradoxes constituted a form of populism, represented the worst gratification that the collective could offer. The fragile nature of command and the transitory aspect of this power paradoxically was not impotence but it was firmly anchored in its time. There were elite Romans who were well known in their day and who were quickly forgotten. Once seen though, the Tomb of Eurysaces the Baker would not so easily have faded from mind.

Other Times, Other Places

I hope readers will bear with me as I now lead them on what might at first appear to be a strange though short diversion, discussing the social make-up of mid to late twentieth century Rome as reflected in the novels and stories of Alberto Moravia. The relevance of this particular diversion will, I think, soon become clear.

Alberto Moravia is probably best known for his books (titles given here in translation) *The Conformist, A Ghost at Noon, The Woman of Rome, Two Women,* and *Roman Tales,* and it is the latter title that I will consider here. *Roman Tales* comprises nineteen short stories or fictional studies set in and around the city, its compendium structure and urban framework obviously owing something to James Joyce's *Dubliners.* Set in the late 1940s, each tale centres on an individual young male working class protagonist, usually unnamed. We often only know their occupation or profession and Moravia uses this knowledge to help the reader to try and interpret their often-opaque characters. Like so many of Moravia's characters the protagonists of *Roman Tales* are people such as lorry drivers, taxi drivers, waiters, gardeners, the unemployed, or people on the fringes of illegality.

Trapped by their circumstances they lead somehow diminished lives, fret over lost opportunities and chances missed, and are often regretful of bad decisions. At first sight these are lives of quiet desperation, shrouded in bleakness, though they are imbued with ideas on the importance of friendship, loyalty, and solidarity. They are lives often led astray by encounters with power, sex, money, subterfuge, and concealment. This existential angst shared by many of the characters is not presented as being a necessarily Roman trait. Looked at together these studies present a middle class author's picture of the lives of working class Romans, people who inhabit their own social space in Roman society and who have their own culture, their own individual and class identities, and modes of expression.

But Moravia's interest in 'the ordinary Roman', the working man, was not some kind of outlier but rather represented one of a number of moments in nineteenth and twentieth century Italian culture when in one medium or another the focus has been turned on this class. The work of social-realist painters, neorealist film-makers, and Italian fascist propaganda-makers marked other such moments.[1] Each of these moments led to the production of written or visual images of Roman workers whose construction in each instance was part of the forging and redefinition of a new Italian character and identity. The creation of these new Italian workers' images in public discourse replaced the self-creation of his or her identity by a worker and subsumed it within a process of open political discourse. Identity was being thrust upon the Italian worker, in a way that never happened in the ancient Roman past with which we are mainly concerned. Of course, just such a fight over the soul of the Italian worker was also played out in the twentieth century between the Italian Communist Party, as best represented in the writings of Antonio Gramsci, and Mussolini's Fascist party.

Social-realist art in nineteenth and early twentieth century Italy placed the image of the worker, both the agricultural labourer and the factory worker, at the forefront of the cultural economy of the time. Works like Giuseppe Pellizza da Volpedo's massive and extremely moving and powerful painting *Il Quarto Stato* or *The Fourth Estate* of c. 1900, depicting a march of striking workers, Enrico Butti's *Il Minatore* or *The Miner* sculpture of c. 1890, and Attilio Pusterla's (1862–1941) realist painted study *Alle Cucina Economiche di Porta Nuova* or *An Economical Canteen at Porta Nuova* of 1887 made potent comments on the severe class divisions within Italian society at the time and demonstrated that the working class protagonists in these artworks were people of dignity and worthy of respect. These images of workers, like Moravia's, had no agency, as most ancient Roman occupational images had.

As for the Italian neorealist film directors of the 1940s and 1950s, such as Vittorio De Sica, Luchino Visconti, Roberto Rossellini, and Federico Fellini, collectively they presented a narrative about contemporary Italian society that in its mix of ancient and modern, and of poverty and opportunity, mirrored the overall narrative of ancient Roman society as expressed through both its public and private art. This ancient art was not a fantasy construction, it was intensely realist in scope and intent, certainly in the case of the work and professional images discussed in this book, but it was also an art about censorship and sometimes human erasure, so that what was omitted or excluded was often as important as what was left in. These artisans would not generally commission art that dealt with mythological themes and strayed away from their daily concerns. The art by which they chose to represent themselves sometimes could metaphorically allude to potential, and to personal and economic empowerment, but never far from the surface was a sense that the tension between progressing and staying put, and between being cosmopolitan like their city and staying rooted, underwrote the narrative and their lives and death.

The depiction of workers in totalitarian art from Russia, Germany, Italy, China, and North Korea formed the subject matter of a seminal art historical study by Igor Golomstock.[2] Here once more the images of these workers were purely symbolic, drawn along on the tides of history and the forward momentum of the creation of a bold new totalitarian world. Such images Golomstock categorised as 'genre' images, along with landscapes, still lifes, and nudes, all of these being considered by him as peripheral in the hierarchy of genres, at whose centre was the official portrait of the leader or leaders, historical painting, and battle pictures or sculptures.[3] Yet, Italian Fascism more than the other regimes listed here attempted to place 'labour' at the heart of its official art, perhaps in some ways because of the national tradition of social realist art.

If German Nazi propaganda at first had a fixation with images of peasants, reflecting the ideological links between land and race, then images of factory workers soon came to usurp this position, as German industry was geared up to come to terms with the practicalities of preparing for a permanent state of war.

In the Constructivist art, photography and cinema of early post-revolutionary Russia the image of the worker became a kind of new Russian icon. As the state became a totalitarian one the image of the Soviet worker in the factories and fields continued to hold some sort of pre-eminent place in the iconology of the country, though celebration of this image had now given ground to its use as crude propaganda, though not without interest as a contested image.[4] Images of workers appeared in many media but earlier Soviet era art was particularly exceptional in placing such images not only in paintings, sculptures, on posters, and so on but also on many of the ceramic plates and figurines produced at the former Imperial Porcelain Factory in St Petersburg.[5] As Stalinism changed the focus of the revolution's ideas and ideals, so state propaganda, in the opposite route to the Nazi regime, placed the image of the peasant ahead of that of the worker as the notion that a nation at war required feeding above all else took hold. However, in both eras the image being presented was of an anonymous worker, a universal symbol for all the workers of the Soviet Union. The identity of this worker was defined for him or her; it was not chosen for presentation by the worker themselves.

Much of the propaganda artwork produced under the Nazi and Stalinist regimes blended both ideas of labour and struggle into single emotional images, works which, as Golomstock put it, 'give the impression of a desperate battle against an invisible enemy'. Work was here one of the virtues, if not actually the supreme virtue, of a true citizen. 'Man no longer simply worked – he struggled for the plan, for victory, for his own liberation.'

Unlike Soviet Russia, in the USA large factories became somehow detached from the overarching political system, though a sort of transcultural logic meant that the factory became a public symbol of progress in both these very different political regimes. In America though there was still at best a tradition which represented the public civic culture in which labour had a distinct dignity and value. This was most vividly made clear during the Second World War in the United States with the propaganda drive for increased productivity centred around the fictitious figure of Rosie the Riveter, the subsequent reception of the Rosie myth subtly altering and enhancing the original creation.

There is a certain degree of confusion around which Rosie came first, the lean and improbably glamorous working Rosie on the cover of the sheet music for the 1942 popular song or the rather more authentic Rosie painted by Norman Rockwell and immortalised by the reproduction of the painting on the cover of the Saturday Evening Post in May 1943. Rockwell's Rosie is a no-nonsense figure, caught during her lunch break eating a sandwich. Dressed in overalls her rivet gun is set down to one side. A real factory-line worker was signed up to appear as 'Rosie' on propaganda posters and leaflets.

Accompanied by the bold, lean slogan *We can do it!* another all-American factory-working woman appeared on a 1942 poster that is probably the most iconic American image of the war, and which became mistakenly cited as a poster of 'Rosie the Riveter' many years later. Clad in deep blue work-wear overalls and with her hair up and tied with a red spotted headscarf, she poses with one hand in the crook of the other arm, as a strongman would do to mime power and strength. However, the pose might have offended some Italian Americans for whom this gesture possibly denoted something offensive. That the protagonist here was a woman 'fighting' on the home front would not have been lost on its target audience of female factory workers in armament factories and dockyards up and down the country. She was a universalising figure: strong, proud, independent but patriotic, femme and butch at the same time. Or so it might seem. However, this strong figure at the time went unnamed, and the Rosie the Riveter moniker was only attached to her in the 1970s when the image was appropriated by the feminist movement in America. *We can do it!* changed its meaning from 'we can up production of guns and planes and win the war through women's work' to 'we can defeat the patriarchy by being strong women and playing them at their own game'.

Different versions of Rosie appeared in a feature film in 1944 and in a popular song of 1942, strengthening the message conveyed by the poster girl Rosie depending on the individual viewpoint of viewers and listeners. The creators of Rosie realised that a generalised strong figure was required for the image itself but that this figure would be more relateable if 'she' had a name, one that was short and memorable, something achieved by using the alliterative form for Rosie the Riveter.

My own mother, coincidentally called Rose, started the war by volunteering to undertake work in a munitions factory far from her Yorkshire home and inadvertently cut off the end of one of her fingers in a machine at a factory in Aston, Birmingham, distracted by the sound outside of an air raid. Unaware of what she had done, she finished her shift. Women like my mother would have been swayed by images of equivalent British figures on posters like Rosie the Riveter or the *We can do it!* woman worker.

There are numerous other modern artworks and studies that have helped me theorise my exploration of Roman workers' images and helped inform my interpretations, including, Diego Rivera's Detroit murals; the emotionally detached cityscapes of Charles Sheeler; the documentary photographs of Margaret Bourke-White; and the writings generated by the Mass Observation project.

These modern wartime exemplars might at first sight appear to bear no resemblance to the kinds of Roman images of workers with which this book is primarily concerned, however, there are ideological connections, as there are with the images of workers in totalitarian art which have also been discussed here. We need to ask if the complex history of the reception of the image and persona of Rosie the Riveter might in any way be reflected in the changing perception and reception of the meaning of the Tomb of Eurysaces the Baker, from the time of its construction and dedication in the first century AD up to the time it became incorporated into the Aurelian-Honorian city defences and pretty much disappeared from view and thus from the historical record, up to its rediscovery in the nineteenth century and its study in the years since.

Eurysaces was presenting his societal identity, his family/marriage identity, and his professional identity to the citizens of Rome at the time of his death and for three centuries afterwards. There came a time though when his monument and thus his presented identity lost all relevance and indeed the personal was overtaken by the contingency of the political and the need for the tomb to be sacrificed to make way for new defensive building works here.

The rediscovery of the tomb led to the rediscovery and redefinition of Eurysaces as Eurysaces the Baker whose tomb no longer was simply viewed as an isolated monument but which rather now was contextualised within the complete history of freedmen funerary monuments throughout the whole city of Rome and more widely in Roman Italy. The significance and stature of Eurysaces are probably today much greater than they ever were in his own time. He is undoubtedly the most famous baker of ancient Rome and quite possibly the most famous freedman businessman of the city. Was he viewed like this at the time or was his funerary memorial viewed as some kind of bloated, grand conceit, the manifestation of the overarching aspiration of Rome's nouveau riche freedman class, a baking Trimalchio? A few commentators have noted that the tomb, in its architectural style is remarkably reminiscent of some Italian Fascist structures, curiously almost making it a prescient construction, a harbinger of the Fascist era to come in hauntological terms, emerging butterfly-from-chrysalis-like into the future from its encasing inside the old city walls. Today his tomb is at the same time both obscure and famous.

Before Eurysaces, or whoever was the very first worker or professional to overtly celebrate their professional identity in public in this way, as far as we are aware the Roman state had not said no to such displays but had probably enjoined its citizens not to believe or accept that their social selves should or could be presented in this manner. But unlike the workers celebrated in totalitarian art discussed above these ancient Roman workers created their own images which were somehow both always the same and yet always different. If the very first attempt to place an occupational identity on a public funerary monument for freedmen was the creation of the c. 40 BC family funerary relief of the Gavii, now in *San Giovanni in Laterano* in Rome, then its subtle design must have been crucial to the success of the venture. The relief panel carries four bust portraits of the family members, all of whom were named. Almost incidentally, at the end of the inscription appear the words *fabrei tignuares* or 'carpenters' to identify the two brothers commemorated here. No tools appeared as images, and there were no work scenes. The family members are formally dressed and their appearances are those of respectable citizens whose principal identities are linked to their legal, freed status and to family. A number of other such family tomb reliefs, slightly later in date, can be seen to have refocused and redefined this new convention and included images of tools and work items. For instance, on the relief of the Antestii, in the *Musei Vaticani* in Rome, three portraits appear, an inscription names the three individuals, and images of an assemblage of objects is provided, including metalworking tools and a metal jug. On the relief of the Ampudii, in the British Museum in London, three portraits appear, of a man, named in the inscription, and two women, with an image of a *modius* or corn measure on either side, one of the corn measures bearing the inscription *modi(arius)*, telling us that the man was a grain seller or perhaps a baker (Plate 87). The design of funerary monuments such as those of the Gavii, the Antestii, and the Ampudii probably paved the way for the eventual appearance of fully fledged work scenes such as those on the Tomb of Eurysaces.

When the Italian Marxist art historian Ranucchio Bianchi Bandinelli coined the term *Arte Plebea* or *Plebeian Art* in 1967 to denote a particular strain of non-elite artistic expression in ancient Roman art he did so in the slipstream of the competing ideas of writers like Moravia, the neorealist filmmakers, and of Gramsci, in reaction almost to the idea of the role of the worker promulgated by Italian Fascism. To me, it is difficult to understand why this term is no longer fashionable and simply viewed as irrelevant, even historicist, in Roman art studies today. It still seems a handy shorthand name for a particular strain of cultural production that constituted 'art in the lives of ordinary Romans', as leading American ancient-art historian John Clarke prefers to call the phenomenon.[6] Plebeian culture was not merely based on elite emulation, it was both distinct and distinctive.

Interzone

As I noted at the very start of this book, this study is not intended to be some kind of underground or subcultural history, or unveiling of ancient workers and artisans as secret Romans. Rather such people are there in the archaeological record, hiding in plain sight for all to see. It is museological practices and theories that have moved such people to the peripheries, as we shall now discuss.

In Rome three of the major museums dedicate space to the display of evidence relating to Roman craftsmen and workers, to a greater or lesser degree. In the *Musei Vaticani* the large collection of occupational inscriptions forms part of the overall *Museo*

Lapidaria which is not open to the general public but which can be viewed by researchers by appointment. The inscriptions are mostly displayed set into the walls of a long, high-ceilinged gallery on both sides. They are grouped thematically and two bays of occupational inscriptions number around 120 inscriptions in total. A small number of stele and funerary altars stand on the gallery floor in association with their relevant group. At the time of writing this I understand that the digitisation of the epigraphic collection in the *Museo Lapidaria* is almost complete, with the aim being to provide an accessible and searchable database which should allow everyone access to this incredible educational resource.

In the *Museo Nazionale Romano*, in its *Terme di Dioclezione* buildings a large room is dedicated to the display of a significant number of occupational inscriptions from Rome. Indeed, if the visitor takes the time to carefully inspect the items on display and read discrete summary captions, in Italian, a remarkably clear impression will be left on them as to the incredible range of specialist occupational identities presented here. Every time I have visited this gallery in the last ten years I have been the only person in here and it may be that visitors find the display of so many inscriptions here off-putting.

In the *Museo della Civiltà Romana* in Rome's EUR district there is presented what is perhaps the most important series of displays relating to Roman workers and Roman technology in any one single museum. While the two main galleries set aside to present these topics – Room 52 Industry and Craft and Room 55 Commerce and Economic Life – house collections of casts rather than original reliefs and steles, the range of casts, in terms of the types of occupation represented here and the geographical spread of sites and museums where casts were made, including many outside of Italy, represents an astonishing academic achievement. And yet, the motivation for the creation of much of this material was purely ideological, linked to fascist ideas of the dignity of the Roman worker, both in the deep Roman past and in the Italy of the 1920s and 1930s.[7] Indeed, the genesis of the museum's collection lies in the enormous *Mostra Augustea della Romanitá* (MAR) staged by Mussolini's regime in 1937–38 to celebrate the 2,000th anniversary of the birth of Augustus, first emperor of Rome.[8] This enormous exhibition, in the *Palazzo delle Esposizioni* on Via Nazionale was obviously intended as a way of launching Mussolini as the new

Augustus, presenting the Italian Fascist identity to both the people of Rome and Italy, diehard and sceptical alike it was hoped, and to the international community. It held up a mirror to contemporary Italian society and asked it to reflect upon its past and its future, and indeed upon its very destiny, as Fascist ideology saw it.

The exhibition was not just about Augustus and his reign, but rather used this as a jumping-off point for considering the achievements of ancient Rome as a whole, as reflected in the c. 3,000 casts of ancient Roman artworks assembled here – not just from Rome itself but from Italy more broadly and from many of Rome's provinces – including hundreds of models, maps, plans, photographs, explanatory texts, programmes, and academic publications. Indeed, one of the works cited in my bibliography for this book resulted from research linked to the exhibition, Maria Floriana Squarciapino's *Civiltà Romana: Artigianato e Industria, Mostra della Romanità*. The layout of the exhibition gave more than adequate space to the placing of the worker right at the heart of the Augustan and Roman project, linking Roman workers to technological progress and achievement, and marking their true place in the integrated nature of the ancient economic system. This obviously reflected Italian Fascism's view of the significance of the worker in the Italian society of the 1920s and 1930s.

At Ostia the mosaics in the *Piazzale delle Corporazioni* are mostly on display in situ, though covered for their protection each winter, as is the House of the Corn Measurers' mosaic a short distance away. However, having visited the museum at the site many times in the past twenty years it is disappointing to note that not a single one of the many worker's images from the town is on permanent display there and none has ever been out on display in a temporary exhibition when I have visited. Of course, as at any museum appointments can be made by academics to view material in the museum stores there, but given the richness of the assemblage of such material from Ostia I feel an opportunity to present such material to the general public is being missed. A number of terracotta plaques and replicas of plaques bearing occupational images can be seen in their original positions at the highly atmospheric and fascinating *Necropoli di Porto* site a few miles away, once more viewable by appointment only.

In Pompeii, because of restrictions of access to many historic properties at the site, no overall impression can be gained as to the complexity of the working world of the town's inhabitants by a visitor today. Without a museum on the site this problem is further compounded. While many relevant artworks from Pompeii and Herculaneum can be viewed in the *Museo Archeologico Nazionale* in Naples, there is no permanent display themed around occupational images and workers. Of course, many other individual museums in Italy hold multiple artworks bearing occupational images, and I would single out the *Museo Civico Archeologico* in Bologna as a good example. Likewise, in the French, Belgian, and German museums where there are significant collections of workers' funerary monuments, such as in Sens, Dijon, Metz, Arlon, and Trier, all of which I visited while researching this book, the presentation of such monuments is exemplary but quite matter of fact, without thematic structuring.

I certainly do not want to be critical of any museum or museums in particular, but so much of the material I have viewed during research for this book has been in museum storerooms, rather than on permanent display, including many seminal artworks in this field of study, and I wonder if museological practices relating to Roman period material need to be broadened to occasionally move away from an over-reliance on chronological and historical narratives as framing structures for displays, and embrace more diverse categorisations of *Romanitas*.

Writing Identity

The issue and significance of the marking of a manufactured item with a personalised mark has been discussed at length, particularly in the case of the name-stamping of pottery vessels. However, it is worth thinking further about the issue of the image of the stamp as a display of literacy and the expectation of written or visual literacy in the viewer or reader of that stamp. One authority has written about the existence of what she has called 'the performance of literacy' in the Roman world and how analysis of evidence for this can shed light on certain phenomena in Roman society, particularly with regard to information exchange.[9]

If the depiction of people writing and, by extension, of writing equipment itself either in use or on its own in Roman art had a particular meaning as a social statement, then such depictions in a funerary context might also have been of significance. In discussing these themes a clear distinction will be made between those for whom writing was a class or social and socialising activity, and those for whom it was principally a skill employed in professional contexts, in other words a job that we can discuss here in the same way that we have discussed bakers or metalworkers.

At Pompeii and Herculaneum it would appear that there was a well-defined trend towards the depiction in wall paintings of private individuals having themselves portrayed in the act of writing, or at least holding writing equipment, and indeed some of these images are perhaps the best known pictures from the sites. Were the individuals who commissioned such works simply elite individuals who wished to use this common trope to convey messages about their education and standing, or even to suggest their 'wealth and business acumen'? Some of the depictions of women in such contexts probably alluded to particular gender roles and expectations. Certainly the commissioning of such pictures and their discovery in wealthy homes rather than shop or workshop premises suggests that this indeed was the case.

But in terms of professionals consideration will be given here to lawyers, scribes and clerks, book and record keepers, bankers and accountants, teachers, medical practitioners such as doctors, occulists, and pharmacists. Architects as literate professionals have already been discussed above in Chapter One. The presentation of the commodification of knowledge, with writing as an enabling technology, was part and parcel of Roman occupational imagery.

While Cicero would never have described himself as a professional lawyer, though regularly appearing as an advocate in high-profile cases, there certainly emerged what we might call a legal profession from the early empire onwards. But most of those who pursued the law as a profession appear to have preferred to cite their public offices held in their epitaphs and indeed Sandra Joshel does not list any lawyers in her study of Roman occupational inscriptions. However, the early fourth-century AD sarcophagus of the lawyer Caius Valerius Petronianus from Milan and in the *Museo Civico Archeologico* does carry a small legal scene on one of its short sides (Plate 88).

On one of the leaves of the early eighth-century AD illustrated manuscript Bible the *Codex Amiatinus*, in the *Biblioteca Medicea Laurenziana* in Florence, though created in the monasteries of Monkwearmouth and Jarrow in north-eastern England, is depicted the prophet Ezra working as a scribe, sitting on a low bench with a book on his lap which he is writing in. Another book sits on display on a stand in front of him and along one wall of the room in which he works is a large, tall wooden cabinet whose double doors are open to reveal many more books shelved inside. Here labour is quite simply a sacred task, and I have mentioned this early medieval work in this context because the image seems to derive from earlier Roman models.

The number of professional scribes, what would probably be described as clerks today, must have been enormous within the bureaucracy of the Roman state machinery, in provincial and local administration, in the Roman army at all levels, in religious sects, both pagan and Christian, and in private businesses both large and small. A number of funerary monuments to professional scribes are known and an examination of a few of the best of these will now be presented. The interpretation of some of these funerary monuments is further complicated by the fact that the depiction of a high status male elite figure in an image on a tombstone with a clerk in attendance may simply be a way to convey the status and importance of the deceased.

In the *Museo Nazionale Romano* in Rome is a cinerary altar from the necropolis of Via di Porta San Sebastiano in the city. Dating to AD 25–50 this altar is today commonly known as the Altar of the Scribes (Plate 89) and was dedicated by a father to his two sons, Quintus Fulvius and Quintus Fulvius Priscus, being described in the dedicatory inscription as *scribae librarii*, that is secretary scribes, to the aediles or magistrates. On its front face can be seen two registers of scenes. In the upper register two magistrates sit on stools on either side of a low table, on which a scribe clerk is laying out a scroll document for their perusal or for signing. Two other clerks stand by, each clutching a scroll ready in their hands. In the lower register a large crowd of men, women and children gathers, looking up as if to a rostrum or balcony. A man holding a tablet is at the centre of the scene. While not nearly as exciting for the viewer as scenes of baking or metalworking, nonetheless images such as these are important to show how widespread was the practice of recognising and celebrating working and professional achievement in Roman society. In the collections of the same museum is an inscription to Quintus Natronius Rusticus, scribe to the quaestors.

Just as this book was being completed a new theory regarding the significance of the paintings inside the early third century AD *Hypogeum* of the Aurelii on the Esquiline Hill in Rome was published.[10] Given this timing I am only really able to briefly mention it here, without the opportunity to fully weigh up its merits and assess the reactions of other scholars to what is likely to be seen in some quarters as controversial revisionism. This particular *hypogeum* or underground burial chamber, named from an inscription on a floor mosaic here, is particularly famed for its decorative mix of pagan and Christian symbolism and overtly literate use of mythological metaphor, perhaps related to contemporary Gnostic beliefs in its multiple frescos. It might be thought that there was no imagery here relevant to this study of working and professional images: indeed, there is not overtly so. However, the new theory suggests that this *hypogeum* was the collegiate tomb of professional scribes involved in the imperial bureaucracy and that its decoration was not necessarily religious in intent but rather reflected both the demonstration of professional power and of a hard-won status with its roots in the pride of earlier freedmen culture.

A figure of a bearded man sat behind a desk, variously identified as a banker or a scribe, appears on a Christian stele decorated with a mosaic of the late fifth century AD in the Chapel of the Martyrs at Tabarka in Tunisia, one of a number of remarkable Tabarka tombstone mosaics now in the *Musée National du Bardo* in Tunis. A female figure, presumably his wife, appears below in an attitude of prayer.

One particularly common trope in funerary imagery was the depiction of an individual holding a scroll in one hand, but such an image could have related to issues of inheritance rather than to the professional application of literacy. Probably more telling is the appearance of writing equipment on its own on funerary monuments such as those to M. Servius Primigenius from Aquileia; and Statorius Aper from Sulmona, L'Aquila in central Italy. Funerary epitaphs of Latin teachers – *grammatici latinus* – are known, including those of Publius Atilius Septicianus from Como in northern Italy who also had decurial honours bestowed on him by the town council and of Quintus Tuticanus Eros from Verona, also in the north of Italy. Teachers were also honoured on funerary monuments in Gaul and Germany, as the illustrated examples shown from Arlon in Belgium (Plate 90) and Trier in Germany (Plate 91) demonstrate.

The number of depictions of Roman bankers, money changers, or accountants is considerable and we have these not only from Rome and Italy but also from the north-western provinces. However, as might have been expected over half of the inscriptions dedicated to bankers, money changers, and moneylenders come from the city of Rome itself. On my museum research study visits for this book I noted at least twelve banking scenes and there must be many more, though no one has yet catalogued this particular category of image to allow us to be more precise about its ubiquity. The image is normally one of a man sat at a desk quite clearly counting out coins, either on his own, or in the presence of others, the latter implying a formal transaction of some sort and in some cases might depict the collection of taxes in coin. I have chosen to illustrate just one of these scenes involving some form of accountancy taking place, on the face of a mid-third-century AD uninscribed funerary monument from Arlon in Belgium and in the *Musée Luxembourgeois* there (Plate 92). An accountant or tax collector sits at a desk having received a bag of money from a heavily bearded, hirsute man standing in front of the desk, and he is counting out the coins on the tabletop. He looks calm and composed, which is more than can be said for the other man who seems to be in a state of some agitation, gesticulating wildly with one hand and holding a staff in the other. He is obviously not at all happy at having to make this payment. It is a curious image for an accountant or tax collector's funerary memorial but one that displays a sense of humour above all. Such everyday scenes appeared commonly on funerary monuments in this region, as in another scene illustrated here from Trier (Plate 93), with agricultural scenes, cloth trading, transportation of goods, and the paying and verification of accounts each appearing on multiple occasions.

Of course, there were other professions in which literacy would have gone hand in hand with the studying of texts and treatises, and of these the most obvious is the field of medicine.[11] It is unlikely that any doctor in the ancient world was illiterate and unable to use the knowledge to be gained from reading the vast body of written works on medical practice from the Greek world. Many doctors in the Roman world were in any case either Greek or of Greek heritage. Not all doctors in the Roman period were male and the first century AD funerary stele of a woman *medica* is known from Metz, as discussed in Chapter Eight.

Over one hundred graves of doctors have been excavated, graves containing indisputably medical instruments such as forceps and scalpels, rather than items that might have been general toilet implements. At the *Necropoli di Porto*, Isola Sacra, Ostia as we have seen previously, Tomb 100 had two terracotta plaques mounted on the front facade, one to a midwife, Scribonia Attice, and the other to a doctor, M. Ulpius Amerimnus. This is a rare instance of both partners in a professional couple being commemorated together, though the freedwoman Naevia Clara from Rome, described as 'a doctor and scholar' in the first century BC inscription on her tombstone, was married to C. Naevius Philippus who was himself, we are told, a physician and a surgeon.

Other female doctors honoured in funerary inscriptions include Aurelia Alexandria Zosime who may have received instruction in medicine from her husband Aurelius Pontonianos Asclepiades who honoured her in a third or fourth century AD inscription set up in Adada in Pisidia, Turkey. Scantia Redempta on her fourth century AD tombstone now in the *Museo Campano* in Capua, south central Italy was referred to by her parents who dedicated it as 'excelling in the field of medicine'. Somewhat pointedly the parents also took the opportunity to add here that her husband with her death had 'lost his wife, his own personal physician, and his principal source of income'.

A particular specialised type of medical practice that was carried out exclusively by women in the Roman world was that of the midwife – the *obstetrix* – and portrayals of midwives have received detailed study by Natalie Kampen who saw such portrayals as emblematic of women's natural nurturing role, though professionalised.[12]

An early fourth century AD strigillated sarcophagus from Ostia, now in the Metropolitan Museum of Art in New York, carries a small depiction in the centre of its front panel of a seated bearded male doctor, wearing a toga, reading a scroll, presumably a medical text of some sort. He is sitting in front of a large cabinet, with its central double doors open, which appears to contain other medical texts in the form of rolled-up scrolls and a bowl presumably containing medicines of some sort or a receptacle for blood while bleeding patients. On top of the cabinet rests an open case containing his set of medical and surgical instruments, clearly on display here to help the viewer easily identify the man's profession. A number of probes and a scalpel can clearly be made out. The name of the deceased would have appeared on the sarcophagus lid which is now unfortunately lost. The inscription in Greek on the sarcophagus front is a standard warning of the time for others not to reuse or violate this sarcophagus. The inscription mentions fines payable to the authorities of Portus, the port near Ostia, should such desecration take place.

In the *Altes Museum* in Berlin is an uninscribed stele or votive relief depicting another doctor. Dated to some time between 50 BC to AD 50 and presumably from Rome, the scene depicted on the stone is quite detailed and would appear to represent something rather more complex than simply commemorating an individual's life. As on the Metropolitan Museum sarcophagus the doctor is shown seated, holding a scroll in one hand, his cabinet of surgical implements again out on display behind him. A young boy approaches him, holding out another scroll to him. In the foreground is an altar, attended by a figure with their head covered, as if making an offering at the altar. Another figure, a man leading a horse, approaches. A snake twists its sinuous body around a tree in the manner of the symbolic snake around the staff of the healing god Aesculapius, itself a symbol for the medical profession.

In the British Museum in London is the grave stele of the doctor Jason of Athens, 'also known as Decimus' the accompanying inscription tells us (Plate 94). Dating to around 100 BC Jason is depicted seated once more, caught in the process of examining a sick child with an unnaturally distended stomach. To one side is depicted a large bell-shaped cupping vessel, out of scale to the human figures. Such cupping vessels were heated and then cupped on to the body of a sick person to draw blood or pus from a wound.

On another sarcophagus, that of Sosia Iuliana, in the *Museo Nazionale* in Ravenna in Italy, on one of the short ends appears a scene in which a standing doctor or specialist occulist can be seen examining the eyes of a seated woman (Plate 95). Two bell-shaped cupping vessels hang on the wall behind them. It is difficult to know how to interpret this scene in the broader context of the decoration of this second century AD sarcophagus as a whole, particularly as it is a minor side scene. Certainly it would appear that the family was somehow involved with, or interested in, the cult of the goddess

Isis. One authority has suggested that the medical scene could be linked to cult activity, and that the man is the husband of the seated woman, anointing her eyes in preparation for the visions that she is about to experience. If this were the case it is difficult to see why the event appears to be taking place in a room with medical equipment in the form of the cupping vessels hanging ready on the wall.[13]

On the Via Consolare in Pompeii stands the *Casa del Chiurgo* or House of the Surgeon, so called because of the discovery here of a large assemblage of surgical and medical instruments during the early excavations in the town. Unfortunately no evidence was recovered to provide a name for the doctor who lived here. However, outside another house in Pompeii, on the Via dell'Abbondanza and identified by its contents as a *taberna medica* or doctor's surgery, is painted a sign that identifies the presiding doctor as Aulus Pumponius Magonianus.

Just as images of tools could apparently be intended to be representative of a particular trade, so the same would appear to have applied in those few examples we have of the depiction of sets of medical instruments or other items of doctors' equipment on their own. However, it should also be noted that such images just might have simply been symbolic of the healing art in general or of the healing gods such as Aesculapius; indeed, a votive plaque from the Asklepieion in Athens carries a depiction of a folding case of surgical implements, flanked on either side by a cupping vessel.

Professional doctors in the Greek and Roman worlds would not necessarily have made and prepared their own medicines and salves, and it is therefore not altogether surprising that we can identify quite a large number of named individuals who carried out pharmaceutical preparation and have one possible portrayal of such a medicinal chemist at work.[14] This large stone relief, probably part of a funerary monument, dates to the second century AD and comes from Grand, Épinal, Vosges in north-eastern France, and is now in the *Musée Départmental d'Art Ancien et Contemporain* there (Plate 96). Known as the *Meditrina*, depicted here is the interior of a workshop of some kind, under the control of a woman who sits on a seat at the very front centre of the relief, one foot on a small footstool. She would appear to be holding a writing tablet in one hand, resting on her knee, the presence of the tablet implying that she is literate, indeed that she needs to be literate in her profession whatever that was, and that the book could contain recipes or formulae for the cooking up or preparation of whatever is being made in this manufactory. With her other hand, now broken off, she would seem to have been stirring a pot. Behind her, a subordinate (judging by their relative sizes) labours away, again stirring something in a large vat. They are surrounded by numerous baskets, pots, and other containers.

Many different interpretations of this scene have been offered by academics and there is no general consensus as to what we are actually seeing here. The lack of an inscription naming the main woman and giving her profession is unfortunate. It has been variously suggested that she is a pharmacist making medicines, that she is making soap or perfumes, making beer perhaps, and most improbably that she is making glass. Most recently, it has been suggested that she is making cheese, although this particular interpretation has not been widely accepted.

Of course, it is also possible that what we are actually seeing here is a representation of a goddess rather than a mortal woman, but that seems unlikely given the uniqueness of the scene and the lack of any signifying attributes of a deity. She could be Hygeia or her sister Meditrina (hence the common but confusing name for the relief), both daughters of the healing god Aesculapius, or even the powerful goddess Juno.

However, the seated posture of the female overseer and the allusion to her literacy recalls the stylistic manner in which we have just seen a number of male doctors portrayed. It is not always noted in the academic discussion of this relief that there are in fact two other fragmentary statues from Grand, again probably derived from funerary monuments, that depict scenes of the stirring of vats and the filling of pots and receptacles with some product, implying that whatever procedure was being carried out on the *Meditrina* relief it was perhaps a wider, specialised local industry involving a number of individual workshops and a large workforce, arguing against the *Meditrina* relief being a unique portrayal of a female deity.

There is no reason why the woman on the Grand *Meditrina* relief should not have been a workshop manager or overseer, or that her literacy and ability to record or consult recipes or formulae for a product or to keep records and accounts was particularly unusual. It was a common trope in Roman art to explore an issue such as female literacy through images of writing or of writing equipment, or to portray writing equipment in order to make a more general point about accounting and record-keeping. Indeed implying through such images that the individual portrayed was professional, competent, and wealthy was quite common. Accounting scenes in the funerary art of Gallia Belgica were most often associated with men, as we have seen above, as indeed were scenes of seated doctors with scrolls in Roman art more generally, and so the mixing of these tropes on the *Meditrina* relief is of considerable interest. There is a considerable amount of evidence that women played an often significant role in the urban economy at this time. Their occupations and resulting social connections were part of the phenomenon or result of the emergence of what might be called a middle class in Roman and then provincial society, even if they were excluded by their gender from belonging to a *collegium* or other such professional association. For instance, there is evidence from the examination and cataloguing of brick stamps to show that in a few instances individual women owned brick and tile works or oversaw production there. The same would appear to be true in the case of the manufacture of lead water pipes, judging by evidence from inscriptions on pipes.

If there have to be doubts about the precise meaning of makers' stamps on pottery vessels or on bricks and tiles, then there can be no such doubt attached to occulists' stamps. Made of stone of various kinds these stamps were used to mark blocks of medicinal preparations for eye diseases. Around the thin edges of the stamps were cut letters in reverse that spelled out the individual occulist's name and the name of the medicine being stamped. It is interesting to note that such stamps are found almost exclusively in the north-western provinces of Germany, Gaul, and Britain. They are generally not found in Rome and Italy, possibly because herbs used in these medicinal recipes were easily available in fresh or dried form there, so that eye salves and ointments could be made up on the spot whenever required.

As one can sometimes trace the working practices of individual potters, so in one instance can we do this for an individual doctor, Quintus Postumius Hyginus, whose name appears on an occulist's stamp from Vidy in Switzerland and which also appears in an inscription set up in Avenches by Hyginus and his fellow *medicus* Postumius Hermes, also his freedman incidentally. Both present themselves as members of a *collegium* of doctors and teachers. The two sites are some 30 or so miles apart, making this a lucky but nonetheless remarkable coincidence.

Endgame

It will already be apparent to many readers that a considerable number of the funerary images of workers discussed in this book locate representations of workers quite specifically, in workshops, smithies, foundries, bakeries, inside mints, in shops, in taverns, at market stalls, and so on. The importance of the setting in such cases was rarely simply topographical but it was most certainly significant and integral, embedding the working protagonists meaningfully in both space and time, and placing the viewer inside the room and inside the action. On a few rare occasions a worker was fused with some specific feature of the workplace, for example identified with a complex or unique piece of machinery as in the case of Verrius Euhelpistus and his curious grinding machine depicted on a plaque and mosaic at his tomb in the *Necropoli di Porto* cemetery at Isola Sacra, Ostia (Plate 97). Even on a very few occasions we can assume that the veristic portrayals of workers and the highly complex automated reaping machine known as the *vallus* in operation on three funerary stele from Buzenol (Plate 98) and Arlon in Belgium and Trier in Germany represented something more than the use of an agricultural scene for metaphorical purposes. The images were figurative rather than strictly realistic: the surface image was constantly interrupted or disrupted on occasions by metaphor or symbolic modes which served to extend the frame of reference to points of conflict and change in society, while at the same time suggesting stability. This was part of the envelope of cultural references inherent in the Roman work image genre.

There is no modern 'off the shelf' social or political theory whose structures and ramifications can be brought to bear on the Roman data, to illuminate their meanings and workings. However, in the writings of the Italian Marxist theorist Antonio Gramsci certain pathways to interpretation can be found in terms of his crucial recognition that culture and cultural phenomena and manifestations needed to be seen as situated within political systems.[15] Before Gramsci there was little or no consideration of culture and the arts, particularly popular culture, in Marxist writings where economic issues predominated. Gramsci identified a clear distinction between the cultural territories of the dominant and the dominated in any society, as there was in political, economic, and social matters. The apparent autonomy of much popular culture he saw as illusory, given that the dominant not only overtly controlled certain aspects of cultural performance, production, and reproduction but at the same time covertly directed such areas. This hegemony, as he called it, was a mediating force that once identified and isolated could be turned back on itself by strength and subversion and by knowledge and awareness. Popular culture informed by hegemonic discourse could therefore express and assert its own unmediated values and concerns.

Roman occupational images perhaps corresponded both to the expectations of viewers and to reality, marking a move away from the picturesque and the idealised towards realism and an almost documentary style, a kind of what we might today call authenticity.

The gendered nature of some of these occupational images may have been significant at the time of their creation and deployment. Most obviously images of working women provided counter evidence to the contemporary image of the cloistered Roman matron. It has been suggested that some images of women workers could have provided an erotic charge for some male viewers, and that some images of female workers might have been subject to a male gaze which in the case of some individual male viewers could have included a sexual fetishisation of the image both because of the gender of the protagonist portrayed and because of the nature of the act of labour itself. Might the same have applied to viewers of some images of male workers? Indeed in the same vein some images of male workers in hyper-masculine roles might too have delivered a frisson of sexual tension in some viewers, even if unintentionally.

The Latin sexual vocabulary equated many occupations and tools of certain trades with metaphorical images of sex and eroticism and this may well have extended to visual vocabulary too.[16] In the Latin sexual vocabulary the metaphorical uses of the names and actions of certain occupations and trades in sexual allusions and references were common, as indeed were the names of tools. Thus, for instance, ploughing, digging, sowing, grinding, kneading, beating, and hammering each contributed towards the creation of Latin double entendres, while hammers, grinding stones, ploughshares, sickles, ovens, awls, and the word for a tool in general – *instrumentum* – became handy euphemisms for sexual organs or for alluding to sexual acts. This metaphorical link between production and reproduction in language was certainly connected to a sexualisation of work processes and certain kinds of workers. Such metaphors may indeed have had their origins in the rituals of production. In this vein, butchers and the sawing of cuts of meat springs immediately to mind, but sexual metaphor might also have included references to a miller's grindstone or a smith's raised hammer, and so on.

Of considerable relevance to any discussion of work-metaphor language, is the study of English occupational folk songs of the seventeenth to nineteenth centuries, both of pre-industrial England and of the industrialised country.[17] Popular song, either transmitted from singer to singer or through published 'broadsides' or pamphlets, represented a truly plebeian art form. This category of song included both work songs, which accompanied work and mimicked its rhythm, and generalised labour or narrative songs. Thousands of such songs have been recorded by researchers and fieldworkers and their analysis of the corpus has found that very few occupations went totally unrepresented in song. Occupations acted as signifiers in the songs and it will perhaps come as no surprise to learn that in the English song tradition as in the Latin sexual vocabulary the sexual nature of songs about or involving butchers was a common trope.

It would seem then that the celebration of a professional identity became a typically Roman trait from the time of the late Republic, from the second century BC onwards. Numbers of such images peaked in the first half of the second century AD and we see a subsequent increase in mainly Christian contexts in the fourth century. A good illustration of how this phenomenon was particularly Roman can be found in the area of Aegean Thrace where the repertoire of motifs employed on figured grave reliefs remained local and Greek for centuries before Roman rule and influence. However, among the Romanising aspects on this particular facet of regional Greek culture was the occasional allusion to the occupation of the deceased on some of the local grave markers, even though the ethnic mix of the population did not appear to change.

The earliest employment of a working or professional image must have come about as an extension of, and complementary to, contemporary social ritual and a growing sense of group identity. Émile Durkheim has suggested that the first cultural expression of this identity or of a particular occupational calling would have been through ritual, and it is therefore hardly surprising that it was in the funerary sphere where images of Roman workers first became widespread.

The kind of activity detailed in this book constitutes part of what might be called the cultural and social elements of the Roman economy. The economic system that emerged in ancient Rome was not all about the money; rather, it also involved the city's elite in a kind of voluntary engagement in cooperative and benevolent social behaviour that allowed them to obtain or enhance their prestige and status in return. This might have been manifested most obviously in the endowment of public buildings, a kind of architectural benefaction known as euergetism, but it also arose more naturally from the interaction of capital, construction, urbanism, and employment which created cultural space that allowed for the emergence and public celebration of the working and professional identities of the workers within the economy. To some extent this mirrored or was mirrored by the microcosmic world of the Roman army wherein traditional structures linked to power, discipline, and anonymity allowed for the retention and expression of personal identity in certain cultural and social contexts, such expressions tending towards the strengthening of the whole rather than its weakening by atomisation into uncontrollable parts.

This whole book has been about ideas of identity and belonging, the opposing of the banality and boredom of many working lives. Workers' images have been used as a lens to explore Roman society through works which engaged with both genre and social and gender experimentation and which questioned the modes of acceptable display which enabled and nurtured this art, while other cultural forms were on the cusp of obsolescence. We should not underestimate the ability of art such as this to have moved and physically engaged its contemporary audience in the same way as it does us today beyond its purely figurative or representational function. It was somehow infectious, seeping into Roman culture, affecting both its form and its traditional narratives. The notion of belonging could change at different times and in different contexts and the trajectories of these material manifestations and their metaphorically personalised set of meanings and sense of place can perhaps be traced through analysing occupational art from its first emergence through to Late Antiquity.

The very earliest workers' funerary images must have vibrated, clashed, and brought a new kind of thought into being by their inherent vitality and truth. There would have been a point at which such images came to 'think' for themselves, as literary or film critics would term it, beyond the constraints of the human imagination. In reality, the trouble with Roman art had not been its technical limitations but the demands of broad society and the need to constantly compromise. There could have emerged a plebeian art of cruelty, contamination, and sensation: instead, Roman occupational imagery expanded and ruptured the expected repertoire of that art and gave rise to, or resulted from, new forms of thinking. The physical presence of viewers of funerary monuments, as opposed to the absence of individual bodies often portrayed in artworks there, allowed the art to conjure forth rather than simply represent bodies.

Much writing on Roman art omits the kind of art discussed in this book. This is usually reasonable given the titles and scope of many studies, focusing on elite, imperial, or state art. However, workers' images became part and parcel of what we now understand as Roman art in its totality and this art also became part of contemporary discourse about Roman culture. Discourse is not fixed, and indeed there are always struggles for meaning, and the fact that discourse over Roman culture changed across time is significant. Most fundamentally, it can be argued that the sorts of knowledge produced within these discourses did not simply concern sets of facts about the external world, they were also about the kinds of people the Romans were. They were bound up with the contemporary sense of self. They related to larger narratives, both national and imperial, as well as private and intimate notions of identity They dealt with issues of family, fracture, memory, grief, and the strangeness that infused the seemingly real, normal, and banal. The number, richness, and complexity of these images of working people suggests that they inhabited all kinds of intellectual and imaginary spaces, even if only to disrupt and dismantle existing frames of reference.

The images' needs and desires were potentially tragic in their intensity and at the same time capable of fulfilment in their simplicity. To view them was to be confronted with the immediacy of the entire gamut of emotions from despair to hope, from forgetfulness, through memory, into recognition. They gave form to their future absence, marking a tussle between the urge to reveal and the instinct to suppress, so deep was their shading of motive and consequence, bringing a sense of resolution, a feeling of closure through a kind of artistic intersectionality at play there.

If we view these images of working men and women as evidence of causation in the past, some kind of visual and conceptual mirror, then it might be thought that they acted to desacralize the visual field. To some extent this study might have been by and large one of absence and omission. What we do not see is often most significant and what is hidden, glossed over, or left out entirely cannot merely be ignored. These images seemed to permit no division between salvation and utility, empire and economy; here, radiant ideal and sober reality could be brought into some kind of apparently logical perceptual correspondence, a new kind of social realism for its time.

There was generally no place for representations of ordinary people in Roman historical reliefs or in imperial art, unless the narratives required this.[18] In the programme of relief images on Trajan's Arch at Benevento the emperor required the people to be there to receive his largesse and to give him acclaim, no more, no less.[19] The recording in a wall painting in the House of Actius Anicetus Castre(n)sis in Pompeii, now in the *Museo Archeologico Nazionale* in Naples, of the amphitheatre riot of AD 59, when local Pompeians fought with townspeople from neighbouring Nuceria, is certainly an exception in this respect.[20] Admittedly this incident was deemed so serious and so unseemly that it was also written about by the Roman historian Tacitus who also described the judicial aftermath and intervention by the Senate in Rome. Quite recently a monumental tomb was excavated in the San Paolino area outside Pompeii's Porta Stabia and there was discovered a detailed relief that included scenes of gladiatorial combat and of the brawl in the arena that sparked off the riot, the riot also being referenced in the hugely long and detailed dedicatory inscription at the tomb. An incidental element in the riot painting is the depiction of temporary stalls set up outside the amphitheatre, their owners either having abandoned them to save themselves and their goods or to join in the mayhem of the riot themselves.

Obviously, slaves were regularly portrayed in Roman art in many different media but usually in almost incidental roles – serving food or drink, attending on their master or mistress, combing hair, holding up mirrors, proffering jewellery boxes and so on. However, very occasionally slaves were portrayed in narrative episodes that placed them within the story and they thus became part of that story, though in both the cases to be cited here as examples there was a sexual undertow to both portrayals.[21] The first such image is on the silver vessel known as the Warren Cup in the British Museum in London. As two naked men have sex on a bed a third man, presumably a slave, surreptitiously watches the coupling through a partially open door. Is he a sexual voyeur? Was he spying for some other reason? Do the men on the bed know he is there? The other image appears on a wall painting in the House of Caecilius Iucundus in Pompeii, and this time involves a heterosexual coupling whose viewing is complicated by the fact that a third person, a woman stands at the foot of the bed, almost in an attitude of attendance. Was she a bedroom servant, an interpretation which seems most likely?

Because so many of the workers' images and occupational names discussed in this book were employed in funerary contexts – on name plates in *columbaria*, on stele or tombstones, on tombs and mausolea, or on funerary altars – such images became part of Roman devotional life, certainly in the city of Rome itself and in northern Italy but also in certain of the provinces, as we have seen. These monuments infused their cultural environment with a sacrality which was at the same time quotidian and profane. Their form often would have had the ability to link memory, visual and written literacy, and tactility. Their presence in many cemeteries, juxtaposed with other types of grave memorial, would have broken down the marked oppositions between sacred and profane, life and the afterlife, decoration and devotion, and beauty and *pietas*. The value and potency of such objects may have rested in their balancing of levels of reality and illusion by the interplay between text and image.

The contemporary viewers of these funerary monuments of workers, artisans, and professionals had to draw out the visual, rhetorical, and metaphorical clues provided in these images in order to interpret the varied associations offered. The same image might have created different experiences, including understanding, incomprehension, emulation, annotation, meditation, or inattention. The great power of these memorials was their capacity to encompass multiple meanings, to cross boundaries of culture and propriety, and to set up and embrace contradictions. Workshop interiors in images echoed all the ways workspace was arranged for practical usage but in a funerary context these spaces became otherwise inhabited by the spirits of the departed and domestic cares intruded into the celebration of the afterlife and religious rites.

Perhaps the problem with presenting information in museum contexts about workers, artisans, and professionals in the Roman world is the fact that their story does not form a coherent, ordered, or orderly narrative. Yet a self-reflexive analysis of the way the archaeological record acquires, stores, and uses information from the past could help overturn this situation. I am not suggesting for a minute that there is some kind of conspiracy in operation today to suppress an understanding of the complex interdependency of the various social classes in Roman society but rather that there should be room for a modern model of ancient identity which reunites all these different atomised social identities back into their social world and presents that world back to the lay public as an academic project and practice. The move towards creating difference in terms of a Freudian 'narcissism of small differences' has made difference a defining characteristic of ancient Roman life rather than its unifying mode.

Identity was, and is, socially produced, socially embedded, to a greater or lesser extent depending on the nature of the society in question, and is worked out in people's everyday social and working lives. Other issues tend to cohere around identity, but must always have included in the past a concern with memory, with small and grand narratives, a concern with sameness and difference at all levels, a concern with the interaction of private and public worlds, a concern with agency and its limits, and today an overriding concern with authenticity of various sorts.

The wider cultural narrative around which the definition of identity among Roman and Romanised workers and professionals took place was that of Roman history. There would have been no Roman empire without the city's architects and builders, its masons and carpenters, its bakers and butchers, its metalworkers, its textile workers and shoemakers, its potters and glassmakers, its musicians and entertainers, and, of course its soldiers and slaves. Eurysaces the Baker and others like him forged their identity through a series of creative acts in which they interpreted and reinterpreted their memory and experiences, articulated within the contemporary historical narrative and by way of a cultural mode of expression, that is Roman art, which allowed them to propose a way for others to understand this identity themselves and to situate it within their own personal experience.

It must be understood that there was no prohibitive, denying force working from the rulers and upper echelons of Roman society to stop those lower down the social scale forming, proclaiming, and exhibiting their own identities within the framework of first and foremost being Roman. Thus, while this study could be thought to be about cityscapes and the people within them they are primarily interior constructions.

It is interesting quite how specialised Roman craft and industry became, and how the Latin language had to grow to take in the names for each of these trades.[22] In an earlier chapter it was mentioned that there were eight or more different names for makers or repairers of different types of shoes, boots, sandals, and slippers, so it should come as no surprise to learn that in total 160 different trades are recorded in the city of Rome from inscriptions and other texts, 85 in Pompeii, with around 225 in total known from the Roman west as a whole. Following industrialisation, nineteenth century Birmingham in the English midlands became known as 'the city of a thousand trades', most of those trades being connected to metalworking of one kind or another and in many ways we should think of Rome as much as 'a city of multiple trades' as a city of empire. Each trade had its own trade tools, images of which were often used symbolically (Plate 99), as we have seen.

While there was unlikely to have been much mobility between trades or professions, sometimes this can be seen to have occurred. If Eurysaces began life as a humble baker and made his way up to owning his own bakery and becoming a contractor and businessman in the process then that seems quite logical. Less easy to understand is the career of Lucius Nerusius Mithres from Magliano, in southern Tuscany, as set out in the inscription on his tombstone, which tells us that he started out selling goatskins or wool and worked his way up from there. 'I dealt in popular goods, my rare honesty was praised always and everywhere. My life was happy, I built myself a tombstone of marble, I lived free from care, always paid my taxes, was honest in all my contracts, just to all men as far as I could be, often helped a petitioner...' Here Mithres is not only emphasising his humble beginnings but also making an attempt to occupy the moral high ground by emphasising how honest and open he had been in his commercial dealings, as far as was possible he adds as some form of insurance against any disgruntled former customer who might have been viewing his tombstone. From Lyon in central southern France come two lengthy inscriptions that show a remarkable degree of occupational diversity: Marcus Primius Secundianus is not only a *sevir augustales*, but occupationally is described as a boatman or boat owner but also as a carpenter and a trader in brine; Toutius Incitatus was also a boatman, but also a sackcloth maker and grain dealer.

The new times of empire had to be represented concretely and conceptually. Artistic commissions had to reify the key forces involved in the transformation of Rome as reflected in the lives of its workers and develop a discourse which would express the changes not only as physical phenomena but as concepts. The physical forces included new lands and new, and more, raw materials to be worked and transformed, leading to new ideas centred around labour identity, power, and productivity. The images discussed in this book were therefore located in a nexus of responses to the changing times.

Though the main thesis of this book has been the great visibility of workers and professionals in the Roman world and their forging of individual, group, and class identities, in passing discussion has also included topics such as child labour, industrial accidents, workers' riots, and slavery. To learn that a child such as Quartulus or Quintus Artulus died so young probably through work in a mine or that the slave Hermas died after falling off insecure scaffolding or a faulty ladder, or that the mintworkers of Rome rioted in AD 271 to bloody effect, sets the issue of identity in a more causatory context. Almost three quarters of slaves in Rome who were recorded in inscriptions with an occupational title were tied to a wealthy owner, family, or household rather than operating in any kind of free market. A significant proportion of these household slaves would have been children. Even apprenticeships did not necessarily provide a safe environment for all child workers, as is evidenced by the case of an apprentice worker blinded by his irate cobbler employer.[23]

Earlier in the book I referred to the idea of identity as performance, a theory first formulated by Erving Goffman and subsequently elaborated on by others. This is undoubtedly a very useful tool for analysing Roman sculpture and funerary monuments in general, but perhaps less so for the kind of workers' funerary monuments discussed in this book. Of course, a classic performance is provided by the portrait image on the funerary stele of the Roman shoemaker Caius Iulius Helius (discussed in Chapter Three) in particular. It is surprising perhaps that of the numerous workers, artisans, and professionals whose funerary monuments have been discussed in this book only a few took the opportunity, or had that opportunity taken for them by their families or heirs, to have their portraits sculpted on their memorials, in addition to or in lieu of the use of an image or images of their professions.[24] Notable exceptions to this were the silversmith Publius Curtilius Agatho, perhaps Eurysaces the Baker and his wife, and Septimia Stratonice of Ostia whose stele image was big enough and detailed enough to be considered a portrait, presumably commissioned by her good and admiring friend Marcus who dedicated the memorial to her and to his son. When portraits were additionally commissioned it would appear that issues other than simply those connected to occupational identity were at play. There would appear to have been a kind of brutal honesty on display in the case of many of the other funerary images and texts used by some Romans to present their working identities, as discussed above. This makes their analysis in terms of performance unrewarding and questions their very authenticity.

Eurysaces and his ilk proposed a way to understand Roman society in a way that did not involve the unfurling of grand narratives and the working of historical processes. However, these images were social products rather than simply unproblematic and transparent reflections of social reality. We often have to try and go beyond such representations of lives to consider the reality of the lives themselves and beyond their descriptive essence to consider the context of what they described. Once images of workers became common we need also to consider issues around intertextuality: were later images of workers created by implicitly or explicitly drawing on and referring to earlier workers' images in some cases?

As this study reaches its end it is worth reflecting on the outcome of the whole endeavour. Readers will have gathered that

I am not supportive of the stance taken by some writers on the ancient world that the history of the forging of public identities by workers and professionals in the Roman world through art and representation is lost in time and that the lives of these workers therefore constitute some kind of hidden history. But there has been no conspiracy here, no attempt to erase such people from the historical record. Rather it is a situation brought about by academic priorities and the reflection of this in museological practice. Academic priorities have shifted greatly in the almost forty years since Natalie Kampen and Gerhard Zimmer published their ground-breaking studies on images of working Romans,[25] and scarcely a month goes by without a new academic book appearing on some aspect of the Roman economy and the workers that drove that system. Yet, as one art historian has quite recently written on Roman workers' images: 'museums and their storage areas are filled with such objects, but proportionately few find their way into the histories of Roman art or sculpture.'[26] Indeed. Even as recently as 2005, one academic writing about Roman glass noted that 'in common with the majority of skilled artisans in the ancient world, little is known about the glassworkers as individuals'.[27]

Much of this book has been about named individuals who by necessity have become subsumed within the general category of Roman workers. The trend towards the depersonalising of designs on funerary monuments meant that these workers' images could be approached not as an aggregation of individual expressive subjects but as a conceptual consistency. Like a literary cut-up, the images viewed/read in different orders could and did dislocate established narratives, break habits, and allowed new associations to coalesce around the generalised identity of the worker. Ultimately it became what it was originally a reaction against, that is the dismantling of identity, with individuals cast into an indifferent sea with no object of personal identification other than their name and trade. The existing identities no longer served as anchors. In many ways, we have been able to map their presence and their anxieties onto the physical geography of the city of Rome and onto that of many other towns across the western empire. Every one of these images, after the very first one, became both a hypotext and a hypertext, that is both the model for and the product of reception. In other words the process became self-perpetuating. In these occupational images experiences were not merely represented, rather they were transformed through their articulation. It was their potency and resonance that made such enlargements of meaning and their depths possible.

It might be thought that the composer Jean Sibelius's well-known quip that 'no one ever put up a statue to a critic' could equally be applied to ancient Rome where many might have thought that no one would put up a monument to commemorate a baker or a butcher, yet in the absence of such public recognition they did it themselves, as this book has demonstrated.

Notes

Preface
1. Kampen 1981.
2. Zimmer 1982.
3. Wilson and Flohr 2016.
4. Joshel 1992. For earlier statistical work see Kühn 1910.
5. Mayer 2012.

1 The Dignity of Labour: Presentation or Performance?
1. On Greek and Roman attitudes to the idea of work see, for example, Joshel 1992, pp. 63–68; Verboven 2014; and Vernant 1956.
2. On Christian attitudes to the idea of work see, for example, Arbesmann 1973; MacCormack 2001; and Ovitt 1994.
3. Seneca. *Epistulae Morales* 56.1–2.
4. Artemidorus. *Oneirocritica* 1.51 and 2.20.
5. Cicero. *De Officiis* 1.150–151.
6. Aristotle *Ethica Nicomachea* 5.10.7.
7. Aristotle *De Generatione Animalium* 2.730b.20–23.
8. Aristotle *Politica* 7.1329a.
9. Seneca. *Epistulae Morales* 90.
10. St Augustine. *De Civitate Dei* 22.24.
11. Suetonius. *Vespasianus* 1.
12. Synesius. *Epistulae* 57.26.
13. Tacitus. *Annales* 15.34 and *Historiae* 1.37.2.
14. On the Balbus inscription see Bond 2016a and Guarnieri 2010, p. 35.
15. On the Severina inscription see Guarnieri 2010, p. 24.
16. On Trimalchio's wall painting see Petronius. *Satyrica* 29.3–6.
17. On slave labour see, for example, Bernard 2016, pp. 65–69; George 2013; Joshel 1992, pp. 145–161; Joshel and Petersen 2015; Kirschenbaum 1987; Laes 2008; Lenski 2013; and MacLean 2018.
18. On freedmen and freedwomen and Roman culture and life see, for example, Borg 2012; Broekart 2016a; D'Ambra and Métraux 2006; Garnsey 1981;

George 2006; Joshel 1992, pp. 128–144; Kirschenbaum 1987; Leach 2006; López Barja De Quiroga 1995; Maclean 2018; Marcone 2016; Mihăilescu-Bîrliba 2018; Mouritsen 2001, 2005, and 2011; Petersen 2006 and 2009; and Verboven 2012. On the idea of the ancient 'middle class' see Mayer 2012 and Veyne 2000. On various aspects of freedmen and freedwomen and their relationship with art and culture see specifically Petersen 2006.

19. On the Tomb of the Haterii see Kleiner 1992, pp. 196–199; Leach 2006; and Zimmer 1982, pp. 160–161.
20. Ammianus Marcellinus. *Res Gestae* 17.4.15.
21. On the Trier *Adventus* Ivory see, for instance, Brubaker 1999; Chatterjee 2018; Holum and Vikam 1979; Wilson 1984; and Wortley 1980.
22. On the Obelisk of Theodosius see, for example, MacCormack 1981, pp. 56–57.
23. On the *Hypogeum* of Trebius Justus see, for instance, Casalone 1962; Petrassi 1976; and Rea 2004.
24. On Roman architects see Van Beek 2017 and Von Hesberg 2015.
25. On the Basilica Aemilia see, for example, Kampen 1991 and Kleiner 1992, pp. 88–89.
26. On the building work on Trajan's Column see, for example, Ferris 2000, pp. 65–66.
27. On Roman building work and builders see, for instance, Adams 1994; Bernard 2016 and 2018; Bodei Giglioni 1974; Cohon 2010; DeLaine 2003; Favro 2011; Taylor 2003; Wright 2009; and Zimmer 1982, pp. 153–161. On Roman marble workers see, for instance, Claridge 2015; Fant 2001; Jockey 1998; Russell 2017; and Strong and Claridge 1976.
28. On signatures on mosaics see Dunbabin 1999, pp. 269–278.
29. On Roman woodworking principally see Ulrich 2007 and 2008a and Zimmer 1982, pp. 139–142.
30. On Diocletian's Edict of Maximum Prices see, for instance, Bernard 2016, pp. 8–83; Groen-Vallinga and Tacoma 2016; and Reynolds 1981.
31. On Minerva and cloth workers at Pompeii see principally Flohr 2013a and 2013b.
32. On the Virgin Mary Annunciate see Taylor 2018. Proclus. *Homilies* 1.431.
33. On Vulcan see, for instance, Brommer 1973 and 1978.
34. On Prometheus 'making man' see Mayor 2018, pp. 114–127.
35. Parker 2007, 409.
36. Antonio Gramsci 1912.
37. Joshel 1992.

2 Feeding the City: The Baker and His Wife

1. On Eurysaces the Baker see Brandt 1993; Ciancio Rossetto 1973; Coates-Stephens 2005/2006; Kleiner 1992, pp. 105–109; MacLean 2018, pp. 5–15; Petersen 2003 and 2006, pp. 84–120; Wilson and Schörle 2009; and Zimmer 1982, pp. 106–109.
2. MacLean 2018, p. 11.
3. On *arte plebea* see original article Bianchi Bandinelli 1967. A useful recent reassessment is Petersen 2015a. On Roman plebeian culture see, for instance

Courrier 2014 and 2016; Evans 2017; Huttunen 1974; Logghe 2017; Maxey 1938; Purcell 1994 and 1999; and Veyne 2000.
4. Zimmer 1982, pp. 106–120.
5. On the Trastevere relief see Wilson and Schörle 2009
6. On bakers at Pompeii see Monteix 2016a. On the idea of the 'ignoble (Roman) baker' see Bond 2016a, pp. 153–159. On preserved environmental evidence see Ciaraldi 2007.
7. On Trajan's arch at Benevento see, for example, Kleiner 1992, pp. 224–229.
8. Libanius. *Orations* 19–23.
9. On Roman butchers see Bond 2016a, pp. 109–112 and Zimmer 1982, pp. 93–106.
10. Kampen 1981, pp. 99 and 154.
11. Joshel 1992.
12. On this personalised mosaic at Pompeii see Curtis 1984.

3 Threads: Clothing the City

1. On textile work and workers see, for instance, Alfaro *et al.* 2004; Balzer 1983; Béal 2006–2007; Bevis 2014; Cardon and Feugère 2000; Cottica 2007; Cüppers 1968; D'Ambra 1989 and 1993; Deniaux 1995; De Ruyt 2001; Dickmann 2013; Dixon 2001; Drexel 1920; Drinkwater 1982 and 2001; Droß-Krüpe 2016a; Dumitrache 2018; Flohr 2011, 2013a, 2013b, and 2017; France 2004; Gillis and Nosch 2007; Gleba 2004; Gleba and Pásztókai-Szeőke 2013; Harlow and Nosch 2014; Holliday 1993; Hughes 2007; Larsson Lovén 1998a, 1998b, 2000, 2001, 2002, 2003, 2007a, 2007b, 2013, and 2014; Liu 2009 and 2013a; Moeller 1971; Monteix 2012 and 2013; Petersen 2009; Radman-Livaja 2013; Schwinden 1989; Setälä 1989 and 2002; Taylor 2018; Vicari 2001; Wild 1970, 2000, 2004, and 2008; Young 2000; and Zahn 1982. On fullers in particular see, for instance, Bevis 2014; De Ruyt 2001; and Flohr 2011, 2013a, 2013b, and 2017.
2. On the Forum Transitorium frieze see D'Ambra 1993.
3. Joshel 1992.
4. Zimmer 1982, pp. 120–132.
5. On the textile economy of northern Italy see Roncaglia 2018, pp. 89–100 and Vicari 1994. On the Modena stamped loom weights see Roncaglia 2018, p. 93.
6. See Chapter One: Note 30.
7. On the Valcamonica rock art images see, for example, Bevan 2006.
8. On the Igel Column see, for example, Balzer 1983; Béal 2006–2007; Cüppers 1968; Drexel 1920; Drinkwater 1982 and 2001; France 2004; Veyne 1986; and Zahn 1982.
9. On Titus Aelius Evangelus see Holliday 1993.
10. On the fullers of Pompeii see principally Flohr 2011, 2013a, 2013b, and 2017.
11. On the Verecundus paintings see, for example, Clarke 2003, pp. 105–112.
12. On *purpurarii* see, for instance, Hughes 2007 and Napoli 2004.
13. On the Siscia lead tags see Radman-Livaja 2013.
14. On theoretical ideas about shoe symbolism see, for instance, Nahshon 2008.
15. Joshel 1992.

16. On shoemakers and leather workers see, for instance, Baratta 2008; Leguilloux 2004; Van Driel-Murray 2008 and 2016; and Zimmer 1982, pp. 132–139. On tanners in particular and the taboo aspects of their work see Bond 2016a, pp. 97–125. On inscriptions naming tanners see Bond 2016a, Appendix III, pp. 203–207.
17. Petersen 2015, p. 448.
18. On Septimia Stratonice see Kampen 1981, pp. 64–69.
19. Clarke 2003, p. 216.
20. Zimmer 1982, pp. 132–139.
21. On the *Tomba del Calzolaio* at Nocera see Dé Spagnolis 2000, particularly pp. 52–56 and pp. 62–76.

4 Metal and Transformation: Metal Postcards
1. See Chapter One: Note 33.
2. Zimmer 1982, pp. 179–196 and on metalworking and tools see also Mattusch 2008 and Pernot 2011.
3. Joshel 1992.
4. On the Linares relief principally see Sandars 1905.
5. On the child miner Quartulus see Mander 2013, pp. 49–50 and p. 217 No. 259. On child workers see, for instance, Laes 2008 and 2011; Mander 2013, pp. 49–50 and 217; Martinez 2012; Sandars 1905; and Vuolanto 2015.
6. On Roman mining see, for instance, Healy 1978; Hirt 2010; Martinez and Garcia 2015; Millar 1984; and Sandars 1905. On condemnation to hard labour see Millar 1984.
7. On Arthur Munby see Hudson 1972. On other photographers and Welsh women miners see Lord 1998, pp. 152–153.
8. On the Atimetus altar see, for instance Clarke 2003, pp. 121–123.
9. On the Ostian Meleager sarcophagus see D'Ambra 1988.
10. On Roman mints see, for instance, Bond 2016a, pp. 126–141 and 2016b and Woytek 2012.
11. Eutropius. *Breviarium Historiae Romanae* 9.14; Aurelius Victor. *Epitome de Caesaribus* 35.6; *Scriptores Historiae Augustae. Aurelianus* 38.2-4. On the riots see also Bond 2016a, pp. 133–134 and 2016b, pp. 237–238 and Conway 2006.
12. See Chapter One: Note 30.
13. St Augustine. *De Civitate Dei* 7.4.
14. On the paintings in the House of the Vettii see, for instance, Clarke 2003, pp. 98–195; De Angelis 2011; Monteix 2016b; and Tameanko 1990.
15. Hobbs 2018 and Richard Hobbs *pers. comm.*, and for the broader background see Canepa 2017.
16. On miniature votive offerings see Kiernan 2009, particularly pp. 195-210 on the *Mithrassymbole*.

5 Making a Mark: Word as Image
1. On Greek signatures see, for instance, Hurwit 2015 and Keesling 2018. On stamping and identity see also Perkins 2000, pp. 204–208.
2. On Roman pottery stamps see, for instance, Fulford 2017; Fülle 1997; Hartley *et al.* 2008–2012; Kenrick 2004; Marichal 1988; and Presicce 2016.

On brick stamps see, for instance, Setälä 1989 and 2002. On stamped lead pipes see, for instance, Aubert 1993, pp. 176–178 and Bruun 2012.
3. On Binchester Roman fort see Ferris 2010.
4. On *Monte Testaccio* see, for example, Almeida 1984; Donkin 2017; Holleran 2012, pp. 76–78; and Tchernia 2016, pp. 250–252.
5. Joshel 1992.
6. Zimmer 1982, pp. 199–201, and on the relief of the potter and his wife see also Dobbins 1985.
7. On the scabrous *graffito* from the *Praedia* of Iulia Felix see Clarke 2003, pp. 95.
8. On Roman glass workers see, for instance, Baldoni 1987; Barag 1987; Caron 1997; Foy 2017; Foy and Nenna 2001; Harrison 1987; Leon 1941; Naumann-Steckner 1991; Stern 1999; Trowbridge 1930; and Whitehouse 1999.
9. On the Roman artist see, for example, Ling 2000; Squire 2015; Toynbee 1951; and Volkommer 2015. On Roman sculptors see, for instance, Charles-Picard 1961 and Erim and Roueché 1982.
10. On the Kerch painter see Goldman 1999. On the female painter trope see, for example, Ling 2000, pp. 93–94.
11. Pliny. *Naturalis Historia* 40.147–148.
12. On the 'painter burials' see Carroll 2006, p. 145 and Note 98.
13. Zimmer 1982, pp. 156–158. See also Chapter One: Note 27.
14. On the concept of 'the making of ancestors' on the *Testamentum* relief see D'Ambra 1995.
15. On retrospective signatures and the 'epigraphy of appropriation' see Keesling 2018.

6 An Empire on the Move
1. On Longidienus see, for instance Clarke 2003, pp. 118–121 and Zimmer 1982, pp. 143–144.
2. Clarke 2003, p. 120.
3. Zimmer 1982, pp. 144–148.
4. On Theokritos see Trimble 2017, pp. 121–123. On the Monument of C. Munatius Faustus see Petersen 2006, pp. 65–69.
5. On the Ostia sarcophagus see Kampen 1981, pp. 44–51.
6. On Roman transport see, for example, Adams 2012; Bakker; Béal 2006–2007; Bérard 2012; and Lund 2011.
7. On Minicius see Zimmer 1982, pp. 141–142.
8. On the Cabrières-d'Aigues monument principally see Cavalier 2008.
9. See Chapter Three: Note 8.
10. On the Colonzelle monument see principally Blanc 1976.
11. On Roman traders and trade see, for instance, Adam 2012; Broekaert 2011 and 2013; Evers 2017; Rice 2016; Schörle; and Wilson and Bowman 2017.
12. Joshel 1992.
13. See Chapter Six: Note 5.
14. On retail, shop workers, market traders and hawkers see, for instance, Caleresu and Van Den Hevel 2016; Ellis 2018; Holleran 2011, 2012a, 2012b, 2016, 2017, and Forthcoming; Kampen 1981, pp. 52–64 and 1982; Larsson Lovén 2018; Pirson 2007; Putzeys and Lavan 2007; Schoevaert 2018; and Treggiari 1980.

15. On the hawker figures and lamp bearers see, for instance Holleran 2016, pp. 28–30 and Lenski 2013, pp. 136–146.

7 Illusion and Metaphor

1. On metaphorical 'work' motifs on children's sarcophagi principally see Huskinson 1996, pp. 16 and 100.
2. On Quintus Sulpicius Maximus see Nelson 1903.
3. On the Mausoleum and sarcophagus of Santa Costanza (Constantina) see, for instance, Ferris 2015, pp. 61–62.
4. See Chapter Four: Note 14. On ancient perfume production see, for instance, Brun 2000; Brun and Monteix 2009; and Mattingly 1990.
5. On the idea of 'technical culture' see Cuomo 2007 and Monteix 2016b. On representations of technical processes see Ulrich 2008a. The quote is from Monteix 2016b, p. 211.
6. On the Vienna Dioscorides see Brubaker 2002.
7. Garland 1995.
8. On Roman entertainers such as actors and mimes see Dunbabin 2016, pp. 114–120 and 124–127 and Vincent 2012.
9. On Bassilla see Scrinari 1972, p. 117.
10. On the Antonine Wall legionary distance slabs see Breeze and Ferris 2016; Ferris Forthcoming; Keppie 1976, 1979, and 1988; and Keppie and Arnold 1984.
11. On the enamel vessels see Breeze 2012 and Henig 2011.
12. On the *agrimensores* see Dilke 1971.
13. See Chapter One: Note 26.
14. On hauntology see, for instance, Fisher 2014, pp. 97–182.

8 A Community of Workers: Strength in Numbers

1. Joshel 1992.
2. On spatial patterns in occupational funerary stele see, for instance, Reddé 1978, especially pp. 44–47 and p. 48 Fig. 1 and for patterns in textile production Vicari1994 Carte 2–5.
3. On urban crafts and craftsmen see, for example, Antonaras 2016; Béal and Goyon 2002; Brun 2016; Erdkamp 2012; Flohr and Wilson 2016; Goodman 2016; Hartnett 2017; Hawkins 2016; Holleran Forthcoming; Láng 2016; Larsson Lovén 2016; Loane 1938; MacMahon and Price 2005; Monteix 2011; Monteix and Tran 2011; Morel 1987; Mouritsen 2001; Papi 2002; Presicce 2016; Tran 2016; Wilson 2002; and Wilson and Flohr 2016. On the products of various Roman crafts see Strong and Brown 1976.
4. On the *Necropoli di Porto* see, for instance, Baldassarre *et al.* 1996.
5. On the *Piazzale delle Corporazioni* at Ostia see Rohde 2012.
6. On *columbarium* tombs see principally Borbonus 2014 and Hasegawa 2005.
7. Weatherill 1996.
8. On the clustering of artisans see Goodman 2016. On commerce and topography in Rome see, for instance, Carroll 2006, pp. 248–249; Droß-Krüpe 2016a, pp. 345–347; Goodman 2016, pp. 320–323; and Morel 1987.
9. On the idea of workers being classed as 'invisible Romans' see Knapp 2011.

10. On Roman *collegia* and associations see, for instance, Arnaoutoglou 2016; Ascough *et al.* 2012; Bérard 2012; Bond 2016a, pp. 8–10; Broekart 2011; Diosono 2007; Dondin-Payre and Tran 2012; Gabrielsen 2016; Hemelrijk 2008; Kloppenborg 1996; Liu 2009, 2013a, and 2013b; Patterson 1992 and 1994; Perry 2006; Rubio Rivera 1993; Tran 2006, 2013, and 2019; Van Haeperen 2012; Van Nijf 1997; Venticinque 2016; and Verboven 2002, 2007, 2011a, and 2011b.
11. Callistratus. *Digest* 50.6.6.12.
12. *Scriptores Historiae Augustae. Alexander Severus* 33.2.
13. On the Augustales see Petersen 2006, pp. 58–83 and Laird 2015.
14. Verboven 2016, p. 198.
15. On porphyry see, for instance, Del Bufalo 2012 and Malgouyres and Blanc-Richel 2003.
16. On the *ostaka* from *Mons Porphyrites* see Sheridan and Roth 1992. On *Mons Claudianus* see, for instance, Bülow-Jacobsen 2009.
17. On the *murex* industry see, for example, Giner 2016.
18. On the trade in wild animals see Ferris 2018, pp. 119–127.
19. On images of working women see Kampen 1981. The academic literature on women and work is vast, but see, for instance, Balielo 2016; Becker 2016; Boscolo 2005; D'Ambra 1989 and 1993; Dixon 2004; Dobbins 1985; Eichenauer 1988; Ferris 2015; Flemming 2007; Gardner 1999; Groen-Vallinga 2013; Haines-Eitzen 1998; Hemelrijk 2008 and 2012; Hemelrijk and Woolf 2013; Kampen 1982, Larsson-Lovén 1998a, 1998b, 2002, 2003, 2007a, 2007b, 2012, 2013, and 2016; Le Gall 1970; Morretta 1999; Parker 1997; Shelton 1998; Strong 2016; Taylor 2018; and Treggiari 1975a, 1976, 1979a, and 1979b.
20. See Chapter Four: Note 7.
21. On working couples see, for instance, Larsson Lovén 2016, pp. 210–211.
22. On women business owners see, for example, Dixon 2004, pp. 62–64.
23. On the carpenters' procession at Pompeii see, for example, Clarke 2003, pp. 85–87.
24. On occupational art in the catacombs see, for example, Bisconti 2004; Carletti 1982; Du Bourguet 1965; Fasola 2011; Stevenson 1978; and Wilpert 1903.

9 *Roman Tales: A Cacophony of Voices*

1. On later twentieth century Italian mass culture see, for example, Affron 1997; Forgacs and Gundle 2007; and Painter 2005 and 2018.
2. Golomstock 2011.
3. On the hierarchy of propaganda images see Golomstock 2011, pp. 254–260.
4. On Soviet/Stalinist images see also Baburina 1985; Becker and Caiger-Smith 1995; Bonnell 1997; Gale and Sidlina 2017; and Ward 2007.
5. On the products of the former Imperial Porcelain Factory see Kudryavtseva 2004.
6. Clarke 2003.
7. On Mussolini see, for instance; Affron 1997; Becker and Caiger-Smith 1995, pp. 12–17; Forgacs and Gundle 2007, pp. 198–247; Golomstock 2011, pp. 114–120, 209–213; and Painter 2005 and 2018.

8. On this exhibition see Squarciapino 1942.
9. On the significance of images of writing principally see Eckardt 2017, pp. 139–157 and 204–207. On female scribes see Eckardt 2017, pp. 155–157 and Haines-Eitzen 1998.
10. On the *Hypogeum* of the Aurelii see, for instance, Bradley 2019.
11. On Roman doctors and literacy see, for instance, Eckardt 2017, pp. 204–207 and on doctors in general Jackson 1988.
12. On this and other midwife images see Kampen 1981, pp. 33–44.
13. On Sosia Iuliana see Egger 1951 and Kampen 1981, p. 88.
14. On the *Meditrina* stele from Grand see Bouvier 2006.
15. On Gramsci see, for instance, Fiori 1970; Hoare and Smith 1971; Lawner 1979; and Spriano 1979.
16. On the Latin sexual vocabulary see Adams 1987.
17. On English occupational folk songs see Porter1992.
18. On 'ordinary Romans' and art see Clarke 2003.
19. See Chapter Two: Note 6.
20. On the riot at Pompeii see Moeller 1970. On the abandoned stalls see Holleran 2017, p. 162.
21. On these two sex scenes involving slaves see Clarke 1998, pp. 61–78 and 160–161 and Ferris 2015, pp. 180–182.
22. Joshel 1992.
23. Laes 2011, p. 193.
24. On the latest thoughts on Roman portraits see Fefjer 2008 and 2015, but see also Kleiner 1977 and 1987.
25. Kampen 1981 and Zimmer 1982.
26. Petersen 2015, p. 448.
27. Price 2005, p. 174.

Bibliography

Adam, J.-P. (1994) *Roman Building: Materials and Techniques*, London: Batsford.

Adams, C. (2012) 'Transport', in W. Scheidel (ed) 2012, pp. 218–240.

Adams, J.N. (1987) *The Latin Sexual Vocabulary*, London: Duckworth.

Affron, M. (1997) *Fascist Visions: Art and Ideology in France and Italy*, Princeton: Princeton University Press.

Alfaro, C., J.P. Wild, and B. Costa (eds) (2004) *Purpureae Vestes: Textiles et Tintes del Mediterráneo en Época Romana*, València: Consell Insular d'Eivissa I Formentera.

Almeida, E.R. (1984) *Il Monte Testaccio: Ambiente, Storia, Materiali*, Rome: Edizioni Quasar.

Amedick, R. (1991) *Die Antiken Sarkophagreliefs. Die Sarkophage mit Darstellung aus dem Menschengenleben. Vita Privata auf Sarkophagen 4*, Berlin: Gebr. Mann.

Antonaras, A. (2016) *Arts, Crafts and Trades in Ancient and Byzantine Thessaloniki: Archaeological, Literary and Epigraphic Evidence*, Regensberg: Schell and Steiner.

Arbesmann, R. (1973) 'The Attitude of St Augustine Toward Labor', in D. Neiman and M. Schatkin (eds) 1973 *The Heritage of the Early Church. Essays in Honor of the Very Reverend Georges Vasilievich Florovsky*, Rome: Orientalia Christiana Analecta 195, pp. 245–259.

Arnaoutoglou, I. (2016) 'Hierapolis and its Professional Associations: a Comparative Analysis' in A. Wilson and M. Flohr (eds) 2016, pp. 278–300.

Ascough, R.S., P.A. Harland and J.S. Kloppenborg (eds) (2012) *Associations in the Greco-Roman World. A Sourcebook*, Berlin: De Gruyter.

Atkin, M. and R. Osborne (eds) (2006) *Poverty in the Roman World*, Cambridge: Cambridge University Press.

Aubert, J.-J. (1993) 'Workshop Managers', in W. Harris (ed) 1993 *The Inscribed Economy: Production and Distribution in the Roman Empire in the Light of Instrumentum Domesticum, Proceedings of a Conference Held at the American Academy in Rome on 10th–11th January 1992*, Ann Arbor: University of Michigan Press, pp. 171–181.

Aubert, J.-J. (1994) *Business Managers in Ancient Rome. A Social and Economic Study of Institores, 200 B.C.–A.D. 250*, Leiden: Brill.

Augenti, E.D. (2016) *Gente dell'Antica Ostia. Una Ricerca Epigrafica*, Rome: Arbor Sapientiae Editore.

Baburina, N. (1985) *The Soviet Political Poster 1917–1980*, Harmondsworth: Penguin.

Bakker, L. (1990a) 'Apollon-Grannus und Weintransport: Zwei Neue Steindenkmäler aus Augusta Vindelicum, Stadt Augsburg, Schwaben', *Das Archäeologische Jahr in Bayern* 1990, pp. 107–109.

Bakker, L. (1990b) 'Weinverkauf und Kontorzene auf dem Grabmal des Pompeianius Silvinus aus Augsburg', *Das Archäeologische Jahr in Bayern* 1990, pp. 129–130.

Baldassarre, I, I. Bragantini, C. Morselli and F. Taglietti (1996) *Necropoli di Porto, Isola Sacra*, Rome: Libreria dello Stato.

Baldoni, D. (1987) 'Una Lucerna Romana con Raffigurazione di Officina Vetaria: Alcune Considerazioni sulla Lavorazione del Vitro Soffiato nell'Antichità', *Journal of Glass Studies* 29, pp. 22–29.

Balielo, A. (2016) 'Il Lavoro delle Donne nella Produzione Laterizia: Tracce dal Silencio', in C.P. Presicce (ed) 2016, pp. 24–25.

Balme, M. (1984) 'Attitudes to Work and Leisure in Ancient Greece', *Greece and Rome* 31, pp. 140–152.

Balzer, M. (1983) 'Die Alltagsdarstellungen der Treverischen Grabdenkmäler. Unterschungen zur Chronologie, Typologie und Komposition', *Trierer Zeitschrift* 46, pp. 8–151.

Banaji, J. (2015) *Exploring the Economy of Late Antiquity*, Cambridge: Cambridge University Press.

Barag, D. (1987) 'Recent Important Epigraphic Discoveries Related to the History of Glassmaking in the Roman Period', *Annales du 10th Congrès de l'Association Internationale pour l'Histoire du Verre (Madrid-Segovie 1985)*, pp. 109–116.

Baratta, G. (2008) 'La Produzione della Pelle Nell'Occidente e Nelle Province Africane', in J. González, P. Ruggeri, C. Vismara, and R. Zucca (eds) 2008 *L'Africa Romana: le Richezze dell'Africa: Risorse, Produzioni, Scambi. Atti del XVII Convegno di Studio, Sevilla, 14–17 Dicembre 2006*, Rome: Carocci, pp. 203–222.

Béal, J.-C. (1999) 'Remarques sur l'Imagerie du Pilier Funéraire d'Igel', in N. Blanc and A. Buisson (eds) 1999 *Imago Antiquitatis: Religion et Iconographie du Monde Romaine, Mélanges Offerts à Robert Turcan*, Paris: De Boccard, pp. 95–104.

Béal, J.-C. (2006–2007) 'Transporteurs et Propriétaires Terriens en Gaule Romaine: Un Bilan', *Revue Archéologique du Centre de la France* 45–46, pp. 9–21.

Béal, J.-C. and J.-C. Goyon (eds) (2002) *Les Artisans dans la Ville Antique*, Archéologie et Histoire de l'Antiquité 6, Lyons: Université Lumière Lyon-2.

Becker, H. (2016) 'Women in the Urban Economy: Occupations, Social Connections, and Gendered Exclusions', in S. Budin and J. Turfa (eds) 2016 *Women in Antiquity: Real Women Across the Ancient World*, London: Routledge, pp. 915–931.

Becker, L. and M. Caiger-Smith (eds) (1995) *Art and Power: Images of the 1930s*, London: Hayward Gallery.

Bellia, A., A. De Siena and G. Gruppioni (eds) (2017) *Solo Tombe di 'Musicisti' a Metaponto?: Studio dei Restei Ossei e degli Strumenti Musicali Contenuti nei Corredi Funerari*, Telestes 3, Pisa and Rome: Istituti Editoriali e Poligrafici Internazionali.

Bellingham, D.C. (1984) 'Review of G. Zimmer 1982 *Römische Berufsdarstellungen* and N.B. Kampen 1981 *Image and Status: Roman Working Women in Ostia*', *Journal of Roman Studies* 74, pp. 227–229.

Bérard, F. (2012) 'Les Corporations de Transport Fluvial à Lyon à l'Époque Romaine', in M. Dondin-Payre and N. Tran (eds) 2012, pp. 135–198.

Bernard, S.G. (2016) 'Workers in the Roman Imperial Building Industry', in K. Verboven and C. Laes (eds) 2016, pp. 62–86.

Bernard, S.G. (2018) *Building Mid-Republican Rome: Labor, Architecture, and the Urban Economy*, Oxford: Oxford University Press.

Bevan, L. (2006) *Worshippers and Warriors. Reconstructing Gender and Gender Relations in the Prehistoric Rock Art of Naquane National Park, Valcamonica, Brescia, Northern Italy,* British Archaeological Reports International Series 1485, Oxford: Archaeopress.

Bevis, E. (2014) 'Looking Between Loom and Laundry: Vision and Communication in Ostian Fulling Workshops', in M. Harlow and M.-L. Nosch (eds) 2014, pp. 306–322.

Bianchi Bandinelli, R. (1967) 'Arte Plebea', *Dialoghi di Archeologia* 1.1, pp. 7–19.

Bisconti, F. (2000) *Mestieri nelle Catacombe Romane. Appunti sul Declino dell'Iconografia del Reale nei Cimiteri Cristiani di Roma*, Vatican City: Pontificia Commissione di Archeologia Sacra.

Bisconti, F. (2004) 'Il Programma Decorativo dell'Ipogeo di Trebio Giusto tra Attitudine e Autorappresentazione', in R. Rea (ed) 2004 *L'Ipogeo di Trebio Giusto sulla Via Latina. Scavi e Restauri,* Vatican City: Pontificia Commissione di Archeologia Sacra, pp. 133–147.

Blanc, A. (1976) La Scène de Halage de Colonzelle (Drôme), *Revue Archéologique Narbonnaise* 9, pp. 247–250.

Bodei Giglioni, G. (1974) *Lavori Pubblici e Occupazione nell'Antichità Classica,* Bologna: Pàtron.

Bolle, K. (2018) 'Inscriptions Between Text and Texture: Inscribed Monuments in Public Spaces – a Case Study at Late Antique Ostia', in A. Petrovic, I. Petrovic and E. Thomas (eds) 2018 *The Materiality of Text: Placement, Perception, and Presence of Inscribed Texts in Classical Antiquity*, Leiden: Brill, pp. 348–379.

Bond, S. (2016a) *Trade and Taboo: Disreputable Professions in the Roman Mediterranean*, Ann Arbor: University of Michigan Press.

Bond, S. (2016b) 'Currency and Control: Mint Workers in the Later Roman Empire', in K. Verboven and C. Laes (eds) 2016, pp. 227–245.

Bonnell, V. (1997) *Iconography of Power: Soviet Political Posters Under Lenin and Stalin*, Berkeley: University of California Press.

Borbonus, D. (2014) *Columbarium Tombs and Collective Identity in Augustan Rome*, Cambridge: Cambridge University Press.

Borg, B. E. (2012) 'The Face of the Social Climber: Roman Freedmen and Elite Ideology', in S. Bell and T. Ramsby (eds) 2012 *Free at Last!: the Impact of Freed Slaves on the Roman Empire*, London: Bloomsbury Academic, pp. 25–49.

Borg, B. E. (ed) (2015) *A Companion to Roman Art*, Malden: Wiley-Blackwell.

Borg, B. E. (2019) *Roman Tombs and the Art of Commemoration: Contextual Approaches to Funerary Customs in the Second Century CE*, Cambridge: Cambridge University Press.

Boscolo, F. (2005) 'Aurelia Nais, Piscatrix de Horreis Galbae e i Piscatores di Roma', *Rivista Storica dell'Antichità* 35, pp. 181–188.

Bouvier, M.M. (2006) 'Une Nouvelle Intérpretation des Stèles de Grand (Vosges)', *Bulletin de la Société Nationale des Antiquaires de France* 2006, pp. 267–282.

Bowman, A. and A. Wilson (eds) (2009) *Quantifying the Roman Economy: Methods and Problems*, Oxford: Oxford University Press.

Bradley, J. (2019) *The Hypogeum of the Aurelii: a New Interpretation as the Collegiate Tomb of Professional Scribae*, Oxford: Archaeopress.

Bradley, K. (1985) 'Child Labour in the Roman World', *Historical Relections/ Réflexions Historiques* 12.2, pp. 311–330.

Brandt, O. (1993) 'Recent Research on the Tomb of Eurysaces', *Opuscula Romana* 19, pp. 13–17.

Breeze, D. (ed) (2012) *The First Souvenirs. Enamelled Vessels from Hadrian's Wall*, Kendal: Cumberland and Westmorland Antiquarian and Archaeological Society.

Breeze, D. and I.M. Ferris (2016) 'They Think It's All Over. The Face of Victory on the British Frontier', *Journal of Conflict Archaeology Online*.

Brewster, E.H. (1917) *Roman Craftsmen and Tradesmen of the Early Empire*, New York: Burt Franklin 1972 Edition.

Broekaert, W. (2011) 'Partners in Business: Roman Merchants and the Potential Advantages of Being a *Collegiatus*', *Ancient Society* 41, pp. 221–256.

Broekaert, W. (2013) *Navicularii et Negotiantes: a Prosopographical Study of Roman Merchants and Shippers*, Rahden; Marie Leidorf.

Broekaert, W. (2016a) 'Freedmen and Agency in Roman Business' in A. Wilson and M. Flohr (eds) 2016, pp. 222–253.

Broekaert, W. (2016b) 'The Economics of Culture. Shared Mental Models and Exchange in the Roman Business World', in K. Droß-Krüpe, S. Föllinger and K. Ruffing (eds) 2016, pp. 163–184.

Broekaert, W. and A. Zuiderhoek (2013) 'Industries and Services', in P. Erdkamp (ed) 2013, pp. 317–335.

Brommer, F. (1973) *Der Gott Vulkan auf Provinzialrömischen Reliefs*, Cologne: Böhlau-Verlag.

Brommer, F. (1978) *Hephaistos, Der Schmiedegott in der Antiken Kunst*, Mainz: Von Zabern.

Brubaker, L. (1999) 'The Chalke Gate, the Construction of the Past, and the Trier Ivory', *Byzantine and Modern Greek Studies* 23(1), pp. 258–285.

Brubaker, L. (2002) 'The Vienna Dioskurides and Anicia Juliana', in A.R. Littlewood, H. Maguire, and J. Wolschke-Bulmahn (eds) 2002 *Byzantine Garden Culture*, Washington: Dumbarton Oaks Research Library and Collections, pp. 189–214.

Brun, J.-P. (2000) 'The Production of Perfumes in Antiquity: The Cases of Delos and Paestum', *American Journal of Archaeology* 104, pp. 277–308.

Brun, J.-P. (ed) (2009) *Artisanats Antiques d'Italie et de Gaule. Mélanges Offerts à Maria Francesca Buonaiuto*, Naples: Centre Jean Bérard.

Brun, J.-P. (2016) 'The Archaeology of Roman Urban Workshops: a French Approach?' in A. Wilson and M. Flohr (eds) 2016, pp. 23–54.

Brun, J.-P. and N. Monteix (2009) 'Les Parfumeries en Campanie Antique', in J.-P. Brun (ed) 2009, pp. 115–133.

Bruun, C. (2012) 'New Prosographical Data Derived from Roman Lead Pipe Inscriptions', *Arctos* 46, pp. 19–31.

Bülow-Jacobsen, A. (ed) (2009) *Mons Claudianus. Ostraca Graeca et Latina IV. The Quarry Texts*, Cairo: Institut Français d'Archéologie Orientale du Caire.

Bibliography

Burford, A. (1972) *Craftsmen in Greek and Roman Society*, London: Thames and Hudson.

Calaresu, M. and D. Van Den Hevel (eds) (2016) *Food Hawkers: Selling in the Street from Antiquity to the Present*, London: Routledge.

Campbell, B. (2012) *Rivers and the Power of Ancient Rome*, Chapel Hill: University of North Carolina Press.

Canepa, M. (2017) *The Two Eyes of the Earth: Art and Ritual of Kingship Between Rome and Sasanian Iran*, Berkeley: University of California Press.

Cardon, D. and M. Feugère (eds) (2000) *Archéologie des Textiles: Des Origines au Ve Siècle. Actes du Colloque de Lattes, Octobre 1999*, Montagnac: Monique Mergoil.

Carletti, S. (1982) *Guide to the Catacombs of Priscilla*, Rome: Pontificia Commissione di Archeologia Sacra.

Carlsen, J. (2016) 'Le Attività Agricole e dell'Allevamento', in A. Marcone (ed) 2016, pp. 225–264.

Caron, B. (1997) 'Un Fragment de Lampe Représentant un Four de Verrier', *Journal of Glass Studies* 39, pp. 197–198.

Carroll, M. (2006) *Spirits of the Dead: Roman Funerary Commemoration in Western Europe*, Oxford: Oxford University Press.

Casalone, C. (1962) 'Note sulle Pitture dell'Ipogeo di Trebio Giusto a Roma', *Cahiers Archéologiques* 12, pp. 57–64.

Cavalier, O. (ed) (2008) *La Scène de Halage de Cabrières-d'Aigues*, Avignon: Imprimerie Laffont.

Cefalo, G. (2019) 'La Rappresentazione del Sé e la Ricerca del Prestigio Sociale Attraverso il Ricordo della Professione e la Sepoltura ad Sanctos', *Aiônos. Micellanea di Studi Storici* 21 (2017), pp. 209–231.

Chardron-Picault, P. (2008) *Hommes de Feu. L'Artisanat en Pays Éduen. Catalogue de l'Exposition 22 Septembre 2007–Janvier 2008*, Autun: Musée Rolin.

Charles-Picard, G. (1961) 'Sur une Famille de Sculpteurs d'Aquitaine, d'Apres une Stele Funéraire du Musée de Bordeaux', *Revue Archéologique* 2, pp. 96–100.

Chatterjee, P. (2018) 'Iconoclasm's Legacy: Interpreting the Trier Ivory', *The Art Bulletin* 100(3), pp. 28–47.

Ciancio Rossetto, P. (1973) 'Il Sepolcro del Fornaio Marco Virgilio Eurisace a Porta Maggiore', in *I Monumenti Romani* 5, Rome: pp. 1017–1018.

Ciaraldi, M. (2007) *People and Plants in Ancient Pompeii: a New Approach to Urbanism from the Microscope Room*, Accordia Specialist Studies on Italy Volume 12, London: University of London.

Claridge, A. (2010) *Rome. An Oxford Archaeological Guide*, Second Edition, Oxford: Oxford University Press.

Claridge, A. (2015) 'Marble Carving Techniques, Workshops, and Artisans', in E.A. Friedland and M.G. Sobocinski (eds) 2015, pp. 107–122.

Clarke, J.R. (1998) *Looking at Lovemaking. Constructions of Sexuality in Roman Art 100 BC–AD 250*, Berkeley: University of California Press.

Clarke, J.R. (2003) *Art in the Lives of Ordinary Romans. Visual Representation and Non-Elite Viewers in Italy, 100 B.C.–A.D. 315*, Berkeley: University of California Press.

Clarke, J.R. (2014) 'Sexuality and Visual Representation', in T.K. Hubbard (ed) 2014, pp. 509–533.

Clarke, J.R. and M. Larvey (2003) *Roman Sex: 100BC to 250 AD*, New York: Harry J. Abrams.

Coarelli, F. (2014) *Rome and Environs: An Archaeological Guide*, Updated Edition, Berkeley: University of California Press.

Coates-Stephens, R. (2005/2006) 'Un Pistrinum Tardo-Repubblicano a Porta Maggiore', *Rendiconti della Pontificia Accademia Romana di Archeologia* 78, pp. 473–498.

Cohon, R. (2010) 'Tools of the Trade: A Rare, Ancient Roman Builder's Funerary Plaque', *Antike Kunst* 53, pp. 94–100.

Connolly, S. (2010) *Lives Behind the Laws: The World of the Codex Hermogenianus*, Bloomington: Indiana University Press.

Conway, C.P.M. (2006) 'Aurelian's *Bellum Monetarium*: An Examination', *Past Imperfect* 12.

Cornell, T.J. (1987) *Art and Production in the World of the Caesars*, Milan: Olivetti.

Cottica, D. (2007) 'Spinning in the Roman World: From Everyday Craft to Metaphor of Destiny', in C. Gillis and M.-L. Nosch (eds) 2007, pp. 220–228.

Courrier, C. (2014) *La Plébe de Rome e Sa Culture (Fin du IIer Siècle av. J.-C.-Fin du Ier Siècle ap. J.-C.)*, Rome: École Française de Rome.

Courrier, C. (2016) 'Plebeian Culture in the City of Rome, from the Late Republic to the Early Empire', in L. Grig (ed) 2016 *Popular Culture in the Ancient World*, Cambridge: Cambridge University Press, pp. 107–128.

Craven, W. (1986) *Colonial American Portraiture: The Economic, Religious, Social, Cultural, Philosophical, Scientific, and Aesthetic Foundations*, Cambridge: Cambridge University Press.

Cristofori, A. (2016) 'Lavoro e Identità Sociale', in A. Marcone (ed) 2016, pp. 149–174.

Croisille, J.-M. (2010) *Paysages dans la Peinture Romaine*, Paris: Picard.

Cuomo, S. (2007) *Technology and Culture in Greek and Roman Antiquity*, Cambridge: Cambridge University Press.

Cupcea, G. and R. Varga (eds) (2018) *Social Interactions and Status Markers in the Roman World*, Archaeopress Roman Archaeology 37, Oxford: Archaeopress.

Cüppers, H. (1968) 'Arbeiten und Beobachtungen an der Igeler Säule', *Trierer Zeitschrift* 31, pp. 222–226.

Curtis, R.I. (1984) 'A Personalised Floor Mosaic from Pompeii', *American Journal of Archaeology* 88/4, pp. 557–566.

Cussini, E. (2017) 'The Pious Butcher and the Physicians: Palmyrene Professions in Context', in T. Long and A.H. Sørensen (eds) 2017, pp. 84–96.

D'Ambra, E. (1988) 'A Myth for a Smith: a Meleager Sarcophagus from a Tomb in Ostia', *American Journal of Archaeology* 92/1, pp. 85–99.

D'Ambra, E. (1989) 'The Cult of Virtues and the Funerary Relief of Ulpia Epigone', *Latomus* 48, pp. 392–400.

D'Ambra, E. (1993) *Private Lives, Imperial Virtues. The Frieze of the Forum Transitorium in Rome*, Princeton: Princeton University Press.

D'Ambra, E. (1995) 'Mourning and the Making of Ancestors in the Testamentum Relief', *American Journal of Archaeology* 99(4), pp. 667–681.

D'Ambra, E. (1998) *Roman Art*, Cambridge: Cambridge University Press.

D'Ambra, E. and G.P.R. Métraux (eds) (2006) *The Art of Citizens, Soldiers, and Freedmen in the Roman World*, BAR International Series 1526, Oxford: Archaeopress.

D'Arms, J.H. (1981) *Commerce and Social Standing in Ancient Rome*, Cambridge Massachusetts: Harvard University Press.

De Angelis, F. (2011) 'Playful Workers. The Cupid Frieze in the Casa Dei Vettii', in E. Poehler, M. Flohr, and K. Cole (eds) 2011 *Pompeii. Art, Industry and Infrastructure*, Oxford: Oxbow Books, pp. 62–73.

DeFelice, J. (2001) *Roman Hospitality: The Professional Women of Pompeii*, Warren Centre: Shangri-La Publications.

DeLaine, J. (2003) 'The Builders of Roman Ostia: Organisation, Status and Society', Proceedings of the First International Congress on Construction History, 20th–24th January 2003 Madrid: Instituto Juan de Herrera, pp. 723–732.

DeLaine, J. (2005) 'The Commercial Landscape of Ostia', in A. MacMahon and J. Price (eds) 2005, pp. 29–47.

Del Bufalo, D. (2012) *Porphyry. Red Imperial Porphyry: Power and Religion*, Turin: Allemandi.

Demarolle, J.-M. (2001) 'Un Corpus en Question: L'Iconographie Lapidaire des Métiers en Gaule Belgique', in M. Polfer (ed) 2001, pp. 31–42.

Dembin, E.Z. (2018) 'Voicing the Past: The Implications of Craft-Referential Pottery in Ancient Greece', in E. Simpson (ed) 2018 *The Adventure of the Illustrious Scholar: Papers Presented to Oscar White Muscarella*, Leiden: Brill, pp. 537–563.

Deniaux, E. (1995) 'L'Artisanat du Textile en Gaule: Remarques sur Quelques Inscriptions', *Cahiers du Centre G. Glotz* 6, pp. 195–206.

De Robertis, F.M. (1963) *Lavoro e Lavorati nel Mondo Romano*, Bari: Adriatica Editrice.

De Ruyt, C. (2001) 'Les Foulons, Artisans des Textiles et Blanchisseurs', in J.P. Descoeudres (ed) 2001 Ostia. Port et Porte de la Rome, Geneva: Musée Rath, pp. 186–191.

Dé Spagnolis, M. (2000) *La Tomba del Calzolaio Dalla Necropolis Monumentale Romana di Nocera Superiore*, Rome: Bretschneider.

Dickmann, J.-A. (2013) 'A 'Private' Felter's Workshop in the Casa dei Postumii in Pompeii', in M. Gleba and J. Pásztókai-Szeőke (eds) 2013, pp. 208–228.

Dilke, O.A. (1971) *The Roman Land Surveyors: An Introduction to the Agrimensores*, Newton Abbot: David and Charles.

Diosono, F. (2007) *Collegia: Le Associazioni Professionali nel Mondo Romano*, Rome: Quasar.

Di Stefano Manzella. I. (2017) 'Due Libarii Concorrenti a Pompei: Ipotesi Interpretative dei Criptici Graffiti CIL IV, 1768–1769', *Sylloge Epigraphica Barcinonensis* 15, pp. 199–213.

Dixon, S. (2001) 'How Do You Count Them If They're Not There? New Perspectives in Roman Cloth Production', *Opuscula Romana* 25/26, pp. 7–26.

Dixon, S. (2004) 'Exemplary Housewife or Luxurious Slut: Cultural Representations of Women in the Roman Economy', in F. McHardy and E. Marshall (eds) 2004 *Women's Influence on Classical Civilization*, London: Routledge, pp. 56–74.

Dixon, S. (2008) 'Gracious Patrons and Vulgar Success Stories in Roman Public Media', in S. Bell and I.L. Hansen (eds) 2008 *Role Models in the Roman World: Identity and Assimilation*, Ann Arbor: University of Michigan Press, pp. 57–68.

Dobbins, J.J. (1985) 'A Roman Funerary Relief of a Potter and His Wife', *Arts in Virginia* 25, pp. 24–33.

Dobres, A.-M. (2001) 'Meaning in the Making: Agency and the Social Embodiment of Technology and Art', in B. Schiffer (ed) 2001 *Anthropological Perspectives on Technology*, Albuquerque: University of New Mexico Press, pp. 47–76.

Dobres, A.-M. and C. Hoffman (1994) 'Social Agency and the Dynamics of Prehistoric Technology', *Journal of Archaeological Method and Theory* 1, pp. 211–258.

Donderer, M. (1989) *Die Mosaizisten der Antike und Ihre Wirtschaftliche und Soziale Stellung. Eine Quellenstudie*, Erlangen: Universitätsbibliothek Erlangen.

Donderer, M. (1996) *Die Architektenderspäten Römischen Republik Undder Kaiserzeit: Epigraphische Zeugnisse*, Erlangen: Universitätsbibliothek Erlangen.

Dondin-Payre, M. and N. Tran (eds) (2012) *Collegia: le Phénomène Associatif dans l'Occident Romain*, Bordeaux: Ausonius.

Donkin, L. (2017) 'Mons Manufactus: Rome's Man-Made Mountains Between History and Natural History (c. 1100–1700)', *Papers of the British School at Rome* 85, pp. 171–204.

Drexel, F. (1920) 'Die Bilder der Igeler Säule', *Deutsches Archaologisches Institut: Römische Abteilung Mitteilungen* 35, pp. 82–142.

Drinkwater, J.F. (1982) 'The Wool Textile Industry of Gallia Belgica and the Secundinii of Igel: Questions and Hypotheses', *Textile History* 13, pp. 111–128.

Drinkwater, J.F. (2001) 'The Gallo-Roman Woollen Industry and the Great Debate. The Igel Column Revisited', in D.J. Mattingly and J. Salmon (eds) 2001 *Economies Beyond Agriculture in the Classical World*, London: Routledge, pp. 297–308.

Droß-Krüpe, K. (2016a) 'Spatial Concentration and Dispersal of Roman Textile Crafts' in A. Wilson and M. Flohr (eds) 2016, pp. 334–351.

Droß-Krüpe, K. (2016b) 'Prinzipale und Agenten im Römischen Handel. Fallstudien zum Antiken Handel im Spiegel der Neuen Institutionenökonomik', in K. Droß-Krüpe, S. Föllinger and K. Ruffing (eds) 2016, pp. 63–76.

Droß-Krüpe, K., S. Föllinger and K. Ruffing (eds) (2016) *Antike Wirtschaft und Ihre Kulturelle Prägung*, Wiesbaden: Harrassowitz Verlag.

Du Bourguet, P. (1965) *Early Christian Painting*, London: Weidenfeld and Nicolson.

Dumitrache, I. (2018) 'Latin Occupational Titles in Roman Textile Trade', in G. Cupcea and R. Varga (eds) 2018, pp. 23–46.

Dunbabin, K.M.D. (1999) *Mosaics of the Greek and Roman World*, Cambridge: Cambridge University Press.

Dunbabin, K.M.D. (2016) *Theater and Spectacle in the Art of the Roman Empire*, Ithaca: Cornell University Press.

Durkheim, E. (1912) *The Elementary Forms of the Religious Life*, Translated by J.W. Swain, London: Allen and Unwin (1964 edition).

Durkheim, E. (1924) *Sociology and Philosophy*, Translated by D.F. Pocock, London: Cohen and West (1965 edition).

Eckardt, H. (2017) *Writing and Power in the Roman World: Literacies and Material Culture*, Cambridge: Cambridge University Press.

Egger, R. (1951) 'Zwei Oberitalienische Mystensarkophage', *Mitteilungen des Deutschen Archäologischen Institut Rom* 4, pp. 35–64.

Eichenauer, M. (1988) *Unterschungen zur Arbeitswelt der Frau in der Römischen Antike*, Frankfurt an Main: P. Lang.

Ellis, S.J.R. (2018) *The Roman Retail Revolution: The Socio-Economic World of the Taberna*, Oxford: Oxford University Press.

Erdkamp, P. (2012) 'Urbanism', in W. Scheidel (ed) 2012, pp. 241–265.

Erdkamp, P. (ed) (2013) The Cambridge Companion to Ancient Rome, Cambridge: Cambridge University Press.

Erdkamp, P. and C. Holleran (eds) (2018) *The Routledge Handbook of Diet and Nutrition in the Roman World*, London: Routledge.

Erdkamp, P., K. Verboven and A. Zuiderhoek (eds) (2015) *Ownership and Exploitation of Land and Natural Resources in the Roman World*, Oxford: Oxford University Press.

Erim, K.T. and C.M. Roueché (1982) 'Sculptors from Aphrodisias: Some New Inscriptions', *Papers of the British School at Rome 50*, pp. 102–115.

Espérandieu, É. (1907–1949) Recueil Général des Bas-Reliefs, Statues et Bustes de la Gaule Romaine, Volumes 1–13, Paris: Imprimerie National.

Evans, R. (ed) (2017) *Mass and Elite in the Greek and Roman Worlds. From Sparta to Late Antiquity*, London: Routledge.

Evers, K.G. (2017) *Worlds Apart Trading Together: The Organisation of Long-Distance Trade Between Rome and India in Antiquity*, Archaeopress Roman Archaeology 32, Oxford: Archaeopress.

Fant, J.C. (2001) 'Rome's Marble Yards', *Journal of Roman Archaeology* 14, pp. 167–198.

Fasola, U.M. (2011) *The Catacombs of Domitilla and the Basilica of the Martyrs Nereus and Achilleus*, Fourth Edition, Rome: Pontificia Commissione di Archeologia Sacra.

Fava, A.S. (1969) *I Simboli nelle Monete Argentee Republicane e la Vita dei Romani*, Turin: Museo Civico di Torino.

Favro, D. (2011) 'Construction Traffic in Imperial Rome', in R. Laurence and D.J. Newsome (eds) 2011 *Rome, Ostia, Pompeii: Movement and Space*, Oxford: Oxford University Press, pp. 332–360.

Fejfer, J. (2008) *Roman Portraits in Context*, Berlin: De Gruyter.

Fefjer, J. (2015) 'Roman Portraits', in B.E. Borg (ed) 2015, pp. 233–251.

Ferdière, A. (2001) 'La "Distance Critique": Artisans et Artisanat dans L'Antiquité Romaine et en Particulier en Gaule', *Les Petits Cahiers d'Anatole* 1, pp. 2–31.

Ferdière, A. (2005) 'L'Artisanat en Gaule Romaine', in L. Rivet (ed) 2005 *Société Française d'Étude de la Ceramique Antique en Gaule, Actes du Congrèes de Blois, 5th–8th May 2005, Marseilles*, pp. 7–14.

Ferris, I.M. (2000) *Enemies of Rome. Barbarians Through Roman Eyes*, Stroud: Sutton Publishing.

Ferris, I.M. (2010) *The Beautiful Rooms Are Empty. Excavations at Binchester Roman Fort, County Durham 1976–1981 and 1986–1991*, Durham: Durham County Council Excavation Monograph.

Ferris, I.M. (2012) *Roman Britain Through Its Objects*, Stroud: Amberley Publishing.

Ferris, I.M. (2015) *The Mirror of Venus. Women in Roman Art*, Stroud: Amberley Publishing.

Ferris, I.M. (2018) *Cave Canem. Animals and Roman Society*, Stroud: Amberley Publishing.

Ferris, I.M. Forthcoming 'Building an Image: Soldiers' Labour and the Antonine Wall Distance Slabs'.

Fiori, G. (1970) *Antonio Gramsci: Life of a Revolutionary*, London: NLB.

Fisher, M. (2014) *Ghosts of My Life: Writings on Depression, Hauntology and Lost Futures*, Winchester: Zero Books.

Flemming, R. (2007) 'Women, Writing and Medicine in the Classical World', *The Classical Quarterly* 57(1), pp. 257–279.

Flohr, M. (2011) 'Exploring the Limits of Skilled Craftmanship. The *Fullonicae* of Roman Italy', in N. Monteix and N. Tran (eds) 2011, pp. 87–100.

Flohr, M. (2013a) *The World of the Fullo: Work, Economy, and Society in Roman Italy*, Oxford: Oxford University Press.

Flohr, M. (2013b) 'Ulula, Quinquatrus and the Occupational Identity of Fullones in Early Imperial Italy', in M. Gleba and J. Pásztókai-Szeőke (eds) 2013 *Making Textiles in Pre-Roman and Roman Times. Peoples, Places, Identities. Ancient Textiles Series Vol. 13*, Oxford: Oxbow Books, pp. 192–207.

Flohr, M. (2016) 'Constructing Occupational Identities in the Roman World' in K. Verboven and C. Laes (eds) 2016, pp. 147–172.

Flohr, M. (2017) 'Beyond Smell: The Sensory Landscape of the Roman *Fullonica*', in E. Betts (ed) 2017 *Senses of the Empire: Multisensory Approaches to Roman Culture*, London: Routledge, pp. 39–53.

Flohr, M. and A. Wilson (2016) *The Economy of Pompeii*, Oxford: Oxford University Press.

Flohr, M. and A. Wilson (2016) 'Roman Craftsmen and Traders: Towards an Intellectual History' in A. Wilson and M. Flohr (eds) 2016, pp. 23–54.

Forgacs, D. and S. Gundle (2007) *Mass Culture and Italian Society from Fascism to the Cold War*, Bloomington: Indiana University Press.

Formigli, E. (1985) Tecniche dell'Oreficeria Etrusca e Romana: Originali e Falsificazioni, Florence: Sansoni.

Foy, D. (2017) 'An Overview of the Circulation of Glass in Antiquity', in A. Wilson and A. Bowman (eds) 2017, pp. 265–300.

Foy, D. and M.-D. Nenna (2001) *Tout Feu, Tout Sable. Mille Ans de Verre Antique dans le Midi de la France*, Aix en Provence: Musées de Marseille et Édisud.

France, J. (2004) 'Les Monuments Funéraires et le "Capitalisme" des Élites Trévires', in J. Andreau, J. France and S. Pittia (eds) 2004 Mentalités et Choix Économiques des Romaines, Pessac: Ausonius, pp. 149–178.

Freeman, J.B. (2018) *Behemoth: A History of the Factory and the Making of the Modern World*, New York: W.W. Norton.

Freu, C. (2016) '*Disciplina, Patrocinium, Nomen*: The Benefits of Apprenticeship in the Roman World' in A. Wilson and M. Flohr (eds) 2016, pp. 183–199.

Friedland, E.A. and M.G. Sobocinski (eds) (2015) *The Oxford Handbook of Roman Sculpture*, Oxford: Oxford University Press.

Fulford, M. (2017) 'Procurators Business? Gallo-Roman Sigillata in Britain in the Second and Third Centuries A.D.', in A. Wilson and A. Bowman (eds) 2017, pp. 301–326.

Fülle, G. (1997) 'The Internal Organization of the Arretine *Terra Sigillata* Industry: Problems of Evidence and Interpretation', *Journal of Roman Studies* 87, pp. 111–155.

Gabrielsen, V. (2016) 'Be Faithful and Prosper: Associations, Trust and the Economy of Security', in K. Droß-Krüpe, S. Föllinger and K. Ruffing (eds) 2016, pp. 87–112.

Gale, M. and N. Sidlina (eds) (2017) *Red Star Over Russia: a Revolution in Visual Culture 1905–55*, London: Tate Publishing.

Garçon, A.-F. (2011) 'Le Savoir Professionnel des Métiers de l'Antiquité: Constantes et Spécificités. Conclusions et Questions', in N. Monteix and N. Tran (eds) 2011, pp. 135–140.

Gardner, J.F. (1999) 'Women in Business Life: Some Evidence from Puteoli', in P. Setälä and L. Savunen (eds) 1999 *Female Networks and the Public Sphere in Roman Society*, Rome: Institum Romanum Finlandiae, pp. 11–27.

Garland, R. (1995) *The Eye of the Beholder: Deformity and Disability in the Graeco-Roman World*, Ithaca: Cornell University Press.

Garnsey, P. (ed) (1980) *Non-Slave Labour in the Greco-Roman World*, Cambridge: Cambridge Philological Society.

Garnsey, P. (1981) 'Independent Freedmen and the Economy of Roman Italy Under the Principate', *Klio* 63, pp. 359–371.

George, M. (2006) 'Social Identity and Dignity of Work in Freedmen's Reliefs', in E. D'Ambra and G.P.R. Métraux (eds) 2006, pp. 22–28.

George, M. (ed) (2013) *Roman Slavery and Roman Material Culture*, Toronto: University of Toronto Press.

Gillis, A.-C. (2014) *Corps, Travail et Statut Social. L'Apport de la Paléoanthropologie Funéraire aux Sciences Historiques*, Villeneuve d'Ascq: Presses Universitaires du Septentrion.

Gillis, C. and M.L.B. Nosch (eds) (2007) *Ancient Textiles: Production, Craft and Society*, Oxford: Oxbow Books.

Giner, C.A. (2016) 'Purple in the Ancient Mediterranean World: Social Demand and the Exploitation of Marine Resources', in T. Bekker-Nielsen and R. Gertwagen (eds) 2016 *The Inland Seas: Towards an Ecohistory of the Mediterranean and the Black Sea*, Stuttgart: Franz Steiner Verlag, pp. 138–159.

Gleba, M. (2004) 'Linen Production in Pre-Roman and Roman Italy', in C. Alfaro, J.P. Wild, and B. Costa (eds) 2002, pp. 29–38.

Gleba, M. and J. Pásztókai-Szeőke (eds) 2013 *Making Textiles in Pre-Roman and Roman Times. Peoples, Places, Identities. Ancient Textiles Series Vol. 13*, Oxford: Oxbow Books.

Goldman, B. (1999) 'The Kerch Easel Painter', *Zeitschrift für Kunstgeschichte* 62 Band H1, pp. 28–44.

Golomstock, I.N. (2011) *Totalitarian Art in the Soviet Union, the Third Reich, Fascist Italy, and the People's Republic of China*, London: Duckworth.

Goodman, P. (2016) 'Working Together: Clusters of Artisans in the Roman City', in A. Wilson and M. Flohr (eds) 2016, pp. 301–333.

Graham, S. (2005) 'Of Lumberjacks and Brick Stamps: Working with the Tiber as Infrastructure', in A. MacMahon and J. Price (eds) 2005, pp. 106–124.

Groen-Vallinga, M.J. (2013) 'Desperate Housewives? The Adaptive Family and Female Participation in the Roman Urban Labour Market', in E. Hemelrijk and G. Woolf (eds) 2013, pp. 295–312.

Groen-Vallinga, M.J. and L.E. Tacoma (2016) 'The Value of Labour: Diocletian's Prices Edict', in K. Verboven and C. Laes (eds) 2016, pp. 104–132.

Guarnieri, C. (ed) (2010) *Sarsina: Parole di Pietra. Le Epigrafi del Museo Archeologico Nazionale di Sarsina*, Cesena: Il Vicolo Divisione Libri.

Gummerus, H.G. (1913) 'Darstellungen aus dem Handwerkaufrömischen Grab-und Votivsteinen in Italien', *Jahrbuch des Deutschen Archäologischen Instituts* 28, pp. 63–126.

Haines-Eitzen, K. (1998) 'Girls Trained in Writing': Female Scribes in Roman Antiquity and Early Christianity', *Journal of Early Christian Studies* 6, pp. 629–646.

Harlow, M. and M.-L. Nosch (eds) 2014 *Greek and Roman Textiles and Dress: An Interdisciplinary Anthology*, Oxford: Oxbow Books.

Harries, J. (2018) 'Saturninus the Helmsman, Pliny and Friends. Legal and Literary Letter Collections', in A. König and C. Whitton (eds) 2018 *Roman Literature Under Nerva, Trajan and Hadrian: Literary Interactions, AD 96–138*, Cambridge: Cambridge University Press, pp. 260–279.

Harris, W.V. (2017) 'The Indispensible Commodity: Notes on the Economy of Wood in the Roman Mediterranean', in A. Wilson and A. Bowman (eds) 2017, pp. 211–236.

Harrison, G.W.M. (1987) 'Martial 1.41: Sulphur and Glass', *Classical Quarterly* 37.1, pp. 203–207.

Hartley, B.R., B.M. Dickinson and G.B. Dannell (2008–2012) *Names on Terra Sigillata: An Index of Makers' Stamps and Signatures on Gallo-Roman Terra Sigillata (Samian Ware), Volumes 1–9*, London: Institute of Classical Studies.

Hartnett, J. (2017) *The Roman Street: Urban Life in Pompeii, Herculaneum, and Rome*, Cambridge: Cambridge University Press.

Hasaki, E. (2019) *Potters at Work in Ancient Corinth: Industry, Religion, and the Penteskouphia Pinakes*, Athens: American School of Classical Studies at Athens.

Hasegawa, K. (2005) *The Familia Urbana During the Early Empire: A Study of Columbaria Inscriptions*, British Archaeological Reports International Series 1440, Oxford: Archaeopress.

Hawkins, C. (2012) 'Manufacturing', in W. Scheidel (ed) 2012, pp. 175–196.

Hawkins, C. (2013) 'Labour and Employment', in P. Erdkamp (ed) 2013, pp. 336–351.

Hawkins, C. (2016) *Roman Artisans and the Urban Economy*, Cambridge: Cambridge University Press.

Healy, J. (1978) *Mining and Metallurgy in the Greek and Roman World*, London: Thames and Hudson.

Heilmeyer, W.D. (2004) 'Ancient Workshops and Ancient 'Art'', *Oxford Journal of Archaeology* 23, pp. 403–415.

Heinrich, F. (2018) 'Cereals and Bread', in P. Erdkamp and C. Holleran (eds) 2018, pp. 101–115.

Hemelrijk, E. (2008) 'Patronesses and 'Mothers' of Roman *Collegia*', *Classical Antiquity* 27.1, pp. 115–162.

Hemelrijk, E. (2012) 'Public Roles for Women in Cities of the Latin West', in S. Dillon and S.L. James (eds) 2012 *A Companion to Women of the Ancient World*, Chichester: Wiley-Blackwell, pp. 478–490.

Hemelrijk, E. and G. Woolf (eds) (2013) *Women and the Roman City in the Latin West*, Leiden: Brill.

Henig, M. (2011) 'Souvenir or Votive? The Ilam Pan', *Bulletin of the Association for Roman Archaeology* 20, pp. 13–15.

Hin, S. (2013) *The Demography of Roman Italy: Population Dynamics in an Ancient Conquest Society 201 BCE–14 CE*, Cambridge: Cambridge University Press.

Hirt, A.M. (2010) *Imperial Mines and Quarries in the Roman World: Organizational Aspects, 27 BC–AD 235*, Oxford: Oxford University Press.

Hoare, Q. and G.N. Smith (eds) (1971) *Selections from the Prison Notebooks of Antonio Gramsci*, London: Lawrence and Wishart.

Bibliography

Hobbs, R. (2018) 'Divine Silver: Elite Relations Between Rome and Its Eastern Rivals', Unpublished Paper, Roman Archaeology Conference April 2018, Edinburgh.

Hollander, D.B. (2018) *Farmers and Agriculture in the Roman Economy*, London: Routledge.

Hollander, D.B., T.R. Blanton and J.T. Fitzgerald (eds) (2019) *The Extramercantile Economies of Greek and Roman Cities: New Perspectives on the Economic History of Classical Antiquity*, London: Routledge.

Holleran, C. (2011) 'Street Life in Ancient Rome', in R. Laurence and D.J. Newsome (eds) 2011 *Rome, Ostia, Pompeii*, Oxford: Oxford University Press, pp. 245–261.

Holleran, C. (2012) *Shopping in Ancient Rome: The Retail Trade in the Late Republic and the Principate*, Oxford: Oxford University Press.

Holleran, C. (2012) 'Women and Retail in Roman Italy', in E. Hemelrijk and G. Woolf (eds) 2013, pp. 313–330.

Holleran, C. (2015) Review of A.-C. Gillis 2014 *Corps, Travail et Statut Social. L'Apport de la Paléoanthropologie Funéraire aux Sciences Historiques*, Classical Review 66 No. 1, pp. 235–237.

Holleran, C. (2016) 'Getting a Job: Finding Work in the City of Rome', in K. Verboven and C. Laes (eds) 2016, pp. 87–103.

Holleran, C. (2016) 'Representations of Food Hawkers in Ancient Rome', in M. Calaresu and D. Van Den Hevel (eds) 2016, pp. 19–42.

Holleran, C. (2017) 'Finding Commerce: the Taberna and the Identification of Roman Commercial Space', *Papers of the British School at Rome 85*, pp. 143–170.

Holleran, C. (2018) 'Market Regulation and Intervention in the Urban Food Supply', in P. Erdkamp and C. Holleran (eds) 2018, pp. 283–295.

Holleran, C. (Forthcoming) *Earning a Living: The Organisation of Labour in Ancient Rome*.

Holleran, C. (Forthcoming) 'The Retail Trade', in A. Claridge and C. Holleran (eds) Forthcoming *A Companion to the City of Rome*, Oxford: Wiley-Blackwell.

Holliday, P.J. (1993) 'The Sarcophagus of Titus Aelius Evangelus and Gaudenia Nicene', *J. Paul Getty Museum Journal* 21, pp. 85–100.

Holum, K. and G. Vikam (1979) 'The Trier Ivory, *Adventus* Ceremonial, and the Relics of St Stephen', *Dumbarton Oaks Papers* 33, pp. 115–133.

Hope, V. (2000) 'Status and Identity in the Roman World', in J. Huskinson (ed) 2000, pp. 125–152.

Hope, V. (2009) *Roman Death: The Dying and the Dead in Ancient Rome*, London: Continuum.

Horsley, G.H.R. (1982) *New Documents Illustrating Early Christianity Volume 2: A Review of the Greek Inscriptions and Papyri Published in 1977*, Sydney: The Ancient History Documentary Research Centre MacQuarie University.

Hoyer, D. (2018) *Money, Culture, and Well-Being in Rome's Economic Development 0–275 CE*, Leiden: Mnemosyne Supplement 412.

Hudson, D. (1972) *Munby, Man of Two Worlds. The Life and Diaries of Arthur J. Munby, 1828–1910*, London: John Murray.

Hughes, L. (2007) "Dyeing' in Ancient Italy? Evidence for the *Purpurarii*', in C. Gillis and M.-L. Nosch (eds) 2007, pp. 87–92.

Hunter, M. (2016) *The Face of Medicine: Visualising Medical Masculinities in Late Nineteenth-Century Paris*, Manchester: Manchester University Press.

Hurwit, J.M. (2015) *Artists and Signatures in Ancient Greece*, Cambridge: Cambridge University Press.

Huskinson, J. (ed) (2000) *Experiencing Rome. Culture, Identity and Power in the Roman Empire*, London: Routledge and the Open University.

Huttunen, P. (1974) *The Social Strata in the Imperial City of Rome*, Acta Universitatis Ouluensis, Oulu: University of Oulu, Finland.

Jackson, R. (1988) *Doctors and Diseases in the Roman Empire*, London: British Museum Press.

Jackson, R. B. (2002) *At Empire's Edge: Exploring Rome's Egyptian Frontier*, New Haven: Yale University Press.

Jahn, O. (1861) 'Darstellungen Antiker Reliefs, Welche sich auf Handwerk und Handelsverkehr Beziehen', *Sächsischen Akademie der Wissenschaften zu Berlin* 13, pp. 346–374.

Jahn, O. (1870) 'Über Darstellungen des Handwerks und Handelsverkehr auf Antiken Wandgemälden', *Sächsischen Akademie der Wissenschaften zu Leipzig* 5, pp. 163–318.

Jaritz, G. (2009) 'The Visual Representation of Late Medieval Work: Patterns of Context, People and Action', in J. Ehmer and C. Lis (eds) 2009 *The Idea of Work in Europe from Antiquity to Modern Times*, Aldershot: Ashgate, pp. 125–148.

Jockey, P. (1998) 'Les Réprésentations d'Artisans de la Pierre dans le Monde Gréco-Romain et Leur Éventuelle Exploitation Par l'Historien', *Topoi* 8.2, pp. 625–652.

Jones, N.B. (2019) *Painting, Ethics, and Aesthetics in Rome*, Cambridge: Cambridge University Press.

Joshel, S.R. (1992) *Work, Identity and Legal Status at Rome: A Study of the Occupational Inscriptions*, Norman: University of Oklahoma Press.

Joshel, S.R. and L.H. Petersen (2015) *The Material Life of Roman Slaves*, Cambridge: Cambridge University Press.

Kampen, N.B. (1981) *Image and Status: Roman Working Women in Ostia*, Berlin: Gebr. Mann Verlag.

Kampen, N.B. (1982) 'Social Status and Gender in Roman Art: The Case of the Saleswoman', in N. Broude and M.D. Garrard (eds) (1982) *Feminism and Art History*, New York: Harper and Row, pp. 63–77.

Kampen, N.B. (1991) 'Reliefs of the Basilica Aemilia', *Klio* 73, pp. 448–458.

Keegan, P. (2017) 'Traces of the Unfamiliar: Epigraphic Evidence for Extended Families on the Margins of Roman Italy', in S.R. Huebner and G.S. Nathan (eds) 2017 *Mediterranean Families in Antiquity: Households, Extended Families, and Domestic Space*, Malden: Wiley Blackwell, pp. 95–120.

Keesling, C.M. (2018) 'Epigraphy of Appropriation: Retrospective Signatures of Greek Sculptors in the Roman World', in D.Y. Ng and M. Swetnam-Burland (eds) 2018 *Reuse and Renovation in Roman Material Culture: Functions, Aesthetics, Interpretations*, Cambridge: Cambridge University Press, pp. 84–111.

Kehoe, D. (2012) 'Contract Labour', in W. Scheidel (ed) 2012, pp. 114–132.

Kenrick, P. (2004) 'Signatures on Italian Sigillata: A New Perspective', in J. Poblome, P. Talloen, R. Brulet, and M. Waelkens (eds) 2004 *Early Italian Sigillata: The Chronological Framework and Trade Patterns*, Leuven: Peeters, pp. 253–262.

Keppie, L.J.F. (1976) 'Distance Slabs from the Antonine Wall; Some Problems', *Scottish Archaeological Forum* 7, pp. 57–65.

Keppie, L.J.F. (1979) *Roman Distance Slabs from the Antonine Wall. A Brief Guide,* Glasgow: Hunterian Museum.

Keppie, L.J.F. (1998) *Roman Inscribed and Sculptured Stones in the Hunterian Museum University of Glasgow,* Britannia Monograph Series No. 13, London: Society for the Promotion of Roman Studies.

Keppie, L.J.F. and B.J. Arnold (1984) *Scotland: Great Britain Volume 1 Fascicule 4 Corpus Signorum Imperii Romani,* Oxford: British Academy and Oxford University Press.

Kiernan, P. (2009) *Miniature Votive Offerings in the North-West Provinces of the Roman Empire,* Mainz: Verlag Franz Philipp Rutzen.

Kirschenbaum, A. (1987) *Sons, Slaves and Freedmen in Roman Commerce,* Washington: Catholic University of America Press.

Kleiner, D.E.E. (1977) *Roman Group Portraiture. The Funerary Reliefs of the Late Republic and Early Empire,* New York: Garland Publishing.

Kleiner, D.E.E. (1987) *Roman Imperial Funerary Altars with Portraits,* Rome: Bretschneider.

Kleiner, D.E.E. (1992) *Roman Sculpture,* New Haven: Yale University Press.

Kloppenborg, J.S. (1996) 'Collegia and Thiasoi: Issues in Function, Taxonomy, and Membership', in J.S. Kloppenborg and S.G. Wilson (eds) 1996 *Voluntary Associations in the Graeco-Roman World,* London: Routledge, pp. 16–30.

Knapp, R. (2011) *Invisible Romans,* Cambridge, Massachusetts: Harvard University Press.

Kristensen, T.M. (2012) 'Introduction: *Ateliers* and Artisans in Roman Art and Archaeology', in T.M. Kristensen and B. Poulsen (eds) 2012, pp. 6–12.

Kristensen, T.M. and B. Poulsen (eds) (2012) *Ateliers and Artisans in Roman Art and Archaeology,* Journal of Roman Archaeology Supplementary Series 92, Portsmouth.

Kudryavtseva, T. (2004) *Circling the Square: Avant-Garde Porcelain from Revolutionary Russia,* London: Fontanka.

Kühn, G. (1910) *De Opificum Romanorum Condicione Privata Quaestiones,* Halle: Wischan and Burkhardt.

Laes, C. (2008) 'Child Slaves at Work in Roman Antiquity', *Ancient Society* 38, pp. 235–283.

Laes, C. (2011) *Children in the Roman Empire: Outsiders Within,* Cambridge: Cambridge University Press.

Laird, M.J. (2015) *Civic Monuments and the Augustales in Roman Italy,* Cambridge: Cambridge University Press.

Laird, M.J. (2018) 'The Vigiles, Dynastic Succession and the Symbolic Reappropriation in the Caserma dei Vigili at Ostia', in D.Y. Ng and M. Swetnam-Burland (eds) 2018 *Reuse and Renovation in Roman Material Culture: Functions, Aesthetics, Interpretations,* Cambridge: Cambridge University Press, pp. 51–83.

Láng, O. (2016) 'Industry and Commerce in the City of Aquincum' in A. Wilson and M. Flohr (eds) 2016, pp. 352–376.

Langellotti, M. (2017) 'Occupations and Naming Trends in First-Century Tebtunis and Philadelphia', in M. Nowak, A. Łajtar and J. Urbanik (eds) 2017 *Tell Me Who You Are: Labelling Status in the Graeco-Roman World,* U Schyłku Starozytności Studia Źródloznawcze 16, Truskaw: Sub Lupa Academic Publishing, pp. 147–182.

Larsson Lovén, L. (1998a) 'Male and Female Professions in the Textile Production of Roman Italy', in L. Bender Jørgensen and C. Rinaldo (eds) 1998 *Textiles in European Archaeology, Report from the 6th NESAT Symposium, 7–11 May 1996 in Borås*, Göteborg: Göteborg University, pp. 73–78.

Larsson Lovén, L. (1998b) '*Lanam Fecit*-Woolworking and Female Virtue', in L. Larsson Lovén and A. Stromberg (eds) 1998 *Aspects of Women in Antiquity*, Jonsered: Paul Astroms Förlag, pp. 85–95.

Larsson Lovén, L. (2000) 'Representations of Textile Production in Gallo-Roman Funerary Art', in D. Cardon and M. Feugère (eds) 2000, pp. 235–240.

Larsson Lovén, L. (2001) 'Images of Textile Manufacture in Funerary Iconography', in M. Polfer (ed) 2001, pp. 43–53.

Larsson Lovén, L. (2002) *The Imagery of Textile Making. Gender and Status in the Funerary Iconography of Textile Manufacture in Roman Italy and Gaul*, Göteborg, Göteborg University.

Larsson Lovén, L. (2003) *The Imagery of Textile Making: Gender and Status in the Funerary Iconography of Textile Manufacture in Roman Italy and Gaul*, Göteborg: Department of Classical Archaeology and Ancient History University of Göteborg.

Larsson Lovén, L. (2007a) 'Wool Work as a Gender Symbol in Ancient Rome: Roman Textiles and Ancient Sources', in C. Gillis and M.-L. Nosch (eds) 2007 *Ancient Textiles: Production, Craft and Society*, Oxford: Oxbow Books, pp. 229–236.

Larsson Lovén, L. (2007b) 'Male and Female Work in Roman and Gallo-Roman Funerary Iconography', in E. Hartmann, U. Hartmann and K. Pietzner (eds) 2007 *Geschlechterdefinitionen und Geschlechtergrenzen in der Antike*, Stuttgart: Steiner, pp. 169–186.

Larsson Lovén, L. (2012) 'Roman Family Reliefs and the Commemoration of Work: Text, Images, and Ideals', in M. Harlow and L. Larsson Lovén (eds) 2012 *Families in the Roman and Late Antique World*, London: Continuum, pp. 141–156.

Larsson Lovén, L. (2013) 'Female Work and Identity in Roman Textile Production and Trade: A Methodological Discussion', in M. Gleba and J. Pásztókai-Szeőke (eds) 2013, pp. 109–125.

Larsson Lovén, L. (2014) 'Roman Art: What Can It Tell Us about Dress and Textiles? A Discussion on the Use of Visual Evidence as Sources for Textile Research', in M. Harlow and M.-L. Nosch (eds) 2014, pp. 260–278.

Larsson Lovén, L. (2016) 'Women, Trade, and Production in Urban Centres of Roman Italy' in A. Wilson and M. Flohr (eds) 2016, pp. 200–221.

Larsson Lovén, L. (2018) 'Shopping in Roman Iconography', Unpublished Paper, Roman Archaeology Conference April 2018, Edinburgh.

Lassus, J. (1969) 'Antioche en 459 d'Apres la Mosaique de Yakto', in J. Balty (ed) 1969 *Apamée de Syrie. Bilan des Recherches Archéologiques 1965–1968. Actes du Colloque Tenu à Bruxelles les 29 et 39 Avril 1969*, Brussels: Fouilles d'Apamée de Syrie Miscellanea 6, pp. 137–146.

Laurence, R. (2007) *Roman Pompeii: Space and Society*, Second Edition, London: Routledge.

Lavan, L., E. Swift and T. Putzeys (eds) (2007) *Objects in Context. Objects in Use: Material Spatiality in Late Antiquity*, Leiden: Brill.

Lawner, L. (ed) (1979) *Antonio Gramsci: Letters from Prison*, London: Quartet Books.

Leach, E.W. (2006) 'Freedmen and Immortality in the Tomb of the Haterii', in E. D'Ambra and G.P.R. Métraux (eds) 2006 *The Art of Citizens, Soldiers and Freedmen in the Roman World*, BAR International Series 1526, Oxford: Archaeopress, pp. 1–18.

Lefèbvre, L. (1990) *Le Musée Luxembourgeois*, Brussels: Ludion.

Le Gall, J. (1970) 'Métiers des Femmes au Corpus Inscriptionum Latinarum', in *Mélanges Marcel Durry par Ses Collègues et Ses Amis*, Paris: Les Belles Lettres, pp. 123–130.

Leguilloux, M. (2004) *Le Cuir et la Pelleterie à l'Époque Romaine*, Paris: Éditions Errance.

Lennon, J. (2017) 'The Contaminating Touch in the Roman World', in A.C. Purves (ed) 2017 *Touch and the Ancient Senses. The Senses in Antiquity*, London: Routledge, pp. 121–133.

Lenski, N. (2013) 'Working Models: Functional Art and Roman Conceptions of Slavery', in M. George (ed) 2013, pp. 129–157.

Leon, H.J. (1941) 'Sulphur for Broken Glass (Martial 1.41.3–5)', *Transactions and Proceedings of the American Philological Association* 72, pp. 233–236.

Levin-Richardson, S. (2019) *The Brothel of Pompeii, Sex, Class, and Gender at the Margins of Roman Society*, Cambridge: Cambridge University Press.

Ling, R. (2000) 'Working Practices', in R. Ling (ed) 2000 *Making Classical Art: Process and Practice*, Stroud: Tempus, pp. 91–107.

Lis, C. and H. Soly (2012) *Worthy Efforts: Attitudes to Work and Workers in Pre-Industrial Europe*, Leiden: Brill.

Lis, C. and H. Soly (2016) 'Work, Identity and Self-Representation in the Roman Empire and the West-European Middle Ages: Different Interplays Between the Social and the Cultural' in K. Verboven and C. Laes (eds) 2016, pp. 262–290.

Liu, J. (2009) *Collegia Centonariorum: The Guilds of Textile Dealers in the Roman West*, Leiden: Brill.

Liu, J. (2013a) 'Trades, Traders and Guilds(?) in Textiles: The Case of Southern Gaul and Northern Italy (1st–3rd Centuries AD)' in M. Gleba and J. Pásztókai-Szeőke (eds) 2013, pp. 126–141.

Liu, J. (2013b) 'Professional Associations', in P. Erdkamp (ed) 2013, pp. 352–368.

Loane, H.J. (1938) *Industry and Commerce of the City of Rome (50 BC–200 AD)*, Baltimore: Johns Hopkins University Press.

Logghe, L. (2017) 'Plebeian Agency in the Later Roman Republic', in R. Evans (ed) 2017, pp. 63–81.

Long, T. and A.H. Sørensen (eds) (2017) *Positions and Professions in Palmyra*, Copenhagen: Royal Danish Academy of Sciences and Letters.

López Barja de Quiroga, P. (1995) 'Freedmen Social Mobility in Roman Italy', *Historia* 44, pp. 326–348.

Lord, P. (1998) *The Visual Culture of Wales: Industrial Society*, Cardiff: University of Wales Press.

Lund, J. (2011) 'Handling and Use of Transport Amphorae in the Roman Period', in M.L. Lawall and J. Lund (eds) 2011 *Pottery in the Archaeological Record: Greece and Beyond*, Aarhus: Aarhus University Press, pp. 51–60.

MacCormack, S. (1981) *Art and Ceremony in Late Antiquity*, Berkeley: University of California Press.

MacCormack, S. (2001) 'The Virtue of Work: an Augustinian Transformation', *Antiquité Tardive* 9, pp. 219–237.

MacLean, R. (2018) *Freed Slaves and Roman Imperial Culture: Social Integration and the Transformation of Values*, Cambridge: Cambridge University Press.

MacMahon, A. and J. Price (eds) (2005) *Roman Working Lives and Urban Living*, Oxford: Oxbow Books.

Malgouyres, P. and C. Blanc-Riehl (2003) Porphyre: La Pierre Pourpre des Ptolémées à Bonaparte, Paris: Réunion des Musées Nationaux.

Mander, J. (2013) *Portraits of Children on Roman Funerary Art*, Cambridge: Cambridge University Press.

Marcone, A. (ed) 2016 *Storia del Lavoro in Italia. L'Età Romana. Liberi, Semiliberi e Schiavi in una Società Moderna*, Rome: Castelvecchi.

Marconi, C. (ed) (2015) The Oxford Handbook of Greek and Roman Art and Architecture, Oxford: Oxford University Press.

Marichal, R. (1988) 'Les Graffites de La Graufesenque', *Gallia Supplement* 47.

Martinez, J.-L. (ed) (2012) *Arles, Les Fouilles du Rhône: Un Fleuve Pour Mémoire*, Paris: Louvre Éditions.

Martinez, L.A. and E.A. Garcia (2015) 'Infantile Individuals: the Great Forgotten of Ancient Mining and Metallurgical Production', in M.S. Romero, E.A. Garcia, and G.A. Jiménez (eds) 2015 *Children, Spaces and Identity, Childhood in the Past Monograph Series* 4, Oxford: Oxbow Books, pp. 105–121.

Marzano, A. (2007) *Roman Villas in Central Italy: a Social and Economic History*, Leiden: Brill.

Mattingly, D.J. (1990) 'Paintings, Presses and Perfume Production at Pompeii', *Oxford Journal of Archaeology* 9/1, pp. 71–90.

Mattusch, C. (2008) 'Metalworking and Tools', in J.P. Oleson (ed) 2008, pp. 418–438.

Maxey, M. (1938) *Occupations of the Lower Classes in Roman Society as Seen in Justinian's Digest*, Chicago: University of Chicago Press.

Mayer, E. (2012) *The Ancient Middle Classes: Urban Life and Aesthetics in the Roman Empire 100 BCE–250 CE*, Cambridge, Massachusetts: Harvard University Press.

Mayor, A. (2018) *Gods and Robots: Myths, Machines, and Ancient Dreams of Technology*, Princeton: Princeton University Press.

McInerney, J. (2019) 'Interpreting Funerary Inscriptions from the City of Rome', *Journal of Ancient History* 7(1), pp. 156–206.

Michele, G. (2006) 'Social Identity and the Dignity of Work in Freedmen's Reliefs', in E. D'Ambra and G.P.R. Metraux (eds) 2006 *The Art of Citizens, Soldiers and Freedmen in the Roman World*, British Archaeological Reports International Series 1526, Oxford: Archaeopress, pp. 19–30.

Mignone, L.M. (2017) 'Living in Republican Rome: Shanty Metropolis', in R. Evans (ed) 2017, pp. 100–117.

Mihăilescu-Bîrliba, L. (2018) 'The Professions of Private Slaves and Freedmen in Moesia Inferior', in G. Cupcea and R. Varga (eds) 2018, pp. 47–56.

Millar, F. (1984) 'Condemnation to Hard Labour in the Roman Empire, from the Julio-Claudians to Constantine', *Papers of the British School at Rome* 54, pp. 124–147.

Miller, J.F. and J.S. Clay (eds) (2019) *Tracking Hermes, Pusuing Mercury*, Oxford: Oxford University Press.

Moeller, W.O. (1970) 'The Riot of A.D. 59 at Pompeii', *Historia* 19, pp. 84–95.

Moeller, W.O. (1971) 'The Felt Shops of Pompeii', *American Journal of Archaeology* 75(2), pp. 188–189.

Monteix, N. (2011) 'De "l'Artisanat" aux Metiers. Quelques Réflexions sur les Savoir-Faire du Monde Romain à Partir de l'Exemple Pompeien, in N. Monteix and N. Tran (eds) 2011, pp. 7–26.

Monteix, N. (2012) 'Caius Lucetius ... Marchand de Couleurs de la Rue du Fabricant de Courroies: Réflexions Critiques sur les Concentrations de Métiers à Rome', in G. Sanidas and A. Esposito (eds) 2012 *Quartiers Artisanaux en Grèce Ancienne: une Perspective Méditerranéenne*, Villeneuve d'Ascq: Presse Universitaires du Septentrion, pp. 333–352.

Monteix, N. (2013) 'The Apple of Discord: Fleece Washing in Pompeii's Textile Economy', *Journal of Roman Archaeology* 26, pp. 79–88.

Monteix, N. (2016a) 'Contextualizing the Operational Sequence: Pompeian Bakeries as a Case Study' in A. Wilson and M. Flohr (eds) 2016, pp. 153–182.

Monteix, N. (2016b) 'Perceptions of Technical Culture Among Pompeian Élites: Considering the Cupids Frieze of the Casa dei Vettii', in K. Droß-Krüpe, S. Föllinger and K. Ruffing (eds) 2016, pp. 199–222.

Monteix, N. and N. Tran (eds) (2011) *Les Savoirs Professionnels des Gens de Métier. Études sur le Monde du Travail dans les Sociétés Urbaines de l'Empire Romain*, Collection du Centre Jean Bérard 37: École Française de Rome.

Morel, J.-P. (1987) 'La Topographie de l'Artisanat et du Commerce dans la Rome Antique', in École Francaise de Rome (ed) 1987 *L'Urbs: Espace Urbain et Histoire*, Rome: École Francaise de Rome, pp. 127–155.

Morel, J.-P. (1989) 'L'Artigiano', in A. Giardina (ed) 1989 *L'Uomo Romano*, Rome: Laterza, pp. 233–269.

Morretta, S. (1999) 'Donne Imprenditrici nella Produzione Commercio dell'Olio Betico (I–III Sec. d.C.)', *Saitabi* 49, pp. 229–245.

Morwood, J. (1991) 'Aeneas, Augustus, and the Theme of the City', *Greece and Rome* 38(2), pp. 212–223.

Mouritsen, H. (2001) 'Roman Freedmen and the Urban Economy: Pompeii in the First Century AD', in F. Senatore (ed) 2001 *Pompei tra Sorrento e Sarno: Atti del Terzo e Quarto Ciclo di Conferenze di Geologia, Storia e Archeologia*, Pompei, Gennaio 1999–Maggio 2000, Rome: Bardi, pp. 1–27.

Mouritsen, H. (2005) 'Freedmen and Decurions: Epitaphs and Social History in Imperial Italy', *Journal of Roman Studies* 95, pp. 38–63.

Mouritsen, H. (2011) *The Freedman in the Roman World*, Cambridge: Cambridge University Press.

Nahshon, E. (ed) (2008) *Jews and Shoes*, Oxford: Berg.

Napoli, J. (2004) 'Art Purpuraire et Légalisation a L'Époque Romaine', in C. Alfaro, J.P. Wild, and B. Costa (eds) 2004, pp. 123–136.

Nappa, C. (2018) *Making Men Ridiculous: Juvenal and the Anxieties of the Individual*, Ann Arbor: University of Michigan Press.

Naumann-Steckner, F. (1991) 'Depictions of Glass in Roman Wall-Paintings', in M. Newby and K. Painter (eds) 1991 *Roman Glass: Two Centuries of Art and Invention*, London: Society of Antiquaries of London, pp. 86–98.

Nelson, J.R. (1903) 'The Boy Poet Sulpicius: A Tragedy of Roman Education', *The School Review* 11.5, pp. 384–395.

Nochlin, L. (2018) *Misère: The Visual Representation of Misery in the 19th Century*, London: Thames and Hudson.

O'Connell, S.D. (2018) 'Visual Evidence: Picturing Food and Food Culture in Roman Art', in P. Erdkamp and C. Holleran (eds) 2018, pp. 26–35.

Oleson, J.P. (ed) (2008) *The Oxford Handbook of Engineering and Technology in the Classical World*, Oxford: Oxford University Press.

Ovitt, G. (1994) 'The Cultural Context of Western Technology: Early Christian Attitudes Towards Manual Labour', in A.J. Frantzen and D. Moffat (eds) 1994 *The Work of Work: Servitude, Slavery, and Labor in Medieval England*, Glasgow: Cruithne Press, pp. 71–95.

Painter, B. W. (2005) *Mussolini's Rome: Rebuilding the Eternal City*, New York: Palgrave MacMillan.

Painter, B. W. (2018) 'Mussolini and Rome', in C. Holleran and A. Claridge (eds) (2018), *A Companion to the City of Rome*, Oxford: Wiley-Blackwell, pp. 683–698.

Papi, E. (2002) 'La *Turba Inpia*: Artigiani e Commercianti del Foro Romano e Dintorni (I sec. a.C.–64 d.C.)', *Journal of Roman Archaeology* 15/1, pp. 45–62.

Papini, M. (2016) 'Una Storia dell'Arte Senza Nomi? Opere "Firmate" e Officine nella Scultura Tardorepubblicana e Imperiale', in C.P. Presicce (ed) 2016, pp. 55–60.

Parker, H.T. (1997) 'Women Doctors in Greece, Rome, and the Byzantine Empire', in L.R. Furst (ed) 1997 *Women Physicians and Healers: Climbing a Long Hill*, Lexington: University of Kentucky Press, pp. 131–150.

Parker, R. (2007) *Polytheism and Society at Athens*, Oxford: Oxford University Press.

Patterson, J.R. (1992) 'Patronage, *Collegia* and Burial in Imperial Rome', in S. Bassett (ed) 1992 *Death in Towns: Urban Responses to the Dying and the Dead, 100–1600*, Leicester: Leicester University Press, pp. 15–27.

Patterson, J.R. (1994) 'The *Collegia* and the Transformation of the Towns of Italy in the Second Century AD', in 1994 *L'Italie d'Auguste a Dioclétien*, Actes du Colloque International de Rome 25–28 Mars 1992, Rome: Collection de l'École Française de Rome 198, pp. 227–238.

Peachin, M. (ed) (2011) *The Oxford Handbook of Social Relations in the Roman World*, Oxford: Oxford University Press.

Peña, J.T. and M. McCallum (2009) 'The Production and Distribution of Pottery at Pompeii: a Review of the Evidence; Part 1, Production', *American Journal of Archaeology* 113.1, pp. 57–79.

Perkins, P. (2000) 'Power, Culture and Identity in the Roman Economy', in J. Huskinson (ed) 2000, pp. 183–212.

Pernot, M. (2011) 'Quels Métiers les Arts des Plombiers, Bronziers et Orfèvres Impliquent-Ils?', in N. Monteix and N. Tran (eds) 2011, pp. 101–118.

Perry, J.S. (2006) *The Roman Collegia: The Modern Evolution of an Ancient Concept*, Leiden: Brill.

Petersen, L.H. (2003) 'The Baker, His Tomb, His Wife, and Her Breadbasket: The Monument of Eurysaces in Rome', *The Art Bulletin* 85(2), pp. 230–257.

Petersen, L.H. (2006) *The Freedman in Roman Art and Art History*, Cambridge: Cambridge University Press.

Petersen, L.H. (2009) '"Clothes Maketh the Man": Dressing the Roman Freedman Body', in T. Fögen and M.M. Lee (eds) 2009 *Bodies and Boundaries in Graeco-Roman Antiquity*, Berlin: De Gruyter, pp. 181–214.

Petersen, L.H. (2015a) '"Arte Plebeia" and Non-Elite Roman Art', in B.E. Borg (ed) 2015, pp. 214–230.

Petersen, L.H. (2015b) 'Non-Elite Patronage', in E.A. Friedland and M.G. Sobocinski (eds) 2015, pp. 436–450.

Petrassi, M. (1976) 'Torna alla Luce L'Ipogeo di Trebio Giusto', *Capitolium 51*, pp. 17–22.

Petrikovits, H. von (1981) 'Die Spezialisierung des Römischen Handwerks', in H. Jankuhn, W. Janssen, R. Schmidt-Wiegand and H. Tiefenbach (eds) 1981 *Das Handwerk in Vor-und Fruhgesichhtlicher Zeit*, Göttingen: Vandenhoeck and Ruprecht, pp. 63–152.

Pierce, E., A. Russell, A. Maldonado and L. Campbell (eds) (2016) *Creating Material Worlds: The Uses of Identity in Archaeology*, Oxford: Oxbow Books.

Pirson, F. (2007) 'Shops and Industries', in J.J. Dobbins and P.W. Foss (eds) 2007 *The World of Pompeii*, London: Routledge, pp. 457–473.

Poblome, J. (2016) 'The Potters of Sagalassos Revisited' in A. Wilson and M. Flohr (eds) 2016, pp. 377–404.

Polfer, M. (ed) (2001) *L'Artisanat Romain: Évolutions, Continuités et Ruptures (Italie et Provinces Occidentales), Actes du 2e Colloque d'Erpeldange (26–28 Octobre 2001)*, Montagnac: Monique Mergoil.

Pomeroy, A.J. (1991) 'Status and Status Concern in the Greco-Roman Dreambooks', *Ancient Society 22*, pp. 51–74.

Porter. G. (1992) *The English Occupational Song*, Stockholm: University of Umeå with Almquist and Wiskell International.

Presicce, C.P. (ed) (2016) *Made in Roma. Marchi di Produzioni e di Possesso nella Società Antica*, Rome: Gangemi Editori.

Price, J. (2005) 'Glass-Working and Glassworkers in Cities and Towns.', in A. MacMahon and J. Price (eds) 2005, pp. 167–190.

Purcell, N. (1983) 'The *Apparitores*: A Study in Social Mobility', *Papers of the British School at Rome 51*, pp. 125–173.

Purcell, N. (1994) 'The City of Rome and the Plebs Urbana in the Late Republic', in J.A. Crook, A. Lintott and B. Rawson (eds) 1994 *Cambridge Ancient History Volume IX The Last Age of the Republic 146–43 BC*, 2nd Edition, Cambridge: Cambridge University Press, pp. 644–688.

Purcell, N. (1999) 'The Populace of Rome in Late Antiquity: Problems of Classification and Historical Description', in W.V. Harris (ed) 1999 *The Transformations of Urbs Roma in Late Antiquity, Proceedings of a Conference Held Feb. 13–15 1997 in the American Academy in Rome and the University of Rome 'La Sapienza'*, Portsmouth: Journal of Roman Archaeology Supplementary Series 33, pp. 135–161.

Putzeys, T. (2007) 'Productive Space in Late Antiquity', in L. Lavan, E. Swift and T. Putzeys (eds) 2007, pp. 63–80.

Putzeys, T. and L. Lavan (2007) 'Commercial Space in Late Antiquity', in L. Lavan, E. Swift and T. Putzeys (eds) 2007, pp. 81–109.

Radman-Livaja, I. (2013) 'Craftspeople, Merchants or Clients? The Evidence of Personal Names on the Commercial Lead Tags from Siscia', in M. Gleba and J. Pásztókai-Szeőke (eds) 2013, pp. 87–108.

Rainer, J.M. (1990) 'Bauen und Arbeit im Klassichen Römischen Recht', *Zeitschrift der Savigniy-Stiftung für Rechtsgeschichte Romanistiche Abteilung* 107, pp. 376–381.

Ransel, D.L. (2008) 'Neither Nobles nor Peasants: Plain Painting and the Emergence of the Merchant Estate', in V.A. Kivelson and J. Neuberger (eds) 2008 *Picturing Russia: Explorations in Visual Culture*, New Haven: Yale University Press, pp. 76–80.

Rawson, E. (1975) 'Architecture and Sculpture: The Activities of the Cossutii', *Papers of the British School at Rome* 43, pp. 36–47.

Rea, R. (2004) *L'Ipogeo di Trebio Giusto sulla Via Latina. Scavi e Restauri*, Vatican: Pontificia Commissione di Archeologia Sacra.

Reddé, M. (1978) 'Les Scènes de Métier dans la Sculpture Funéraire Gallo-Romaine, *Gallia* 36, pp. 43–63.

Revell, L. (2009) *Roman Imperialism and Local Identities*, Cambridge: Cambridge University Press.

Revell, L. (2015) *Ways of Being Roman: Discourses of Identity in the Roman West,* Oxford: Oxbow Books.

Reynolds, J. (1981) 'Diocletian's Edict on Maximum Prices: The Chapter on Wool', *Zeitschrift für Papyrologie und Epigraphik* 42, pp. 283–284.

Rice, C. (2016) 'Mercantile Specialization and Trading Communities: Economic Strategies in Roman Maritime Trade' in A. Wilson and M. Flohr (eds) 2016, pp. 97–114.

Richardson, L. (1992) *A New Topographical Dictionary of Ancient Rome*, Baltimore: Johns Hopkins University Press.

Richter, G. (1951) 'Who Made the Roman Portrait Statues-Greeks or Romans?', *Proceedings of the American Philosophical Society* 95, pp. 184–191 and 193–208.

Robinson, O.F. (1992) *Ancient Rome. City Planning and Administration*, London: Routledge.

Rohde, D. (2012) 'Der Piazzale delle Corporazioni in Ostia: Wirtschaftliche Funktionund Soziale Bedeutung', *Marburger Beiträge zur Antiken Handels-, Wirtschafts-und Sozialgeschichte* 27, pp. 31–61.

Roncaglia, C.E. (2018) *Northern Italy in the Roman World from the Bronze Age to Late Antiquity*, Baltimore: Johns Hopkins University Press.

Roueché, C. and K.T. Erim (1982) 'Sculptors from Aphrodisias: Some New Inscriptions', *Papers of the British School at Rome* 50, pp. 102–115.

Rubio Rivera, R. (1993) '*Collegium Dendrophorum*: Corporación Profesional y Confradía Metroaca', *Gerión* 11, pp. 175–183.

Ruffing, K. (2008) *Die Berufliche Spezialisierung in Handel und Handwerk. Untersuschungen zu Ihrer Entwicklung und zu Ihren Bedingungen in der Romischen Kaiserzeit im Ostlichen Mittelmeerrraum auf der Grundlage Griechischer Inschriften und Papyri*, Rahden: Leidorf.

Ruffing, K. (2016) 'Driving Forces for Specialization: Market, Location Factors, Productivity Improvements' in A. Wilson and M. Flohr (eds) 2016, pp. 115–131.

Russell, B. (2017) 'Stone Use and the Economy: Demand, Distribution, and the State', in A. Wilson and A. Bowman (eds) 2017, pp. 237–264.

Salvaterra, C. (2006) 'Labour and Identity in the Roman World: Italian Historiography During the Last Two Decades', in B. Waaldjik (ed) 2006 *Professions and Social Identity: New European Historical Research on Work, Gender and Society*, Pisa: Pisa University Press, pp. 15–38.

Bibliography

Salvaterra, C. and A. Cristofori (2016) 'Twentieth-Century Italian Scholarship on Roman Craftsmen, Traders, and Their Professional Organizations' in A. Wilson and M. Flohr (eds) 2016, pp. 55–76.

Sandars, H. (1905) 'The Linares Bas-Relief and Roman Mining in Spain', *Archaeologia* 59, pp. 311–332.

Scheidel, W. (ed) (2012) *The Cambridge Companion to the Roman Economy*, Cambridge: Cambridge University Press.

Schoevaert, J. (2018) *Les Boutiques d'Ostie: l'Économie Urbaine au Quotidien: Ier s. av. J.-C. Ver ap. J.-C.*, Rome: Collection de l'École Française de Rome.

Schörle, K. (2015) 'Pearls, Power, and Profit: Mercantile Networks and Economic Considerations of the Pearl Trade in the Roman Empire', in F. De Romanis and M. Maiuro (eds) 2015 *Across the Ocean: Nine Essays on Indo-Mediterranean Trade*, Leiden: Brill, pp. 43–54.

Schwinden, L. (1989) 'Gallo-Römisches Textilgewerbe Nach Denkmälern aus Trier und dem Trevererland', *Trier Zeitschrift* 52, pp. 279–318.

Scrinari, V.S.M. (1972) *Museo Archeologico di Aquileia: Catologo delle Sculture Romane*, Rome: Istituto Poligrafico dello Stato P.V..

Seland, E.H. (2016) 'Ancient Trading Networks and New Institutional Economics: The Case of Palmyra', in K. Droß-Krüpe, S. Föllinger and K. Ruffing (eds) 2016, pp. 223–234.

Setälä, P. (1989) 'Brick Stamps and Women's Economic Opportunities in Rome', in A. Angerman (ed) 1989 *Current Issues in Women's History*, London: Routledge, pp. 61–74.

Setälä, P. (2002) 'Women and Brick Production. Some New Aspects', *Acta Instituti Romani Finlandiae* 25, pp. 181–201.

Shaw, J.W. (1967) 'A Double-Sheaved Pulley Block from Kenchreai', *Hesperia* 36, pp. 389–401.

Shelton, J.-A. (1998) 'Working Women', in *As the Romans Did: A Sourcebook in Roman Social History 2nd Edition*, Oxford: Oxford University Press.

Sheridan, J.A. and Roth, J. (1992) 'Greek Ostraka from Mons Porphyrites (Gebel 'Abu Dukhan)', *Bulletin of the American Society of Papyrologists* 29 (3/4), pp. 117–126.

Smith, R.R.R. (2008) 'Sculptors' Workshops: Inscriptions, Images and Archaeology', in R.R.R. Smith and J. Lenaghan (eds) 2008 *Roman Portraits from Aphrodisias*, Istanbul: YKY, pp. 102–119.

Smyth, W.R. (1947) 'Statius *Silvae* 1.6.73–4 and Martial 1.41.3–5', *Classical Review* 61, pp. 46–47.

Sobocinski, M.G. and E.W. Thill (2018) 'Dismembering a Sacred Cow: the Extispicium Relief in the Louvre', in B. Longfellow and E. Perry (eds) 2018 *Roman Artists, Patrons, and Public Consumption: Familiar Works Reconsidered*, Ann Arbor: University of Michigan Press, pp. 38–62.

Spriano, P. (1979) *Antonio Gramsci and the Party: The Prison Years*, London: Lawrence and Wishart.

Squarciapino, M.F. (1942) *Civiltà Romana: Artigianato e Industria*, Mostra della Romanità, Rome: C. Colombo.

Squire, M. (2015) 'Roman Art and the Artist', in B. E. Borg (ed) 2015, pp. 172–194.

Stern, E.M. (1999) 'Roman Glassblowing in a Cultural Context', *American Journal of Archaeology* 103, pp. 441–484.

Stevenson, J. (1978) *The Catacombs: Life and Death in Early Christianity*, London: Thames and Hudson.

Strong, A.K. (2016) *Prostitutes and Matrons in the Roman World*, Cambridge: Cambridge University Press.

Strong, D. and A. Claridge (1976) 'Marble Sculpture', in D. Strong and D. Brown (eds) 1976, pp. 195–208.

Strong, D. and D. Brown (eds) (1976) *Roman Crafts*, London: Duckworth.

Talbert, R. and F. Naiden (eds) (2017) *Mercury's Wings: Exploring Modes of Communication in the Ancient World*, Oxford: Oxford University Press.

Tameanko, M. (1990) 'Goldsmith's, Mint, or Jewelry Factory? A New Interpretation of the Wall Painting from the House of the Vettii, Pompeii', *Minerva* 1, pp. 42–46.

Taylor, C.G. (2018) *Late Antique Images of the Virgin Annunciate Spinning: Allotting the Scarlet and the Purple*, Leiden: Brill.

Taylor, R. (2003) *Roman Builders: A Study in Architectural Process*, Cambridge: Cambridge University Press.

Tchernia, A. (2016) *The Romans and Trade*, Oxford: Oxford University Press.

Terpstra, T. (2013) *Trading Communities in the Roman World: A Micro-Economic and Institutional Perspective*, Leiden: Brill.

Terpstra, T. (2017) 'Communication and Long-Distance Trade', in R. Talbert and F. Naiden (eds) 2017, pp. 45–61.

Terpstra, T. (2019) *Trade in the Ancient Mediterranean: Private Order and Public Institutions*, Princeton: Princeton University Press.

Thompson, E.P. (1971) *The Making of the English Working Class*, Harmondsworth: Penguin.

Todeschini, G. (2008) 'Theological Roots of the Medieval/Modern Merchants' Self-Representation', in M.C. Jacob and C. Secretan (eds) 2008 *The Self-Perception of Early Modern Capitalists*, New York: Palgrave MacMillan, pp. 17–46.

Toynbee, J.M.C. (1951) *Some Notes on Artists in the Roman World*, Brussels: Collection Latomus.

Tran, N. (2006) *Les Membres des Associations Romaine: le Rang Social des Collegiati en Italie et en Gaules Sous le-Haut Empire*, École Francaise: Rome.

Tran, N. (2011) 'Les Gens de Métier Romains: Savoirs Professionnels et Supériorités Plébéiennes', in N. Tran and N. Monteix (eds) 2011, pp. 119–133.

Tran, N. (2013) 'Conceptions du Travail et Formes de Fierté Professionelle dans les Milieux de l'Artisanat et du Commerce', in N. Tran (ed) 2013 *Dominus Tabernae: le Statut de Travail des Artisans et des Commercants de l'Occident Romain (Ier Siècle av. J.-C.-IIIe Siècle ap. J.-C.)*, Rome: École Française de Rome, pp. 187–252.

Tran, N. (2016) 'The Social Organization of Commerce and Crafts in Ancient Arles: Heterogeneity, Hierarchy, and Patronage' in A. Wilson and M. Flohr (eds) 2016, pp. 254–277.

Treggiari, S. (1973) 'Domestic Staff at Rome in the Julio-Claudian Period, 27 B.C. to A.D. 68', *Histoire Sociale/Social History* 6(12), pp. 241–255.

Treggiari, S. (1975a) 'Jobs in the Household of Livia', *Papers of the British School at Rome* 43, pp. 48–77.

Treggiari, S. (1975b) 'Family Life Among the Staff of the Volusii', *Transactions of the American Philological Association* 105, pp. 393–401.

Treggiari, S. (1976) 'Jobs for Women', *American Journal of Ancient History* 1, pp. 76–104.

Treggiari, S. (1979a) 'Lower-Class Women in the Roman Economy', *Florilegium: Carleton University Annual Papers on Classical Antiquity and the Middle Ages* 1, pp. 65–86.

Treggiari, S. (1979b) 'Questions on Women Domestics in the Roman West', in Groupe International de Recherches sur l'Esclavage Ancien (GIREA) (eds) 1979, *Schiavitù, Manomissione e Classi Dipendenti nel Mondo Antico, Atti del Colloquio Internazionale di Bressanone, 25–27 Novembre 1976*, Padova: University of Padova, pp. 185–201.

Treggiari, S. (1980) 'Urban Labour in Rome: Mercennarii and Tabernarii', in P. Garnsey (ed) 1980, pp. 48–64.

Trimble, J. (2017) 'Communicating with Images in the Roman Empire', in R. Talbert and F. Naiden (eds) 2017, pp. 106–127.

Trowbridge, M.L. (1930) *Philological Studies in Ancient Glass*, Urbana: University of Illinois Press.

Ulrich, R.B. (2007) *Roman Woodworking*, New Haven: Yale University Press.

Ulrich, R.B. (2008a) 'Representations of Technical Processes', in J.P. Oleson (ed) 2008, pp. 35–61.

Ulrich, R.B. (2008b) 'Woodworking', in J.P. Oleson (ed) 2008, pp. 439–464.

Van Beek, B. (2017) *The Archive of the Architektones Kleon and Theodoros (P. Petrie Kleon)*, Collectanea Hellenistica VII, Leuven: Peeters.

Van den Hoven, B. (1996) *Work in Ancient and Medieval Thought: Ancient Philosophers, Medieval Monks and Theologians and Their Concept of Work, Occupations and Technology*, Amsterdam: J.C. Gieben.

Van Driel-Murray, C. (2008) 'Tanning and Leather', in J.P. Oleson (ed) 2008, pp. 483–495.

Van Driel-Murray, C. (2016) 'Fashionable Footwear: Craftsmen and Consumers in the North-West Provinces of the Roman Empire' in A. Wilson and M. Flohr (eds) 2016, pp. 132–152.

Van Haeperen, F. (2012) 'Collèges de Dendrophores et Autorités Locales et Romaines', in M. Dondin-Payre and N. Tran (eds) 2012, pp. 47–62.

Van Nijf, O.M. (1997) *The Civic World of Professional Associations in the Roman East*, Amsterdam: J.C. Gieben.

Varga, R. (2018) 'The Professionals of the Latin West', in G. Cupcea and R. Varga (eds) 2018, pp. 9–22.

Venault, S., S. Deyts, Y. Le Bohec, and Y. Labaune (2009) 'Les Stèles Funéraires de la Nécropole de Pont-l'Évêque à Autun: Contextes de Découverte et Étude du Corpus', Antiquité, Archéologie Classique 2009, pp. 129–204.

Venticinque, P.F. (2016) *Honor Among Thieves: Craftsmen, Merchants and Associations in Roman and Late Roman Egypt. New Texts from Ancient Cultures*, Ann Arbor: University of Michigan Press.

Verboven, K. (2002) *The Economy of Friends: Economic Aspects of Amicitia and Patronage in the Late Republic*, Brussels: Éditions Latomus.

Verboven, K. (2007) 'The Associative Order: Status and Ethos Among Roman Businessmen in Late Republic and Early Empire', *Athenaeum* 95, pp. 861–893.

Verboven, K. (2011a) 'Professional Collegia: Guilds or Social Clubs?', *Ancient Society* 41, pp. 187–195.

Verboven, K. (2011b) 'Resident Aliens and Translocal Merchant Collegia', in O. Hekster and T. Kaizer (eds) 2011 *Frontiers in the Roman World: Proceedings of the Ninth Workshop of the International Network Impact of Empire Durham 16–19 April 2009*, Leiden: Brill, pp. 335–348.

Verboven, K. (2012) 'The Freedmen Economy of Roman Italy', in S. Bell and T.R. Ramsby (eds) 2012 *Free At Last! The Impact of Freed Slaves on the Roman Empire*, London: Bristol Classical Press, pp. 88–109.

Verboven, K. (2014) 'Attitudes to Work and Workers in Classical Greece and Rome', *Tijdschrift voor Sociale en Economische Geschiedenis* 11, pp. 67–87.

Verboven, K. and C. Laes (2016) 'Work, Labour, Professions. What's In a Name? in K. Verboven and C. Laes (eds) 2016, pp. 1–20.

Verboven, K. and C. Laes (eds) (2016) *Work, Labour and Professions in the Roman World*, Leiden: Brill.

Vernant, J.-P. (1956) 'Aspects Psychologiques du Travail dans la Grèce Ancienne', *La Pensée* 66, pp. 80–84.

Veyne, P. (1986) 'Les Cadeaux des Colons à Leur Propriétaire: la Neuvième Bucolique et le Mausolée d'Igel', *Revue Archéologique* 1986, pp. 245–252.

Veyne, P. (2000) 'La "Plèbe Moyenne" Sous le Haut-Empire Romain', *Annales, Histoire, Sciences Sociales* 55, pp. 1169–1199.

Vicari, F. (1994) 'Economia della Cispadana Romana: la Produzione Tessile', *Rivista Storica dell'Antichità* 24, pp. 239–260.

Vicari, F. (2001) *Produzione e Commercio dei Tessuti Nell'Occidente Romano*, British Archaeological Reports International Series No. 916, Oxford: Archaeopress.

Vincent, A. (2012) 'Les Collèges de Musiciens. Pratiques Professionnelles et Insertion Civique', in M. Dondin-Payre and N. Tran (eds) 2012, pp. 183–198.

Volkommer, R. (2015) 'Greek and Roman Artists', in C. Marconi (ed) 2015, pp. 107–135.

Von Hesberg, H. (2015) 'Greek and Roman Architects', in C. Marconi (ed) 2015, pp. 136–151.

Vuolanto, V. (2015) 'Children and Work: Family Strategies and Socialisation in the Roman and Late Antique Egypt', *Acta Instituti Romani Finlandiae* 42, pp. 97–112.

Wallace-Hare, D.A. (2018) 'Seeing the Silva Through the Silva: the Religious Economy of Timber Communities in Aquitania and Gallia Narbonensis', in J. Wolf and J. Shack (eds) 2018 *Proceedings of the Harvard Celtic Colloquium 38*, Cambridge Massachusetts: Harvard University Press, pp. 251–273.

Ward, A. (2008) *Power to the People. Early Soviet Propaganda Posters in the Israel Museum, Jerusalem*, London: Lund Humphreys.

Ward, W.D. (ed) (2017) *The Socio-Economic History and Material Culture of the Roman and Byzantine Near East: Essays in Honour of S. Thomas Parker*, Piscataway, New Jersey: Gorgias Press.

Weatherill, L. (1996) *Consumer Behaviour and Material Culture in Britain 1660–1760* (2nd edition), London: Routledge.

Whitehouse, D. (1999) 'Glass in the Epigrams of Martial', *Journal of Glass Studies* 41, pp. 73–81.

Wild, J.P. (1970) *Textile Manufacture in the Northern Roman Provinces*, Cambridge: Cambridge University Press.

Wild, J.P. (2000) 'Textile Production and Trade in Roman Literature and Written Sources', in D. Cardon and M. Feugère (eds) 2000, pp. 209–214.

Wild, J.P. (2004) 'The Roman Textile Industry: Problems But Progress', in C. Alfaro, J.P. Wild, and B. Costa (eds) 2004, pp. 23–28.

Wild, J.P. (2008) 'Textile Production', in J.P. Oleson (ed) 2008, pp. 465–482.

Wilpert, G. (1903) *Le Pitture delle Catacombe Romane*, Volumes 1 and 2, Rome: Desclée, Lefebvre.

Wilson, A. (2002) 'Urban Production in the Roman World: The View from North Africa', *Papers of the British School at Rome* 70, pp. 231–273.

Wilson, A. and A. Bowman (eds) (2017) *Trade, Commerce, and the State in the Roman World*, Oxford: Oxford University Press.

Wilson, A. and M. Flohr (eds) (2016) *Urban Craftsmen and Traders in the Roman World*, Oxford: Oxford University Press.

Wilson, A. and K. Schörle (2009) 'A Baker's Funerary Relief from Rome', *Papers of the British School at Rome* 77, pp. 101–123.

Wilson, L.J. (1984) 'The Trier Procession Ivory: A New Interpretation', *Byzantion* 54, pp. 602–614.

Wortley, J. (1980) 'The Trier Ivory Reconsidered', *Greek, Roman, and Byzantine Studies* 21, pp. 381–394.

Woytek, B.E. (2012) 'System and Product in Roman Mints from the Late Republic to the High Principate: Some Current Problems', Revue Belge de Numismatique et de Sigillographie CLVIII, pp. 85–122.

Wright, G.R.H. (2009) *Ancient Building Technology, Volume 3; Construction*, Leiden: Brill.

Young, A. (2000) 'Representations of Cloth Vendors and the Cloth Trade on Funerary Reliefs in Roman Gaul and Italy', in D. Cardon and M. Feugère (eds) 2000, pp. 215–233.

Zahn, E. (1982) *Die Igeler Säule in Igel bei Trier*, Cologne: Rheinisch Kunststätten.

Zanker, P. (1975) 'Grabreliefs Römischer Freigelassener', *Jahrbuch des Deutschen Archäologischen Instituts* 90, pp. 267–315.

Zanker, P. and B.C. Ewald (2012) *Living with Myth: The Imagery of Roman Sarcophagi*, Oxford: Oxford University Press.

Zimmer, G. (1982) *Römische Berufsdarstellungen*, Berlin: Deutsches Archäologisches Institut, Gebr. Mann Verlag.

Zimmer, G. (1985) 'Römische Handwerker', *Aufstieg und Niedergang der Römischen Welt* 12/2, pp. 205–228.

Zimmermann, C. (2002) *Handwerkervereine im Griechischen Osten des Imperium Romanum*, Mainz: Verlag des Römisch-Germanischen Zentralmuseums in Kommission bei Habelt.

Named Roman Workers

Listed in order of appearance in the text

Named Roman Workers

Index

Unless discussing individual monuments in the city I have omitted the word Rome from the index as so much of the book is concerned with the city and its workers. The word funerary is omitted for the same reason of multiple references.

Also available from Amberley Publishing

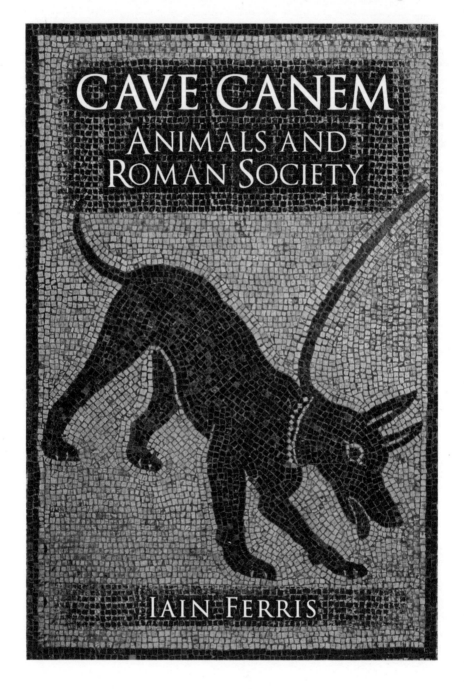

CAVE CANEM
ANIMALS AND
ROMAN SOCIETY

IAIN FERRIS

Available from all good bookshops or to order direct
Please call **01453-847-800**
www.amberley-books.com